16 –
nc

American Popular Music

Folk

American Popular Music

Blues
Classical
Country
Folk
Jazz
Rhythm & Blues, Rap, and Hip-Hop
Rock and Roll

General Editor: Richard Carlin

Editorial Board:

Barbara Ching, Ph.D., University of Memphis

Ronald D. Cohen, Ph.D., Indiana University-Northwest

William Duckworth, Bucknell University

Kevin J. Holm-Hudson, Ph.D., University of Kentucky

Nadine Hubbs, Ph.D., University of Michigan

Craig Morrison, Ph.D., Concordia University (Montreal)

Albin J. Zak III, Ph.D., University at Albany (SUNY)

American Popular Music

Folk

Richard Carlin

Foreword by Ronald D. Cohen, Ph.D.
Indiana University-Northwest

Facts On File
An imprint of Infobase Publishing

American Popular Music: Folk

Copyright © 2006 by Richard Carlin

Facts On File, Inc.
An imprint of Infobase Publishing
132 West 31st Street
New York NY 10001

Library of Congress Cataloging-in-Publication Data

Carlin, Richard, 1956–
    American popular music : folk / Richard Carlin ; foreword by Ronald D. Cohen.
        p. cm.
    Includes bibliographical references (p.   ), discographies, and index.
    ISBN 0-8160-5313-8 (hc : alk. paper)
    1. Folk music—United States—Encyclopedias. I. Title.
    ML102.F66C37 2005
    781.62'13'003—dc22   2005000445

Text design by James Scotto-Lavino
Cover design by Nora Wertz

Printed in the United States of America

VB FOF 10 9 8 7 6 5 4 3 2 1

This book is printed on acid-free paper.

Contents

Foreword

Richard Carlin has crafted a wide-ranging and creative guide to understanding the history of folk music in the United States and Great Britain throughout the 20th century. The reader might be curious as to why another folk music encyclopedia is necessary at this time. After all, there is no dearth of encyclopedias and other research tools that cover the history of folk music broadly defined, which would include country/western, string-bands, blues, gospel, cajun, singer-songwriters, and much more. To take one very simple example, biographical information on Bob Dylan is readily available, as is the case with many of the individuals and topics here represented.

Carlin does not attempt a rigid definition of folk music or folk songs, since these terms and categories have become more fluid in recent decades. His argument that "folk music means many different things to different people" is surely the best definition at this time. What is of greater importance, however, concerns his choice of topics and individuals. Encyclopedias often include numerous contributors, but in this case Richard Carlin has compiled all of the entries, which makes this volume very unique. The entries thus reflect not only his expertise and research but also his interests, insights, and aesthetic judgments. He includes numerous biographies of musicians, the majority of his entries, but also information on folklorists, instruments, record companies, institutions, magazines, songs, and much more, all written from his unique perspective.

Every editor has to make discrete and difficult choices in selecting the finite number of entries that can reasonably be included in a one-volume encyclopedia. Carlin has been very successful in accomplishing this difficult task. There are biographies not only of American musicians, but also those from England, Ireland, and Scotland. He not only locates these musicians within the contexts of their traditional music, but he also details their strong transatlantic connections, particularly since the 1960s. Carlin is also interested in numerous obscure southern and British musicians, individuals as well as groups, particularly those who have used string instruments and who often are not included in the numerous country, pop, and blues music encyclopedias previously published. On the other hand, some major country music figures are not here included as separate entries, such as Bill Monroe, Earl Scruggs, the Carter Family, Jimmie Rodgers, or Johnny Cash, because they are covered in the *Country* volume of the Encyclopedia of American Popular Music. Moreover, Carlin's focus is on the 20th century, and somewhat beyond, thereby updating and expanding our understanding of the individuals and topics covered. As is usual in music encyclopedias, Carlin discusses the musicians' important recordings, for which he gives his musical/aesthetic judgments. Again, the reader should understand that there is no such thing as a purely objective or neutral encyclopedia, for the writers, in this case one person, cannot avoid giving their personal views.

The editor's interest in the subject is evident not only in understanding what individuals/topics are included but also in what are excluded. There is, for example, more of an emphasis on white rather than black musicians, but again Carlin avoids duplication of the entries in the blues and rhythm and blues volumes in this series. Celtic music and musicians are readily evident, and klezmer music is defined, but most other aspects of what is today referred to as "world music" are not included. There are no listings for musicians from Africa, Asia, South America, for example, and even most of Europe, even though many have performed and recorded in the United States for many years. Their exclusion is a matter of both the editor's interests as well as space limitations, but it should be clear that this volume is certainly not definitive, but only a rich starting point for those interested in exploring not only individual entries but also a broader understanding of the topic.

The history of folk music in the United States and Britain in the twentieth century is rich and complex and touched upon in the books listed in the bibliography. But perhaps a brief overview will help in understanding the topic. Musical styles and instruments from Ireland, England, and Scotland, as well as Africa, came to the New World beginning in the 17th century, leaving a rich and vibrant legacy. By the mid-19th century there was a large body of British folk songs and ballads performed throughout the country, particularly in the southern backwoods. African Americans, both slave and free, maintained their own musical styles, which were borrowed and parodied by the white minstrel shows that were so popular before the Civil War. The five-string banjo, based on an instrument originally from Africa, fiddles, and parlor pianos were the most popular instruments, although the guitar would soon emerge as the standard folk instrument (in the 20th century). By century's end there was a dynamic folk music culture, partly shared through the widespread availability of sheet music.

Technological innovations would permanently transform the performance and reach of folk music throughout the 20th century. The invention of the phonograph in the 1880s, followed by the advent of radio in the 1920s, and eventually television, would create an influential commercial marketplace. The first blues records would appear in the early 1920s, quickly followed by the recording of hillbilly performers, broadening the reach and influence of both black and white roots musicians. Moreover, there were numerous recordings of European and other ethnic musicians, which found a niche market that would stretch throughout the century. Folklorists had begun collecting and publishing black spirituals in the mid-19th century, followed by Harvard professor Francis Child, who published a large collection of British ballads before 1900. The survival of such "Child ballads" among southerners quickly fascinated collectors, particularly British scholar Cecil Sharp, who found a rich legacy of these ballads. At the same time, John Lomax published a book of cowboy compositions, making a case for collecting songs that had domestic rather than perceived ancient British roots.

Beginning in the 1920s, numerous published collections of folksongs and ballads—sea shanties, traditional songs, blues tunes, cowboy and work songs, spirituals and gospel tunes, and much else—proliferated. The poet Carl Sandburg's *The American Songbag* (1927) brought a rich compilation of folk songs into homes throughout the country and would always remain in print. Country music radio programs quickly sprang up, capturing a national interest; the most successful was Nashville's Grand Ole Opry, still airing into the 21st century, but initially it was only one among many. Record companies, large and mall, recorded a plethora of black and white performers, while a few, such as Jimmie Rodgers and the Carter Family, became very influential and popular.

Folk music was never as commercially popular as mainstream popular music and jazz, but it found a stable market, although this rich musical legacy declined during the 1930s. The depression killed off some of the smaller record labels and discouraged others, but folk music continued to flourish on the radio, and now through the numerous folk festivals and contests that had sprung up. Economic disaster also led to an increasing interest in the preservation and promotion of the country's musical legacy as a means of promoting a national energy and spirit. The federal government had already established the Archive of American Folk Song in the Library of Congress, which encouraged collecting and sharing this legacy. Moreover, labor-union organizers and those connected with the Communist Party believed that folk-styled songs, newly written, could energize the working class on the picket lines. The Industrial Workers of the World, a radical union formed in 1905, had already used songs, many written by Joe Hill, to promote their agenda. The connection between folk songs and labor/political organizing would last for many decades.

By the late 1940s folk music, broadly defined, had become established as part and parcel of America's musical legacy, although it was not yet a major commercial success. In particular, performers such as Woody Guthrie and Huddie Ledbetter (aka Lead Belly) had made recordings for commercial companies as well as the Library of Congress, thanks to the diligent work of folklorist Alan Lomax, but they were not yet significant figures. This would change with the surprising commercial success of the Weavers, a quartet who had a number of major hits from 1950 to 1952. After a brief period of being blacklisted for their political beliefs, they resurfaced in 1955, and for the remainder of the decade a mini-folk revival existed. Harry Belafonte stimulated a brief calypso craze, and there was an increasing interest in recording folk musicians, particularly among the smaller labels, such as Elektra, Riverside, Tradition, Vanguard, and particularly Folkways. But the amazing success of the Kingston Trio, beginning in 1958, signaled the coming of a major folk revival that would peak within a few years.

It is somewhat difficult to understand why folk music became such a commercial success for a few years, although the vast numbers of young people searching for new musical sounds provides one answer. In any case the proliferation of folk groups and individuals flooded the college campuses, while the sale of guitars and banjos skyrocketed. Joan Baez appeared as the first of the female folk divas, soon followed by Bob Dylan as the best of the singer-songwriters. The height of folk's commercial phase was reached by the ABC-TV *Hootenanny* show in 1963–1964 and the use of the label "hootenanny" to sell a range of products: records, songbooks, paper dolls, hand lotion, Halloween costumes. Folk music not only connected the performers, whether professionals or amateurs, and their audiences to a fascinating, historic past but also to the vibrant present. While topical songs had always been part of the folk legacy, in the 1960s this became more urgent when they became connected to the escalating civil rights movement, closely followed by anti-war organizing, the women's movement, and other activist causes. But by decade's end, folk music, and its offshoot folk-rock, had commercially subsided, while Dylan and most of the other singer-songwriters now focused on writing introspective songs about feelings and personal experiences rather than social/political issues.

Over the years since, however, folk music has managed to hold its own, as the entries in this encyclopedia clearly demonstrate. Folk festivals continue to draw large crowds throughout North America and Britain. Record companies continue to produce albums of both contemporary artists as well as reissues of older recordings, and now it is possible to hear virtually all musicians who have ever been recorded. Amateur and professional musicians alike continue to make music, some copying traditional songs and styles, while others follow in the footsteps of the singer-songwriters who have dominated the folk music scene since the 1960s. What has particularly become popular in recent decades, however, has been the rise of what is termed *world music,* that is, traditional musical forms and styles from particularly Africa, Central and South America, Asia, and the Caribbean. This latter category can also include Celtic music, however, which Carlin covers in some depth, but public radio programs such as Afropop

Worldwide attest to a much broader concept of folk music that has recently developed. While it is evident that popular music from the United States has a worldwide audience, the opposite is also true; sounds from other countries have become part of the domestic folk music world. Folk music has always been a dynamic musical form, as this encyclopedia readily demonstrates, and the future holds similar promise. The reader will be delighted by discovering both old and new musical friends, as well as strong links between the British Isles and the United States. It is hoped that these entries will inform as well as stimulate the reader to explore this music farther.

Ronald Cohen

Preface

American popular music reflects the rich cultural diversity of the American people. From classical to folk to jazz, America has contributed a rich legacy of musical styles to the world over its two-plus centuries of existence. The rich cross-fertilization of cultures—African-American, Hispanic, Asian, and European—has resulted in one of the unique musical mixtures in the world.

American Popular Music celebrates this great diversity by presenting to the student, researcher, and individual enthusiast a wealth of information on each musical style in an easily accessible format. The subjects covered are:

Blues
Classical music
Country
Folk music
Jazz
Rock and Roll
Rhythm and Blues, Rap, and Hip-Hop

Each volume presents key information on performers, musical genres, famous compositions, musical instruments, media, and centers of musical activity. The volumes conclude with a chronology, recommended listening, and a complete bibliography or list of sources for further study.

How do we define *popular music?* Literally, any music that attracts a reasonably large audience is "popular" (as opposed to "unpopular"). Over the past few decades, however, as the study of popular music has grown, the term has come to have specific meanings. While some might exclude certain genres covered in this series—American classical music leaps to mind—we felt that it was important to represent the range of musical styles that have been popular in the United States over its entire history. New scholarship has brought to light the interplay among genres that previously were felt to be unrelated—such as the influence of folk forms on classical music, opera's influence on jazz, or the blues' influence on country—so that to truly understand each musical style, it is important to be conversant with at least some aspects of all.

These volumes are intended to be introductory, not comprehensive. Any "A to Z" work is by its very nature selective; it's impossible to include *every* figure, *every* song, or *every* key event. For most users, we hope the selections made here will be more than adequate, giving information on the key composers and performers who shaped each style, while also introducing some lesser-known figures who are worthy of study. The Editorial Board and other outside advisers played a key role in reviewing the entry lists for completeness.

All encyclopedia authors also face the rather daunting task of separating fact from fiction when writing short biographies of performers and composers. Even birth and death dates can be "up for grabs," as artists have been known to subtract years from their lives in their official biographies. "Official" records are often unavailable, particularly for earlier artists who may have been born at home, or for those whose family histories themselves are shrouded in mystery. We have attempted to draw on the latest research and most reliable sources whenever possible, and have also pointed out when key facts are in dispute. And, for many popular performers, the myth can be as important as the reality when it comes to their lives, so we have tried to honor both in writing about their achievements.

Popular music reflects the concerns of the artists who create it and their audience. Each era of our country's history has spawned a variety of popular music styles, and these styles in turn have grown over the decades as new performers and new times have arisen. These volumes try to place the music into its context, acknowledging that the way music is performed and its effect on the greater society is as important as the music itself. We've also tried to highlight the many interchanges between styles and performers, because one of the unique—and important—aspects of American cultural life is the way that various people have come together to create a new culture out of the interplay of their original practices and beliefs.

Race, class, culture, and sex have played roles in the development of American popular music. Regrettably, the playing field has not always been level for performers from different backgrounds, particularly when it comes to the business aspects of the industry: paying royalties, honoring copyrights, and the general treatment of artists. Some figures have been forgotten or ignored who deserved greater attention; the marketplace can be ruthless, and its agents—music publishers, record producers, concert promoters—have and undoubtedly will continue to take advantage of the musicians trying to bring their unique voices to market. These volumes attempt to address many of these issues as they have affected the development of individual musicians' careers as well as from the larger perspective of the growth of popular music. The reader is encouraged to delve further into these topics by referring to the bibliographies in each volume.

Popular music can be a slave itself to crass commercialism, as well as a bevy of hangers-on, fellow travelers, and others who seek only to make a quick buck by following easy-to-identify trends. While we bemoan the lack of new visionary artists today like Bessie Smith, Miles Davis, Pauline Oliveros, or Bob Dylan, it's important to remember that when they first came on the scene the vast majority of popular performers were journeymen musicians at best. Popular music will always include many second-, third-, and fourth-tier performers; some will offer one or two recordings or performances that will have a lasting impact, while many will be celebrated during their 15 minutes of fame, but most will be forgotten. In separating the wheat from the chaff, it is understandably easier for our writers working on earlier styles where the passing of time has helped sort out the important from the just popular. However, all the contributors have tried to supply some distance, giving greatest weight to the true artists, while acknowledging that popular figures who are less talented can nonetheless have a great impact on the genre during their performing career—no matter how brief it might be.

All in all, the range, depth, and quality of popular musical styles that have developed in the United States over its lifetime is truly amazing. These styles could not have arisen anywhere else, but are the unique products of the mixing of cultures, geography, technology, and sheer luck that helped disseminate each style. Who could have forecast the music of Bill Monroe before he assembled his first great bluegrass band? Or predicted the melding of gospel, rhythm and blues, and popular music achieved by Aretha Franklin during her reign as "Queen of Soul"? The tinkering of classical composer John Cage—who admitted to having no talent for creating melodies—was a truly American response to new technologies, a new environment, and a new role for music in our lives. And Patti Smith's particular take on poetry, the punk-rock movement, and the difficulties faced by a woman who leads a rock band make her music particularly compelling and original—and unpredictable to those who dismissed the original rock records as mere "teenage fluff."

We hope that the volumes in this series will open your eyes, minds, and, most important, your ears to a world of musical styles. Some may be familiar, others more obscure, but all are worthy. With today's proliferation of sound on the Web, finding even the most obscure recording is becoming increasingly simple. We urge you to read deeply but also to put these books down to listen. Come to your own conclusions. American popular music is a rich world, one open to many different interpretations. We hope these volumes serve as your windows to these many compelling worlds.

Richard Carlin,
General Editor

Introduction

This volume documents folk music as it has been a part of American popular music history. It covers a wide range of material, from traditional ballads and dance tunes to the work of popular singer-songwriters.

The first question that any writer on this subject faces is the age-old one of what, exactly, is meant by the term *folk music*? Is it music made by "the folks"? If so, wouldn't that include all types of music, from classical symphonies to advertising jingles? Even within the "folk music" world itself, there have been different meanings given to this term over the years. This makes it hard for anyone to say for certain what is "folk music" and what is not.

The classic definition given by folklorists is of a type of music that is passed down from one singer or instrumentalist to another. This is commonly called "oral transmission" because there is no written score or guidelines used to teach a song. In this process subtle changes may occur, resulting in changes to the words, melody, or tempo; called the "folk process," this means that there can be dozens—if not hundreds—of different versions of a single song—even fairly recent songs like the folk ballad "John Henry," which dates from the late 19th century. These songs were not "composed" by songwriters but were said to arise out of the folk communities themselves, a natural product of the need to express their feelings about local concerns and events. Folksongs were said to "survive" best in communities that did not come into contact with more modern popular music, so collectors often traveled deep into the Appalachian Mountains or visited places like prisons, where they

felt older traditions might still be heard. Folk performers are usually not "professionals" but rather play the music for their own amusement and the entertainment of their friends and neighbors.

However, this classic definition of folk music and its performers has come under question over the last few decades as many of the assumptions that the original folk scholars made have been shown to be only partially true. Many folk musicians were professional performers, at least in terms of the communities where they performed; they may not have toured widely or performed in concert halls, but they still made their living as performers and were viewed by their community as "professional." Further, many songs entered the folk repertory in the same way as other popular music did, through published sheet music, traveling shows, and (from the 1920s) recordings or radio broadcasts. Songs once thought to be "traditional"—such as the popular cowboy song "Home on the Range"—were actually not written by "the people" but composed by lyricists and musicians just like other popular songs, and were widely published in newspapers—which is how the "folk" learned them!

This history is further complicated when we take into account the "folk revival" that began in the 1940s and blossomed in the late 1950s through the mid-60s. At this time "folk groups"—mostly made up of young, college-educated musicians who learned folk music at camp, from songbooks, or from records, not from older relatives—enjoyed success on the pop charts. Groups such as the Kingston Trio had major pop hits with songs like

"Tom Dooley," a song based on a real story of the hanging of Thomas C. Dula, who murdered his girlfriend in Wilkes County, North Carolina, on May 6, 1868. This success spawned many other groups, and many of these groups began composing their own "folk songs"—or at least pop songs in the style of folk songs. In reaction, the so-called folk purists were dismayed by the great popularity of these groups, who they felt diluted the true power of "real" folk music.

The most influential songwriter of the early 1960s—indeed of the next few decades—was a young guitarist from Minnesota who arrived in New York City in 1961. His name was Bob Dylan, and he soon showed how contemporary songs could be written that drew on folk traditions but still reflected the unique events—and attitudes—of their times. In the popular press Dylan and his contemporaries—Judy Collins, Tom Rush, Joan Baez, Phil Ochs, and dozens more—were labeled as "folk musicians," even though true folklorists would not have considered them to be so. The image of the guitar-strumming, nasal-voiced, singer/songwriter singing about contemporary events became a stereotype for many of what folk music is.

In the 1970s and 1980s still another definition of folk music arose as individual musicians became more interested in regional styles and the musical heritage preserved by different immigrant groups. Cajun music, klezmer Jewish music, Tex Mex music, and dozens more styles were suddenly embraced by and became part of folk music. While earlier folk performers had performed some "international" music (Israeli and African songs), they often presented them in versions that reflected their own musical styles. Now an attempt was made to more carefully learn the instruments, musical styles, and languages of the original songs, whether they originated abroad or were sung here by the descendants of immigrant musicians.

All of this is a roundabout way of saying that folk music means many different things to different people. This encyclopedia tries to embrace as many of these meanings as possible, while highlighting the key musicians, styles, and musical instruments that are popular today. Like all the volumes in this series, it is meant to serve as an introduction, not an end point, in your journey. Each of these musicians had influences and subsequently influenced other performers; by following these threads, a rich world of music will unfold. I hope this collection inspires your further explorations in the rich world of American folk music.

A-to-Z Entries

Abshire, Nathan (1913–1981) *accordionist*

Born in Gueydan, Louisiana, on June 12, 1913, Abshire was inspired by his accordion-playing parents to take up the instrument at age six. He was befriended by the early Cajun recording artist/local musician Amédée Ardoin, who encouraged him to play for dances. Abshire made his first recordings in 1934 for Bluebird (the budget division of RCA Victor), but really came into his own as a recording artist in the 1950s and 1960s, when he worked for local producer Jay Miller, among other small, local labels. Abshire had a regional hit with his "Pine Grove Blues," a mixture of Cajun and African-American blues stylings. He often worked with the BALFA BROTHERS, perhaps the best known of the Cajun bands thanks to their performances on the folk-revival circuit. Abshire continued to record and perform until his death on May 13, 1981, in Basile, Louisiana.

accordions

Accordions are most commonly described as large, piano-keyboard instruments. However, there is an entire family of free-reed instruments that have been marketed under a variety of names, including piano and button accordions, melodeons, and concertinas, all of which have played a role in folk music. In fact, the piano accordion was a relatively late development, coming into popularity in the late 1920s, about a century after the original accordions were made. However, once it was introduced, it tended to sweep away the many earlier variants, because of its great versatility, amazing sound, and use by popular orchestras and singers.

A free reed instrument is one that produces sound through the vibration of a metal reed, secured at one end to a metal frame, which vibrates "freely" under air pressure. You might compare this with a single reed (such as found in a clarinet), which is also secured at one end, but its tip beats against the upper edge of the instrument's mouthpiece, or a double reed (such as found in BAGPIPES or an oboe), which consists of two thin reeds, also secured at one end, that beat against each other. Free reeds were unknown in Europe until a Chinese instrument, called a *sheng*, was brought to France in the late 18th century; subsequently mouth organs (HARMONICAS), reed organs, and accordions were developed using this new technology.

The names "accordion," "melodeon," and "concertina" were applied rather haphazardly to a number of different instruments. All featured hand-operated bellows that were drawn in and out to produce the air pressure necessary to make the reeds sound. Some play a different note when the bellows are pressed in or out, while others play the same note. Some feature buttons that play chords for accompaniment, while others require the musician to press several buttons at once to play chords. Some were relatively inexpensive and produced in great numbers, while others were more expensive and thus less likely to be played by folk musicians.

The accordion and its relatives had several advantages for use in dance halls and in noisy bars where folk music is often performed. Most accordions are louder than fiddles, mandolins, or banjos, thanks to the carrying power of metal reeds. Accordions also give musicians the ability to play both melody and accompaniment, offering a richer-sounding instrumental accompaniment to songs and eliminating the need for two or three musicians to play for a dance. Finally, thanks to mass production, accordions became readily available and relatively inexpensive; mail order catalogs made them even easier to buy in places not served by music stores.

The Irish were among the first to embrace accordion-family instruments in their dance music, particularly inexpensive melodeons and concertinas. In the United States Cajun musicians also embraced the inexpensive melodeon, using it as the primary melody instrument—along with the fiddle—in their dance music. The small concertina is associated in the popular mind with sailors and songs of the sea. The piano accordion became a popular instrument in WESTERN SWING bands in the 1930s, mirroring its popularity in dance bands throughout the country.

Today there are many virtuoso musicians known for their playing on the accordion. In Irish music JOE BURKE is one of the leading exponents on the button accordion. NATHAN ABSHIRE and CLIFTON CHENIER were both well-known Cajun accordionists, as is MARC SAVOY.

See also BANJO, FIVE-STRING; FIDDLE; MANDOLIN.

Albion Band   See HUTCHINGS, ASHLEY.

Alger, Pat (b. 1947) *guitarist, songwriter, and vocalist*

Pat Alger first emerged in several different projects organized by Happy and Artie Traum, including the various incarnations of the Woodstock Mountains Revue, a loosely knit group of musicians from the greater Woodstock area including bluegrasser John Herald, the Traums, MARIA MULDAUR, and others. Alger contributed some of the more country-flavored songs to the group's repertoire, including

"Old Time Music" and "Southern Crescent Line." Alger hooked up with folk/country singer NANCI GRIFFITH in the mid-1980s, cowriting several of her hits, including "Once in a Very Blue Moon" and "Lone Star State of Mind." In 1988 Kathy Mattea covered "Goin' Gone," a song Alger had cowritten for Griffith, which launched his career in new Nashville circles. Alger made three solo albums in the early 1990s, featuring backup by many current Nashville stars, including Griffith, Mattea, and Lyle Lovett. Alger continues to work, primarily as a songwriter and producer, in Nashville.

See also TRAUM, HAPPY AND ARTIE.

Allen, Jules Verne (1883–1945) *cowboy singer*

Allen was born in Waxahachie, Texas, on April 1, 1883, began ranch work at the age of 10, and was soon an accomplished horseman. During the 1890s he worked on several cattle drives in the Plains and into Mexico, performed at local rodeos, and sang occasionally on an amateur basis. After serving in World War I, Allen briefly returned to ranching, but the growth of radio led him to believe he could make a living as a performer. He landed his first radio work in the early 1920s in Dallas and was also employed in San Antonio and Los Angeles through the 1920s. He took various stage names, including "Longhorn Luke" and "The Original Singing Cowboy."

During 1928–29 Allen made 24 recordings for Victor Records, which have come to be viewed as classic examples of "real" cowboy singing. These included such evergreen cowboy favorites as his first record, "Little Joe the Wrangler" and classics like "The Dying Cowboy" and "The Days of '49." In 1933 Allen published a book of cowboy stories and songs that was printed locally in Texas. After that Allen faded from the scene, although he continued to play locally at rodeos and on the radio.

Allen, Red (1930–1993) *bandleader and performer*

Harley "Red" Allen was born on February 12, 1930. He first came to prominence as the lead singer and guitarist for the OSBORNE BROTHERS in the mid-1950s, but he soon broke away to form his own band, the Kentuckians. In the early 1960s he recorded and performed with innovative MANDOLIN players Frank Wakefield and DAVID GRISMAN. His band became very popular on both the folk and bluegrass circuits and was one of the most influential of the second-generation groups during the 1960s.

In the early 1970s Allen hooked up with progressive banjo player J. D. Crowe to sing lead in the first version of the band the New South. Allen performed through the 1970s and 1980s, grooming the careers of his three sons, who formed the Allen Brothers band in the mid-1970s. He died of cancer on April 3, 1993. His sons recorded a couple of albums of contemporary country and bluegrass compositions in tight three-part harmonies.

Allen, Terry (b. 1943) *composer, performer, and songwriter*

Allen was born in Wichita, Kansas, on May 7, 1943. Trained as an architect and a sometimes art teacher, Allen recorded a number of concept LPs in the 1970s and early 1980s, collaborated with David Byrne on the soundtrack for his *True Stories* movie, and accompanied Joe Ely and Butch Hancock on their recordings. His most interesting LPs are *Juarez*, a 1975 song cycle that relates the story of four Californians who migrate to Mexico in search of a better life, and *Lubbock on Everything*, a double-LP set peopled with archetypical Texan misfits and desperados. His best-known songs are "New Delhi Freight Train," covered by Little Feat, and the slightly skewed "Cocktail Desperado," which he performed in Byrne's film. He also scored Wolf Echart's film on the American influence on Southeast Asia during the Vietnam War, called *Amerasia*, which is probably the world's only country-"eastern" record, because it features Allen accompanied by traditional Thai instrumentalists. Allen is also a painter whose work has been shown around the world. In the mid-1990s, after a period of inactivity recording, Allen cut two records for the Sugar Hill label.

Allen Brothers

Born in Sewanee, Georgia, Austin (banjo and lead vocal, 1901–59) and Lee (GUITAR, kazoo, and vocals, 1906–81) were raised in Chattanooga, Tennessee. They were well educated and aspired to be vaudeville stars. They fell in love with jazz and blues songs that they heard played by local performers such as a guitar player named May Bell, who was a popular performer on the riverboats that cruised up and down the Mississippi, and a group known as the Two Poor Boys, who were familiar street singers. The brothers were also influenced by jazz-era orchestras and pop crooners.

The Allens first recorded for Columbia in Chattanooga under the direction of famed producer Frank Walker. Their first record, "SALTY DOG BLUES," sold well and became their signature number; the jazzy "hey-hey-hey" chorus set their version apart from others. It led to a second session producing another jazz-age number, "Chattanooga Blues," featuring a "wow-wow-wow wow" chorus echoing their earlier "hey-hey" chant in "Salty Dog," and a ragtime-influenced guitar break by brother Lee.

The Allens recorded prolifically through the mid-1930s, focusing on songs that at least had "blues" in the title. These songs were pop jazz numbers, many with topical themes, including songs that commented on the plight of the farmer ("Price of Cotton Blues") and the rise of mass-market chain stores that were threatening the local mom-and-pop venues ("Chain Store Blues"). They moved into "hokum" (slightly sexually suggestive) novelty numbers in the second half of their career, including their hit, "(Mama Don't Allow) No Low Down Hanging Around," from 1930, a version of the ever-popular jazz novelty that was widely copied by other country acts. They also rerecorded their first song, now called "New Salty Dog Blues," which helped keep the song in circulation through the late 1930s.

The Depression and the advent of radio conspired to put a bite into the profitability of many recording labels. The Allens, like many other country acts, saw their sales suffer. In the early 1930s they were performing in vaudeville and eventually ended up in New York, where in 1934 they made their last recordings, mostly remakes of their earlier hits. Older brother Austin remained in the city, but his younger sibling returned to Tennessee, where he eventually became an electrician.

Almanac Singers, The   See WEAVERS, THE.

Altan

An Irish folk revival band, Altan achieved its greatest success in the late 1980s to early 1990s. The band centered on the husband-and-wife duo flutist Frankie Kennedy and fiddler/vocalist Mairéad Ní Mhaonaigh. Natives of West Donegal, the pair formed their first band in the late 1970s, and then recorded together as a duo in 1983. With the addition of bouzouki player Ciarán Curran and Mark Kelly on GUITAR, they toured the United States in 1986, where they were heard by Wendy Newton of Green Linnet Records, who signed the as-then nameless band to a recording contract. Their first album took its name from Loch Altan, a lake near Mhanoaigh's hometown and the inspiration for a reel that she composed. Altan subsequently became the name of the band. Various other musicians came and went through 1994, when Kennedy died after a long-running battle with cancer. Mhanoaigh then became the de facto leader, and the band moved into a folk-pop direction that emphasized her vocals.

Anderson, Eric (b. 1943) *guitarist, singer, and songwriter*

Although born in Pittsburgh, Pennsylvania, on February 14, 1943, Anderson was raised in Amherst, Massachusetts, taking up the GUITAR as a teenager in the late 1950s. While attending Hobart College he began playing local clubs, and by the early 1960s left school to travel to Boston, where a vibrant folk scene was developing. He quickly formed a Kingston Trio–like group called the Cradlers, who played throughout New England but did not record. After the group disbanded, Anderson moved to New York City to perform in its Greenwich Village coffeehouses. In 1964 he signed with Vanguard Records, then the leading folk label. Thanks to songs like 1966's "Thirsty Boots" (inspired by the CIVIL RIGHTS MOVEMENT), Anderson was hailed as the next Bob Dylan. He also focused on the ups and downs of romantic love in songs such as "Hey Babe, You've Been Cheatin'," an area that BOB DYLAN had also explored. Moving to electric instrumentation and a singer-songwriter orientation, Anderson switched first to Warner Bros. in 1969 and then to Columbia two years later, recording his most commercially successful album, 1972's *Blue River*. Anderson's career has been spotty since then, including a few additional albums, tours, and collaborations with other 1960s–1970s–era FOLK-ROCK performers such as Rick Danko.

Archive of American Folk Song, The

Founded in 1928 as part of the Library of Congress, the Archive of American Folk Song has played a vital role in collecting and preserving traditional American music. The first director of the archive was Robert Gordon, a folklorist who had made nearly 1,000 cylinder recordings of traditional American songs and also wrote popular columns on folk song for newspapers and magazines. In 1933 the famous folklorist John Lomax began a 10-year association with the archive, enlisting his son Alan Lomax to serve as his assistant in a series of groundbreaking field trips. Alan became "Assistant in Charge" of the archive in 1937 and conducted a series of interviews with major musicians, including WOODY GUTHRIE, LEAD BELLY, and jazz musician Jelly Roll Morton, to add to the collection. In 1941 a Recording Laboratory was established as part of the archive. From the 1940s the archive occasionally issued 78s and later LP recordings of its holdings (many reissued on CD by Rounder Records).

In 1971 the archive was renamed the Archive of Folk Culture to reflect a broader mission beyond the preservation simply of music. In turn, seven years later, the archive was incorporated into the American Folklife Center.

See also LOMAX, JOHN AND ALAN.

Ardoin family

The Ardoin family has spawned a long line of famous Cajun/ZYDECO musicians, beginning with Amédée Ardoin (c. 1896–1941), born in L'Anse Rougeau, Lousiana. The family were Creoles, of mixed white and African-American heritage, and worked on a farm owned by the Rogeau family. Ardoin began playing ACCORDION at a young age, influenced by another local musician, Adam Fontenot. Ardoin began playing for dances with various musicians. Around 1921 he was working as a sharecropper on Oscar Comeaux's farm near Chataignier, where he met white fiddler DENNIS MCGEE. The two formed a duo, an unusual arrangement as white performers did not usually "mix" with Creoles. In 1929 McGee and Ardoin were among the first Cajun musicians to record, making their first, which were noteworthy for Ardoin's intense vocals and accordion work. They recorded three more times through 1934, and these records had a great influence on the next generation of Cajun musicians. Later in the 1930s Ardoin partnered with fiddler Sady Courville. He died in 1941, apparently a victim of venereal disease.

Amédée's nephew is Alphonse "Bois Sec" (literally "Dry Wood") Ardoin (b. c. 1915), who began his musical career playing triangle for his uncle. Bois Sec primarily performed with fiddler Canray Fontenot (1922–95), son of his uncle's mentor, Adam Fontenot; the two first worked together in 1948. The duo made an appearance at the National Folk Festival in Washington, D.C., in 1966, which led to their first recordings. By the early 1970s they had built a band, mostly featuring Bois Sec's sons, notably Lawrence "Black" Ardoin (b. unknown) on drums, and eventually Lawrence's two sons, Chris (accordion, b. 1981) and Sean (drums; b. unknown). The band continued to perform through Fontenot's death from cancer in 1995. Since the mid-1990s Chris and Sean have played together in the group Double Clutchin'.

Arkie the Arkansas Woodchopper

(1915–1981) *dance caller, fiddler, and guitarist*

Born Luther William Ossenbrik, near Knob Noster, Missouri, on September 21, 1915, Arkie performed as a boy guitarist/fiddler/dance caller. In 1928 he made his debut on Kansas City radio, and a year later joined the prestigious *National Barn Dance* program broadcast out of Chicago on WLS. One of the longest-running stars of the program, Arkie continued on air with them until the original show was canceled in 1960, then for a further decade on a revived version of the show.

His colorful name and handle—"Country boy from the Ozarks"—was given to him by WLS staff—even though he was not from the Ozark region at all. He made a few country-novelty recordings in the 1930s and 1940s, but was best loved for his on-air monologues about country life. In 1940 he published a book of SQUARE DANCE calls, and a year later he recorded an album of 78s with calls and music. This helped spur further interest in square dancing among city dwellers, as did Arkie's tours as a caller.

After 1970, when the second incarnation of the *National Barn Dance* went off the air, Arkie retired from active performing. He died on June 23, 1981.

Armstrong, Frankie (b. 1941) *ballad singer*

Born in Worthington, Cumbria, England, Armstrong has worked professionally as a social worker since the mid-1960s, while also performing, primarily as an unaccompanied ballad singer and singer of topical material addressing women's subjects. She worked with EWAN MACCOLL's Singer's Group, an informal group of young performers, from the mid-1960s through 1971, when she began a solo performing career. Armstrong recorded most prolifically from 1972 through the early 1980s, when she decided to retire from professional performing to focus on teaching and social work. She has since recorded on occasion, notably in the late 1980s, but has been generally less active as a performer/recording artist. In 1989 she appeared on an album of songs by Bertholt Brecht along with American blues revivalist DAVE VAN RONK, an unusual move for both artists.

Armstrong Twins (b. 1930) *performers*

Born in rural Dewitt, Arkansas, but raised in Little Rock, Lloyd (vocals, MANDOLIN) and Floyd (vocals, GUITAR; both born on January 24, 1930) were performing professionally by age nine. Influenced by the popular country brother duos the Blue Sky Boys and the Monroe Brothers, they developed a tight harmony sound with a modern, slightly jazz-influenced bounce to their accompaniments. Besides being young and cute, the boys had the added attraction of being twins, so they soon had quite a strong following. They remained local favorites on various Little Rock–based radio shows through 1947, when they decided to relocate to Southern California, which had a growing country music scene.

They quickly established themselves in California, becoming favorites on radio and in live performances. They also made their first recordings, mostly of well-known songs, although they also cut some original mandolin instrumentals and a few novelty numbers. In 1952 they left California for Odessa, Texas, where they had their own radio and TV shows. They began touring with honky-tonk star Johnny Horton and performing on the popular *Louisiana Hayride* radio program. They briefly returned to California toward the end of the 1950s, working on television and radio.

By the early 1960s the brothers had retired to their home state because their musical style was out of fashion. In 1979 a selection of their earlier recordings was reissued, bringing them a new audience in the old-time music revival. They toured through the 1980s, until Floyd's health began to fail, forcing them to curtail their activities.

Arthur, Emry (c. 1900–1966) *singer*

Arthur was raised on a small farm in southern Kentucky, where both his brothers, Sam and Henry, were musicians. A hunting accident damaged one of his hands, so Emry was a rather limited musician, but a talented singer. Around 1925 the brothers moved to Indianapolis in search of work; there, two years later, they were heard by a talent scout from a small record label. In early 1928 Henry and Emry recorded 10 songs in Chicago, including the first recording of "I Am a Man of Constant Sorrow." The song was native to Kentucky; Dick Burnett (of the popular performing/recording duo BURNETT AND RUTHERFORD), who lived close to the Arthur family farm, published the song in one of his songbooks in 1913 and may have been Emry's source for it. Arthur's recording was a source for traditional singers Sarah Ogan Gunning (who renamed it "Girl of Constant Sorrow") and, eventually, the Stanley Brothers. The song was given a considerable boost in 2000, when it was featured in the film *O Brother, Where Art Thou?*, as performed by the film's fictional country trio, the "Soggy Bottom Boys."

Emry recorded through summer 1929, but then seems to have faced a life crisis. His wife left him and the Depression struck; he eventually moved to Wisconsin, where he was hired by the Wisconsin Chair Company (who manufactured phonographs and records under the Paramount label). When his employers discovered that Emry had previously had hit records, they invited him into their studios in the early 1930s, but these recordings did not fare well. In 1934 Arthur made his last recordings for Decca, including country blues and novelty numbers, along with remakes of some of his earlier hits. Emry died in Indianapolis in 1966.

See also STANLEY BROTHERS AND RALPH STANLEY.

Asch, Moses (1905–1986) *founder of Folkways Records*

Asch, the son of noted novelist Sholem Asch, was born in Russia on December 2, 1905, but his family soon fled due to the unrest before the Russian Revolution. He began his career as a sound engineer, training in Germany, and then eventually moving to New York City. Asch founded the Disc and Asch labels in the early 1940s, recording jazz, folk, and blues performers such as PETE SEEGER, WOODY GUTHRIE, and JOSH WHITE. In 1949 he started Folkways Records as a means of documenting all types of music and speech.

From the beginning, Folkways played a central role in the revival of interest in folk music. In 1952 an eccentric filmmaker and record collector named HARRY SMITH approached Asch about issuing a six-record set of recordings from the 1920s and 1930s that he called *The Anthology of American Folk Music.* Smith had an excellent collection and peerless taste, and selected many key artists for representation on this set, many of whose recordings had long been unavailable or had never been available in urban areas. These six records were highly prized by the first generation of folk revivalists, who in turn passed along the songs to another generation of performers.

Meanwhile, Asch was recording Pete Seeger throughout the 1950s, when Seeger was blacklisted for his Communist sympathics, as well as issuing albums by traditional artists such as BASCOM LAMAR LUNSFORD and LEAD BELLY.

In 1959 young folklorist MIKE SEEGER approached Asch about issuing an album he called *Mountain Music Blue Grass Style;* this was the first album of bluegrass music issued for a city audience. Seeger's group, the NEW LOST CITY RAMBLERS, were the first old-time stringband revivalists, and they recorded for Folkways throughout the 1960s. Meanwhile, group members Seeger and JOHN COHEN produced albums of traditional country musicians, both rediscovered artists from the 1920s and 1930s such as DOCK BOGGS and newly found masters such as ROSCOE HOLCOMB. Folkways also issued albums by traditional banjo players WADE WARD and Pete Steele.

Because Asch believed that all of his records should remain in print, even if they sold only a few copies each year, all of this material remained available until the time of his death on October 19, 1986, influencing many generations of musicians. The Smithsonian Institution purchased the label and Asch's archives after his death, and has been slowly reissuing the better material on compact disc, while keeping everything available through special-order cassettes and CDs.

See also RECORDING.

Ashley, Tom (1895–1967) *banjoist and guitarist*

Born Clarence Earl McCurry in Bristol, Tennessee, on September 29, 1895, Clarence was raised by his maternal grandfather, Enoch Ashley, in the Mountain City area of northeastern Tennessee (he later legally took his grandfather's surname). He was already performing on banjo and GUITAR in local medicine shows around 1910. He performed on record with a number of bands, usually as guitarist, including the famed old-time trio the Carolina Tar Heels, Byrd Moore and his Hotshots, and the Blue Ridge Mountain Entertainers.

The Tar Heels recorded many sides in the late 1920s and early 1930s, usually featuring Ashley on guitar and lead vocals, either Gwen Foster or Garley Foster (no relation) on HARMONICA, guitar, and tenor vocals, and Doc Walsh on banjo and baritone vocal. Ashley "composed" the folk ballad "My Home's across the Blue Ridge Mountains" for the group, which became popular in the folk revival repertoire after BASCOM LAMAR LUNSFORD recorded it for the Library of Congress. In 1928 Ashley also cut solo play-party songs on the banjo, most notably his versions of "The Coo Coo Bird" and "The House Carpenter," which were much copied during the early days of the folk revival in the 1950s and 1960s.

Ashley was "rediscovered" at the Galax, Virginia, fiddlers convention in 1960 by folklorist RALPH

RINZLER. Rinzler encouraged him to take up banjo playing again, an instrument he had stopped playing in the early 1940s due to a hand injury. Ashley had in turn discovered and tutored a number of younger musicians in northwest North Carolina, where he had been living, including guitarists Clint Howard and ARTHEL "DOC" WATSON plus fiddler Fred Price. The quartet was brought to New York City by Rinzler in 1961–62 to record a series of influential albums as well as to perform for folk-revival audiences. Watson was such a standout that he was quickly performing as a solo act, recording for the then-major folk label Vanguard Records. Ashley continued to make appearances at folk festivals and in concerts and made one further album before he died on June 2, 1967.

Atcher, Bob (1914–1993) *singer*

Born James Robert Owen Atcher in Hardin County, Kentucky, on May 11, 1914, Atcher was raised in North Dakota. His father was a champion fiddler, and many other members of his family played musical instruments and sang, so he was exposed to both Southern folk songs and songs of the West from an early age. By his late teens he had moved to Chicago, which at the time had a thriving country-music scene, primarily centered on a number of popular radio shows. Atcher, with his smooth tenor voice and good looks, was a natural for the role of singing cowboy, and he appeared on a number of Chicago-based radio shows from 1931 on and signed with Columbia Records in 1937 (where he remained for 21 years).

Atcher's fame grew after he joined Chicago's *National Barn Dance* in 1948, where he performed both as a soloist and in duet with a string of partners all going by the radio name of "Bonnie Blue Eyes." He remained with the *Barn Dance* for 22 years. Toward the end of his career, Atcher turned his attention to local politics, serving as mayor of Schaumburg, Illinois (a Chicago suburb) for 16 years. He died on October 31, 1993.

Axton, Hoyt (1938–1999) *singer and songwriter*

Son of noted pop tunesmith Mae Boren Axton (who wrote Elvis Presley's early hit "Heartbreak Hotel"), Axton was born on March 25, 1938, raised in rural Comanche, Oklahoma, and was greatly influenced by the topical music of fellow Oklahoman WOODY GUTHRIE. Axton's first big hit was "Greenback Dollar," a rewrite of "I Don't Want Your Millions, Mister," a Depression-era song popularized by Guthrie. Through the 1960s, he placed other songs, primarily with country acts.

Axton's big break into pop music came when the rock group Steppenwolf recorded his "The Pusher" in 1969, which was featured on the soundtrack of the influential film *Easy Rider*. Thanks to this success he was signed to Columbia in the same year and released an album in a soft, singer-songwriter style.

Axton next wrote "Joy to the World," a megahit for Three Dog Night in 1971; this was followed by the silly "No No Song" for Ringo Starr four years later, another number one pop hit. Axton recorded two more folk-country–styled discs in the mid-1970s, scoring minor hits with 1974's "When the Morning Comes" and 1976's "Flash of Fire." A year later he had moved to a new label, recording "Snow Blind Friend," about the evils of cocaine, and producing the hit satire "You're the Hangnail in My Life." Axton recorded a pure country album in 1979, with minor success on the story songs "Delta and the Dealer" and "Rusty Old Halo"; however, after that, Axton's career as a songwriter and performer went into decline.

In the 1980s Axton worked as a film actor, appearing in a number of Steven Spielberg–produced films, including *Gremlins* and *E.T.* Axton suffered a stroke in 1995, and although he made a few appearances and attempted to make some recordings, he subsequently passed away four years later on October 26, 1999.

Baez, Joan (b. 1941) *singer and songwriter*
Although born on Staten Island, New York, on January 9, 1941, she was raised in Palo Alto, California. Baez's father was of Mexican heritage, and worked as a physicist; her mother had Irish ancestry. Like many teens of her generation, she was a big fan of early rock and roll stars, including Elvis Presley and Bill Haley, and so she took up the GUITAR. The family moved back east after Baez graduated from high school so her father could take a position at the Massachusetts Institute of Technology. Baez began sitting in at local folk clubs while beginning college and became a favorite particularly at the well-known Club 47 in Cambridge, Massachusetts. In early 1959 Chicago-based folksinger BOB GIBSON heard her play at a local club there, which led him to invite her to be a guest during his set at that summer's NEWPORT FOLK FESTIVAL. She was an immediate sensation, and a year later signed with the folk label Vanguard.

Baez's early repertory leaned toward traditional ballads and folk songs, but she soon began incorporating the work of contemporary songwriters into her act and recordings. She was particularly important in the early career of BOB DYLAN, as she made some of the first recordings of many of his songs, invited him to appear with her at the height of her popularity, and also ceaselessly promoted him as the best songwriter of his generation. She was also active in the civil rights and antiwar movements, marrying fellow activist David Harris in 1968. He was briefly imprisoned for his refusal to serve in Vietnam, and Baez made freeing her husband—and

spreading the antiwar message—a major focus of her recordings and concert appearances.

Baez reached her greatest popularity as a commercial recording artist in 1972, with her recording of "The Night They Drove Old Dixie Down" hitting number five, her highest-charting pop record. She moved to A&M Records that same year and recorded her first album of her own compositions, while continuing to record and perform antiwar material. In 1975 she had her last major hit with the title track of the album "Diamonds and Rust," very much in the confessional style of singer-songwriters of the day. From fall 1975 she toured for the next 18 months with Bob Dylan's fabled Rolling Thunder Revue, appearing in the semifictional film based on the tour, *Renaldo and Clara*.

However, Baez's career was fading. She made her last U.S. album for seven years in 1980, although she remained popular in Europe. She has recorded sporadically since, mostly for smaller labels, with an occasional major label "comeback" (such as the album *Play Me Backwards* in 1992 for Virgin, featuring the minor hit single "Stones in the Road," penned by Mary Chapin Carpenter). Baez has remained a tireless worker for world peace and human rights, often playing benefit concerts and contributing time to various peace-oriented organizations.

bagpipes
The bagpipes are among the oldest traditional instruments, found in many different parts of the world. In Great Britain there are three main varieties

of bagpipes. The best known are the Scottish or Great Highland bagpipes, because they are heard so often in parades and on special occasions. However, the Irish, Uillean, or Union pipes and the Northumbrian small pipes are more often heard in traditional music.

All bagpipes work on the same principles. One pipe, known as the chanter, plays the melody; one or more other pipes, known as drones, play single harmony notes. The sound itself is produced by a thin wooden reed that is mounted inside each pipe. The chanter has finger holes (and keys) that enables the player to play melodies, while the drones have no holes so are limited to single notes. The reeds are powered by air pressure, supplied either by blowing into or bumping a "bag" (traditionally made of animal skin or leather). When the bag is inflated, pressure builds until there is enough to make the reeds sound.

The Scottish or Great Highland pipes are very loud and were developed to be played outdoors; their musical themes were used as signals, often in battles, so it was important that they could be heard for miles around. A highly elaborate tradition of pipe melodies developed during the 18th century, known as pibroch, which were handed down from master piper to novice (often father to son).

The Irish pipes—also known as Uillean or Union pipes—are played when the performer is sitting down. Unlike the Scottish bagpipes where the player blows into a tube to fill the bellows, the Irish pipes feature a small pump—like a fireplace bellows—to provide the air flow. They also feature a special type of pipe called regulators, which play several notes at once to provide harmonies, in addition to the usual drones. The Irish pipes are considered very difficult to master because of the intricate technique involved. Great Irish pipers include the folklorist SEAMUS ENNIS, WILLIE CLANCY, and Leo Rowsome.

The Northumbrian small pipes are, as might be expected, much smaller in size and softer in volume than either the Scottish or Irish versions. They are also powered by a small, external bellows and feature a chanter with one, two, or three drone pipes. Over the last century great players such as the legendary Billy Pigg developed a highly ornate style of playing the pipes, featuring virtuosic arpeggios and quickly executed scale runs. Current players of the small pipes include Alistair Anderson and Kathryn Ticknell.

Bailes Brothers, The

Hailing from a West Virginia farming community, the Bailes Brothers—guitarists Johnnie (June 24, 1918–December 1989) and Walter (January 17, 1920–November 2000)—performed together with their other siblings at home and church from an early age. Their father was a Baptist preacher. In 1937 Johnnie began working as a musician, and by the later 1930s Walter had joined him. They worked as a duo on local radio.

In 1942 the two brothers were brought by Roy Acuff to Nashville's *Grand Ole Opry*, where they remained popular performers for six years. They were signed to Columbia, where they recorded many of their classic compositions, including "I Want to Be Loved (But Only by You)," "Oh, So Many Years," and "Give Mother My Crown." The duo became particularly well known for their gospel songs, and together they wrote many country gospel classics, including "Dust on the Bible." In 1948 the Bailes switched to the rival *Louisiana Hayride* program, performing for one more year before the act dissolved. Although Johnnie and Walter continued to work sporadically as a gospel duo through the early 1950s, Walter eventually curtailed his performing to focus on the ministry.

Bain, Aly   See BOYS OF THE LOUGH.

Baker, Etta (b. 1913) *guitarist*

Etta Baker was born in Caldwell County, North Carolina, on May 31, 1913. She was raised in a musical family and learned GUITAR from her father. Like fellow Carolinian ELIZABETH COTTON, Baker developed a relaxed, ragtime-influenced picking style that is common to the Piedmont/Carolina region. She might have remained simply a local musician if not for PAUL CLAYTON meeting her in the mid-1950s and recording her for the album, *Instrumental Music of the Southern Appalachians,* first issued in 1956 (and remaining in print for more than 20 years). Still, unlike other "discoveries" of the folk revival, Baker did not begin performing and touring until decades later. She made her first solo album in 1991, still playing very much in the same style she used in the 1950s; a second album followed in 1999. She also produced a 1996 instructional video teaching her guitar technique.

Baker, Kenny (b. 1926) *fiddle player*

Baker was born in Jenkins, Kentucky, on June 26, 1926, to a line of coal miners and fiddlers; he is said to have first taken up the FIDDLE at age eight, but his father apparently did not feel he had sufficient talent to become a fiddler. Consequently, Baker switched to GUITAR in his high school years, returning to the fiddle in his early twenties. After serving in World War II Baker returned home to work in the mines. However, in 1953 country singer Don Gibson hired him as the fiddler for his backup band. Three years later, when Bill Monroe heard him playing with Gibson, he immediately offered him a job.

Baker joined Monroe's band at a time when bluegrass music had temporarily lost its popularity. Monroe had difficulty meeting the band's payroll, so consequently Baker often returned to mining in order to support his family. He first worked with Monroe from 1956 to 1959; during this period he shared fiddle duties with Bobby Hicks, and the two were featured on Monroe's classic instrumentals "Scotland" and "Panhandle County," recorded in 1958. Baker then left the band, but briefly returned in 1962–63, appearing on Monroe's recording of "Sailor's Hornpipe," featuring Monroe's latest discovery, Boston-born banjo player Bill Keith. Baker then returned to mining, but the pull of a musical career was too strong, and in 1967 he finally returned to Monroe for good.

A year later Baker made the first in a series of solo albums for County Records. County appealed to the old-time music revivalists, who were taken with Baker's great technique. In 1969 Monroe issued his classic album, *Uncle Pen,* a tribute to his fiddle-playing uncle. Baker played an important role in this work; Monroe felt that only Baker had the necessary roots in traditional styles to honor his uncle's music. *Uncle Pen* was a landmark in Monroe's career and further enhanced Baker's reputation as a premier bluegrass fiddler. Baker returned the favor by recording an album of Monroe instrumentals for County in 1976.

Baker became a fixture in Monroe's later bands, remaining with the master until 1986, when he began an association with DOBRO player Josh Graves. The two recorded and performed as a duo, and also as part of the Masters, which also featured Eddie Adcock on banjo and Jesse McReynolds (of Jim & Jesse fame) on MANDOLIN. Baker has continued to record as a solo artist as well, and regularly tours the bluegrass circuit. In 1999 he was inducted into the International Bluegrass Music Hall of Fame.

See also BANJO, FIVE-STRING.

Balfa Brothers, The

The leading Cajun band of the folk revival years, the Balfas were popular performers at major festivals and on college campuses in the 1960s and 1970s, helping to introduce Cajun music to a (primarily) urban audience.

The band centered on fiddlers Dewey (March 20, 1927–January 17, 1992) and Will (d. February 6, 1979), guitarist/vocalist Rodney (1934–February 6, 1979); another brother, Harry, played ACCORDION with the group in its earliest days. The brothers began playing together for local dances and parties in the late 1940s. The group made one recording in 1951, but then Dewey broke off to work as a solo performer, and also in partnership with accordionist NATHAN ABSHIRE, an association that lasted through the mid-1960s.

In 1967, inspired by the growing folk revival audience and interest in Cajun traditions, Dewey,

Rodney, Will, and Dewey's daughter Nelda (triangle/vocals) began touring; nonfamily member Hadley Fontenot took the accordion chair. The band began recording in the United States for Swallow and in Europe for Sonet; they also were featured in the 1975 documentary, *The Good Times Are Killing Me*. On February 6, 1979, an automobile accident took the lives of Rodney and Will. Dewey continued to head a band with various members through his death on January 17, 1992.

Following Dewey's passing, his daughters Christine (guitar, vocals) and Nelda, along with Christine's husband Dirk Powell (fiddle, accordion, vocals), formed Balfa Toujours, dedicated to carrying forward their father's and uncle's legacy.

Ball, E. C. (1913–1978) and Orna (b. 1907)
husband and wife singing duo

Estil "E. C." Ball and his wife, Orna, along with their group the Friendly Gospel Singers, were traditional gospel singers from the Virginia/North Carolina border. The Balls ran a general store/gas station, and were "discovered" in 1938 by JOHN AND ALAN LOMAX, who recorded them for the Library of Congress. With the old-time music revival of the 1960s, they were "rediscovered," recording first for County Records in 1967, and then for the new Rounder label five years later. They also appeared occasionally at folk festivals, although they mostly limited their performing to their home area. E. C. had a pleasant baritone voice, which was perfectly complemented by his wife Orna's higher-pitched, more traditional-sounding vocals; E. C. was also celebrated for his tasteful GUITAR playing, featuring a two-finger melodic picking style influenced by country guitarist/record star Merle Travis.

banjo, five-string

The five-string banjo, developed in the mid-19th century, probably derived from earlier African instruments. White minstrel star Joel Walker Sweeney is generally credited with adding the short fifth or drone string to the banjo, which previously had been made in four-, six-, eight-, and 10-string models. Early banjos were generally made with wooden bodies and rims, a fretless neck, and a skin head. The original banjo-playing style has been variously called clawhammer, frailing, rapping, or knocking. It involves brushing the back of the hand across the strings while catching the thumb on the fifth string. There are many different varieties of clawhammer styles, from highly melodic to highly percussive.

Around the turn of the last century, ragtime players such as Fred Van Epps and Vess L. Ossmann popularized a picked style using three fingers; this style is known as "classical" or "ragtime" banjo today. Improved instrument designs helped increase the banjo's popularity. Makers like the Vega Company out of Boston introduced new metal tone rings that helped project the instrument's sound so it could be heard in a band setting. The famous instruments of the teens and twenties, such as Vega's Whyte Laydie and Tubaphone models, were favored by banjoists working both as soloists or in a band.

In the mid-1940s a new style of playing the banjo helped transform it from a background (or accompaniment) role to prominence as a melody instrument. Two-finger and three-finger picking styles existed among folk banjoists at least from the turn of the last century, particularly in North Carolina and the upper South. These evolved into bluegrass-style picking, originally introduced by Earl Scruggs as a member of Bill Monroe's Blue Grass Boys. Here three fingers are used, with metal picks, to play rapid chord rolls and melody parts. Bluegrass musicians began playing a newly styled banjo marketed by the Gibson Company called the Mastertone; it featured further improvements in the design of the tone ring, including a raised head, as well as a full resonator to further increase the instrument's sound.

One person can be credited with popularizing the five-string banjo among folk musicians: PETE SEEGER. Beginning as a member of the WEAVERS in the late 1940s and then through a long and distinguished solo career, Seeger brought the sound of the banjo to millions of listeners. He self-published in the early 1950s what would become the standard beginner's instruction book for the instrument among folk players, and without

exaggeration there isn't a single folk-style banjo player who didn't first get started either by hearing Seeger or working from his book. Seeger introduced an innovation in banjo design also, lengthening the standard neck to enable him to play in lower keys (more suited to group singing). He convinced the Vega Company to begin making the long-necked or Seeger-style banjos, and they remain popular among folk players.

From the 1960s forward, folk revivalists have rediscovered many of the great banjo players of the past century, from country stars such as BASCOM LAMAR LUNSFORD and Uncle Dave Macon to more roots-oriented players such as FRED COCKERHAM and Pete Steele. Earlier forms of the instrument—such as the fretless banjo and even minstrel-era designs featuring gourd-shaped bodies—have been revived in an attempt to capture the real sound of these styles. Second only to the GUITAR, the banjo is a key instrument in the folk revival.

A Vega Tubaphone Banjo # 2 from the mid-1920s (Courtesy George Gruhn)

Battlefield Band

The Battlefield Band is a long-lived Scottish folk-revival group, which has featured many different musicians in its 30-plus year run.

The original group was formed in 1969 and centered around keyboard player/vocalist Alan Reid and fiddler/vocalist Brian McNeill. Originally playing acoustic instruments and featuring traditional tunes and songs, the band developed over the next decade to feature a more aggressive, folk-rock sound. Reid switched to synthesizers and McNeill amplified his FIDDLE; the addition of guitarists Pat Kilbride (1978) and Ged Foley (1980–84) to the lineup produced some of their best-known work. Further personnel shakeups followed through the 1980s, and McNeill left the band in 1990. Reid has soldiered on as the band's leader, bringing in new players John McCusker (fiddle/vocals), who replaced McNeill in 1990, and later regulars Davy Steele (GUITAR/cittern) and Mike Katz ("bagpipes"), who both joined in 1997. In 2002 Pat Kilbride returned to the lineup, pleasing the band's earlier fans.

Beausoleil

One of the best-known Cajun revival bands, Beausoleil is led by fiddler/vocalist Michael Doucet (b. February 14, 1951, in Scott, Lousiana), who has done much to preserve CAJUN MUSIC and culture. Doucet began playing rock music in high school, and then became interested in folk rock, after hearing FAIRPORT CONVENTION. He traveled to France in 1973 and spent the next few years there and in London. In 1976 he returned home and formed the first version of Beausoleil. Since then the band has featured both traditional Cajun music and Doucet's own songs. The band has performed and recorded widely, notably appearing on Mary Chapin Carpenter's 1991 hit "Down at the Twist and Shout" which celebrates Cajun music.

Belafonte, Harry (b. 1927) *actor and singer*

Harold George Belafonte Jr. was born in Harlem, New York City, on March 1, 1927; his parents had roots in the Caribbean. When he was eight years old, his mother, a Jamaican, split from his father, taking her son back to her native country, where he lived until he was 13 years old. He returned to New York to complete his schooling, then enlisted in the navy. On his discharge he came back to New York, hoping to establish himself as an actor. He initially found success in musical theater and began singing in nightclubs. In 1949 he made his first recording in a pop style for the small Jubilee label.

In the early 1950s Belafonte was introduced to folk music and began performing this material with a guitarist. His acting career continued to develop, and was given a major boost when director Otto Preminger hired him to appear in the 1955 film *Carmen Jones*. This led to a recording contract with RCA, and Belafonte's first album was released in 1956. In early 1957 Belafonte had a major hit with the Calypso-flavored song "Banana Boat (Day-O)," which launched a major craze for the music.

Belafonte's recording career flourished from the mid-1950s through the early 1960s, buoyed by the revival of interest in folk music and his dynamic performances. In the early 1960s he became active in the CIVIL RIGHTS MOVEMENT and other progressive causes while continuing to perform. However, the British Invasion of the pop charts ended his period of greatest commercial success, although Belafonte remained a major star on television, in nightclubs, and in films.

Belafonte's humanitarian work preoccupied him through most of the 1970s and 1980s. In 1985 he was one of the key players in the "We Are the World" fund-raiser recording to benefit starving Africans. He has continued his humanitarian work since that time, while occasionally performing.

Berline, Byron (b. 1944) *fiddle player*

A country boy with a college education, Berline was born in Caldwell, Kansas, on July 6, 1944, to an old-time fiddling father, Luke, and a piano-playing mother. His father was a big fan of Texas or "contest"-style fiddling, and the boy picked up this style when he began to play at age five. Byron beat his father in a local contest when he was 10, and soon was taking many regional titles. Meanwhile, an athletic scholarship took him to the University of Oklahoma, where he began to perform in a college band.

At college he heard bluegrass music for the first time when the popular band the DILLARDS performed on campus. He met banjo player Doug Dillard after the concert, and they soon discovered that both of their fathers shared a love of old-time fiddling. Berline was invited to perform on the Dillards' next album, *Pickin' and Fiddlin'*. The band performed many Texas favorites on this album in the highly ornamental competition style that Berline had picked up playing at countless fiddlers' conventions.

After finishing college in 1967, Berline performed briefly with Bill Monroe before joining the army; during his stint with Monroe, he recorded "Sally Goodin," originally recorded by Eck Robertson in 1922, complete with the many variations that have made the piece a competition

Byron Berline in the mid-1970s (Courtesy Flying Fish Records)

favorite. After he was discharged, Berline rejoined Doug Dillard on the West Coast as a member of the country-rock outfit Dillard and Clark. He performed with The Flying Burrito Brothers in the early 1970s, which soon after became the first version of COUNTRY GAZETTE.

Thanks to the mid-1970s bluegrass revival, Berline was able to return to playing acoustic music in a variety of formats. As a band leader, he recorded bluegrass, newgrass, and jazz-influenced music with his group, Sundance; as a member of the trio Crary, Hickman, and Berline, he recorded in a more straightforward traditional vein. Since the mid-1990s he has led his own Byron Berline Band, continuing to play in a variety of styles.

See also FIDDLE.

Bikel, Theo[dore] (b. 1924) *actor and singer*

Bikel was born in Vienna, Austria, on March 2, 1924. His Jewish family fled the country in 1938, settling in British Palestine and becoming British citizens. Aspiring to be an actor, Bikel appeared with a Tel Aviv theater troupe from 1943 to 1945, leading to study in London. He appeared in the first British production of Tennessee Williams's *A Streetcar Named Desire* in 1947, leading to small roles in films and further dramatic work.

In 1955 Bikel came to New York and soon began performing folk songs at local coffeehouses along with his theatrical appearances. He was signed to Elektra Records, recording a mix of American and world folk and folk-styled songs. In 1959 he premiered on Broadway as the original Baron von Trapp in the Rodgers and Hammerstein musical *The Sound of Music.*

Although Bikel continued to record and perform as a folk singer through the early 1970s, he was increasingly known as an actor/performer/ personality.

Binkley Brothers Dixie Clodhoppers

The Binkley Brothers' band, an early rural string band, was made famous by their appearances on the *Grand Ole Opry* from 1926 to 1939. Fiddler Gale and his brother banjo player Amos Binkley were Nashville natives who eventually owned and operated a successful watch repair business, which was still open as late as 1960. Guitarist Tom Andrews was from nearby Franklin, Tennessee, and was said to be an associate of Kirk and SAM MCGEE.

The Binkley band first appeared on the *Opry* on October 10, 1926, and in 1932 became official *Opry* members, playing from that point forward every other week on the show until they were dropped in 1939. Various members came and went, but the basic old-time style of the band remained unchanged. Probably this is the reason they were summarily dropped in 1939, because their music was, by then, considerably out of date.

The Binkleys were among the first bands to record in Nashville, during the famous September 1928 sessions held by the Victor label. However, when they arrived at the studios, the engineers were unhappy with the Binkleys' singing. They quickly enlisted the help of singer/guitarist Jack Jackson. Jackson was a Lebanon, Tennessee, native, known as the "Singing Yodeler" (this before Jimmie Rodgers had made yodeling an integral part of country blues recording). He provided the vocals on the 10 numbers the Binkleys recorded, including their "hit" versions of "I'll Rise When the Rooster Crows," a song popularized by Uncle Dave Macon on a 1925 recording. Gale Binkley's smooth fiddling was a perfect complement to Jackson's modern singing style, and the record enjoyed wide success. However, the Binkleys never recorded again.

After they left the *Opry*, apparently the two brothers were happy to pursue their jewelry business and leave music making to others.

Blake, Norman (b. 1938) *Dobro player, guitarist, and mandolin player*

Blake was born on March 10, 1938, in Chattanooga, Tennessee, but raised in Georgia. By his teen years he could play a number of instruments. In the mid-to-late 1950s Blake began his professional career playing MANDOLIN with a number of bluegrass-flavored bands. After serving in the army in the early 1960s, Blake returned to his native Georgia to discover that traditional music was on the wane. Determined not to shortchange his talents, he took to teaching GUITAR while playing in a local dance band on the side.

Blake was "discovered" by June Carter, wife of Johnny Cash, who invited him to join her road show in the late 1960s. He began performing with both husband and wife, moving to Nashville in the spring of 1969. He was one of the young musicians featured on BOB DYLAN's *Nashville Skyline* album, further enhancing his reputation both as a guitarist and DOBRO player. He toured with Kris Kristofferson's band in 1970, and then joined JOHN HARTFORD's influential country-bluegrass band of the early 1970s, which also featured fiddler Vassar Clements, dobroist Tut Taylor, and bassist Randy Scruggs.

After leaving Hartford's group in 1972, Blake's solo career began with a number of low-keyed albums, featuring both original material and recreations of traditional bluegrass, country, and old-time songs. His song "Last Train from Poor Valley," featured on his 1974 album *The Fields of November*, was widely covered in bluegrass circles.

From the later 1970s through the mid-1980s Blake often performed as a duo with his wife, Nancy, a classically trained cellist. After a period of separation, they have been performing together again since the later 1990s. With the addition of bluegrass fiddler James Bryan, who had previously played with Bill Monroe, they formed a trio that performed together informally through the 1980s. Blake was one of many country players who was featured on the 2000 film soundtrack *O Brother, Where Art Thou?*, which helped revive interest in his music.

Boggs, Dock (1898–1971) *banjoist*

Born Moran Lee Boggs in Dooley, Virginia, on February 7, 1898, Dock was raised in a traditional mountain community. His entire family was musical, being particularly fond of the banjo. (See BANJO, FIVE-STRING.) Boggs began playing the instrument at the age of 12, impressed by the bluesy playing of a local black banjoist who picked the strings with two fingers and a thumb.

After his wedding in 1918, Boggs continued to play the banjo, while working as a coal miner. His fame spread locally, and in 1927 he was approached by a scout from Brunswick Records to make some recordings. He recorded 24 songs in 1927–28. His biggest hit was "Country Blues," a banjo song that showed the influence of African-American song. The balance of his recordings were less successful, and Boggs stopped playing the banjo when he retired in 1954.

Mike Seeger (left) accompanies Dock Boggs at a concert in Boston in 1963. Seeger "rediscovered" Boggs and brought him north to perform in the early 1960s. (Photo © John Byrne Cooke, http://www.cookephoto.com)

In the early 1960s folklorist MIKE SEEGER came to the mountains, looking for some of the older recording artists. One artist he particularly wanted to find was Boggs, and through a stroke of luck he located him living not too far from his place of birth. A series of albums of music and interviews followed, and Boggs was also soon performing at the NEWPORT FOLK FESTIVAL and also on the folk-revival circuit. Boggs died on February 7, 1971.

Boggs's career was highlighted by culture/music critic Greil Marcus in his influential 1997 book, *Invisible Republic: Bob Dylan and the Basement Tapes*. Thanks to this book, Boggs's Folkways recordings were reissued on CD, as were his original 1928 recordings.

Bok, Gordon (b. 1939) *singer and songwriter*
Although born in Pennsylvania on October 31, 1939, Bok is closely associated with the music and lore of the Maine fishing industry. His mother played folk songs on a classical GUITAR, encouraging her son to take up the instrument at age nine. After high school he worked summers on fishing boats, which inspired him to begin to learn traditional sea chanteys and other songs. By his young adult years he was working as a carpenter in Maine. In the mid-1960s he was discovered by Noel "Paul" Stookey, of PETER, PAUL, AND MARY fame, who produced Bok's first album. Five years passed before Bok was heard again, but he then recorded and performed prolifically from the early 1970s. He has written his own songs in the style of traditional ballads, and also created longer "cante-fables," half-sung, half-spoken works, often based on traditional stories and lore.

Bok performed and recorded with friends and fellow folksingers Ann Mayo Muir and Ed Trickett; Muir plays harp and FLUTE, and Trickett plays hammer dulcimer and guitar. They perform a mix of traditional songs and their own compositions.

Bothy Band, The
Although short-lived and suffering many changes in personnel, the Bothy Band was one of the most influential of the new Irish revival bands of the 1970s. In 1975 bouzouki player Donal Lunny left PLANXTY, another revival band, to form his own record label, Mulligan. He assembled an all-star cast of musicians, including FLUTE and whistle player Matt Malloy, piper Paddy Keenan, and fiddler Paddy Glackin to form a new band; to add vocals to the mix, he enlisted Michael (GUITAR) and Triona ni Domhnaill (harpsichord and keyboards), brother-and-sister performers who came from a long line of traditional singers. Before the group made its debut recording in 1975, Glackin was replaced by fiddler Tommy Peoples; he in turn was replaced shortly thereafter by KEVIN BURKE. The group combined the strong lead vocals of Triona and Michael with the energetic ensemble playing of Malloy, Kennan, and Burke to create a hard-driving, acoustic sound. After two more albums and a live collection, the

group disbanded in 1979, although its various members continued to work together in different combinations over the next decades.

Bowers, Bryan (b. 1940) *autoharp player*
Bowers was born in St. Petersburg, Virginia. After dropping out of college he began playing GUITAR, and then other folk instruments, eventually hearing a friend play the autoharp. He moved briefly to Seattle in the early 1970s, and then worked his way back east performing and settled in Washington, D.C. Bluegrass performers the DILLARDS heard him play at a local club and urged him to perform on the bluegrass circuit, where his unique ability to play complicated melodies on the autoharp made him an immediate sensation. The Dillards' label, Flying Fish, signed him, and he issued his first solo album in 1977, followed by three more (including 1982's live album, *Home, Home on the Road*), before taking an 18-year break from recording. Bowers continues to perform live, although he has never again enjoyed the great popularity that his initial concerts and recordings inspired.

Boys of the Lough
The Boys of the Lough combine the traditional musical styles of Ireland, Scotland, and Shetland in a virtuosic ensemble. Irish performers vocalist/concertina player Robin Morton (b. 1939, Portadown, Ireland) and vocalist/flutist Cathal McConnell (b. 1944, Enniskillen, Ireland) had been performing as a folk duo in the late 1960s and early 1970s. They were booked to appear at a folk festival in 1970, where Shetland fiddler ALY BAIN (b. 1946, Lerwick, Shetland) was scheduled to perform along with guitarist Mike Whelan. Informally jamming together, they decided to perform as a quartet, and the group was born. Whelan quickly left and was replaced, briefly, by singer/guitarist Dick Gaughan for the group's first album, released in 1972. Gaughan, however, wished to pursue a solo career, and was replaced by multi-instrumentalist Dave

Richardson (b. 1948, Corbridge, Northumberland, England). It was this version of the band that achieved the greatest success, performing together through the 1970s and touring Europe and the United States many times. Led by the virtuoso playing of Bain and McConnell, the group was one of the first great instrumental bands of the revival period, although they also performed a repertoire of songs and ballads. They served as a bridge between the first wave of Irish revival bands and the more rock-influenced groups such as PLANXTY and the BOTHY BAND that formed in the mid-1970s.

In 1979 Morton left the group to pursue a career as a record producer. He was replaced by Dave Richardson's brother, guitarist Tich Richardson. Tich's playing had a jazz-swing feeling to it, surprisingly changing the group's overall sound. This line-up lasted until 1983, when Tich was killed in an automobile accident. At this point Bain, Dave Richardson, and O'Connell incorporated as full members of the band. To augment the group, they hired as supporting musicians Irish piper Christy O'Leary (b. 1955, Rathcoole, Dublin) and pianist John Coakley (b. 1951, Cork, Ireland).

From the mid-1980s to today, the band has continued to record and tour, but they often have suspended activities so group members could pursue other musical interests. Bain has been the most active as a freelancer, performing as a solo artist and also in a duo with accordionist Phil Cunningham. In the early 1990s Coakley was replaced by John Newman. In 1997 O'Leary and Newman left the band and were replaced by ACCORDION player Brendan Begley and Garry O'Briain on GUITAR and piano.

Brady, Paul (b. 1947) *singer and songwriter*
Irish singer/songwriter Paul Brady was born on May 19, 1947, in Strabane, County Tyrone, Ireland. He began working as a professional musician as a teenager, but did not begin playing folk music until he was hired as an accompanist for the Irish folk-

revival group the JOHNSTONS in the late 1960s through 1974. Brady then was in an early version of PLANXTY (although he did not record with the group), and during 1976–77 he toured and recorded with ANDY IRVINE. During this period Brady often worked as an accompanist to traditional musicians, including Tommy Peoples. Brady's last album that featured traditional material was made in 1978; since that time he has focused on performing and recording his own compositions. Several of his songs have been covered by Bonnie Raitt among other popular performers.

Brand, Oscar (b. 1920) *broadcaster and musician*

Brand was born on January 7, 1920, in rural Winnipeg, Canada, but his family migrated to the United States while he was still young, settling first briefly in Minneapolis and Chicago before finally reaching New York City. Brand attended high school in Brooklyn in the mid-1930s and heard his first folk concerts. He attended Brooklyn College while honing his folk instrumental skills on the side, taking up GUITAR and banjo, and then served in World War II. On his discharge in 1945, he joined the staff of local public radio station WNYC, broadcasting a folk music show that has continued to be part of its schedule for nearly six decades. Meanwhile, Brand performed on the local coffeehouse circuit.

In the mid-1950s, when the new Elektra label was founded in New York, Brand was among its first artists. His series of albums of "Bawdy Songs"— slightly racy and suggestive material from different musical traditions—helped establish the label and made Brand a star of the early folk revival. A prolific recording artist, Brand turned out dozens of albums, for Elektra, Folkways, Riverside, Tradition, Caedmon, and other labels through the mid-1960s, usually focusing on a topic (*Songs for Golfers, Songs for Skiers, Songs for Doctors*) or historical period (*Election Songs of the U.S.*).

Although Brand recorded less after the early 1970s, he continued to be an advocate for folk music, primarily through his radio broadcasts and concerts.

Broadside magazine

A mimeographed newsletter founded in 1962 by folk singers/activists AGNES "SIS" CUNNINGHAM (1899–2004) and her husband, Gordon Friesen (b. 1909). Disillusioned with the folk song revival's commercialism, and even *SING OUT!* MAGAZINE's lack of political orientation, *Broadside* was founded to publish the best topical songs of the day, and soon attracted young songwriters including BOB DYLAN, PHIL OCHS, and TOM PAXTON, as well as first-generation activists PETE SEEGER and MALVINA REYNOLDS. The magazine was particularly influential in introducing Dylan's songs to folksingers (his own recording career was just beginning, and it was often easier to understand his lyrics on paper than in performance). In 1963 MOSES ASCH of Folkways Records started a related record label to issue the home-made tapes of new singers that Cunningham and Friesen recorded in order to transcribe the songs. However, after the folk song revival and protest song movement cooled in the mid-1960s, *Broadside* was much less influential, although Cunningham and Friesen continued to publish the journal irregularly until 1988. In 2000 Smithsonian/Folkways records issued a boxed set, *The Best of Broadside*, documenting the magazine and record label.

Bromberg, David (b. 1945) *bandleader and guitarist*

Born on December 19, 1945, in Philadelphia, Pennsylvania, Bromberg first attracted attention as a session guitarist working with BOB DYLAN and others in the early 1970s. Signed to Columbia Records, Bromberg recorded a series of albums combining blues, country, and acoustic jazz stylings. In the mid-1970s he formed a large touring band, featuring fiddler Jay Ungar and several other luminaries on the folk and bluegrass scene, and also

David Bromberg at the Philadelphia Folk Festival, c. early 1980s (Photo © Larry Sandberg)

signed with Fantasy Records. In 1980 he more or less retired to focus his attention on instrument building. A new solo album appeared in 1990 on Rounder Records, but it failed to attract much attention.

Broonzy, Big Bill (1898–1958) *guitarist and singer*

Broonzy was born on June 26, 1898, in rural Scott, Mississippi, and his family moved often through the Mississippi-Arkansas region during the early years of his life, sharecropping and working as hired farm hands. Broonzy was already working as an informal entertainer as a teenager, said to have been an able fiddler and also working occasionally as a preacher; about this time he made his first GUITAR out of a discarded wooden crate. He enlisted in the army and served in World War I from 1917 to 1919, then settled in Chicago on his discharge.

Broonzy's career as a recording artist began in 1923, and he recorded prolifically for the next decade, mostly country blues and his own new songs commenting on the plight of Southern blacks who had come to Chicago to work in the factories, railroads, and warehouses of that major industrial hub. Broonzy's ragtime-flavored guitar playing and pleasant voice made him attractive to a sophisticated city audience, while his subject matter drew on traditional rural topics, including love gone wrong, the urge to ramble, and the tough life faced by blacks in a segregated society. Broonzy added to the topics, particularly in his early to mid-1930s recordings, by creating new songs including "House Rent Stomp," "Unemployment Stomp," and even "In the Army Now," recorded at the beginning of World War II. Broonzy emphasized upbeat numbers and specialized in fingerpicked instrumentals that showed his virtuosity on the guitar.

A major figure on the Chicago blues scene by the mid-1930s, Broonzy was introduced to a wider audience thanks to an invitation to appear at John Hammond's famous "From Spirituals to Swing" concert in 1938 at New York's Carnegie Hall. It took a while for Broonzy to build on this new audience, but by the late 1940s he was appearing regularly on Studs Terkel's radio program out of Chicago, which appealed to the new, urban folk-revival audience. Broonzy began simplifying his guitar style and directing his repertory toward older blues that appealed to this audience. A successful European tour in 1951 also built his audience base, and he would make several more successful tours there. He recorded for a number of folk revival labels, including Folkways, which helped him reach this new audience. In 1954 he dictated an autobiography to the Belgian jazz writer Yannick Bruynoghe, which appeared as *Big Bill Blues* a year later. However, Broonzy's health began to fail, and he succumbed to cancer on August 14, 1958.

Following his death, many new albums appeared that popularized Broonzy in the early 1960s folk revival, as well as keeping his name in front of European jazz and blues fans. For a while many diehard blues fans dismissed Broonzy as a folk-styled performer based on being familiar only with his 1950s-era work. However, the early 1970s acoustic blues revival led to a rediscovery of his earlier recordings and a reappraisal of his considerable talents as a guitarist.

Brozman, Bob (b. 1954) *guitarist*

Robert Brozman was born in New York City on March 2, 1954. He came from a musical family; his uncle was the famous club owner Barney Josephson, who presented Billie Holiday and LEAD BELLY at his club, Café Society, in New York City in the 1940s. Before his teen years he began playing GUITAR, and at age 13 first saw and heard a metal-bodied National Steel guitar. Drawn to its unusual sound, he began learning to play fingerpicked and slide-guitar blues. Pursuing his interest in the blues, he attended college at St. Louis's Washington University, where he took a degree in ethnomusicology. He also became interested in other styles of music played on the steel guitar, most notably Hawaiian "slack key" (so called because the strings are tuned to open chords)

Bob Brozman at the Philadelphia Folk Festival (Photo © Larry Sandberg)

style. He released his first album in 1981 on the small Kicking Mule label, and has since over a dozen solo albums to his credit. He has also performed in duet with traditional Hawaiian musicians, including slack key guitarist Led Kaapana. Brozman also performed for a brief period in the 1980s with artist R. Crumb's 1920s-style novelty group, the Cheap Suit Serenaders. Brozman has also written a comprehensive history of the National Steel guitar and related instruments.

Brumley, Albert E. (1905–1977) *gospel song-writer and music publisher*

Brumley was born on October 29, 1905, in Spiro, Oklahoma. He attended many local gospel singing schools and conventions on the Oklahoma/Arkansas border. But most important, as a teenager he enrolled at Hartford (Arkansas) Music Institute, where he encountered Virgil O. Stamps, the founder of the Stamps Quartet. After his marriage in 1931 Brumley settled in the rural Ozarks in the small town of Powell, Missouri; that same year he wrote his first (and perhaps most famous) gospel classic, "I'll Fly Away" (recorded hundreds of times, and revived most recently in the 2000 film *O Brother, Where Art Thou?*).

Brumley eventually penned more than 800 songs, many of them standards in the folk, country, and bluegrass repertoire. Among his classics are "Rank Stranger to Me" (1942), which became one of the favorites in the STANLEY BROTHERS repertoire, and "Turn Your Radio On" (1938), revived in 1971 by JOHN HARTFORD. Other favorites include "Jesus Hold My Hand" (1933), "There's a Little Pine Log Cabin" (1937), and "I've Found a Hiding Place" (1939).

Brumley also formed the Albert E. Brumley Music Company to publish his gospel songbooks, beginning in the 1930s. These songbooks helped spread his songs throughout the South and West, and many artists used them as resources for their radio or record work. In the late 1940s Brumley purchased the Hartford Music Company, which

owned the rights to his earliest songs. He continued to live in Powell, Missouri, until his death on November 15, 1977.

Brumley's children have all been active in the music business. His son Al Jr. began his performing career in honky-tonk music, primarily working in California. However, for the last two decades, he has made a career out of performing his father's songs on the gospel circuit. Tom Brumley is perhaps the most famous of Albert's children; he played steel guitar with Buck Owens's Buckaroos in the mid-1960s and then cofounded one of the first country rock bands, the Stone Canyon band, with singer Rick Nelson. Both Tom and Al are involved with *The Brumley Music Show*, which is staged in the family theater in Branson, Missouri, as are their children. Brumley's other children are also involved in the music publishing business that he founded.

Bud and Travis

Paris-born Bud Dashiell served in the Korean conflict, where he met Collin Edmonson, who introduced him to his GUITAR-playing brother, Travis, who had been performing with the Gateway Singers. By 1958 Bud and Travis were recording and performing together, specializing in a mix of traditional folk, Edmonson's own compositions, and Spanish-language material. They were signed to the West Coast pop label Liberty, and although their albums sold well, they never had hit singles on the pop charts, like other folk revivalists such as the KINGSTON TRIO. Although they were both talented guitarists and harmonized well onstage, they did not get along well as individuals. Nonetheless, they enjoyed great success through 1965, releasing 10 albums. After the duo split, Bud played for a while with another folk group, The Kinsmen, and then performed as a solo artist in the 1970s, until moving in the 1980s to Los Angeles, where he taught GUITAR. He died of a brain tumor in 1989. Travis also performed as a solo artist in the 1970s.

Buffalo Gals, The

One of the first all-female, revival bluegrass bands, the Buffalo Gals spotlighted progressive banjoist Susie Monick (b. 1952). The band was formed originally when Monick, guitarist Debby Gabriel, and dulcimer player Carol Siegel were undergraduates together at Syracuse University. Siegel took up MANDOLIN, and they formed an old-time/bluegrass trio. Gabriel decided to pursue a career as a painter, and was replaced by vocalist/guitarist Martha Trachtenberg and bassist Nancy Josephson. By 1974 fiddler Sue Raines was on board, and the quintet was playing bluegrass and folk festivals.

The band's notoriety came mostly from their all-female makeup; it was not only unusual for women to play bluegrass, women were also rarely showcased as hot pickers, and the band members could certainly hold their own with any of the other progressive bluegrass bands of the day. By 1976 new members Lainie Lyle on mandolin and fiddler Kristin Wilkinson had replaced Raines and Siegel, and the band relocated to Nashville. At about the same time, Monick released a solo banjo LP, *Melting Pots,* a mix of far-out instrumentals along with Celtic-flavored and other experimental banjo sounds. The band went through more personnel changes before it finally folded in 1979.

During the 1990s Monick performed as a mandolin and button ACCORDION player in State of the Heart, a country-folk ensemble led by Nashville songwriter Richard Dobson. In the later 1990s she began displaying her clay art, including many figures based on traditional musicians.

Another (unrelated) group by the same name, playing in a Western Swing style, has performed on the popular radio show *A Prairie Home Companion.*

See also BANJO, FIVE-STRING; DULCIMER (APPALACHIAN); DULCIMER (HAMMERED).

Bumgarner, Samantha (c. 1878–1960)
banjoist, fiddle player, and singer

Born Samantha Biddix in Silva, North Carolina, Bumgarner was an early country banjoist, fiddler, and vocalist who is best known for 12 recordings made in April 1924 along with guitarist Eva Davis, among the earliest old-time recordings. She was among the first banjoists to record in this style, male or female. Bumgarner appeared at the first Mountain Dance and Folk Festival in 1928, organized by another legendary banjoist, BASCOM LAMAR LUNSFORD, in Asheville, North Carolina, and continued to be a favorite at this festival for the next 31 years until her death. The daughter of an old-time fiddler, Bumgarner was a talented performer on both banjo and FIDDLE, winning numerous contests in her day, an unusual feat at the time for a woman. She continued to perform through the 1950s, gaining regional fame as a performer of traditional banjo tunes and songs.

See also BANJO, FIVE-STRING.

Burke, Joe (b. 1939) *accordionist*

Burke was born in Kilnadeema, County, Galway, Ireland, and was raised in a musical household; his mother played the single-row Irish melodeon, as did his uncle, Pat. Burke claims to have begun playing at age four when his uncle showed him a few tunes. During his childhood he also picked up the FIDDLE, wooden flute, and tin whistle. By his mid-teens Burke had obtained a two-row button ACCORDION, and quickly established himself as an expert player. From 1955 to 1962, he played with the Leitrim Céili Band, a group that he had cofounded. In 1959–60 he won the All-Ireland Senior Accordion championships; he then retired from competition. Also in 1959 he made his first recordings.

Burke made his first tour of the United States in 1961 with the Irish cultural group Comhaltas Ceoltóirí Éireann (he eventually made nine such tours of the United States and six of England with the CCE). In 1962 he settled in New York, where he lived for the next three years. He played regularly with various New York–based céili bands and musicians, including Bronx-born fiddler Andy McGann. In 1965 Burke made what became a landmark album with McGann in honor of famed fiddler MICHAEL COLEMAN, which helped establish his reputation as a master on the button accordion. In 1979 the duo reunited for another album, *The Funny Reel*.

Returning to Ireland in 1966, Burke formed a new musical partnership with fiddler Sean Maguire. The two recorded a duet album in 1971 called *Two Champions*. At the same time Burke also recorded a solo disc. Burke remained active in Ireland both as a solo artist and as a guest on various recordings and tours. From 1988 to 1992 he returned to the United States, settling in St. Louis, where he worked in local bars and had his own radio show. In 1990 he married musician Anne Conroy, who plays accordion and guitar, and the two have performed as a duo since. In 1992 they returned to Ireland to live on a farm in Burke's hometown of Kilnadeema.

Burke, Kevin (b. 1948) *fiddler*

Born in southeast London, Burke began classical violin lessons as an eight-year-old. He was exposed to traditional Irish FIDDLE music through recordings. As a teenager he began playing in local Irish pubs, and was invited to join the Glenside Céili Band; Burke was a member when the band took an "All-Ireland" title in 1966. In the early 1970s Burke was visiting Ireland, where by chance he met the American folksinger ARLO GUTHRIE. On his return to the United States, Guthrie invited Burke to come to America to appear on his next album. Burke traveled to Los Angeles via New York (where he met legendary fiddler Andy McGann) in 1972 and appeared on Guthrie's album *Last of the Brooklyn Cowboys* (1973). He also recorded his first solo album for a small folk label; it went unissued until 1977.

In 1974 Burke was invited to join revival singer/instrumentalist Christy Moore's band in Dublin, which played both acoustic and electric music. Meanwhile, in the early 1970s, the BOTHY BAND had formed around instrumentalist DONAL LUNNY. The original band featured fiddler Paddy Glackin, but he was quickly replaced by Tommy Peoples for their first album. Peoples left soon after, and Burke was invited to join the group in 1976. The group featured acoustic arrangements of traditional tunes that showed the influence of pop and

rock arrangements and rhythms, and, while not as popular as DE DANAAN or PLANXTY, they were leaders in the 1970s revival of Irish traditional music. Also in the group was singer/guitarist Michael O'Domhnaill. When the group broke up in 1979, Burke and O'Domhnaill formed a duo and toured through the early 1980s. Burke and O'Domhnaill settled in Portland, Oregon, and recorded two albums, which featured a more laidback approach than their previous band work.

In the early 1980s Burke began working with ACCORDION player Jackie Daly, who had previously played with Planxty. This led to the formation of a new band, Patrick Street, featuring ANDY IRVINE (also ex-Planxty) and, originally, guitarist Arty McGlynn. The band began recording and touring in the mid-1980s; after a break in the early 1990s, the group returned in the later 1990s with the addition of singer/guitarist Ged Foley, previously with the Battlefield Band.

In 1992 Burke formed a more wide-ranging band, Open House, which remained together with varying personnel through 1999. The group explored a variety of music, influenced by new age, jazz, and rock, as well as Irish traditional music. Meanwhile, also in 1992, Burke toured with Scottish fiddler JOHNNY CUNNINGHAM (ex-Silly Wizard) and Breton fiddler Christian LeMaitre under the name "The Celtic Fiddle Festival." A second tour followed in 1997, and the trio released two CDs drawn from live recordings from each tour. Beginning in 1999, Burke began touring as a solo artist, preferring to feature the fiddle unadorned by other instruments.

Burnett and Rutherford

Richard D. Burnett (b. Elk Spring Valley, Kentucky, October 8, 1883–January 1977) was a talented musician who began playing the dulcimer, banjo, and FIDDLE from an early age. Both his father and grandfather were dedicated churchgoers, and Burnett remembers singing hymns from the age of four. Burnett lost both parents by the time he was 12, inspiring him to write "The Orphan Boy" which became one of his most popular numbers.

Burnett began working as an oil field hand around 1901. Six years later, when returning from work one night, he was robbed and shot in the face; the bullet struck his optic nerve, blinding him. Unable to continue work, he fell back on his musical skills, becoming a wandering performer. Around 1914 he approached a local family, the Rutherfords, to ask them if their young, fiddle-playing son Leonard (b. Somerset, Kentucky, c. 1900–1954) could serve as his musical companion and guide-boy. The parents agreed, and the Burnett and Rutherford duo was born.

By the mid-1920s the duo was in great demand throughout the Kentucky-Tennessee-Virginia area. In 1926 they were performing in Virginia when a local store owner heard them perform and recommended them to Columbia Records. Burnett's expressive vocals and Rutherford's smooth fiddling made their records stand out, and they often recorded over the coming years.

Burnett's older style of performing—including a good deal of clowning around onstage—irritated the younger, more serious Rutherford. By the late 1920s they were already recording with other musicians, although they continued to perform together sporadically until Rutherford's death. The Depression effectively ended their recording careers, but they were still well-known street performers through the early 1950s. Later Burnett took up chair caning and retired from music.

See also BANJO, FIVE-STRING; DULCIMER (APPALACHIAN); DULCIMER (HAMMERED).

Byrds, The

Formed in 1964, the Byrds pioneered folk-rock music. Lead vocalist/guitarist Jim McGuinn (later he changed his name to Roger) and second guitarist/vocalist David Crosby had both worked in professional folk-revival groups; GENE CLARK (lead vocals, GUITAR) was a Los Angeles–based singer-songwriter; and bass player/harmony vocalist Chris Hillman's background was in bluegrass. The group's members were inspired by the Beatles to take up electric instruments.

From the beginning the group's repertoire reflected a folk and country orientation. They were among the first to record and popularize BOB DYLAN's songs on the pop charts, beginning with their first hit, 1965's "Mr. Tambourine Man." The same year, they took PETE SEEGER's "Turn Turn Turn," a setting of a verse from the book of Ecclesiastes, to number one.

Clark left the group in 1966 because of his fear of flying, and Crosby soon left to form the pop trio Crosby, Stills, and Nash, leaving the Byrds a three-member group, with McGuinn, Hillman, and drummer Michael Clarke. The band's transformation was completed in 1968 with the addition of singer/songwriter Gram Parsons. The new Byrds, with McGuinn, Hillman, Parsons, and drummer Kevin White, along with guests Clarence White and JOHN HARTFORD, recorded *Sweetheart of the Rodeo*. Besides remakes of country classics such as "An Empty Bottle, A Broken Heart, and You're Still on My Mind," the group recorded Parsons's neocountry ballad "Hickory Wind," pointing the direction for a new country-rock fusion.

Determined to pursue the country-rock direction, Hillman and Parsons left the band to form the Flying Burrito Brothers; session guitarist Clarence White came on board along with bassist John York (later replaced by Skip Battin). This group lasted for four years, producing the hits "Ballad of Easy Rider," sung by McGuinn for the soundtrack of the film of the same name, as well as the 1971 minor hit "Chestnut Mare." In 1975 the original five-man Byrds reunited for an album for Asylum Records, but the old group magic was gone.

In the mid-1970s McGuinn went solo, recording a couple of ill-received albums, as well as touring with Bob Dylan's Rolling Thunder Review. In the early 1980s he reunited with Hillman and Gene Clark to form a trio, and they recorded two albums. In the mid-1980s Hillman formed the country-rock Desert Rose Band, and Clark returned to a solo career (and eventually committed suicide in the early 1990s); McGuinn has continued to perform as a solo artist.

See also MCGUINN, ROGER.

Cajun music

Cajun music—the music created in southern Louisiana by the descendants of French, French-Canadian, African-American, and Native American musicians—has enjoyed popularity among folk musicians since the 1950s.

The Acadians originally hailed from the island of Acadia, a French colony off of Canada (now known as Nova Scotia); when the French ceded the island to the British in 1713, the settlers moved south to what was then still French territory in Louisiana. There they intermixed with English, Spanish, and African-American settlers, while developing their own unique language (known as Louisiana French or Creole) and musical style. Throughout the 19th century the musical styles of Europe—waltzes, quadrilles, cotillions, mazurkas—came to the area and entered the musical repertoire. While in the 18th century, the FIDDLE and triangle were the primary musical instruments, the 19th century brought the newly introduced ACCORDION and its many relatives as well as, later in the century, the GUITAR.

Cajun music was first recorded in the 1920s, when the record industry was quickly discovering the commercial potential for music directed at specific regional groups. Fiddlers DENNIS MCGEE and Saday Courville made the first, legendary twin-fiddle recordings. In the 1930s and 1940s WESTERN SWING and pop styles swept the area, and several Cajun musicians modernized the music to reflect these outside influences.

The FOLK REVIVAL of the late 1950s and early 1960s led to a renewed interest in more traditional Cajun music. Groups such as the NEW LOST CITY RAMBLERS added Cajun music to their act, and traditional family bands such as the BALFA BROTHERS from Mamou, Louisiana, were successful on the festival and folk-revival trail. Accordionist NATHAN ABSHIRE, who had originally recorded in the 1930s without much success, was rediscovered and became a big attraction on the concert scene.

Along with Cajun music, its sister sound, known as zodico or ZYDECO, gained new popularity also in the 1970s and 1980s. Zydeco is the wedding of African-American blues and jazz styles with Cajun dance and song; its proponents are mostly African-American Creoles. One of the greatest zydeco musicians was CLIFTON CHENIER, an accordionist who recorded extensively through the 1960s and 1970s.

Revival bands began springing up in the 1970s to cater to a more educated, upscale market. Fiddler MICHAEL DOUCET was one of the most active of the younger Cajun musicians; eventually he formed the group BEAUSOLEIL, a wedding of Cajun sounds with folk-rock instrumentation. Other popular Cajun and zydeco revivalists include Rockin' Dopsie and the Twisters (who appeared on Paul Simon's *Graceland* album), Rockin' Sydney (who popularized the much-recorded "My Toot Toot"), and Jo-El Sonnier.

Camp, Hamilton (b. 1934) *actor, singer, and songwriter*

Born as Robert Camp on October 30, 1934, Camp began working as a child actor at age 12. By his late teen years he was living in Chicago, where he became active on the folk scene. In 1960 he partnered with the popular singer/performer BOB GIBSON, under his birth name of "Bob Camp." The duo were very popular on the college circuit and in folk clubs, and performed and recorded together for a little over a year. They also composed several folk-styled songs together; PETER, PAUL, AND MARY covered their song "Well, Well, Well" in 1962, and Simon and Garfunkel covered Camp and Gibson's song "You Can Tell the World" on their debut album in 1964.

Camp then struck out on his own, changing his name to "Hamilton Camp" in 1964. On his debut solo album that year, he recorded his own song "Pride of Man," which later was covered by GORDON LIGHTFOOT on his first album and, most famously, by the San Francisco psychedelic rock band Quicksilver Messenger Service on their debut album. By 1967 Camp had settled in California, where he began a long career as a TV and film actor, a career he has pursued to the present. He continued to perform folk-rock music on the Los Angeles scene, releasing two albums in the later 1960s, featuring many accompaniments by a varied crew of local players, including pianist/composer Van Dyke Parks and guitarist Felix Pappalardi of Mountain.

In the mid-1970s Gibson and Camp reunited briefly for a reunion concert and a new album released on the small Mountain Railroad label. They reunited again in 1986 for a 25th anniversary concert and another album. In 1999 Camp released his first solo album in more than two decades.

Carawan, Guy (b. 1927) *singer and activist*

Guy Carawan was born in Los Angeles on July 27, 1927. Carawan began singing folk songs in the early 1950s, making several visits to the American South. In 1959 he began working as the music director of Tennessee's Highlander Research and Education Center, which was dedicated to improving conditions among the rural poor and promoting civil rights. There he met his wife-to-be, Candie, and the two became active participants in the growing CIVIL RIGHTS MOVEMENT. Carawan is credited with adapting the old hymn "I Shall Overcome" into the Civil Rights era anthem, "We Shall Overcome." With his wife, he published several influential songbooks of civil rights material and also produced several albums for Folkways Records. The duo also recorded the traditional singers of Georgia's Sea Islands. In the mid-1970s, inspired by his son, Evan, Carawan took up the hammered dulcimer, and the duo made several records together through the early 1990s.

See also DULCIMER (HAMMERED).

Carlin, Bob (b. 1953) *banjoist*

Robert Mark Carlin was born on March 17, 1953, in New York City, and raised in suburban New Jersey. He first worked as a blues guitarist in the mid-1970s before switching to performing old-time music. Originally playing bass with the New York old-time string band the Delaware Water Gap, Carlin produced and performed on 1977's *Melodic Clawhammer Banjo* album. This album was quite popular among young pickers, and established Carlin as a banjo soloist.

He released his first solo album in 1980, in which he played in a more traditionally oriented style, followed by a second album with an eclectic mix of old-time banjo numbers, duets with progressive banjoist TONY TRISCHKA, and adaptations of Rolling Stones songs to an old-time style. A third album featured duets with a number of fiddlers, including James Bryan (a relaxed, old-styled bluegrass fiddler who works with NORMAN BLAKE), and Brad Leftwich. Carlin and Bruce Molsky released a cassette of old-time songs and instrumentals soon after. His next recording was a fiddle-banjo duet album made with JOHN HARTFORD in 1995; Carlin subsequently recorded and toured with the John Hartford String Band until Hartford's death in June 2001, while continuing to work as a solo act. His self-released *Mr. Spaceman* CD was issued in 1997.

As a producer Carlin has released anthologies of old-time banjo picking as well as a tribute album to fiddler Tommy Jarrell. He also hosted a traditional music radio program out of Philadelphia for more than a decade. During the 1990s he worked as an artist-in-residence in North Carolina and Virginia while continuing to perform and produce recordings.

See also BANJO, FIVE-STRING.

Carolina Tar Heels

A low-key North Carolina–based string band led by guitarist/banjoist/entertainer Doc Walsh (b. Doctor Coble Walsh, Wilkes County, North Carolina, July 23, 1901–May 1967) that had some success in the late 1920s as a recording band.

Little is known of Walsh's early life. He was apparently a street singer who worked the mill towns of North Carolina; in 1925 he made his first recordings as a solo artist. A year later, he teamed with Gwen Foster, and the two formed a band. In 1927 they were signed to Columbia and given the Carolina Tar Heels name.

During the band's short recording history, they had several different lineups. Gwen Foster appeared on the first three sessions, then left the fold; he was replaced by another friend of Walsh's, also a harmonica player, and also with the surname Foster, although Garley Foster (Wilkes County, North Carolina, January 10, 1905–October 1968) was no relation to Gwen. Besides harmonica playing, Garley was billed as "The Human Bird" because of his whistling capabilities.

By fall 1928 Clarence "TOM" ASHLEY joined the group. Already a popular solo recording artist, Ashley was primarily a BANJO player. However, because Walsh already played banjo and was the group's leader, Ashley switched to GUITAR during his approximate one-year stint with the band. The group's biggest hit came as a trio on "My Home's Across the Blue Ridge Mountains." After Ashley left, Walsh and Foster were again a duo.

In 1931 an unrelated group took the Carolina Tar Heels name, broadcasting out of Atlanta. This led the Walsh-Foster duo to bill themselves alternatively as the Pine Mountain Boys or the "Original" Carolina Tar Heels. By 1932 with the Depression leading to less opportunity for country bands to record and perform, the group made its last recordings, this time with Walsh and original member Gwen Foster.

The 1960s folk revival led many folklorists to try to find stars of the 1920s and 1930s. Gene Earle and Archie Green brought Doc Walsh and Garley Foster back together to form a new Carolina Tar Heels, along with Doc's son, Drake. They recorded an album for the small Folk Legacy label, which showed that Garley's human bird capabilities were still intact. They also made a few appearances at folk festivals.

Carroll, Liz (b. 1956) *fiddler*

Carroll was born on September 19, 1956. Her father played the old-fashioned single-row melodeon, and her maternal grandfather was a fiddler. Both parents emigrated from Ireland to Chicago, where she was born. She began to play the FIDDLE at age nine, and soon was a regular in local sessions. In 1975 she took the All-Ireland fiddle title both as a soloist and in duet with ACCORDION player Jimmy Keane. Two years later, she recorded her first album with two other local Chicago musicians, accordion player Tommy Maguire and pianist Jerry Wallace. She then joined the popular Green Fields of America tours, organized by MICK MOLONEY, continuing to tour with them through the 1970s and early 1980s. As well as playing traditional tunes, Carroll is credited with composing nearly 200 of her own tunes. Besides her solo work, she formed a trio called Trian with accordionist Billy McComiskey and guitarist Daithi Sproule in the early 1990s for recording and touring. She has won the National Heritage Fellowship twice, in 1994 and 1999.

Carroll's style is contemporary and clean; she shows the influence of the new generation of Irish revivalists who have been active since the mid-1970s (many of whom are her contemporaries). She emphasizes a full tone, clean execution of melody and ornamentation, and a light, lilting swing. Her playing style, while not so distinctive as more steeped-in-the-tradition players like Tommy Peoples, is still easily recognizable as her own.

Carthy, Martin (b. 1940) *guitarist and singer*
Born on May 21, 1940, in Hatfield, Hertfordshire, England, Martin Carthy has been one of the most influential performers in the British folk revival scene since the mid-1960s. He first performed as a member of the Three City Four, a folk group specializing in social-protest material; another band member was songwriter Leon Rosselson. In 1963 Carthy made his first solo album for Philips Records, a major U.K. label, and continued to record for this label through 1968, one of the few British folk performers to record for a commercial label. He soon formed a partnership with fiddler DAVE SWARBRICK, and the two became among the most innovative and influential performers on the British folk scene. Carthy and Swarbrick recorded several albums together, developing elaborate arrangements of traditional British ballads such as "Prince Heathan," in which extended melodic solos by Swarbrick complemented Carthy's complex GUITAR accompaniment.

In 1968 Swarbrick left to join FAIRPORT CONVENTION, and Carthy went solo again, only to join the folk-rock group STEELEYE SPAN the next year. However, by 1971 Carthy returned to solo recording. His albums of the mid-1970s were very influential, most notably 1976's *Crown of Horn,* featuring his unusual, rhythmic guitar playing and stylized vocals. During the late 1970s Carthy returned briefly to Steeleye Span, and then formed a trio with concertina/accordion master JOHN KIRKPATRICK and trumpeter Howard Evans. By the mid-1980s this group had expanded to become Brass Monkey. Meanwhile, Carthy also performed as a member of the vocal a cappella group, the Watersons, along with his wife, Norma Waterson. In the mid-1990s Carthy and Swarbrick reunited with several tours of the United Kingdom and America, and recorded two "reunion" albums. During the later 1990s into the first decade

of the 21st century, Carthy has alternated solo albums with recordings featuring his wife and daughter, Eliza Carthy, who has herself established a career in both folk and singer/songwriter styles. They perform as Waterson-Carthy and have recorded several albums. In 1998, he was awarded an M.B.E. by Queen Elizabeth II of Great Britain.

Cephas and Wiggins
The acoustic blues duo of guitarist/vocalist John Cephas (b. Washington, D.C., September 4, 1930) and harmonica player Phil Wiggins (b. Washington, D.C., May 8, 1954) has helped keep alive the tradition of classic blues duos like SONNY TERRY and BROWNIE MCGHEE. The two met at the National Folklife Festival in 1976 and soon were performing together as members of Big Chief Ellis's backup band, the House Rockers. They struck out on their own in 1984, playing a mix of Piedmont/ragtime-style blues songs. In addition to traditional blues, they have expanded to include country, gospel, and jump jive material in their act, along with their own original blues-styled compositions. Their albums have won numerous honors, including the W. C. Handy award for Best Blues Album for their 1986 *Dog Days of August* album.

Chad Mitchell Trio
The Chad Mitchell Trio was born at Gonzaga University in 1958, in Spokane, Washington, where vocalists Mitchell, Mike Kobluk, and Mike Pugh were students. On graduation, seeking to make it as folk performers, the trio went to New York, where they met folk producer/publisher Milt Okun who became their manager. Pugh was replaced by Joe Frazier, who was trained as an opera singer, and Okun landed the new group an important slot in a 1961 Carnegie Hall concert with HARRY BELAFONTE, who was already a major star. Appearances on television and in concert followed, and the group soon established itself for its playful onstage humor, slick arrangements, and sometimes satirical songs. Their third album, *Live at the Bitter End,* captures a late

1962 appearance when the group was at its best. Unlike the Kingston Trio, the Mitchell Trio made an effort to record topical material, particularly after PETER, PAUL, AND MARY had a huge hit with their cover of BOB DYLAN's "Blowin' in the Wind." A number of accompanists were hired to work with the group, including guitarist Jim (later ROGER) MCGUINN (founder of the BYRDS), studio bassist Bill Lee (who sessioned on many folk recordings during this period, and is the father of filmmaker Spike Lee), and multi-instrumentalist Paul Prestopino.

Mitchell left the group in 1965 for a solo career and was replaced by a young singer/songwriter, John Denver. The group was now named the Mitchell Trio, and continued to record and perform through 1968. They recorded Denver's "Leavin' on a Jet Plane," which inspired Peter, Paul, and Mary to cover it in 1967 for a major hit. After the group folded, Denver went on to be a popular solo artist, but the other members faded from view. The original group, with Denver, reunited in 1994 for a reunion album/concert.

Chandler, Len (b. 1935) *performer and songwriter*

Len Chandler was born in Akron, Ohio, on May 27, 1935. His parents encouraged his interest in music, and he was studying classical piano at age 12, and oboe soon after; as a high school senior he was invited to play oboe with the Akron Symphony. He was introduced to traditional folk music in college, and then settled in New York to work as a counselor. He began attending the informal folk jams in Washington Square Park in the early 1960s, and soon was writing his own songs and performing in Greenwich Village clubs. He became a regular contributor to BROADSIDE MAGAZINE, writing topical songs addressing the CIVIL RIGHTS MOVEMENT. He began traveling as a songleader and activist in the South in the mid-1960s. In the late 1960s he recorded two albums for major label Columbia, but neither achieved much success. By the early 1970s he settled in Los Angeles, where he founded the Alternative Chorus-Songwriters Showcase. In the

mid-1970s he also participated in PETE SEEGER's Clearwater concerts designed to promote the cleanup of the Hudson River.

Chapin, Harry (1942–1981) *singer and songwriter*

Harry Chapin was born in New York City's Greenwich Village on December 7, 1942. He formed his first band with his brothers Tom and Steve while still in high school. After college he worked briefly as a documentary filmmaker before returning to performing his own songs around New York City. He signed with Elektra Records in 1972, and enjoyed his greatest success through the mid-1970s with hits "Taxi," "W.O.L.D." (about the life of a radio deejay), and his best-known song, "Cat's in the Cradle" about a father too preoccupied with his business life to nurture his growing child.

Through the mid-1970s Chapin became more politically active, working to fight world hunger through music and through establishing World Hunger Year in 1975 to raise awareness and money. He also authored a Broadway musical, *The Night That Made America Famous*, which ran from late February through mid-April 1975. Chapin continued to record through the end of the decade, though with less popular success. He was killed when his car was rear-ended by a tractor-trailer on July 16, 1981. A memorial fund established after his death has raised millions of dollars for various charities near to Chapin's heart. Brother Tom established himself as a prominent children's music performer beginning in the mid-1980s.

Chapman, Tracy (b. 1964) *singer and songwriter*

Born on March 20, 1964, in Cleveland, Ohio, Chapman combined in her music elements of the bluesy vocal style of ODETTA with the confessional singer-songwriter work of Joan Armatrading. Chapman began playing GUITAR as a teenager, writing her own songs as early as her high school years. She won a scholarship to attend Tufts University in

Boston, where she became active on the local folk scene in the early 1980s. She made a demo tape of her songs at the college's radio station, which was heard by a fellow student who happened to be the son of noted music producer Charles Koppelman. Koppelman was impressed and signed her to a management and recording contract in 1986.

Chapman's unique vocal style and the content of her songs brought great attention to her self-titled debut album, released in 1988. It was helped by the unexpected success of the song "Fast Car," which eventually reached number six on the pop charts. This was unusual for a song with a light acoustic guitar-led accompaniment that addressed issues of poverty and alienation. The album garnered four Grammy Awards, including one for Best New Artist, in 1989.

Like many who enjoy quick success, Chapman had trouble maintaining this momentum over the years. It would have been surprising if she had remained so popular, given the difficult subject matter that she tackled. Nonetheless, in 1995 she did make a comeback with the blues-flavored "Give Me One Reason," perhaps due to the growing popularity of the blues style. Chapman returned to her confessional singer-songwriter style on her following albums.

Charters, Samuel (b. 1929) *producer and writer*

Samuel Barclay Charters was born in Pittsburgh, Pennsylvania, on August 1, 1929. He attended the University of California, Berkeley, where he became interested in folk music. On graduation in 1956, he began recording traditional music, particularly blues, jazz, and the music of the Bahamas. Several of these recordings were issued over the coming years by Folkways and Prestige Records. Charters's 1959 book *The Country Blues* was a landmark in introducing many seminal blues recording artists of the 1920s and 1930s to the folk audience; Charters continued to write prolifically about blues history through the 1960s and 1970s. In the late 1950s Charters also occasionally recorded

and played folk concerts himself, although he did not pursue a performing career.

In 1965 Charters was hired to produce folk and pop acts for Vanguard Records, producing sessions by Chicago blues musicians such as Buddy Guy and FOLK-ROCK acts such as Country Joe and the Fish. In 1970 he moved to Sweden, where he became a producer for Sonet Records, among other labels, including traditional Swedish fiddle music. Charters returned to the United States in the 1990s and continues to write and produce recordings. His wife, Ann Charters, is a noted authority on ragtime, a sometimes ragtime pianist, and a well-known photographer of blues and folk musicians.

Chenier, Clifton (1925–1987) *zydeco accordionist*

Born in Opelousas, Louisiana, on June 25, 1925, Chenier was a leading performer on the ACCORDION in the ZYDECO style. He first recorded in 1954 for the small local Elko label, and then a year later for Specialty Records out of Los Angeles, achieving some regional success as a singer-guitarist. He continued to record sporadically through the 1960s for a variety of labels, finally landing on the folk-revival Arhoolie label in the early 1970s. Chenier became quite popular on the festival circuit and was widely credited with introducing zydeco to a wide audience. Plagued in later life by diabetes, Chenier and his band—featuring his brother and later his son, C. J. Chenier (b. Port Arthur, Texas, December 28, 1957)—continued to tour until Chenier was physically unable to perform. He died on December 12, 1987, and his son has continued the family tradition as an accordionist-bandleader-performer.

Chieftains, The

Among the longest-lived and most successful of all Irish instrumental revival bands, the Chieftains have been performing since the mid-1960s, led by piper Paddy Moloney. Moloney was active in the Irish dance music revival and had played with legendary harper/bandleader Sean O'Raida, who was among the first to work up complicated arrangements of Irish dance music and airs for instrumental ensembles. In the early 1960s Moloney formed a record label, Claddagh, to record traditional Irish music. Moloney and O'Raida formed the first Chieftains with Sean Potts (tin whistle), Martin Fay (FIDDLE), Mick Turbidy (FLUTE, concertina), and David Fallon (bodhran); O'Raida and Fallon were quickly replaced by Sean Keane (fiddle) and Peadar Mercier (bodhran). The group worked on a semiprofessional basis until the early 1970s, when they began to achieve wider acclaim.

The Chieftains presented Irish music in serious, almost chamber music–like arrangements, in marked contrast to the boisterous CLANCY BROTHERS, who specialized in rowdy singalong songs. The Chieftains' productions were low-key in comparison; their albums featured cover paintings, rather than photos of the groups, and were simply named "1," "2," "3," etc., through their first major label release, *The Chieftains 5*, which introduced new band member Derek Bell (harp; Bell died suddenly following surgery in 2002). In 1975 the Chieftains' music was featured on the soundtrack of the film *Barry Lyndon*, which brought them further recognition. They began recording for major labels (Island in the mid-1970s, Columbia in the early 1980s), which brought their music wider distribution.

Later band members include Kevin Conneff, the first vocalist featured with the band (he also played bodhran, replacing Mercier), and master flute player Matt Malloy, who came on board after the BOTHY BAND folded in 1980. In 1988 the Chieftains collaborated with singer/songwriter Van Morrison on his album *Irish Heartbeat*. Since the 1990s they have made several theme albums, featuring country and other popular artists, notably on the 1995 album *Long Black Veil*, which featured vocals by Sting and Mick Jagger.

Civil Rights movement

The Civil Rights movement was an important historical movement to grant equal rights and protections to African Americans. Its seeds were planted during World War II, when many black servicemen served with distinction and were exposed to less segregated and more open conditions than they had previously known at home. The landmark *Brown v. Board of Education* decision by the Supreme Court in 1954, which abolished the legality of "separate-but-equal" schools for black and white children was the first step in a long series of battles—mostly waged in the South—to achieve equal rights. Folk musicians—who had been involved in union organizing in the 1930s and 1940s, and other left-wing causes—were natural allies for the young protesters, and music was a natural way to organize marches and sit-ins. The influence of the black church, which long employed hymns and songs as a means of commenting on (and tacitly criticizing) conditions in the South, was another important source for songs that could be adapted to the cause.

In 1955 a young black woman, Rosa Parks, refused to sit in the back of a public bus—as was the law for all black passengers—in Montgomery, Alabama. This inspired a series of boycotts in the city. HARRY BELAFONTE, Miriam Makeba, and even the CHAD MITCHELL TRIO toured southern cities in the wake of these protests, and all spoke openly to the press about the conditions they observed and the need for change. In 1959 young folksinger/activist GUY CARAWAN was hired by the Tennessee-based Highlander Folk School, which became a seedbed for using traditional songs to help organize protesters. A year later, Carawan organized the first workshop for civil rights workers, introducing old union songs like "We Shall Not Be Moved" and the soon-to-be signature song of the movement, "We Shall Overcome," as tools to be used at demonstrations. Carawan also attended the first meeting of the Student Nonviolent Coordinating Committee (SNCC), founded that year in Mississippi to register voters, leading a group sing for 200 organizers. That same year, a sit-in in Nashville was recorded and issued on LP by Folkways Records, an unusual move at the time, as another means of carrying the message.

The New York folk community was quick to help the growing Civil Rights movement. An early 1961 benefit concert was held at Carnegie Hall, with

Carawan, PETE SEEGER, and other performers, including two groups that had been formed specifically to sing at protests and sit-ins. They were promptly recorded by Folkways, who quickly issued an album titled *We Shall Overcome: Songs of the "Freedom Riders" and the "Sit-ins."* Further recordings appeared through the mid-1960s, and Carawan also published two songbooks, the first, also titled *We Shall Overcome,* appearing in 1963. Southern singer/songwriter Bernice Johnson (Reagon) became a key performer/organizer of these songs, and has since been one of the movement's greatest historians.

Folksinging activists specifically organized several tours to bring further attention to the struggle, as well as to provide inspiration and entertainment for those in the trenches. Pete Seeger, PHIL OCHS, JUDY COLLINS, Julius Lester, and dozens more made appearances. The famous 1963 "March on Washington" linked the folk music and Civil Rights movements together forever in the minds of most Americans, thanks to the involvement and performances by JOAN BAEZ, BOB DYLAN, PETER, PAUL, AND MARY, JOSH WHITE, ODETTA, and others.

During the summers of 1962–64 many college students—on vacation from school—traveled south to help organize voter registration, assist at boycotts and demonstrations, and organize rallies. These "Freedom Riders" were rarely welcomed warmly by the native Southerners, who viewed them (at best) as troublemakers. The ultimate tragedy occurred in August 1964, when three civil rights activists—Andrew Goodman, James Chaney, and Michael Schwerner—were picked up for "speeding" in a small Mississippi town. Their release from jail hours later was leaked to the local KKK, and the three were savagely attacked and murdered. Their bodies were found weeks later, along with their car, sunken in a nearby lake. Several people involved in the incident were charged initially, but the primary figure behind the killings, Edgar Ray Killen, charged with three counts of manslaughter, was not convicted until 2005 at the age of 80, after a hung jury set him free in 1967 during a federal trial.

The passage of the Civil Rights Act of 1964—which came before the brutal murders of Goodman, Chaney, and Schwerner—was a landmark achievement for the movement, and in some ways marked the beginning of its decline. The battle was increasingly being won in Congress and in the courts. Marches continued in the summers of 1965–66, but drew less outside attention. White college students were becoming aware of a more direct threat to their freedom: the Vietnam War, which President Lyndon Johnson was rapidly escalating, requiring an increase in the draft. The folk singer/songwriters quickly responded with songs criticizing the mass mobilization.

Many songwriters drew on events in the Civil Rights movement as an inspiration for songs. Bob Dylan, of course, wrote both general songs ("Blowin' in the Wind"; "The Times They Are A-Changin'") that were inspired by the movement (among other events of the time), as well as songs that drew on specific events. "Oxford Town" is a tongue-in-cheek retelling of the uproar that occurred at the University of Mississippi when the first black student was admitted and sought to attend classes on his first day of school. Phil Ochs also drew on the Civil Rights movement, notably in the ironic "Here's to the State of Mississippi." Although many of the topical songs of the period have long been forgotten as the headlines have faded, the very best have survived as unique documents of their time and reminders of the struggle against racism that still troubles American society.

Clancy, Willie (1918–1973) *bagpiper*

Clancy, along with Seamus Ennis and Leo Rowsome, is remembered as a great master of the Irish or uillean BAGPIPES. He was born in Milltown Mulbray on December 24, 1918, to Gilbert and Ellen Clancy, farmers, who were also amateur singers and musicians. He learned to play the whistle by age five, learning dance and song tunes from his family. His father played the bagpipes, FLUTE, and concertina. As a youth Willie also heard the legendary local piper Garrett Barry, one of the last of the so-called wandering minstrels who performed in return for food and lodging or other handouts. Barry, born blind, was a master with his own repertoire of tunes, many of which became hallmarks of Willie Clancy's repertoire. A second, later influence on his playing was Johnny Doran, another traveling piper, whom Clancy met at age 17.

By the time he was in his 20s Clancy had developed into a piper of the first rank. However, there was little opportunity to make a living as a musician at home. He traveled to Dublin, where he befriended piper John Potts, who hosted an Irish music session at his home (Potts's son, Tommy, would become a well-known FIDDLE player). After his father died in 1957, Clancy returned home to take over the family farm. By this time the folk music revival was beginning, and Clancy's great repertoire of songs and dance tunes made him an attractive figure for both local sessions and eventually radio and recordings. Clancy's fame as a performer spread far beyond his hometown; many musicians made the pilgrimage to his farm to learn from him. After his premature death at age 56, his hometown established a weeklong summer music school devoted to the Irish arts and named in his honor.

Clancy Brothers, The

Natives of Carrick-on-Suir, Tipperary, Ireland, the Clancy Brothers—Tom, Pat, and Liam—were living in New York in the early 1950s, looking for any work they could find. They met Armagh-born singer Tommy Makem, who was also scuffling for work as a sometimes actor, sometimes singer. They began performing at Greenwich Village clubs and formed a record label, Tradition Records, to issue their first albums. An appearance on the *Ed Sullivan Show* in 1961 launched the group on the national stage, and they were signed to Columbia Records. The Clancys popularized Irish songs by arranging them in a style like other folk revival groups of the day, such as the KINGSTON TRIO, with upbeat

accompaniments on guitar and banjo, and rousing sing-along choruses.

In 1970 Makem left to pursue a solo career, followed five years later by Liam Clancy; brother Bobby was enlisted to fill his shoes, along with musician Robbie O'Connell. The group continued to record and perform until Tom Clancy's death in 1990, although different versions of the "Clancy Brothers" have reunited for occasional tours through the 1990s.

Clannad

Irish folk-revival band centering on the extended Brennan family (the group's name, "Clannad," is Gaelic for "family"). Siblings Maire (harp, keyboards), Ciaran (bass, GUITAR, synthesizer), and Pol (FLUTE, whistle) joined with their uncles Padraig (MANDOLIN, guitar) and Noel (guitar) to form the original group in the late 1960s. They won a contest as best new folk group in 1970, landing them a contract with Philips Records. Their debut album appeared in 1973, featuring the Gaelic vocals of the three siblings. Becoming increasingly oriented toward FOLK-ROCK and pop, youngest sister Enya was added to the lineup in 1979; she left in 1982 to pursue a solo career (scoring a major pop hit with "Orinoco Flow [Sail Away]" in 1988). The group reached the height of its success when its music was used as the theme song for the British TV show *Harry's Game* in 1983, and then recorded "In a Lifetime" with guest vocalist Bono of the rock group U2, for a top-20 hit, in 1986. Brother Pol left the group in 1989. Their 1990s work was even more pop-oriented, with less attention given to their original Gaelic roots and more to original material.

Clark, Gene (1941–1991) *guitarist and songwriter*

Born in Tipton, Missouri, on November 17, 1941, Clark began his career in the LA-based FOLK-ROCK band, the BYRDS, contributing some of their better original numbers, including "It Won't Be Wrong,"

"Set You Free This Time," and "Feel a Whole Lot Better," along with his emotional lead vocals. He quit the band in 1966 due to his fear of flying, which was required for touring, and hooked up with the traditional-sounding Gosdin Brothers for an excellent album of original compositions featuring super-guitarists Clarence White and Glen Campbell as well as arranger/pianist Leon Russell, and the Byrds rhythm section; however, the album stiffed on the charts. With Doug Dillard and future Flying Burrito Brother and Eagle Bernie Leadon, he formed Dillard and Clark, a folk-rock outfit that featured country instrumentation (Dillard's banjo, BYRON BERLINE'S FIDDLE, plus DOBRO and MANDOLIN) as well as some classic psychedelic 1960s touches like electric harpsichord!

In the early 1970s Clark made a number of abortive attempts at solo albums backed by various members of the Byrds, Burrito Brothers, and other West Coast country-rock regulars. He had a genuine knack for the contemporary country song, but unfortunately was recording about a decade too soon to gain much popular success, and most of these recordings went unreleased at the time.

Early in the 1980s Clark rejoined with ex-Byrds ROGER MCGUINN and Chris Hillman for two critically acclaimed albums, but again his fear of flying prevented widespread touring and limited the success of the trio. In the late 1980s Clark linked up with former Textones vocalist Carla Olson as an acoustic duo. Always troubled personally and prone to periods of depression, he took his own life on May 24, 1991.

Clark, Guy (Jr.) (b. 1941) *guitarist and songwriter*

Born in Monahans, Texas, on November 6, 1941, and raised by his grandmother (who ran a run-down hotel), Clark learned to play GUITAR as a youngster, playing primarily Mexican folk songs that he heard in his small Texas hometown. He came to Houston in the 1960s, where he immediately began performing in the vibrant club scene that centered on that city, Austin, and Dallas. Clark moved briefly to Los Angeles in the late 1960s (inspiring his song "L.A. Freeway," which later was a hit for JERRY JEFF WALKER), and then settled in 1971 in Nashville, where he recorded for RCA in the mid-1970s and Warners later in the decade. His first album, *Old No. 1*, was critically acclaimed, although it did little on the charts. It featured many of his classic songs, including "Rita Ballou," "That Old Time Feeling," and "Desperados Waiting for a Train." Clark became a patron saint of the new Nashville crowd, recording with and supplying songs for Emmylou Harris, Ricky Skaggs, Rodney Crowell, Waylon Jennings, and Rosanne Cash, among others.

In the mid-1980s Clark recorded a comeback, acoustic-tinged album for the country-bluegrass label Sugar Hill. This led to renewed interest in his music, and he signed with major label Arista in 1992, producing two albums for them, before returning once again to recording for Sugar Hill through the 1990s.

Clayton, Paul (1933–1967) *performer*

Paul Clayton was born in New Bedford, Massachusetts, on March 3, 1933. While attending the University of Virginia, he became interested in folk music and began performing. He began recording traditional performers in the South, recording traditional guitarist ETTA BAKER and BANJO player Hobart Smith. Clayton went to New York City to pursue a performing career, and met the CLANCY BROTHERS there, who were starting a new folk label, Tradition Records. He began recording for them, and also gave them his field recordings from the South for an album that remained in print for several decades, introducing Baker and Smith to a wider audience. Clayton recorded prolifically from the mid-1950s through the early 1960s for almost every folk label, focusing on traditional ballads, sea chantys, and songs; he usually accompanied himself on the Appalachian dulcimer. BOB DYLAN admired Clayton's adaptation of the traditional song "Scarlet Ribbons for Her Hair," and, as he often did, borrowed Clayton's revised melody for his song "Don't

Think Twice, It's Alright." Naturally displeased that he received no credit (or payment) for this use, Clayton sued Dylan, but the two eventually settled. By the mid-1960s Clayton was more or less forgotten; depressed by his lack of success, he took his own life on March 30, 1967.

See also DULCIMER (APPALACHIAN).

Clements, Vassar (1928–2005) *fiddler*

Born Vassar Carlton Clements in Kinard, Florida, on April 25, 1928, Clements worked through the 1950s and 1960s with a number of traditional bluegrass bands, including Bill Monroe's and Jim and Jesse's groups. He accompanied country star Faron Young, and also worked for a while in the late 1960s with a bluegrass-rock amalgam, the Earl Scruggs Revue. His career was given a big boost by JOHN HARTFORD, who hired him to tour and record with him in the early 1970s; he appeared on Hartford's seminal *Aeroplane* album. Clements took the jazz and swing elements that were always present in bluegrass fiddling and brought them to the forefront. He also appeared on the landmark *Will the Circle Be Unbroken* album hosted by the Nitty Gritty Dirt Band, which brought together older and younger musicians. In the mid-1970s he made an album with steel guitarist Doug Jerrigan and hotpicker DAVID BROMBERG called *Hillbilly Jazz* for Flying Fish records; this helped revive the Western Swing style, while establishing Clements as a solo artist. He made a number of albums beginning in the 1970s in a variety of styles, including bluegrass, jazz, swing, blues, and even country rock. He also continued to work as a session musician for a variety of artists and appeared with various bluegrass "supergroups." He died on August 16, 2005.

Clifton, Bill (b. 1931) *concert organizer and performer*

Born William Marburg in Riverdale, Maryland, on April 5, 1931, Clifton's interest in folk music bloomed at the University of Virginia, where he began performing with another folk revivalist,

guitarist PAUL CLAYTON. After graduation the two formed a bluegrass band in 1954, perhaps the first "second-generation" urban group to pick up the bluegrass style. They recorded for Nashville's Starday label, and often included songs from the Carter Family repertoire, which Clifton had enjoyed as a youngster; he began playing the autoharp in the style that the Carters made famous, reintroducing this instrument to folk revivalists such as MIKE SEEGER. He also published a songbook including many gospel and old-time songs that had originally been recorded in the 1920s, 1930s, and 1940s, introducing them to a new musically literate audience.

In 1961 Clifton organized the first bluegrass festival for an urban audience, held outside of Washington, D.C. Two years later, at the height of the folk revival, he left the country to settle in England. In 1967 Clifton took his act to the Philippines when he joined the Peace Corps, and continued to work throughout the Pacific Rim through the mid-1970s, turning up in such far-flung places as New Zealand.

Clifton returned to Britain in the late 1970s, touring Europe and the United States with bluegrass veterans Red Rector and Don Stover as the First Generation Band in 1978. He continues to record and perform, with many of his records originating in Germany, although his style remains frozen in the late 1950s style of the early folk revival.

Cockerham, Fred (1905–1980) *banjoist*

Cockerham was born in Round Peak, North Carolina, on November 3, 1905, where a unique style of banjo and FIDDLE playing developed. Key among the musicians who influenced Cockerham was local banjoist Charlie Lowe, who developed a clean, melodically rich style of playing in the traditional drop-thumb or frailing style. Lowe played with local fiddler Ben Jarrell, and then his son Tommy, developing an intertwined style of playing fiddle-banjo duets that was rhythmically and melodically quite sophisticated. Although Cockerham enjoyed playing the banjo in this style, he was also attracted to more modern sounds; hearing fiddler ARTHUR SMITH on the radio, he began to play the fiddle, incorporating the jazz-influenced style of this famed fiddler.

As a teenager, Cockerham performed locally with various other musicians, including fiddler Ernest East and banjo player Kyle Creed. Cockerham played with several semiprofessional bands, and won several fiddle contest titles at the famous Galax, Virginia, Fiddlers Convention in the mid-1930s, then continued to work professionally through the early 1940s. World War II ended the first phase of Cockerham's musical career, and he turned to doing construction work with his friend Kyle Creed. In 1959, caught in his car during a blizzard, Cockerham nearly died; although he recovered, he had lost his high tenor voice, and from that point sang in a gravelly bass. A year later, his vision was seriously impaired during a failed operation to remove cataracts.

During the 1960s Cockerham began playing music once again. He began working with fiddler Ernest East in the Camp Creek Boys, a sedate old-style string band. But it was when folklorists and record executives Richard Nevins and Charlie Faurot introduced Fred to TOMMY JARRELL that he found his best later-life musical partner. The two formed an immediate bond, and their banjo-fiddle duets were a highlight of several albums issued on the County label. Folk festivals and concert tours followed; Cockerham continued to record and perform until his death on July 8, 1980.

See also BANJO, FIVE-STRING.

Cohen, John (b. 1932) *filmmaker and musician*

Born to a well-educated family in New York City, Cohen was first introduced to folk music through his older brother, Mike, who was a founding member of the Shantyboys, an early folk-revival band in the mid-1950s. He attended Yale University, and then settled into the burgeoning folk music/coffeehouse scene in New York in the mid-1950s; it was there he met another Yale alumnus, Tom Paley,

and MIKE SEEGER. In 1958 the trio became the NEW LOST CITY RAMBLERS, the first, and probably most influential, of the old-time string band revivalists.

Cohen performed with the Ramblers through 1972. He also began making field trips to the South. Focusing on the coal-mining communities of Kentucky, he made a film in 1964 called *The High Lonesome Sound,* which introduced master banjo player ROSCOE HOLCOMB to urban audiences, as well as featuring footage of Bill Monroe. He made several other films, including *The End of an Old Song* (1974), featuring ballad singer Dillard Chandler from North Carolina, as well as recording and producing a number of records for Folkways.

In 1972 Cohen formed the Putnam String County Band with fiddler JAY UNGAR, guitarist Lynn Hardy (then Ungar's wife), and cellist Abby Newton. The band was one of the more innovative of the old-time revival groups, although it lasted only a year or so. Since that time, Cohen has continued to perform with the Ramblers at their various reunion concerts, and teaching filmmaking at the State University of New York at Purchase until his retirement in 1997. He has also become interested in traditional Peruvian music and has produced a film as well as several recordings of this musical style.

Coleman, Michael (1891–1945) *fiddler*

Coleman was born in Knockgrania, County Sligo, Ireland, on January 31, 1891, the youngest child of James Coleman, a farmer and FLUTE player, and Beatrice Ellen (Bessie) Gorman, a housewife and amateur singer. Coleman's next oldest brother, Jim, was a FIDDLE player, and the strongest influence on his early playing style. Coleman began to play fiddle at age six, in duet with his father or brother. He also began stepdancing, and by his mid-teens was admired as both a dancer and musician. Physically small, Coleman was not suited to the hard labor of farm work; also plagued by poor health, his schooling was often interrupted. Coleman dropped out of school first when he was 14, and then permanently ended his education at age 18. That same year he made his first appearance at a fiddle convention in the nearby town of Bunnanadden.

Bunnanadden was the home of a fine fiddler, barkeeper, and shipping agent named P[atrick] J[ames] McDermott. He took the young Coleman under his wing, and after Jim Coleman was the largest influence on Michael's playing. In his honor Coleman would later record "McDermott's Hornpipe," a tune P.J. was said to have learned from a traveling musician. In 1909 and 1910, perhaps with P.J.'s encouragement, Coleman participated in the all-Sligo "Feis Ceoil"; the first year he won first prize as a dancer and placed third on the fiddle, showing that his dance skills were considerable.

Coleman continued to compete and perform locally through 1914, while holding a variety of jobs. He then traveled with a friend to England, settling for the middle months of 1914 in Manchester. One of his older brothers, Pat, was already living there; a physically imposing man (the opposite of Coleman), he worked as a policeman and happily took in his younger sibling. Coleman tried working hauling manure in a wheelbarrow, but his small size made hard physical labor nearly impossible. Soon he was back to music making at local bars and dances. That autumn Michael returned to his hometown in Ireland, and then in October sailed for America.

On his arrival in New York, Michael almost immediately found work as a fiddler for local dances and small concerts; he even toured on the Keith's vaudeville circuit for a while. Coleman's big break came early in 1921, when he made his first recordings. At first he recorded for small labels catering to the Irish market, as well as for some of the mainstream "budget" American labels, such as Vocalion and Columbia. His first major hit was his 1922 recording of "The Boys of the Lough"; it was issued in Ireland by the Beltona label under the pseudonym of "Dennis Molloy." By 1927 Coleman was signed to the prestigious Victor label, which brought further distribution to his recordings.

However, the stock market crash of 1929 and the growth of radio both took their tolls on the recording industry. Much recording of ethnic or traditional music dried up, and work was hard to come by. Nonetheless, Coleman persevered, working locally whenever he could. He was also a regular on New York radio programs geared to the Irish audience. When the economy picked up in the mid-1930s, he was invited to record again, this time for the new Decca label. These records were not so successful due to the changing tastes of the market. By the early 1940s, Coleman's health began failing due to ulcers and other digestive problems; he made some final recordings privately in 1940 and for radio transcriptions in 1944 (these later recordings have never been found). His health failed in late 1944, and he subsequently died on January 4, 1945.

Collins, Judy (b. 1939) *singer*

Born in Seattle, Washington, on May 1, 1939, Collins was raised in Denver, where she studied classical piano as a teenager. At age 13 she performed as a pianist with a local semiprofessional orchestra, but at age 16 abandoned piano for GUITAR and took up folk music. By 1960 she had settled in Chicago, where Collins became a performer in the growing coffeehouse scene. She then moved to New York's Greenwich Village and signed with the folk label Elektra Records in 1961. Her initial albums featured traditional ballads and songs, but she soon began championing the work of younger singer/songwriters, including JONI MITCHELL, TOM RUSH, and Leonard Cohen. Her 1967 album, *Wildflowers,* featured lush string arrangements by classical composer Joshua Rifkin. It also included her version of Joni Mitchell's "Both Sides Now," which became a major hit for the singer. By the mid-1970s she was performing a wide range of popular material, achieving her last major hit with a cover of Stephen Sondheim's "Send in the

Judy Collins (left) and Mimi Fariña performing together at the 1967 Newport Folk Festival. (Photo © John Byrne Cooke, http://www.cookephoto.com)

Clowns." Collins left Elektra in the mid-1980s and has since recorded sporadically for a variety of labels, while continuing to perform on her own and as part of folk-revival concerts.

Collins, Shirley (b. 1935) *singer*

Born on July 5, 1935, in Hastings, Sussex, England, Collins was a major force on the British folk-revival scene from the late 1950s through the 1980s. She assisted Alan Lomax on several field trips in England during the 1950s, and in the U.S. in 1959 and Lomax produced her first album, also in 1959. She then paired with her sister, Dolly, who played Renaissance music on original instruments; Dolly's unique arrangements of traditional ballads and songs combined them with her own work on early organs. In 1970 Shirley wed British folk-rocker ASHLEY HUTCHINGS, who produced her 1971 album, *No Roses,* her first to feature electric instruments. The two collaborated on several recordings through their divorce in the mid-1970s, and Collins also performed as a vocalist with Hutching's electric Albion Band as well as his acoustic group, the Etchingham Steam Band (1974–76). She retired from the music scene after her marriage ended, returning to performing briefly in the late 1980s and early 1990s, but vocal troubles led her to retire again. In 2004 she published a memoir of her early life and career, *America across the Waters.*

See also LOMAX, JOHN AND ALAN.

Cooney, Michael (b. 1943) *performer*

Cooney was born in Carmel, California, but mostly raised in Arizona. His father was an amateur guitarist/singer who had a large repertoire of songs, but his parents divorced when he was quite young so this influence was minimal on the young musician. He began playing in folk clubs as a teenager in the early 1960s in the San Francisco area, and then moved to New York in 1964, then the center of the folk scene. He began writing a song-finder's column for *SING OUT!* MAGAZINE in the late 1960s, which became widely read and influential over the next two decades. He also made his first album, *The Cheese Stands Alone*, in 1968 for the small Folk Legacy label. However, since then he has recorded only sporadically, feeling that he is primarily a live performer whose records don't represent his work adequately.

Like PETE SEEGER, Cooney has mastered many different instruments and musical styles, billing himself as a "One Man Folk Festival." Unlike more recent performers who specialize in a single genre or instrument, he presents a full program of music, from traditional ballads to blues and contemporary folk compositions.

Cooper, Wilma Lee (b. 1921) and Stoney

(1918–1977) *husband and wife performing duo*

Wilma Lee Leary was born on February 7, 1921, in Valley Head, West Virginia, to a family of performers. The Leary Family was a well-known gospel singing group who performed throughout the upper South in the 1930s and 1940s, performing at church-sponsored socials, on radio, and at folk festivals. Her mother was the motivating force behind the group; a talented organist, she arranged the music for her three daughters, with her coal miner husband singing bass. Beginning at age five, Wilma Lee sang with her family group; by her teens the group had grown beyond the limits of family to incorporate other local singers and musicians, including a young fiddler named Stoney Cooper, who was born Dale Troy Cooper in Harmon, West

Virginia, October 16, 1918 and died on March 22, 1977. The two were wed in the late 1930s.

Although they continued to perform gospel with the Leary band, the duo began to perform secular music on their own, performing in the early 1940s through the upper South and as far west as Nebraska, as well as having a number of radio jobs on small stations. In 1947 their big break came when they were hired to join the WWVA Jamboree out of Wheeling, West Virginia, a powerful station that saturated the upper South and West. They also made their first recordings for Rich-R-Tone Records, and then were signed two years later to the bigger and more powerful Columbia label. They remained in Wheeling for 10 years, performing with their band known as the Clinch Mountain Clan.

At this time the Coopers had their greatest country hits with a number of songs either written by Wilma or cowritten by husband and wife, from 1956's "Cheated Too" through 1959's "There's a Big Wheel"; their last charting country song was a remake of the venerable "Wreck on the Highway" in 1961. They also introduced LEAD BELLY's "Midnight Special" to the country charts. They continued to record and perform gospel material, giving a hard-driving sound to newly composed hymns such as "Walking My Lord up Calvary Hill." In 1957 they left Wheeling to join the cast of the *Grand Ole Opry*.

The 1960s were slower times for the duo as recording artists, although they continued to tour widely. In the early 1970s the renewed interest in traditional mountain music brought their old-style country/bluegrass sound back in vogue, and they remained quite active, although Stoney's health was beginning to deteriorate due to heart problems. After his death in 1977, Wilma Lee kept the band together, continuing to take a more traditional direction, while recording for bluegrass revival labels. Daughter Carol Lee also performed with the family band, as well as directing the background singers on the *Grand Ole Opry* stage (known as the Carol Lee Singers). Wilma Lee has continued to perform on the *Opry* stage.

Copper Family, The

A traditional a cappella, harmony-singing family from Rottingdean, Sussex, England, the Coppers have been influential throughout the 20th century British folk revival. The founding fathers of the family were James "Brasser" Copper and his brother Tom. Their harmony singing caught the attention of British folklorist Kate Lee, who brought Brasser to London to perform for the English Folk Song Society in 1889. Brasser's son, Jim, also sang, and passed the singing tradition down to his son, Bob, and nephew, Ron.

In 1950 folklorists Peter Kennedy and Alan Lomax recorded Bob and Ron singing the family's incredible repertory of songs and ballads in their unique harmony style. Many of these recordings were featured on the landmark 10-LP set *Folksongs of Britain and Ireland*, compiled by Kennedy and Lomax for the U.S. Caedmon label in the late 1950s. The first LP of the Coppers was released shortly thereafter by the EFDSS (and by Folk Legacy Records in the United States), further spreading their style. Bob Copper became an important folklorist himself, collecting local songs and legends, and fostering interest in traditional English song.

The Coppers were directly influential on a second generation of British vocal harmony groups, including the Waterson family of Yorkshire and the Young Tradition. Bob's children, John and Jill, recorded with their father and uncle as the Copper Family in the 1970s and 1980s, and have continued the family tradition with their own children. Bob died in 2004.

See also LOMAX, JOHN AND ALAN.

Cotton, Elizabeth "Libba" (1893–1987)
guitarist and songwriter
Born in Chapel Hill, North Carolina, on January 5, 1893 (some sources give 1895), Elizabeth Cotton was one of the most talented performers in the East Coast/Piedmont style of ragtime GUITAR. She learned to play from her brothers, although as a left-handed musician, she had to turn the guitar or BANJO "upside down" to play it (on the guitar, she played the bass strings with her fingers and the treble with her thumb). Her most famous song, "Freight Train"—which she claims to have written as a 12-year-old—became a major FOLK-REVIVAL hit in the late 1950s. After her marriage at age 15, Cotton stopped playing for many years.

In the early 1950s, living in the Washington, D.C., area, she was hired as a live-in maid for the Seeger family. Charles and Ruth Crawford Seeger were both folk music enthusiasts, and their young children, Mike and Peggy, both played guitar. Taking the opportunity to play again, Cotton taught Peggy her song "Freight Train"; Peggy moved to London and in turn taught it to other folk revivalists, and it was a major hit in Britain. Meanwhile, Mike recorded Libba's playing for Folkways, issuing her first LP in 1958 (two others, in 1967 and 1983, followed).

Cotton recorded a wide variety of material, from her own songs to guitar instrumentals that combined 19th-century parlor techniques with the popular ragtime-influenced style prevalent throughout the upper South in the teens and twenties. Cotton became a popular performer on the folk revival circuit and was able to retire from domestic work in 1970. She continued to perform until shortly before her death on June 29, 1987.

See also SEEGER, MIKE; SEEGER, PEGGY; SEEGER, PETE.

Country Cooking

Country Cooking was an Ithaca, New York–based, progressive bluegrass band of the mid-1970s, which spawned many other experimental/"new grass" outfits. They were marked by TONY TRISCHKA's and Peter Wernick's dual banjos (inspired by the Osborne Brothers, who used twin banjos on some of their late 1950s and early 1960s recordings), the jazz-influenced FIDDLE of Kenny Kosek, and Russ Barenberg's progressive GUITAR work. They recorded two influential albums for Rounder in the mid-1970s, and various members performed under different names (including Breakfast Special and the Extended Playboys) and with different lineups through the 1970s.

After the band's demise Trischka became the most influential of the new, progressive banjoists, recording a series of solo albums that mixed his own somewhat spacey improvised compositions with more traditional numbers; Wernick relocated to the Denver area, where he recorded one solo album before forming the influential bluegrass ensemble HOT RIZE. Kosek continued to perform with various bands, as a backing musician, as a duo with Matt Glaser, and as a member of JAY UNGAR's band, Fiddle Fever. Barenberg went on to be a solo artist, and bassist John Miller pursued an interest in blues and jazz guitar.

See also BANJO, FIVE-STRING.

Country Gazette

This group got their first break when they were invited to tour with the last original Flying Burrito Brothers lineup in 1971–72 as a kind of extension of the band; the original trio of fiddler BYRON BERLINE, guitarist Kenny Wertz, and banjoist Herb Pederson would play a bluegrass set in the middle of the Burrito's act and then join the group for their electric country-rock numbers.

Mandolinist Roland White came on board in late 1973 after the death of his brother Clarence, with whom he had been playing traditional bluegrass. Banjoist Alan Munde, who gained fame thanks to a solo album titled *Banjo Sandwich* in the mid-1970s, joined in the same year to replace Pederson, and the two became the nucleus of a new band (at one point they even recorded as a duo under the band name). The group's greatest lineup came together in the late 1970s, with vocalist Michael Anderson and jazz-flavored guitarist Joe Carr joining Munde and White. They recorded two excellent albums, both including classic bluegrass numbers along with more recent songs. Anderson was a strong lead singer with a lot of personality whose voice blended perfectly with White's idiosyncratic harmonies, while Munde provided rock-solid banjo playing that was strongly influenced by bluegrass traditions while still pushing forward into more progressive territory.

This band, like most previous lineups, didn't last long, and soon Carr-Bush-White were recording as a trio, producing a couple of rather lame instrumental albums of standards (marketed as *Festival Favorites* because they were the kind of numbers that are played to death at bluegrass conventions). The band petered out by the late 1980s; Munde went back to solo and session work, while White soon after hooked up with the NASHVILLE BLUEGRASS BAND, one of the most distinguished of the new traditional bands of the 1980s. In the early 1990s Munde assembled a new Country Gazette lineup without White, but it was shortlived.

Country Gentlemen, The

A well-known Washington, D.C., bluegrass revival group, the original band was formed out of the pieces of another group, Buzz Busby's Bayou Boys. When most of the group's members were injured in an automobile accident, banjoist Bill Emerson hired a couple of local players to finish out their gigs, including guitarist Charlie Waller, MANDOLIN player John Duffey, and bassist Larry Lahey. The pairing of Waller and Duffy proved to be an inspired choice; Waller's laconic lead vocals were a perfect match for Duffey's high-energy and unusual tenor harmonies, plus both were able players on their instruments. The group changed its name to the Country Gentlemen in 1958 and signed with Starday Records, a Nashville-based label that was dedicated to traditional bluegrass.

Emerson left the band soon after, and, after a brief period during which bluegrass scholar Pete Kuykendall filled his shoes, Eddie Adcock came on board in mid-1959. Adcock had been playing electric GUITAR in local bars to make a living, but he had previously worked with Bill Monroe and Bill Harrell; Harrell was one the first performers to venture beyond the bounds of the traditional bluegrass sound. Adcock was also an excellent baritone vocalist, and the trio of Waller-Duffey-Adcock became one of the most powerful and distinctive in all of bluegrass.

MIKE SEEGER, another Washington-area denizen who had come under the spell of bluegrass music, brought the group to Folkways Records, an urban outfit whose sales were mostly concentrated among the fledgling folk revivalists. Seeger oversaw their first recording in 1959 for Folkways, an album that featured primarily older mountain songs in keeping with the label's folk orientation, although the group also covered Lefty Frizzell's country hit of the same year, "Long Black Veil," a bold move for a bluegrass band (the song has since become a bluegrass and country-rock standard). They would record three more LPs for the label, becoming the best known of all bluegrass groups among the urban revivalists.

After their first album was released, the band reached its classic lineup with the addition of bassist Tom Gray. Another innovative musician like Adcock, Gray avoided the "boom-chick" patterns of traditional country styles, instead adapting jazz licks and walking bass lines borrowed from bluegrass guitar. The importance of the bass was further emphasized in the band's recordings, particularly when the harmonies came in full force and the other instruments dropped back.

Gray left the band in 1964, ending their classic era, and although the band continued to be active on the bluegrass circuit, they were less evident on the mainstream folk scene. Duffey retired in 1969 due to an internal management dispute; within a few years he had rejoined with Gray to form the SELDOM SCENE, the best-loved bluegrass band in Washington in the 1970s. In 1970 Adcock left to form the II Generation, a progressive bluegrass band that was more instrumentally oriented, leaving only Waller to carry the Country Gentlemen torch. The band signed with another urban folk label in the early 1970s, Vanguard Records, and began a long period of success with many new members passing through, including the return of Bill Emerson, young Ricky Skaggs and Jerry

Douglas, Doyle Lawson (later leader of Doyle Lawson and Quicksilver), and many other soon-to-be progressive bluegrass stars. The band has continued to record for Rebel Records, under Waller's leadership until his death in August 2004.

Cousin Emmy (1903–1980) *banjoist and fiddler*

Born Cynthia May Carver, near Lamb, Kentucky, Emmy was the daughter of a fiddling tobacco farmer. Taking up the FIDDLE at an early age, Emmy won the prestigious National Old-Time Fiddlers Contest in Louisville in 1935, the first woman to take this award. Helped by her performing cousins, the Carver Brothers, Emmy began performing professionally. Her first radio job was with the powerful Wheeling (West Virginia) Jamboree as a member of Frankie Moore's Log Cabin Boys. In 1937 she formed the first Kinfolks Band (a name she used for many years for her backup group), broadcasting first out of Louisville. By this time, besides playing fiddle and banjo-guitar, Emmy was also playing a slew of popular instruments, and even handsaw and rubber glove! (By slowly releasing air out of an inflated glove, she could play "You Are My Sunshine," a trick she continued to use throughout the rest of her career.)

Emmy moved to St. Louis in 1941, where her local radio broadcasts were heard by a local university professor who invited her to participate in his lectures on ancient balladry. In 1947 she made her first impact on the urban FOLK REVIVAL through recordings supervised by noted folklorist Alan Lomax, introducing several traditional folk songs into the folk-revival repertoire, including "Free Little Bird" and "I Wish I Was a Single Girl Again."

Emmy appeared in a few cowboy films in the late 1940s and 1950s, as well as performing at Disneyland. Her adaptation of the traditional banjo song "Reuben/Train 45," which she called "Ruby (Are You Mad at Your Man?)" was the first hit for the Osborne Brothers in 1956, establishing the act on the country circuit. In the 1960s Emmy performed on PETE SEEGER's *Rainbow Quest* television program and made her final LP backed by the old-time revival band the NEW LOST CITY RAMBLERS in 1967. She died on April 11, 1980.

See also LOMAX, JOHN AND ALAN.

Cox, Bill (1897–1968) *singer*

Born William Jennings Cox on August 4, 1897, and raised in rural Kanawah County, West Virginia, Cox had settled in Charleston by the mid-1920s. A hotel clerk during the day, he worked as an entertainer at night. In 1927 he was signed as a performer by local station WOBU, whose studios were conveniently located in the hotel where he worked. The station arranged for an audition with the budget Gennett label, and he traveled to their Richmond, Indiana, studios in late 1929 to make his first recordings. Accompanying himself on GUITAR and HARMONICA, he achieved initial success with a series of satirical looks at the "joys" of married life, including his "Rollin' Pin Woman." Although he recorded for Gennett for only two years, his sides remained in print for years, reissued countless times on Gennett's family of dime-store labels.

In the early 1930s Cox attracted the attention of country producer/manager Art Satherley, who signed him to the American Record Corporation (ARC) label, a slightly higher-quality outfit than Gennett. Satherley gave Cox the nickname of the "Dixie Songbird," and also encouraged him to find a partner so he could record vocal duets, which were popular at the time thanks to the success of the many "brother" acts. Although he had previously performed with his cousin, Woodrow "Red" Sovine (soon to be a country star on his own), Cox was paired on records with another local singer, Cliff Hobbs, who sang tenor to Cox's lead.

On ARC, Cox continued to record humorous songs, but added to his repertoire a number of topical songs, such as "NRA Blues" and "Franklin D. Roosevelt's Back Again," which were later popular-ized during the FOLK REVIVAL by the NEW LOST CITY RAMBLERS. Cox's best-remembered song is the sentimental love ballad "Sparkling Brown Eyes," which has been covered over the decades by various artists, including Webb Pierce (1954) and Dickey Lee (1973). Cox also revived a turn-of-the-last-century hit, "Filipino Baby," which he claimed to have authored. Cox's 1937 recording was widely covered during World War II, when the story of an exotic island sweetheart appealed to serving men assigned to the Pacific, including Ernest Tubb's hit version.

After 1940 Cox's recording career ended. Some 25 years later, he was "rediscovered"—broke and forgotten, but still living in Charleston. Local folklorist Ken Davidson recorded Cox for his tiny Kanawha label a year before Cox's death, performing both his hits and some new compositions written in his original style.

Cox Family, The

Like many traditional bluegrass bands, the Coxes are a real family, hailing from Springhill, Louisiana. Father Willard was an oil refinery worker and amateur musician since the 1960s; his wife, Marie, began her career in a sister harmony act. The two met on the local circuit and began performing together shortly thereafter. In the early 1970s Willard began training his children, one by one, on different bluegrass instruments to make up the family band. His eldest daughter, Lynn, was the group's original bass player (she dropped out of the group before they became popular), and was joined in turn by Evelyn on GUITAR, Suzanne on MANDOLIN, and Sidney on banjo and DOBRO. They recorded a homemade album in 1974 and began working the local bluegrass festival.

However, it would take 16 years for the Coxes to reach the big time. A chance encounter with fiddler/singer Alison Krauss at a Texas bluegrass festival in 1988 led to her becoming a champion of the band, particularly of Suzanne's vocals and Sidney's songwriting abilities. Krauss made a minor hit out of one of Sidney's songs, "I've Got That Old Feeling" (the title track of her 1990 album), and convinced her label, Rounder Records, to sign the group in 1993. They recorded two albums for Rounder, and also joined with Krauss on an all-gospel LP, *I Know Who Holds Tomorrow,* in 1994. Suzanne also became a much in-demand session singer, backing Dolly Parton on her bluegrass albums, as well as Randy Travis and other mainstream country singers. In 2000 the family was featured in the Coen Brothers's film *O Brother Where Art Thou?,* singing the gospel song, "I Am Weary." This led to renewed interest in them, although that July Willard was sidelined due to a serious automobile accident. In 2001 he returned to performing, although confined to a wheelchair, with his children, appearing as part of the "Down from the Mountain" tour, featuring musicians from the *O Brother* film.

See also BANJO, FIVE-STRING.

Crary, Dan (b. 1940) *guitarist*

Born in Kansas City, Missouri, Crary began playing GUITAR at age 12 in local bluegrass bands. He moved to Louisville, Kentucky, in 1968, where he joined Bluegrass Alliance, remaining with this group for two years to return to Kansas City in pursuit of a graduate degree. In 1970 he released the album *Bluegrass Guitar,* which became a landmark for a new generation of flatpicking guitarists. Crary updated the style of Doc Watson and Clarence White to include jazz, new age, and other influences. In 1977 he moved to California, joining with fiddler BYRON BERLINE and banjoist John Hickman in the country-rock group Sundance. Within a year Berline, Crary, and Hickman were touring as a trio, and continued to work together on and off throughout much of the 1980s; Berline and Crary formed the group California to explore a variety of acoustic music styles in 1990. Meanwhile, Crary also cut a number of solo albums of bluegrass instrumentals. He has also recorded and toured with banjoist Lonnie Hoppers and Italian guitarist Beppe Gambetta (as Men of Steel).

Crook Brothers

Like Dr. Humphrey Bate, another early star of the *Grand Ole Opry,* Scottsboro, Tennessee, natives Herman (December 2, 1898–June 10, 1988) and Matthew Crook (June 13, 1896–July 1964) were HARMONICA players, an instrument that was very popular at the turn of the last century in middle Tennessee. They began performing in the early 1920s in the Nashville area, and the duo were soon broadcasting on local radio. George Hay, the founder of the *Grand Ole Opry,* invited them to play on the show during its second year of broadcast, in 1926. While they were *Opry* regulars, they continued to perform on other local radio shows as well.

In 1927 Lewis Crook (no relation; b. Trousdale County, Tennessee, May 30, 1909–April 12, 1997) joined the band on BANJO and GUITAR, giving it more of a traditional string band sound. However, like Bate's band, they had a more subdued sound than the more raucous Georgia-based Skillet Lickers. A year later, Victor Records made the first-ever recordings in Nashville, inspired by the success of the *Opry,* and naturally the Crooks participated. They cut four titles, including their best seller, "My Wife Died on Friday Night." Oddly, the band did not record again until the FOLK REVIVAL of the 1960s.

Matthew Crook retired in the late 1920s to join the Nashville police force. Brother Herman, unable to find another harmonica player to take his place, decided to add a fiddler to the band. For most of the 1930s, this spot was taken by Tennessee-native Floyd Etheridge, who played in a style similar to FIDDLIN' ARTHUR SMITH, whom Etheridge had performed with as a teenager. The band also expanded beyond its repertoire of instrumentals by adding a number of country favorites, with vocals handled by Lewis.

The band continued to find work on the *Opry* in the 1940s. Still featuring Herman's harmonica leads, the group had once again changed its sound by adding a vocal harmony trio to the mix, including Neil Matthews Sr. and Jr.; the latter would later be a member of the popular 1950s country-harmony group the Jordanaires. In the early 1960s the group was discovered by the folk revival and recorded again, this time for the Starday label. Eventually, they were limited to an occasional *Opry* spot, although they continued to perform until Herman's death in 1988, with various members.

Crowe, J. D. (b. 1937) *banjoist*

James Dee Crowe was born in Lexington, Kentucky, on August 27, 1937. He began his career as banjoist for JIMMY MARTIN in Martin's country-bluegrass backup band, the Sunnysiders. He quickly established himself as one of the more innovative bluegrass banjo players, with an interest in rock and roll and blues as well as straight country. After leaving Martin, he formed his band the New South in the early 1970s, along with brothers Tony and Larry Rice on GUITAR and MANDOLIN, respectively. They signed to Starday in 1973, already playing amplified instruments and drawing on contemporary singer/songwriters as well as traditional bluegrass numbers. Crowe's most influential album was his 1975 debut on Rounder Records, when the band featured Tony Rice on guitar, Ricky Skaggs on mandolin, Jerry Douglas on DOBRO, and Bobby Slone on FIDDLE. This album did much to boost Rice's, Skaggs's, and Douglas's careers among young bluegrassers, while the band's style influenced countless other "progressive" outfits.

In the late 1970s Keith Whitley, who had previously performed with Skaggs, joined the band as lead vocalist, and the band began to draw more on a honky-tonk repertoire based on Whitley's ability to recreate the sounds and styles of Lefty Frizzell and Lester Flatt. Other important Crowe alumni of this era are Sam Bush and Jimmy Gaudreau.

Crowe rejoined with Tony Rice, along with bluegrass superstars Doyle Lawson (guitar, vocal), Bobby Hicks (fiddle), and Todd Phillips (bass) to form an unnamed supergroup that recorded five "Bluegrass Albums" for Rounder from the mid-to-late 1980s. These were straightforward, return-to-roots efforts for these artists, all of whom had achieved fame and fortune in a more progressive arena. Meanwhile, Crowe has continued to lead his own band through the 1990s, although it does not enjoy the same level of influence that it did 20 years earlier.

See also BANJO, FIVE-STRING.

Cunningham, Agnes "Sis" See *BROADSIDE* MAGAZINE.

Cunningham, Johnny and Phil See SILLY WIZARD.

d

Dane, Barbara (b. 1927) *activist and singer*
Barbara Stillman was born in Detroit, Michigan, on May 12, 1927. She was singing on the San Francisco Bay area folk scene from the late 1940s, when she was married to singer/guitarist Rolf Cahn. Active in the labor union and CIVIL RIGHTS MOVEMENT, she was divorced from Cahn by 1951, when she briefly joined the Gateway Singers. Like the Weavers, the group combined pop-style arrangements with songs with political messages. She was soon performing as a solo singer, mostly working at labor meetings and rallies. By the late 1950s she had graduated to more upscale folk-oriented clubs such as Los Angeles's Cosmo Alley and Chicago's Gate of Horn, singing blues material as well as social protest songs, sometimes with jazz musicians accompanying her. She also recorded for major labels, including Dot and Capitol. In the 1960s she was active in the Civil Rights and antiwar movements, leading a "Sing in For Peace" at New York's Carnegie Hall in 1966 with her second husband (and *Sing Out!* editor), Irwin Silber. The two also compiled a Vietnam songbook featuring antiwar songs. In 1969 Silber and Dane founded Paredon Records to release social-protest and political music.

See also *SING OUT!* MAGAZINE.

Darby and Tarlton
Guitarist Tom Darby (b. Columbus, Georgia, January 7, 1883–June 1971) and steel GUITAR player Jimmy Tarleton (b. Johnny James Rimbert Tarleton, Chesterfield County, South Carolina, May 8, 1892–1979) came out of South Carolina's textile mills. Tarlton was undoubtedly the more talented of the pair; early on, he took up the banjo, but could play many other instruments well. A fine singer with a clear voice, he apparently traveled around the country performing, covering lots of ground between South Carolina, New York, and California. He first began playing guitar with a bottleneck slide in the blues style popular in the South, but then he met a Hawaiian guitarist when he was bumming around the West Coast around the time of World War I and quickly adopted novelty effects from that musical style.

Exactly when and where Darby and Tarlton met and first performed together is unknown. In April 1927 the duo made their first recordings for Columbia Records in New York, with Darby playing guitar and singing lead vocals and Tarlton on steel guitar providing tenor harmonies. At their second recording session, also held in 1927, the duo recorded two traditional folk blues numbers, both "arranged" by Tarlton: "Birmingham Jail" and "Columbus Stockade Blues." Tarlton received a $75 arranger's fee for these two numbers that have since become folk and country standards.

The duo continued to record together through the early 1930s for a variety of labels, until the Depression led to reduced recording of country music; Tarlton also recorded without Darby.

Davis, Rev. Gary (1896–1972) *influential guitarist*
Gary Davis was born in Laurens, South Carolina, on April 30, 1896. Davis originally performed in his native South Carolina as a teenager with local musician Willie Walker. Sometime in his teen years Davis went blind, although there is disagreement as to exactly when and what was the cause of his affliction. He moved to Durham, North Carolina, by his early 20s, where he began performing as a street musician. There he befriended another blind guitarist, Blind Boy Fuller, and the two made some recordings together with Davis on second GUITAR in the mid-1930s. At the same sessions Davis made his first recordings on his own, recording only gospel material. In 1937 he was ordained a minister. He moved to New York City in 1944, where he began performing on the streets of Harlem. He recorded for a variety of folk labels beginning in the mid-1950s, including Riverside and Prestige. His early 1960s albums on Prestige were highly influential, and Davis became a popular performer on the FOLK-REVIVAL circuit. Although he claimed to prefer religious material, he also played ragtime instrumentals as well as party and (somewhat) risqué numbers. His guitar playing was very inventive, featuring ragtime-flavored syncopation and virtuosic fingerpicking. Revival guitarist Stefan Grossman became a close friend of Davis's, recording him extensively, and publishing several books on his guitar style. Davis continued to perform until shortly before his death on May 5, 1972, although his later recordings were not up to the same level as his 1950s–1960s–era work. Thanks to Grossman, a large number of Davis's recordings, made in informal home sessions as well as in studios, are available. Davis was also an active guitar teacher in New York City, giving lessons to many revivalists, both black and white.

De Danann
Second to the Chieftains, De Danann is one of the longest-lived Irish revival bands, although their music has often strayed far beyond its traditional roots. The heart of the group are its two founding members, fiddler/FLUTE player Frankie Gavin and bouzouki/guitarist Alec Finn, who met at informal gatherings of musicians (known as "sessions") in Galway in the early 1970s. They were joined by melodeon player Charlie Piggot and virtuosic percussionist/bodhran player Johnny "Ringo" McDonagh to form the original band lineup. Their first album, released in 1975, featured vocals by the talented singer Dolores Keane, but she left soon after its recording. Johnny Moyniham, who had previously been a member of Sweeney's Men and PLANXTY, joined briefly as a vocalist for the band's second album, released in 1978, but left by 1980, when ACCORDION player Jackie Daly joined the ranks. This new lineup, Gavin-Finn-Piggot-McDonah-Daly, with the addition of vocalist Maura O'Connell, released the band's first major successful album, *The Star Spangled Molly,* in 1981, which mostly consisted of 1920s era popular Irish songs and dances, although the album's arrangement of "Hey Jude" as an Irish hornpipe garnered the most attention.

Despite this success, Piggot (who was accidentally injured so he could no longer play), O'Connor, and Daly all left the group; accordionist Martin O'Connor and singer Mary Black were brought on as replacements. In 1985 Dolores Keane reenlisted in the band's rank as a second singer. This lineup lasted until 1987 and was the last "classic" lineup of the group. Various personnel have come and gone since then, with the band turning increasingly to experimentation with a wider variety of musical styles, from KLEZMER to world music to unabashed pop. Since 1991 the band has performed on a semi-regular basis, usually regrouping every three to four years, usually with a new vocalist and a slightly different emphasis.

DeMent, Iris (b. 1961) *singer/songwriter and pianist*
Born in rural Paragould, Arkansas, DeMent's farmer family moved when she was three years old to Southern California. Both parents were deeply

religious, performing in the church choir and allowing only gospel music to be played around the house. Her father was also a fiddler, and her older siblings formed a family gospel group called the DeMent Sisters.

DeMent played gospel music on the piano and sang in the church choir like her brothers and sisters until she left home at age 25. Relocating to Kansas City, she began playing the GUITAR and writing original songs, many based on her memories of her musical family, including "Mama's Opry," "After They're Gone," and "Our Town." A demo tape of her songs was given to JOHN PRINE, who recommended that she come to Nashville. After a few showcase performances she was signed to Philo/Rounder and recorded her first album with producer JIM ROONEY, who had previously guided NANCI GRIFFITH's recording career. DeMent's folk-edged, homespun sound was an immediate hit with critics, and major label Warner Brothers quickly signed her and rereleased the album.

DeMent followed in 1994 with *My Life*, an album of introspective songs, and then turned in a harder-edged direction with 1996's *The Way I Should*, with many songs featuring social-protest themes. Since then DeMent has continued to tour and compose. In 2001 she appeared in the film *Songcatcher*, which told the story of a folklorist tracking down a traditional Appalachian ballad singer.

Denny, Sandy (1947–1978) *singer and songwriter*

Born in London, England, on January 6, 1947, Sandy Denny was one of the leading lights on the British FOLK-ROCK scene. Denny began performing as a typical girl-with-a-GUITAR on London's booming folk scene in the mid-1960s. She was enlisted to be the lead singer of the folk-rock band the Strawbs in 1967, and shortly thereafter replaced original vocalist Judy Dyble as lead singer in FAIRPORT CONVENTION. Denny remained with the band for three albums, including 1969's classic *Liege & Lief*, which combined traditional ballads with new songs by Denny and band member RICHARD THOMPSON. Denny left the group in 1970, first forming the band Fotheringay with Australian guitarist Trevor Lucas (who would soon become her husband) and then pursuing a solo career. Her best-known song, "Who Knows Where the Time Goes," originally recorded with Fairport in 1968, was covered in the United States by folksinger JUDY COLLINS, furthering Denny's reputation. Despite this success, Denny's solo career was uneven, and so she followed her husband, Trevor Lucas, back into (a new version) of Fairport Convention in 1974, although this lineup lasted only about a year and a half. One final album appeared in 1977. Denny died after falling down a flight of stairs on April 21, 1978.

Denver, John (1943–1997) *singer and songwriter*

Henry John Deutschendorf was born in Roswell, New Mexico, on December 31, 1943. His father was a career air force pilot. Denver began playing folk music in college, and then moved to New York to try to establish himself on the folk scene. His first break came when he was hired to replace group leader Chad Mitchell in the popular CHAD MITCHELL TRIO in 1965, continuing to record with them until 1969, when the trio dissolved. Soon after, Denver was signed to RCA as a solo artist, recording his first album combining self-penned satirical songs attacking then-president Nixon and the war in Vietnam along with such sentimental pop songs as "(Leaving on a) Jet Plane," which had been a hit for PETER, PAUL AND MARY.

Denver's big break as a performer came in 1971 with his recording of "Take Me Home, Country Roads," followed by a string of country-flavored pop hits, including the sappy ballad "Annie's Song" and the uptempo, enthusiastic "Thank God I'm a Country Boy." Denver began a film-acting career in 1977, showing himself to be an affable comedian. He continued to record his own material through the mid-1980s with limited success, forming his own label later to promote the country album

Higher Ground in 1988, featuring the title hit. Denver died while piloting a small airplane on October 12, 1997.

Dickens, Hazel (b. 1937) *singer*

Born in Mercer City, West Virginia, to a coal mining family, Dickens was well acquainted with the hardships and poverty of southern mountain life. Dickens had to leave high school in order to start work, relocating to Baltimore in search of employment. She ended up doing factory work while beginning to sing at local bars and clubs.

By the early 1960s Dickens was living in Washington, D.C., and was becoming well known in the local country scene. There she partnered with urban-born guitarist/singer ALICE GERRARD, and the two recorded an album together, *Who's That Knocking?*, in 1965. They continued to perform together through the mid-1970s, when Dickens's songwriting began to attract a wider audience. Her song "They'll Never Keep Us Down," was featured in Barbara Kopple's documentary film *Harlan County, U.S.A.;* she sang the song on the film's soundtrack. In 1981 she released her first album, *Hard Hitting Songs for Hard Hit People* (named after the famous songbook compiled by WOODY GUTHRIE, PETE SEEGER, and folklorist Alan Lomax in the 1940s). She continued to record and perform through the 1980s, but has been less active since. The Appalchian-based center Appalshop made a film about her life and career, *It's Hard to Tell the Singer from the Song,* in 1986.

See also LOMAX, JOHN AND ALAN.

Dillards, The

Banjo player Doug (b. East St. Louis, Illinois, March 6, 1937) and guitarist/vocalist Rodney Dillard (b. Salem, Missouri, 1942) were sons of an old-time fiddler who grew up surrounded by traditional dance music. In the mid-1950s a vibrant bluegrass scene developed in metropolitan St. Louis, including the young Dillards along with banjo-picker

JOHN HARTFORD. After hooking up with local country deejay Mitch Jayne, who became the group's spokesperson, they made their debut in 1962 performing at Washington University; soon after, they relocated to California, where they signed with Elektra Records, then an urban-folk label (and soon to become a FOLK-ROCK label). At the same time, they were hired to portray the "Darling" family on TV's *Andy Griffith Show,* giving the band further exposure. Their first two albums were a mix of traditional country and bluegrass songs along with more contemporary numbers by songwriters such as BOB DYLAN.

After recording an influential album of fiddle tunes with guest artist BYRON BERLINE, the band split, with Doug leaving to form a folk-rock group

Banjoist Doug Dillard in the mid-1970s (Courtesy Flying Fish Records)

with ex-Byrd GENE CLARK, and Rodney continuing to lead the band with new banjo player Herb Pederson (later a founding member of the Desert Rose Band). The Dillards took a more folk-rock direction, recording two concept albums that featured popular songs by the Beatles and folk artists such as Tim Hardin.

The Dillards as a band were dormant through much of the early to mid-1970s, but re-emerged with the bluegrass revival of the later half of the decade. Rodney and Doug recorded with old friend John Hartford, while Rodney continued to lead a band, now with mandolinist Dean Webb, Jeff Gilkinson (vocals, bass, cello), banjoist Billy Ray Latham (who was a member of the influential KENTUCKY COLONELS, another California-based bluegrass band), and Paul York (drums). The band recorded sporadically through the 1990s, although they were not so successful or influential as the first incarnation of the group had been.

Dilly and His Dill Pickles

A popular string band of the mid-1920s to early 1930s, Dilly and His Dill Pickles was led by a performer known as the "Seven Foot Dilly," a unique guitarist/singer whose real name was John Dilleshaw; born circa 1896. He came from northern Georgia, where his family were subsistence farmers. At age 17 he suffered a freak accident when he accidentally shot himself in the foot. While recuperating, he began playing GUITAR, taking informal lessons from a local black player. Around 1922 Dilleshaw settled in Atlanta, where he was hired by the fire department. As a musician, he performed with Charles Brook as a guitar duet act known as the Gibson Kings, broadcasting on powerful station WSB around 1924–25, as well as with the Dixie String Band. Around 1926 Dilleshaw's brother-in-law, 18-year-old fiddler Harry Kiker, came to Atlanta and began working with him in various groups. The Dilleshaw string band was completed when the father-son team of Pink and Shorty Lindsey came on board. Pink was a talented multi-

instrumentalist who landed his own contract with Columbia in early 1929 (the sides went unissued, however). Shorty had played tenor banjo for Fiddlin' John Carson and also led his own bands.

The band recorded twice in 1930, covering a wide range of material, including humorous skits ("A Georgia Barbecue at Stone Mountain"), energetic fiddle tunes, and even two "talking blues," featuring Dilleshaw accompanied just by his own guitar. Dilleshaw did more than accompany the band on guitar, however. He provided comic spoken narration as the band worked through the tunes. These loosely structured comic yarns set these records apart from the competitors. With the coming of the Depression, there were no more opportunities to record, but Dilleshaw kept various bands going through 1940, when his health began to fail. He died in 1941.

Dixon Brothers, The

Guitarist and fiddler Dorsey (October 14, 1897– April 17, 1968) and steel guitarist Howard (June 19, 1903–March 24, 1961) Dixon were born in Darlington, South Carolina. The entire Dixon family, parents and seven children, worked as mill hands; Dorsey entered the mills when he was 12 years old. From his mother he learned traditional ballads, play-party songs, and hymns, and as a young teenager learned to play GUITAR and FIDDLE. He teamed up with his younger brother, Howard, to perform at local movie theaters as a novelty act between screenings.

By the early 1930s the brothers were working in a mill in East Rockingham, North Carolina, where they met legendary steel guitar player Jimmie Tarleton (of DARBY AND TARLETON fame) who was also working in the mills. Tarleton inspired them to become professional musicians, and also to play more bluesy-sounding songs, with Howard taking up the steel guitar in emulation of Tarleton's mastery of the instrument. The duo got their big break in 1934, when they appeared on a country radio show out of Charlotte, North Carolina, and two years later were signed to RCA's budget Bluebird label. They recorded 60 numbers over the next two years, including many songs commenting on the hard life in the cotton mills ("Weave Room Blues") and the classic country song "I Didn't Hear Nobody Pray." Although Dorsey wrote both songs, he sold the rights to them to his publisher and never earned a penny from the many recordings of these standards. After 1938 the brothers returned to textile work and abandoned their professional careers.

In the early 1960s Dorsey Dixon was "rediscovered" by folk revivalists, and he performed at various folk festivals and made a couple of new albums of his own material and traditional country songs, as well as recording for the Library of Congress, receiving belated recognition for his contributions to country music history.

Dobro (resophonic guitar)

The Dobro is a unique American musical instrument that has become central to the sound of modern bluegrass music. It has its roots in the craze for Hawaiian music that swept the country in the 1920s. The classical guitar was introduced by Portuguese settlers in the islands around the 1830s; eventually, by the century's end, Hawaiian musicians had taken to playing the GUITAR on their laps, tuning the strings to a full open or partially open chord (known as "slack-key" tuning), and noting the strings with a solid metal bar (hence the term, *steel guitar,* referring to the bar used to damp the notes, not to the material used in making the guitar itself).

Although conventional guitars could be used for Hawaiian music, they weren't very loud (particularly when placed on the player's lap, so that the sound hole faced up into the air). A family of Czechoslovakian immigrant instrument makers, the Dopyera brothers, decided they could invent a better instrument for this music. Brother John is generally credited with designing the original resonator used on dobros, a system that employed a primitive nonelectric pickup mounted on the bridge of the instrument (like the needle used on early acoustic phonographs) that transmitted the sound down into a chamber that held three megaphonelike cones, facing down (or toward the back of the instrument). Dopyera was awarded a patent for his design in 1927, and a year later began producing instruments with his brothers under the National name. These instruments had steel bodies, so are commonly called National steels by today's players. A further refinement of the design came in 1929, when the first Dobro (taken from the name *Do*pyera *Bro*thers) was made. In order to make a cheaper instrument than the National steel, the brothers decided to use a plywood body for their new instrument.

The Dobro probably would have disappeared from the musical scene if it had not been for a couple of influential players. "Bashful Brother Oswald" (aka Pete Kirby) played the instrument in Roy Acuff's influential band from 1939 through the 1950s, appearing weekly on the *Grand Ole Opry*. In bluegrass music the pioneering Flatt and Scruggs band featured a talented player of the dobro, Uncle Josh (b. Burkett) Graves, who took Earl Scruggs's signature banjo roll and adapted it to the instrument. The bluegrass revival of the 1970s helped bring the instrument back to the fore, with young players such as JERRY DOUGLAS showing that the Dobro was not just a relic of the past. Douglas became one of the most in-demand session musicians of the 1980s and 1990s, and many other players have emulated his versatility on the instrument.

Donegan, Lonnie (1931–2002) *founder of skiffle music*

Born Anthony James Donegan in Glasgow, Scotland, on April 29, 1931, Donegan is remembered today as the popularizer of British skiffle music, which helped launch both the British FOLK REVIVAL and, later, British blues and rock. Donegan led a band that featured many homemade instruments, including washtub bass, and emphasized that "anybody" could play his music. His big hit came in 1955 with LEAD BELLY's "Rock Island Line," in an uptempo, jazz-pop–flavored arrangement. Donegan had several more hits in Britain through the end of the decade, influencing scores of young British players to take up the GUITAR. Future Beatle John Lennon's first group, the Quarrymen, formed in 1957 when he was in high school, was very much in the skiffle mold. After the skiffle craze ended, Donegan made periodic "comebacks," but never again matched his original success. He died following a heart attack on November 3, 2002.

Doucet, Michael See BEAUSOLEIL.

Douglas, Jerry (b. 1956) *Dobro player*
Gerald Calvin Douglas was born in Warren, Ohio, on May 28, 1956. He began his career as a teenager playing bluegrass music. He performed with the COUNTRY GENTLEMEN in the early 1970s, where he met another talented young player, Ricky Skaggs. The duo formed a progressive bluegrass ensemble in the late 1970s called Boone Creek to perform more contemporary country material in a bluegrass setting. At the same time he recorded his first two solo outings for Rounder, featuring many contemporary-bluegrass musicians, including Skaggs, TONY RICE, Sam Bush, BÉLA FLECK, and Russ Barenberg.

Douglas relocated to Nashville in the early 1980s and was in immediate demand for session work accompanying the so-called new country artists, including his old friend Skaggs. He has continued to record solo albums, while also working in an acoustic trio with bassist Edgar Meyer and guitarist Russ Barenberg. He has become an in-demand session musician, appearing on just about every bluegrass album recorded in Nashville, including recent bluegrass forays by Dolly Parton and Patty Loveless. In 2001 Douglas became an official member of Allison Krauss's band, Union Station.

Dubliners, The
With various lineups, this early Irish revival group has soldiered on over the decades, although they achieved their greatest artistic and commercial success from the mid-1960s through the mid-1970s. Originally formed in 1962 by guitarist/singer Ronnie Drew, the group had a typical FOLK-REVIVAL sound, much like the more successful CLANCY BROTHERS, although they were considerably rougher around the edges. The band's classic lineup coalesced around 1966, with Drew, banjoist/vocalist Luke Kelly, guitarist/vocalist Ciaran Bourke, fiddler John Sheahan, and tenor banjoist/MANDOLIN player Barney McKenna. In 1967 their recording of the (slightly raucous) drinking song "Seven Drunken Nights" was banned by BBC radio, and became a favorite of the (offshore) radio station Radio Caroline, a well-known pirate station favored by rock fans. The song became a major pop hit and launched the band's greatest period of recording and touring success.

Although successful, the band's members were constantly fighting onstage and off, and the band itself teetered on the edge of folding through much of the next seven years. In 1974 founding member Ronnie Drew retired after being shaken by the sudden, unexpected illness of Ciaran Bourke, who was diagnosed with a brain tumor that left him unable to play. Drew returned five years later, but then in 1984 Luke Kelly (whose distinctive high vocal parts were a hallmark of the band's sound) died, also of a brain tumor. Various replacements came on board to keep the band afloat, and the Irish folk-punk band the Pogues paid homage to the group's legendary reputation by inviting them to appear on their recording of the folk-revival standard "The Irish Rover" in 1987, which was a major chart hit.

In 1996 Drew retired again from the band, yet somehow or other it has continued to perform, although focusing primarily on its "classic hits" rather than on new material.

dulcimer (Appalachian)
The Appalachian dulcimer is a common instrument in the upper South, used primarily to accompany ballads. It usually has three strings, with only one being used to play the melody (the other two are unfretted and strummed for a drone effect). The

player often uses a wooden stick to fret the instrument, sometimes called a noter; traditionally, a quill feather was used to strum across the strings, although most contemporary players use the common flatpick developed for the GUITAR. Instruments are relatively simple to make, so that homemade dulcimers were quite common throughout the South.

The best-known dulcimer player is JEAN RITCHIE. Coming from a traditional Kentucky family, Ritchie was a prominent performer for several decades beginning in the early 1950s FOLK REVIVAL. She authored one of the first dulcimer instruction books. In the 1970s the instrument became associated with the "back-to-Earth" movement, thanks to such books as the popular *Life Is Like a Mountain Dulcimer.* Performers during this period developed more intricate ways of playing the instrument, notably Kevin Roth and Holly Tannen.

dulcimer (hammered)

The hammered dulcimer is unrelated to the Appalachian dulcimer, despite the similar names. Usually trapezoidal in shape, it is something like a "piano without the middleman"; i.e., the player holds two wooden "hammers" (actually slightly bent sticks), one in each hand, and strikes directly on the strings to play melodies. The strings are often paired, and pass over a single bridge, in approximately a two-to-three ratio, so that two notes can be played by each paired set, a fifth apart. Because there are no dampers (as found on a piano, for example) the notes tend to ring out long after the strings are struck, giving the instrument a shimmering sound.

Hammered dulcimers were particularly popular in certain regions of the United States for playing dance music, such as Michigan, upstate New York, and Ohio. The instrument was given a considerable boost in popularity in the mid-1970s when folk revivalist Bill Spence released his first album, simply called *The Hammered Dulcimer,* on his own Front Hall label. Spence also made kits and finished instruments, and soon many new players were enticed to

try it out. As had been the case with the Appalachian dulcimer, new players also expanded on techniques, tunings, and the traditional repertoire.

See also DULCIMER (APPALACHIAN).

Dyer-Bennett, Richard (1913–1991) *guitarist and lute player*

Richard Dyer-Bennett was born in Leicester, England, on October 6, 1913. Within the first years of his life, the family relocated to British Columbia, and then to Berkeley, California, arriving there when he was 10 years old. At age 13 his high tenor voice won him a place in a local children's choir, and after finishing high school he continued his musical studies in Germany from 1929 to 1931. While abroad, he learned GUITAR and began to perform folk songs. Dyer-Bennett returned to complete a degree in English at Berkeley, and then returned to Europe, going to Sweden, where he befriended folksong scholar Sven Scholander. Scholander taught him many songs and encouraged him to take up the lute, believing it to be a more authentic "folk" instrument than the later guitar. Dyer-Bennett's repertoire mixed folk songs, ballads, and sea chantys with medieval and Elizabethan classical songs, all sung in his high tenor voice with his lute accompaniment.

After his Swedish trip Dyer-Bennett returned to Berkeley, where he began performing for small groups. In 1938 he appeared before the San Francisco Women's Club, which attracted the attention of a local music critic, who urged him to go to New York, where he arrived in 1941. Soon he was booked at the Village Vanguard club, a meeting place for New York's liberals and fans of folk music, and gained a loyal following. In 1944 Dyer-Bennett was the first folk performer to play New York's Town Hall. This became an annual event and led to a contract with classical music promoter Sol Hurok. Thanks to Hurok, Dyer-Bennett performed and recorded widely.

Like many folk performers, Dyer-Bennett was blacklisted in the early 1950s due to his association with left-wing causes. He managed to survive by appearing for long engagements at New York's Village Vanguard. In 1955 he formed a record label with the sole purpose of releasing his own albums so he could have full artistic—and financial—control over his work, anticipating the trend toward individual artist labels by many years. His first album was surprisingly successful, and he would go on to record 14 albums, mostly on themes such as Elizabethan songs or the songs of STEPHEN FOSTER. Dyer-Benentt continued to tour and teach through 1972, when a stroke left him unable to play music. After that he devoted his time to a long-running project to set Homer's *Odyssey* to music. He died of complications from lymphoma on December 14, 1991.

Dylan, Bob (b. 1941) *influential singer and songwriter*

Born Robert Allen Zimmerman in Duluth, Minnesota, on May 24, 1941, Dylan began performing as a high school student on GUITAR and piano in various local rock-influenced bands. After enrolling at the University of Minnesota in Minneapolis, he was exposed to the FOLK-REVIVAL movement, particularly to the recordings of singer/songwriter WOODY GUTHRIE. Dylan immediately remolded himself in Guthrie's image, and by 1960 had made his way to New York City, hoping to meet his idol. There he began writing topical songs inspired by Guthrie, attracting the attention of New York folk promoter Israel "IZZY" YOUNG, who produced Dylan's first solo concert, and the activist/publishers AGNES "SIS" CUNNINGHAM and Gordon Friesen, who published his first songs in their *BROADSIDE* MAGAZINE.

Dylan's success on the Greenwich Village folk scene led producer John Hammond to sign him to Columbia Records. Hammond produced Dylan's self-titled debut, a mix of folk standards and his own songs. (When recording for other labels, Dylan took the pseudonym of Blind Boy Grunt to avoid angering Columbia.) Dylan's second album, *The Freewheelin' Bob Dylan* (1963), introduced his versions of several social-protest classics, including

"Blowin' in the Wind." However, it was covers of Dylan's songs by other performers—notably PETER, PAUL, AND MARY's version of this song—that were the major hits.

A trip to England in 1964 inspired Dylan to begin experimenting with electric instrumentation, which culminated in his now infamous appearance at the 1965 NEWPORT FOLK FESTIVAL. Angering some of his folk fans, Dylan performed only new material, accompanied by a rock rhythm section (actually the rhythm section of the Paul Butterfield Blues Band). Numerous legends have arisen around this event, including that PETE SEEGER tried to cut the sound cables with an ax during Dylan's set, and that Dylan's manager ALBERT GROSSMAN got into a wrestling match with famed folklorist Alan Lomax backstage.

Although Dylan supposedly turned his back on folk music at this time, he never really abandoned it. After his famous motorcycle accident in 1966, Dylan returned with a collection of folkish ballads on *John Wesley Harding,* and followed that with a brief flirtation with country rock on 1969's *Nashville Skyline.* The 1970s marked a turn toward a confessional, singer/songwriter style, much in the mold of other popular 1970s performers including JONI MITCHELL and Neil Young. A late 1970s "born again" phase was followed by some lackluster rock-flavored recordings in the mid-1980s.

To everyone's surprise, Dylan returned to acoustic folk in the early 1990s with two albums featuring covers of traditional songs, with just his own guitar and vocals: *Good As I Been to You* (1992) and *World Gone Wrong* (1993). When returning to his own songwriting on 1997's *Time out of Mind,* Dylan synthesized a number of influences, including folk, blues, rockabilly, and other "roots" styles that showed—despite the long arc of his career and the many changes he had gone through—his music maintained a vital connection to the folk songs that he performed more than 35 years earlier. In 2001, *Love and Theft* continued his experimentations with roots styles and folk themes.

See also LOMAX, JOHN AND ALAN.

Eanes, Jim (1923–1995) *bandleader and guitarist*
Homer Robert Eanes Jr. was born in Mountain Valley, Virginia, on December 6, 1923. From about the age of nine, Eanes played GUITAR accompanying his father, a traditional-styled banjo player who worked local dances. When he was a teenager, he began working local radio, and at age 16 was hired by Roy Hall, who had his own show out of Roanoke. Eanes worked with Hall's band for four years before enlisting in the army.

After World War II, Eanes worked with a band called Uncle Joe and the Blue Mountain Boys, which broadcast over several small Virginia-based stations before he finally landed a radio job in Knoxville, Tennessee. There he met Bill Monroe and worked with the legendary father of bluegrass for a few months in 1948. The next year Eanes cut his first records for Capitol, accompanied by bluegrass pioneers Homer Sherrill on fiddle and Snuffy Jenkins on banjo. He then formed a permanent band, the Shendandoah Valley Boys, broadcasting out of Danville, Virginia. After recording for small local labels, Eanes was signed in 1952 to Decca, who polished up his sound to appeal to a broader country audience. However, he failed to produce any hits, and the label dropped him in 1955.

Eanes returned to the bluegrass style for the balance of his 1950s and early 1960s recordings, mostly cut for Starday and a variety of smaller labels. On Starday he had a few minor hits, including "I Wouldn't Change You If I Could," which would later be covered by Ricky Skaggs in 1982 for a number one country hit. In 1956 Eanes also made the first recording of "Your Old Standby," which became his theme song.

Eanes continued to work Virginia-area radio and clubs through the 1960s. The bluegrass revival of the late 1960s led to a series of albums cut with Red Smiley's band, the Bluegrass Cut-ups. When Smiley retired in 1970, Eanes took over the band, now called the Shendandoah Cutups, releasing one album on County before the band broke up. Eanes continued to work through the 1970s, although he took a year off following a heart attack in 1978. He continued to record into the 1990s, until his death on November 21, 1995.

East Texas Serenaders

The East Texas Serenaders were an early string band that straddled the line between old-time music and Western Swing. The group originated around the Hammons family; father Will was a fiddler, and his son Cloet accompanied him on GUITAR, with various others joining from time to time. By the mid-1920s Will was replaced by Daniel Huggins Williams, a left-handed fiddler who specialized in the long-bow, smooth, and slightly jazz-influenced fiddle style that was developing in the greater Dallas region. The group's name came from their practice of often going door to door "serenading" locals; they had very few professional jobs as musicians, and that they were recorded at all is one of the flukes of the history of early country music.

Nonetheless, from 1927 to 1930 they recorded a number of influential sides for Columbia and

Brunswick in four different sessions. They recorded only ragtime-influenced instrumentals and waltzes; none of the older, "traditional" SQUARE DANCE breakdowns were apparently part of their repertoire. The sessions' producers may have requested these more modern dance styles, but other Texas bands of this time also seem to have focused on this repertoire. The band then returned to local work, resurfacing in 1937 for a final session for Decca records.

Fiddler Williams's influence spread to younger players through these recordings and his local teaching. Johnny Gimble, later one of the legendary fiddlers associated with Western Swing pioneer Bob Wills, claimed to have taken lessons from Williams. The Serenaders' "Beaumont Rag," recorded at their last (1937) session, was quickly picked up by Wills and Company, and became one of their major instrumental hits.

Elliott, Ramblin' Jack (b. 1931) *guitarist and singer*

Born Elliott Adnopoz in Brooklyn, New York, on August 1, 1931, Elliott championed WOODY GUTHRIE's music from the late 1950s on, taking on his "Ramblin'" name and identity several years before a young Robert Zimmerman would make a similar transformation—again inspired by Guthrie—into BOB DYLAN.

When Woody Guthrie was hospitalized for a ruptured appendix in 1950, one of his visitors was a would-be cowboy who called himself "Buck Elliott." Elliott latched onto Guthrie, eventually moving in with him, and was the last performer to work with the older singer/songwriter before Guthrie was permanently disabled by Huntington's chorea. In 1955, now under the name "Ramblin' Jack Elliott," the singer/guitarist moved to England and became a major influence on the growing British FOLK REVIVAL, introducing many of Guthrie's songs to a British audience.

In 1961 he returned to New York, again visiting the hospitalized Guthrie. There he met Bob Dylan and became something of a mentor to the young singer. Elliott remained a major performer in the

Ramblin' Jack Elliott at the Philadelphia Folk Festival, early 1980s (Photo © Larry Sandberg)

folk world through the 1960s, even recording briefly for major label Reprise Records. In the mid-1970s, in recognition of his earlier support, Dylan invited Elliott to perform as part of his Rolling Thunder Revue. After that, Elliott did not record much until the mid-1990s, although he continued to perform.

Emerson, Bill (b. 1938) *banjoist*

William Hundley Emerson was born in Washington, D.C., on January 22, 1938. He was an influential banjo player in the Washington, D.C.-Virginia-Maryland area in the 1950s, first working with Buzz Busby and the Bayou Boys, a band that also featured Charlie Waller. After Busby was injured in an automobile accident in 1957, Waller and Emerson formed the first version of the COUNTRY GENTLEMEN. Emerson recorded a couple of singles with the group through 1958.

After leaving the Gentlemen, Emerson worked as a sideman, primarily with Jimmy Martin from 1962 to 1964, then spent a year with RED ALLEN, before returning to Jimmy Martin for another two-year stint. His tasteful single-note picking with Martin was much admired by many younger bluegrass revivalists at the time. After leaving Martin in 1967, he formed a group with Cliff Waldron that recorded for the small Rebel label. In 1970 Emerson rejoined the Country Gentlemen, staying with the band for three years. Emerson introduced the band to a song that he had learned from Waldron, "Fox on the Run," which was written by a British folk-rocker, Manfred Mann. The Country Gentlemen had a great success with the number, and it became a standard for many aspiring bluegrass pickers in the early 1970s.

Emerson left the Gentlemen in 1973 to join the navy, beginning a 20-year stint with the Navy Band. He appeared as a session musician sporadically through the 1970s and 1980s, making two triumphant "comeback" albums for Rebel as a solo banjo player in the late 1980s. Because of his fame in bluegrass circles, Stelling Banjo Company issued a special signature instrument for him in 1992. Emerson left the Navy in 1993, and continues to record and perform on occasion.

See also BANJO, FIVE-STRING.

Ennis, Seamus (1919–1982) *folklorist and performer*

Born in Jamestown, Ireland, on May 5, 1919, Ennis came from a line of pipers, including his father, James, who was well known for recording with the Fingal Trio in the 1930s, as well as appearing regularly on the radio. In the early 1940s and running through 1958, Ennis began his career as a folklorist, working first for Irish radio and then the BBC, collecting traditional music. At the same time he made his first recording, released in the United States on the CLANCY BROTHER's Tradition Records label. He began touring and performing actively in the 1960s through the early 1970s. Besides mastering the Irish or uillean pipes (which feature drones, chanters, and regulators—pipes that play chord harmonies for the melody), Ennis was also an excellent singer and storyteller, performing in both Gaelic and English. A number of albums were released of his performances, including a two-volume set called *Forty Years of Irish Piping* made in 1977 by the American folksinger/piper PATRICK SKY, which brought together recordings made over many decades from various sources. Although Ennis's health began to go into decline toward the end of the 1970s, he continued to perform until shortly before his death on October 5, 1982.

Fahey, John (1939–2001) *guitarist*

Eccentric and elusive, John Fahey was one of the first artists to perform solo acoustic GUITAR instrumentals, inspired by blues performers, but extending the pieces into improvisational works that incorporated the influence of everything from jazz and pop to raga and worldbeat. Fahey was born in Takoma Park, Maryland, on February 28, 1939. He became fascinated with early blues recordings as a teenager, particularly the work of Delta blues guitarist Charley Patton (whom he would later write about as his Ph.D. dissertation). In 1959 he recorded his first album, under the pseudonym of Blind Joe Death, on his own label, Takoma Records; only 95 copies were pressed of the original recording (later in the 1960s, Fahey rerecorded all of the pieces for a second version of this album). Fahey relocated to the Bay Area of California in the 1960s, and Takoma grew to issue not only his own recordings but of like-minded acoustic guitarists, including Robbie Basho and LEO KOTTKE (who was greatly influenced by Fahey), as well as such blues legends as Bukka White. Fahey signed with the FOLK-REVIVAL label Vanguard in the mid-1960s and then recorded for Reprise Records briefly in the late 1960s to early 1970s, before returning to Takoma. He sold the label in the mid-1970s, but continued to record for it sporadically through the early 1980s. Throughout this period Fahey only rarely performed and was known almost exclusively through his records.

Beginning in the mid-1980s Fahey's health began to suffer from a number of problems traced to diabetes and Epstein-Barr syndrome. He relocated to Oregon by the mid-1990s, where he finally resumed performing. His later albums were even more experimental than his early work. He also founded Revenant Records to reissue his favorite musicians from the 78 era, including a complete boxed set of Charley Patton's recordings. However, following a sextuple bypass operation in early 2001, Fahey passed away on February 22 of that year.

John Fahey in the late 1970s (Courtesy Rounder Records)

63

Fairport Convention

The leading British folk-rock group, Fairport Convention has gone through many changes in its three-plus-decade existence. The original group was formed around a nucleus of players who met at guitarist Simon Nicol's parents' house, known as Fairport, to play their favorite folk, blues, and pop songs. The senior member was bass guitarist ASHLEY HUTCHINGS, who brought together the original lineup—guitarists Nicol and RICHARD THOMPSON, vocalists Iain Matthews and Judy Dyble, and drummer Martin Lamble. The group began gigging around London, gaining a following at a new, trendy nightspot called the U.F.O. Club, where they were heard by producer/agent Joe Boyd. Boyd signed the group and became their producer.

After Fairport's first album, consisting primarily of covers of singer-songwriter material by JONI MITCHELL, BOB DYLAN, and other American performers, Dyble was replaced by the more seasoned and powerful singer, SANDY DENNY. Denny had already made a name for herself on the London folk circuit, and she brought a number of traditional songs, along with her own compositions; to the band. Matthews soon left as the attention of the band focused on Denny along with the virtuosic solo guitar work of Richard Thompson. Touring England in a small van, the band built up a loyal following. However, tragedy struck in mid-1969, when, driving home late at night after a gig, the van went off the road, and drummer Martin Lamble was killed and other band members injured. Lamble was subsequently replaced by drummer Dave Mattacks.

The band regrouped during the summer of 1969, adding occasional guest artist, fiddler DAVE SWARBRICK, to the group as a full-time member. Over the preceding months, Ashley Hutchings had become fascinated with traditional British folk music, spending hours researching old ballad texts. The group decided to release a "concept album" of traditional British songs and songs written in the traditional style. The result was the late 1969 release, *Liege & Lief,* which became an instant classic. The album truly can be said to have launched the British FOLK REVIVAL.

Following this release Hutchings wished to explore traditional music more deeply, while Denny and Thompson wanted to emphasize their own songwriting. The result was that Hutchings left (to form STEELEYE SPAN) and Denny went solo. New bass player Dave Pegg joined the group, and the new lineup (Thompson-Swarbrick-Nicol-Pegg-Mattacks) recorded *Full House,* mostly consisting of Thompson-Swarbrick compositions. This group also toured the United States in 1970, appearing at small clubs and the Philadelphia Folk Festival.

Thompson left soon after to pursue a solo career, and the band soldiered on as a quartet, recording two more albums before Simon Nicol left, effectively ending the original era of the group. A caretaker lineup briefly performed until new members could be recruited—guitarist/singer Trevor Lucas and lead guitarist Jerry Donahue, both from Sandy Denny's old band Fotheringay. Denny quickly rejoined the group as lead vocalist, and this version of Fairport made an attempt to achieve mainstream success with a rock-oriented album, *Rising for the Moon,* in 1975; however, the album made little impression, and the lineup soon disbursed. In 1977 Nicol, Pegg, Swarbrick, and new drummer Bruce Rowland returned the band to its folk-rock roots, recording two further albums before officially disbanding in 1979.

A year later Dave Pegg hosted the first of what would become an annual reunion event in his hometown of Cropedy in Oxfordshire. Soon, Pegg, Mattacks, and Nicol were touring again, adding first fiddler Ric Sanders (who had played with Nicol in various versions of the Albion Band) and then multi-instrumentalist Martin Allcock. This group was the longest-running lineup for Fairport, lasting from 1985 to 1997, recording several albums primarily of singer-songwriter material and touring. Allcock left in 1997, replaced by Chris Leslie, who had previously played with Dave Swarbrick's band, Whippersnapper. This group continues to record and perform.

Fariña, Richard (1937–1966) and Mimi (1945–2001)

Richard Fariña was a singer/songwriter active on the Greenwich Village folk scene beginning in the late 1950s. In 1960 he married CAROLYN HESTER, a well-known folksinger who was also performing in the Village. He befriended several young singers, including BOB DYLAN and Eric Von Schmidt; the trio recorded an album together of folk standards that was released in London in 1963.

While bumming around Europe in 1963, Fariña met JOAN BAEZ's sister, Mimi, and the two became lovers. They settled in Big Sur, California, after Fariña divorced Hester, and the couple wed. They began performing together, Richard playing dulcimer and Mimi playing GUITAR, performing primarily Richard's original compositions. His most popular song was "Pack Up Your Sorrows," which was successfully covered by a number of acts, including Baez, Johnny Cash, and JUDY COLLINS. The duo recorded two albums for Vanguard Records that achieved moderate success.

In 1966 Fariña's debut novel, *Been Down So Long It Looks Like Up to Me,* was published to some critical success. Sadly, following a signing party for the book, Fariña was killed in a motorcycle accident on April 30, 1966. A posthumous album was released, and then Mimi partnered with singer/songwriter

Mimi and Richard Fariña relaxing at their Carmel, California, home in April 1966. On April 30 of that year, Fariña died in a motorcycle accident on his way home from a book signing for his novel, Been Down So Long It Looks Like Up to Me. (Photo © John Byrne Cooke, http://www.cookephoto.com)

Tom Jans, releasing an album in 1971. She later organized Bread and Roses, a nonprofit organization in the Bay Area that sponsored an annual festival that featured many folk performers. Mimi made one final solo album in 1985, and then performed sporadically around her home. She died of cancer on July 18, 2001.

fiddle

Perhaps the best-known instrument in all of country music, the fiddle has a long-standing place in the traditional music of the British Isles and Appalachia.

One of the first questions asked by new listeners is: What's the difference between the fiddle and the violin? Actually, the difference does not lie in the structure of the instrument—although many fiddlers modify their violins in several important ways—but in the style of playing the instrument.

The fiddle takes its name from medieval bowed, stringed instruments that were the precursors of the modern violin, known as feydls or viols. The modern violin's story begins in Italy in the late 17th and 18th centuries. There famous builders, such as Stradivarius and Amati, developed new instrument designs that made the instrument easier to play and better sounding. Composer/performers such as Corelli and Vivaldi developed new ways of playing the instrument. By the late 18th century these innovative instruments and playing styles had reached the British Isles.

With the introduction of the violin family, a new virtuosic musician developed. One of the most active center for fiddle composition in the British Isles in the late 18th and early 19th centuries was Scotland, where the Baroque Italian style of variation was applied to traditional and new compositions. The 19th century was also marked by a series of dance crazes that swept Europe. Many originated in eastern music and moved rapidly west, like the waltz (of Austrian/German origin) and the polka (of Polish origin). These tunes, along with the traditional jigs, reels, and hornpipes, entered the fiddle repertoire rapidly, particularly in Scotland and Ireland. By the early 20th century a school of virtuosic Irish fiddlers came to the fore, rivaling and surpassing their Scottish forebears. Noteworthy among this group of musicians was MICHAEL COLEMAN, who made many recordings in the 1920s and 1930s that were popular on both sides of the Atlantic. The English fiddle tradition never seems to have reached the virtuosic heights of the Irish, although many bread-and-butter musicians played for country dances.

English, Irish, and Scottish immigrants came to the United States in several different waves, beginning in the early 18th century and continuing through the 20th century. Each new wave brought their music with them, and new, home-grown fiddle styles also developed, particularly in the South and Southwest. Tunes came from the various British traditions but also from minstrel shows and from the popular classical music of the day. There was also a wealth of composers who added an American sound to the fiddle tradition.

The first fiddle tune collections were published by early music publishers such as Elias Howe in the early 1800s. However, beginning in the Civil War period, American dance music became increasingly popular, leading to more widespread publication. In landmark instruction books written for fife players, who accompanied the troops to battle, tunes were collected and notated in standard versions. The war itself inspired the composition of many tunes, or older tunes were given a new association (named for a battle or event in the conflict). After the war, "mammouth" collections of dance tunes began to appear to meet the needs of amateur fiddlers.

Several regional fiddle traditions have been well documented in the United States. In the South, the area of northern West Virginia bordering the Kanawha River has spawned several well-known fiddlers, including Clark Kessinger, Ed Haley, Franklin George, and the Hammonds family. With perhaps the exception of Kessinger, these players all seem to share a unique repertoire of tunes, a more modal sound, and a less refined or polished manner of playing the instrument.

Another region that has been much studied is the Mount Airy, North Carolina–Galax, Virginia nexus. Galax plays host to one of the oldest fiddlers' conventions in the country. Fiddlers' conventions—where fiddlers compete for prize money and get a chance to exchange tunes—originated sometime in the early 20th century, and perhaps go back further than that. They are often organized by a particular local organization as a way to raise funding for schools or charitable groups. The Galax fiddlers meeting is one of the best known, and it was there in the mid-1960s that an important fiddle player, TOMMY JARRELL, was first "discovered" by folk revival musicians. Jarrell's fiddle style has been much copied and studied; he was in the middle of a fiddle dynasty because his father, Ben, recorded in the 1920s and his son, B.F., played in a more modern, bluegrass style.

Texas has been the home of some of the greatest "show" fiddlers. They have developed a flashy style of playing improvisations on traditional tunes, tinged with jazz and other more modern syncopated dance music. Texas has a long tradition of virtuoso fiddlers, beginning with Alexander Campbell "ECK" ROBERTSON, usually cited as the first southern fiddler to make a record, in 1922. His version of "Sally Goodin" and "The Brilliancy Medley" set the standard for elaborate and breathtaking variations. Over the years Texas has spawned many other virtuosic fiddlers, so that fancy fiddling in general is known as the "Texas" or "contest style."

The fiddle survived as the key melody instrument in both old-time string bands and in bluegrass bands. The 1960s FOLK REVIVAL saw many "new" old-time bands arise, beginning with the NEW LOST CITY RAMBLERS and HOLY MODAL ROUNDERS. Then, in the 1970s, young bluegrass and old-time revivalists began playing the instrument, learning mostly through recordings of earlier musicians and also traveling to their homes. One musician who became particularly prominent as both a Nashville session player and as a soloist was MARK O'CONNOR, who began his career as a teen bluegrass champion.

Alison Krauss has opened a new chapter in bluegrass fiddle history by playing the instrument as leader of her band, Union Station. Prior to her success, the instrument was rarely played by a woman as a bandleader (or even as a backup musician).

See also MINSTREL/TRAVELING SHOWS.

Fiddle Fever   See UNGAR, JAY.

Fink, Cathy (b. 1953) *banjoist, guitarist, and singer*

Born on August 9, 1953, in Baltimore, Maryland, vocalist and banjo and GUITAR player Fink first performed in the early 1970s in Toronto, working

Cathy Fink at the Philadelphia Folk Festival, early 1980s (Photo © Larry Sandberg)

with singer/songwriter Duck Donald. Fink became known for her banjo picking and her yodeling abilities, often leading audiences in a mass yodel. Fink and Donald recorded several albums before splitting up in 1981. At that time Fink began recording children's music, often employing Michigan-born musician Marcy Marxer (guitar, vocals) on her records. The two soon became officially a duo, and have since recorded and performed, primarily focusing on children's material, including their own original songs. Fink has also recorded for an adult audience, notably the 1985 album, *The Leading Role,* in which she celebrated women's contribution to country music. Fink also composed the song "Names" in honor of the AIDS Memorial Quilt, which has become an anthem in the fight against this disease. The duo also partnered with Laurie Lewis, Sally van Meter, and Molly Mason in the all-women's string band, Blue Rose.

See also BANJO, FIVE-STRING.

Fisher, Archie (b. 1939) *singer, songwriter, and television host/producer*

Born on October 23, 1939, in Glasgow, Scotland, Fisher has been a major figure in the Scottish FOLK REVIVAL since the mid-1950s. His family were all singers, and he and his sister Ray began performing in the then-popular skiffle style in the mid-1950s. They recorded a duo album in 1963, and then sister Cilla and her husband, along with the siblings' parents, formed the Fisher Family, releasing one album in 1965. In 1966 Ray moved to London and the band folded.

Archie's solo career was launched with an album in 1968. Soon after, he began composing folk-styled songs for BBC radio documentaries, becoming a leading producer for the radio network in the 1970s and 1980s. His U.S. career was given a boost in 1976, when the Folk Legacy label issued his album *The Man with a Rhyme,* featuring his best-known original folk ballad, "The Witch of the West-Mer Lands." He has toured with Tommy Makem and Liam Clancy in the 1970s and

Canadian singer-songwriter Garnet Rogers in the 1980s. In 1983 he began hosting the BBC series *The Traveling Folk,* celebrating Scottish music and culture, which continues to be broadcast. From 1988 to 1992, he directed the Edinburgh Folk Festival. Despite his long career, Fisher has only rarely recorded and toured.

Fleck, Béla (b. 1958) *bandleader and banjoist*

Born on July 10, 1958, in New York City, Fleck was a teenage banjo prodigy, beginning to perform shortly after first taking up the instrument at age 15. He played with local groups Tasty Licks and Spectrum before being enlisted in a later edition of New Grass Revival, a contemporary bluegrass band, joining in 1981 and remaining through the decade. During this period Fleck also recorded solo albums featuring his own jazz-influenced instrumentals. In 1989 Fleck formed his progressive instrumental

Béla Fleck in the late 1970s (Courtesy Rounder Records)

band, the Flecktones, which features a jazz-funk-pop style. The band has become a popular touring and recording act, and Fleck's banjo style has continued to embrace a wide range of influences. In 2001 Fleck issued his first album of banjo arrangements of classical compositions, *Perpetual Motion*. He has since continued to stretch boundaries with his band and also working with bassist/composer Edgar Meyer.

See also BANJO, FIVE-STRING.

Flores, Rosie (b. 1950) *singer*

Rosalie Durango Flores was born in San Antonio, Texas, on September 10, 1950. Her family moved to Southern California when she was 12 years old. Flores was influenced by a wide range of popular musical styles, and unlike many other women musicians, focused on developing her GUITAR-playing skills. Her first band was a local group called Penelope's Children; an all-female outfit, it played soft-rock and even opened for the Turtles on a West Coast tour. In 1978 she formed a punk-cowboy fusion band Rosie and the Screamers, a band that lasted about five years and played the California alternative music circuit. In 1983 she joined her first successful band, the Screaming Sirens, another all-girl outfit that mixed heavy guitar work with country and rockabilly riffs; in 1987 the band was featured in the TV film *The Running Kind*, gaining them some national notoriety.

Flores became a solo performer in 1987, signing with Warner Brothers Records. Dwight Yoakam's lead guitarist and close associate Pete Anderson served as the producer for her first album, which not surprisingly had the sound and feel of Yoakam's neo-rockabilly recordings. A second album was recorded, but Warners dropped Flores before it could be released (it eventually appeared in 1996 on Rounder). Flores spent the early 1990s recording for Hightone, and increasingly focusing on her guitar work. In 1995 she released an album, *Rockabilly Filly,* that featured duets with two of her rockabilly idols, Wanda Jackson and Janis Martin; a tour with

Jackson followed. Settling in the Austin, Texas, region, Flores released *Dance Hall Dreams* in 1999.

In 2000, besides her own solo touring, Flores teamed up with several other female new-country artists to form Henhouse, which played some gigs in Nashville. In fall 2000 Eminent Records announced they were signing the artist, pairing her with pop producer Rick Vito. The resulting album, *Speed of Sound,* appeared in April 2001.

flutes

Flutes and related wind instruments are heard in many different types of Anglo-American and African-American music. A simple whistle—made, for example, from a short length of dried cane—plays a single note. Cutting a number of canes into different lengths and lashing them together creates the ability to play different notes; this instrument is known as panpipes. African-American panpipe and drum bands have been recorded in Mississippi, a survival perhaps of both earlier African ensembles and Civil War–era groups of fife and drum squads.

A single cane can also be modified to play several notes by boring holes in it. A simple fife can be made in this manner; adding some type of mouthpiece creates a pennywhistle or (with further elaborations) a recorder. Pennywhistles are commonly used in Irish traditional dance music, in which a highly virtuosic style of playing has been developed.

Flutes feature a special kind of oval mouthpiece and are often played in a transverse (held horizontally to the ground) rather than straight up-and-down (vertical) manner (as are pennywhistles and recorders). The earliest flutes were made of wood and featured six holes; keys were added during the 18th century to facilitate playing in more octaves and adding additional scale notes. Eventually, the Boehm system style of flute evolved in the early 19th century, which enabled players to greatly expand the range of the instrument, and the modern flute was born.

Many folk traditions—notably the Irish flute tradition—continue to use earlier wooden, "open-holed" flutes. (The Boehm system features metal covers to the holes.) The open holes allow the player to play semitones by partially opening or closing the hole, whereas on the Boehm flute this is not possible because the keys are either open (and the note sounds) or shut. This is particularly important in Irish dance music, where there are many ornaments added to the basic melody notes, including slides from one note to another, trills, and other interpretative additions that are only possible on an open-hole instrument.

Although fifes and flutes were widely introduced to amateur musicians during the Civil War era in America, the folk tradition of using flutes is fairly limited. Most contemporary folk players draw on either the Irish or British traditions, playing the earlier wooden, open-holed flute, or use the modern, metal, Boehm-system instrument as an additional color in instrumental ensembles.

folk revival, the

For a brief period in the late 1950s and early 1960s, folk music was tremendously successful on the pop music charts. Granted, these hits were mostly produced by professional or at least semiprofessional musicians (not the "folks" themselves) and were often watered-down versions of the true folk styles. Nonetheless, the folk revival had a profound impact on the future direction of pop and country music styles.

There has always been a fascination in the city for the culture of the country, dating back at least to the time when cities first emerged out of the rural background. In the 19th century Romantic poets and philosophers idealized country life, and so influenced the first folklorists to go into the field to collect the traditional songs, dances, and legends of the ordinary "folk." At the turn of the last century, folklorists such as Francis James Child out of Harvard University and John Lomax working out of Texas published influential collections—Child of literary ballads and Lomax of the cowboy songs that he collected throughout the West. The recording

and radio industries that blossomed in the 1920s further spread folk music to the city; it was now possible for a resident of Manhattan to buy a recording of New Orleans jazz or Tennessee string band music. Traditional folk musicians such as WOODY GUTHRIE and AUNT MOLLY JACKSON were brought to major urban areas to perform, sometimes as curiosities and sometimes to support various political causes.

After World War II the first "folk boom" occurred when a group led by banjoist PETE SEEGER called the WEAVERS had a massive pop hit with a version of LEAD BELLY's "GOODNIGHT, IRENE." The Weavers's success was unexpected, but short-lived; because many of the group's members had been involved in radical political causes in the 1930s, the group was effectively silenced during the early 1950s Communist scare. By the late 1950s and early 1960s a new generation of more freshly scrubbed (and less politically adventurous) groups arose to pick up the Weavers' style, beginning with the KINGSTON TRIO (who had a big hit with the traditional banjo blues number "Tom Dooley"), the Rooftop Singers, the CHAD MITCHELL TRIO (who specialized in more politically oriented and satirical material), and, of course, PETER, PAUL, AND MARY. More sophisticated groups like the NEW LOST CITY RAMBLERS were able to ride the crest of the popularity of the mainstream groups, while never achieving quite the commercial success that these other groups enjoyed.

More important to the development of folk music in the long run was the emergence of the SINGER/SONGWRITER MOVEMENT. In pop and country music traditionally, professional songwriters wrote songs that were then recorded by trained singers. A songwriter who couldn't "sing" up to professional standards would never have dreamed of recording his or her own material. Nor was the material itself necessarily an expression of personal feelings; it often was written to meet the needs of a specific audience or market. However, in folk circles (and in early country music), the artists often wrote and performed their own material; musical ability or lack thereof (in terms of mainstream musical talent) was not a deterrent to performing.

Woody Guthrie pointed the way, showing how a singer could be the best interpreter of his own material, despite his rudimentary GUITAR style and nasal voice. BOB DYLAN during the FOLK-REVIVAL days expanded the notion of singer/songwriter, and thousands more arose in his wake: PHIL OCHS, TOM PAXTON, TOM RUSH, JONI MITCHELL, and many more.

By the mid-1960s the energy of the folk revival was pretty much absorbed by rock and roll. Interest in folk music reemerged in the mid-1970s; a more sophisticated revival occurred, with various regional music, from WESTERN SWING to CAJUN MUSIC to old-time string band to TEX-MEX MUSIC, coming to the fore.

See also LOMAX, JOHN AND ALAN.

folk-rock

The enormous success of the Beatles in early 1964 changed the American popular music scene, literally overnight. Folk musicians—particularly those who were working in KINGSTON TRIO/CHAD MITCHELL TRIO–type popular folk groups—were particularly impressed with the Beatles' clever songs and arrangements, sunny harmonies, and simple, but effective, presentation. The Beatles also established the instrumental lineup of GUITAR, bass, and drums; two out of three of these instruments (acoustic guitar and stand-up bass) were already used in folk groups.

The reaction was almost immediate; overnight, folk performers switched to electric instruments and formed Beatles-like groups. Jim McGuinn (later known as ROGER MCGUINN) and David Crosby formed a group they originally called the Beefeaters, in homage to the Beatles's British heritage; soon they switched its name to the BYRDS (whose spelling and animal name, of course, were further links to the Beatles). All five members of the original Byrds came out of the FOLK-REVIVAL movement. New York's Lovin' Spoonful was a kind of electrified folk jug band, led by HARMONICA/guitar player John Sebastian, who had long been active on the city's folk scene. Similarly, the Mamas and the Papas was led by John Phillips, a veteran folk guitarist and singer.

This new musical hybrid came to be known as "folk-rock." Much of the early folk-rock repertoire came from the popular folk songwriters of the day, including BOB DYLAN, TOM PAXTON, and JONI MITCHELL. The individual group members also wrote their own material, drawing on similar political and social topics as the earlier folk songs, but with a more Beatles-influenced beat and arrangement.

The folk-rock movement also had an influence on the British folk scene. Admiring the Americans' ability to present folk material with electric instrumentation and rock arrangements, many British folk musicians turned to this style. Most successful among these groups was FAIRPORT CONVENTION, which initially recorded much of the same singer-songwriter material as its American cousins, and, later, STEELEYE SPAN.

By the late 1960s–early 1970s most of the folk-rock bands had developed into either pure pop bands or full-fledged rock units. The singer/songwriters of the 1970s were the direct descendants of the style, although their songs were more focused on personal relationships and individual issues than political or social ones.

Fontenot, Canray   See ARDOIN FAMILY.

Foster, Stephen (1826–1864) *influential songwriter*

Stephen Collins Foster was born in Lawrenceville, Pennsylvania, a suburb of Pittsburgh, on July 4, 1826. His father was active as a local politician and businessman. Foster may have received some musical training as a youngster in Pittsburgh from a local German musician, but otherwise was self taught. He published his first composition in 1841, shortly before entering college, and his first song followed three years later. Around the mid-1840s he composed songs for amateur minstrel shows presented by a local fraternal organization, probably including his classic "Oh! Susanna."

In 1846 Foster relocated to Cincinnati to work as a bookkeeper in his brother's business. He continued to publish songs while passing manuscripts to key minstrel performers, hoping they'd promote them. One was George Washington Christie, who led the famous Christie Minstrels; Christie took "Oh! Susanna," and published it as his own composition in 1848; many more editions followed, pirated from Christie's publication, and not always credited to Foster. Nonetheless, its success earned Foster a lucrative publishing contract with a New York company, so he could return to his native Pennsylvania to work full time as a songwriter.

The early 1850s saw Foster's greatest period of creativity as a songwriter, producing such classic songs as "Camptown Races" (1850), "Old Folks at Home" (1851), and "My Old Kentucky Home" (1853). However, by later in the decade, Foster's popularity had waned, and he began to drink heavily; he moved to New York in 1860, hoping to revive his career, but lapsed into poverty. He died following a fall on January 13, 1864.

Foster's songs have become American standards, sung everywhere from the Appalachian Mountains to large concert halls. Their success can be attributed largely to his masterly recreation of folk dialects, melodies, and themes. In this sense he served as a model songwriter for future folk-influenced composers, including A. P. Carter, WOODY GUTHRIE, and BOB DYLAN.

See also MINSTREL/TRAVELING SHOWS.

Fraley, J. P. (b. c. 1920) and Annadeene
(1923–1996) *husband and wife fiddler and singer*
Born Jesse Presley Fraley in the early 1920s in rural Hitchins, Kentucky, Fraley learned to fiddle from his father, Richard, working local dances. He also learned from the legendary Kentucky fiddler ED HALEY, a blind musician who was much revered in the region. Like many other rural Kentuckians, Fraley began working in the mines as a teenager, but eventually graduated to selling coal mining equipment, an occupation that took him far beyond his Kentucky home. In 1946 he wed local singer Annadeene Prater, who had been performing on the radio since her early teens. The duo did not begin performing together until the mid-1960s, mostly at local fiddlers' conventions. By the early 1970s they attracted the attention of folklorist Mark Wilson, who recorded them for Rounder Records (*Wild Rose of the Mountains,* released in 1973 and reissued on CD in 1993). Fraley's relaxed fiddling style, playful vocals, and talents as a storyteller made him popular on the old-time revival circuit. The couple recorded one further album together, *Mayville,* in 1995. Annadeene died a year later on April 12, but Fraley has continued to perform, often with his daughter, Danielle. In 1998 Fraley was honored with the Appalachian Treasure Award from Morehead (Kentucky) State University. In 2000 he released an album of fiddle duets with younger fiddler Betty Vornbrock, who performs with the revival band the Reed Island Rounders. Fraley has hosted his "Mountain Music Gatherin'," a country music festival, in Olive Hill, Kentucky, since the mid-1960s.

"Freight Train" (c. 1905) *popular folk song*
Folk-blues guitarist ELIZABETH "LIBBA" COTTON claimed to have written this song when she was about 12 years old. Like many "composed" folk songs, it includes several "floating" verses that are found in many other traditional songs, although the combination of verses, the charming melody, and the clever chorus are unique to it. In the late 1940s Cotton was working for the Seeger family when she first played this song for Mike and Peggy Seeger; Peggy took the song with her to England in the late 1950s, and it became a hit there. Originally credited

as "traditional," Cotton eventually established copyright for the song.

See also SEEGER, MIKE; SEEGER, PEGGY.

Fruit Jar Drinkers

The early string band popular on the *Grand Ole Opry* included George Wilkerson, FIDDLE; Tommy Leffew, MANDOLIN; Howard Ragsdale, GUITAR; and Claude Lampley, banjo.

Although promoted as a group of backwoods hillbillies, the Fruit Jar Drinkers were made up of solidly working-class Nashville residents, all involved in the thriving lumber business by day, and music-making by night. The band's leader was George Wilkerson, a fiddler who originally hailed from northeast Georgia. His two brothers, Charlie and Brownie, were also musicians, and the youngsters soon formed their own homegrown band. The family moved to Nashville when Wilkerson was 16, and he was soon working in the local lumberyards. Along with his brother Charlie on mandolin, he began playing locally, and was on radio by early 1927.

At about this time Wilkerson met another performer who had been playing on occasion as a soloist over the air: mandolinist Tommy Leffew, who worked in a flooring factory. Leffew brought on board his fellow worker, Claude Lampley, who came from a small rural town in Hickman County, about 50 miles southwest of the city. Finally, guitarist Howard Ragsdale, also from Hickman County and another woodworker, joined up. Not only did the four men all share similar occupations, they also all lived in a four-block radius of one another, and held weekly rehearsals at their homes. The band was originally nameless, but sometime in early 1927 they hit on the Fruit Jar Drinkers as having the appropriately rural sound to it, and began playing on the popular radio program the *Grand Ole Opry*.

The history of the band is somewhat complicated because their name was either borrowed or stolen by the flamboyant banjo player Uncle Dave Macon. His label, Vocalion, noting the popularity of string bands, asked Macon to assemble one for his May 1927 recording session. He brought along his sometime accompanists, Sam and Kirk McGee, along with fiddler Mazy Todd, to these sessions. These records were issued as by "Uncle Dave Macon and His Fruit Jar Drinkers."

Despite their popularity on the *Opry*, where they were often featured as the closing act, the original Fruit Jar Drinkers never recorded. Even at the 1928 Victor Nashville sessions—where several of their friends and competitors, such as the CROOK BROTHERS and the Gully Jumpers, were recorded—they were mysteriously overlooked. The Fruit Jar Drinkers continued to play on the *Opry* for decades. By the mid-1930s the band had "modernized" only to the extent that they added a bass player. By this point Wilkerson had earned the nickname "Grandpappy" from Hay, because of his constant on-air bragging about his first grandchild. Wilkerson retired from performing in 1953, shortly before his death, but the band soldiered on with various members until the mid-1970s.

See also BANJO, FIVE-STRING; MCGEE, SAM.

Frumholz, Steve (b. 1945) *singer and songwriter*

Born in Temple, Texas, Frumholz attended Texas State University in 1963, where he met future country star Michael Martin Murphey, and the twosome became a duo, later forming the Dallas Country Jug Band. After college and a brief stint in the navy, Frumholz formed a close relationship with singer/songwriter Dan McCrimmon, and the two took the colorful name of Frummox, recording a country-rock album in 1969; two years later, they briefly worked with Steve Stills as his backup band.

After struggling for a few years on the West Coast, in 1974 Frumholz returned to Austin, where a vibrant outlaw music scene was brewing. He was befriended by Willie Nelson and appeared on Nelson's *Sound in Your Mind* album as a backup singer, as well as providing original material for Nelson to record. In 1976, Frumholz finally made an album that was released, aptly called *A Rumor in My Own Time,* featuring many friends including Nelson, banjoist Doug Dillard, steel guitarist Red Rhodes, and folksinger John Sebastian. Although a cult success, the album was not a commercial one, and after a second equally unsuccessful release, he was dropped by his label.

In 1979 Nelson had his own label, Lone Star, distributed by Columbia, and invited old friend Frumholz to make an album, titled *Jus' Playin' Along.* This also failed to generate much in the way of sales, and Frumholz has since been one of many "local heroes" who play regularly in the greater Austin area.

Gaughan, Dick (b. 1948) *singer*

Born on May 17, 1948, in Leith (part of Edinburgh), Scotland, Gaughan's father was an Irish-born FIDDLE player and his mother a native Scot who sang songs and ballads in both Gaelic and English. Gaughan began performing in local folk clubs in his early 20s, and soon partnered with Shetland-born fiddler Aly Bain. Playing a folk festival in 1973, the duo met Cathal McConnell and Robin Morton; on the spur of the moment they played a set together, and the band the BOYS OF THE LOUGH was born. Gaughan only remained with the group for their debut album; at the same time his classic solo album, *No More Forever*, was released (with fiddler Bain on many tracks). Gaughan has gone on to record many albums, increasingly performing modern singer-songwriter material along with the traditional ballads and songs that made him famous. He was also a member of the Scottish folk-rock band Five Hand Reel in the mid-1970s.

Gavin, Frankie See DE DANAAN.

Georgia Yellow Hammers

A popular Georgia string band of the 1920s—second in popularity only to Gid Tanner and His Skillet Lickers—the Georgia Yellow Hammers are best remembered for their tight harmony singing on gospel and original composed songs. The nucleus of the group came from northern Georgia's Calhoun county, where they were all active as musicians,

songwriters, and had played in various combinations in local bands. FIDDLE and banjo player "Uncle Bud" Landress and fiddler Bill Chitwood had played together on occasion locally, often in a trio with banjoist Fate Norris (later of the Skillet Lickers). In 1924 the duo traveled to New York and recorded for the Brunswick label. Sometime after, they met local music promoter and guitar player Phil Reeve, who put together the first Georgia Yellowhammers group and arranged for them to record in February 1927. Reeve invited local singer/songwriter C. E. Moody to be the group's fourth member; Moody is remembered for his gospel songs that have become bluegrass and country favorites, such as "Kneel at the Cross" and "Drifting Too Far from the Shore." He became the group's final member.

From the start the group emphasized quartet singing over rousing fiddle tunes, although throughout their career they recorded everything from comic songs and skits to sacred-harp numbers. Their biggest seller was Landress's composition "The Picture on the Wall," a Victorian-styled tearjerker about mother and home that is said to have sold more than 100,000 copies on 78 rpm records. Between 1927 and 1930 the group recorded for a variety of labels under a number of names, sometimes recording the same songs for each new pseudonym. It is unclear whether all four musicians attended every session, and other musicians may have been enlisted from time to time. The Depression put an end to most early country recording, and the various Yellow Hammer combinations could no longer find an outlet for their music. Of all the players, Landress remained a professional longest, working locally through the 1940s.

See also BANJO, FIVE-STRING.

Gerrard, Alice (b. unknown) *publisher and singer*

Gerrard was born to a middle-class family and was not exposed to folk music until she enrolled at Antioch College in the early 1960s. Moving to Washington, D.C. after graduation, she became involved in the local bluegrass scene, and soon partnered with singer/songwriter HAZEL DICKENS. The duo recorded their debut album, *Who's That Knocking?*, which was released by Verve/Folkways in 1965, with accompaniment by local bluegrass musicians, including mandolinist DAVID GRISMAN and banjo player Lamar Grier. A second album was recorded soon after, but remained unreleased until 1973. Also in 1973, they partnered with Grier, MIKE SEEGER, and Tracey Schwartz in the short-lived bluegrass band, the Strange Creek Singers, recording one album for the Arhoolie label.

The duo became best known after they released the more country-oriented album *Hazel and Alice* on Rounder Records in 1975. It featured Dickens's best-known song, "Don't Put Her Down (You Helped Put Her There)." Gerrard also began performing with her then-husband Mike Seeger, and the duo released two albums besides making many tours together through the late 1980s. In 1983 she coproduced the film *Sprout Wings and Fly* about the legendary fiddler TOMMY JARRELL. In 1987 Gerrard began publishing *The Old Time Herald*, which has become the best-known magazine chronicling the old-time music revival. In 1995 her first solo album, *Pieces of My Heart*, was released.

See also BANJO, FIVE-STRING.

Gibson, Bob (1931–1996) *banjoist, guitarist, and singer*

Robert Gibson was born in New York City on November 16, 1931. First working as a traveling salesman in the early 1950s, he became interested in folk music after attending a PETE SEEGER concert, and took up the banjo and twelve-string GUITAR. He developed a unique style of playing the twelve-string that was less percussive and bluesy than earlier folk performers such as LEAD BELLY; this would influence others, such as GORDON LIGHTFOOT and HARRY CHAPIN, to take up the instrument. In 1956 promoter ALBERT GROSSMAN invited Gibson and FRANK HAMILTON to be house singers at his new Gate of Horn folk club in Chicago. In 1956 he began his recording career along with the first folk artists on the Riverside label, better known for its jazz offerings.

Gibson met another folk singer in Chicago, Bob Camp (later HAMILTON CAMP), and the two became a popular duo through the early 1960s; their *At the Gate of Horn* live album from 1961 was a best seller. At that point Grossman tried to convince Gibson and Camp that they could be even more successful if they hired a young female singer to make their group into a trio; Gibson turned him down, and Grossman eventually took his idea to Peter Yarrow, resulting in the successful group PETER, PAUL, AND MARY.

Gibson is also credited with helping to launch the careers of younger singers. He presented JOAN BAEZ at her first NEWPORT FOLK FESTIVAL appearance in 1959, and encouraged PHIL OCHS in his early songwriting attempts. Gibson's initial recording career ended after 1964, but he returned to recording in the mid-1970s, although by then his style was fairly dated. In 1994 he wrote a musical play based on the life of CARL SANDBURG that was produced in Chicago. He continued to perform and record until his death on September 28, 1996.

See also BANJO, FIVE-STRING.

Gilmore, Jimmie Dale (b. 1945) *bandleader, singer, and songwriter*

Born in Amarillo, Texas, on May 6, 1945, Gilmore formed his first band while living in Lubbock, Texas, in the late 1960s. The group, the Flatlanders, has achieved near-mythic status, thanks to its line-up including Joe Ely and Butch Hancock, two other Texas singer-songwriters. They recorded one album in 1971 that saw only limited release for 19 years, finally appearing on Rounder Records. Gilmore spent the mid-1970s on the move, first relocating to Austin, center of Texas's hippie-country music community, and then giving up music altogether to pursue a degree in oriental philosophy at the University of Colorado.

Gilmore returned to Austin in 1980 and recorded two albums for the small Hightone label in the mid-1980s. He even managed a number 72 country hit with one of his best-known songs, "White Freight Liner Blues." He signed with Elektra Records in 1991, but by the end of the decade he was releasing his own recordings on his Windcharger imprint. He continues to record and perform.

Gimble, Johnny (b. 1926) *bandleader and fiddle player*

John Paul Gimble was born near Tyler, Texas, on May 30, 1926. He displayed an early facility for music, playing banjo and MANDOLIN. He joined his brothers' group, the Rose City Hipsters, in his early teen years; the band played locally for dances and parties, as well as broadcasting over Tyler's radio station. When he was 17, he was hired to play with the Shelton Brothers, leading to work with Jimmie Davis.

After World War II Western Swing master Bob Wills hired Gimble, originally to play mandolin, although soon his talents as a fiddler showed through. He remained with Wills through the 1950s, and his jazz-influenced fiddling, with its rich tone, became a hallmark of Wills's later recordings. In the 1960s and early 1970s Gimble worked as a Nashville studio musician; he rejoined Wills in 1973 for the Texas Playboys reunion LP that was inspired by Merle Haggard's love for Western Swing; he then performed throughout the 1970s with several alumni of Wills's band, recording several albums.

From 1979 to 1981 Gimble worked with Willie Nelson's touring band. He achieved his greatest chart success accompanying Ray Price on the single "One Fiddle, Two Fiddle" drawn from Clint Eastwood's 1983 film, *Honkytonk Man*. He has since recorded as a solo artist, leading his own band Texas Swing, and also working with various Texas Playboys reunion bands. He has also played sessions with new country stars such as George Strait and older traditionalists such as Haggard. In 1993 his work on Mark O'Connor's *Heroes* album garnered him a Grammy nomination, and a year later he won the award for his arrangement of "Redwing" that was featured on Asleep at the Wheel's *A Tribute to Bob Wills and the Texas Playboys* album. Over the last decade he has hosted "Swing Week" in his native Texas as a learning/workshop for young fiddlers, as well as producing instructional videos.

See also BANJO, FIVE-STRING.

Glazer, Tom (1914–2003) *guitarist and singer*

Thomas Glazer was born in Philadelphia, Pennsylvania, on September 3, 1914. His father, a carpenter, died when Tom was four years old, and Glazer was raised by his mother and relatives. The family moved to New York when he was 17. Glazer attended college for three years, and then moved to Washington, where he got a job at the Library of Congress. There, he met folklorist ALAN LOMAX, who introduced him to political songs and folk songs. Glazer began performing as a singer/guitarist, and became very popular, even making an appearance at a private White House function hosted by Eleanor Roosevelt. He specialized in topical songs focusing on the working man. He made his debut at New York's Town Hall in 1943, and from 1945 to 1947 hosted a national radio program, *Tom Glazer's Ballad Box*. He also began a popular radio program for children. He became known as a talented songwriter, specializing in social causes and children's material.

However, Glazer's mainstream career was cut short in the early 1950s when his name appeared in the notorious conservative publication *Red Channels*. He was labeled as a Communist sympathizer, a charge Glazer vehemently denied. Like many of his contemporaries, he had been active in pro-labor and liberal causes. By 1952 Glazer had lost most of his work as a radio performer, although he never was officially blacklisted. Five years later, Elia Kazan—also a liberal implicated in Communist causes, but who had named names before the House Un-American Activities Committee—hired Glazer to provide songs for his film *A Face in the Crowd*.

Glazer continued to work as a songwriter, and his songs were covered by mainstream singers such as Frank Sinatra ("Melody of Love") and Perry Como ("More"). His greatest hit came in 1963 with his satire of the traditional folk song "On Top of Old Smokey" in a reworked children's version as "On Top of Spaghetti," which became a summer camp favorite. He returned to recording labor and children's songs in the mid-1970s for small labels. Glazer died on February 21, 2003, in Philadelphia.

See also LOMAX, JOHN AND ALAN.

Goins Brothers

Guitarist Melvin (b. Melvin Glen Goins, December 30, 1933) and banjo player Ray (b. Raymond Elwood Goins, January 3, 1936) were born in rural Bramwell, West Virginia. When they were teenagers, they heard groups such as the STANLEY BROTHERS and BILL MONROE broadcasting over local radio and became immediate converts to bluegrass. Melvin joined a local band, the Lonesome Pine Fiddlers, around 1949, and his brother Ray followed in 1951. They recorded with the group in 1952 for RCA and then formed the first Goins Brothers band in late 1953 after the rest of the Fiddlers packed up to move to Detroit. Neither the Fiddlers nor the Goins were successful during their year apart, so when the Fiddlers returned to West Virginia, the Goins were back in the lineup. They worked with the band sporadically through the 1950s and early 1960s, recording with them and appearing on local radio.

In the mid-1960s Ray temporarily retired from music making, and Melvin worked with a number of bands, including his idols, the Stanley Brothers. Besides playing bass with the Stanleys, Melvin also performed classic country-rube comedy onstage, going by the name of "Big Wilbur." The Goins were reunited in the late 1960s and have since performed with a variety of backup musicians. Some of their best recordings were made in the 1970s for Jessup and Rebel Records. They have also hosted their own radio show since 1974, broadcasting out of Hazard/Lexington, Kentucky. Associated groups include the Woodettes, a female gospel quartet featuring Melvin's wife, Willia, and her sisters; and the Stedhouse Trio, a group-within-the-group led by Melvin to perform pure country material.

See also BANJO, FIVE-STRING; GUITAR.

Goldstein, Kenneth S. (1927–1995) *folklorist and producer*

Born in New York City, Goldstein became interested in folk music as a college student. After serving in World War II, he worked for a while as a journalist but also began freelance work as a folk producer, first for the small Stinson label, and then through the 1950s, for almost all the folk labels. Eventually, he would oversee the production of more than 500 albums, helping to introduce artists such as EWAN MACCOLL, A. L. LLOYD, and RICHARD DYER-BENNETT, to name just a few. From 1959 to 1960 he recorded traditional music in Great Britain on a Fulbright Scholarship.

Goldstein was also a pioneer in folklore studies. He founded Folklore Associates to reprint classic works on folk music and traditions. In 1958 he entered the University of Pennsylvania and became one of the first students there to earn a Ph.D. in folklore. He eventually became chair of Penn's Folklore Department, building it into one of the leading centers in the world. He died of cancer on November 11, 1995.

Goodman, Steve (1948–1984) *mandolinist and songwriter*

Born on July 25, 1948, in Chicago, Illinois, Goodman was raised in a middle-class Jewish home. Influenced by the singer-songwriters of the FOLK REVIVAL, Goodman began writing his own songs as a teen and in college, returning home after graduation to perform at local clubs. Performing as an opening act for country songwriter Kris Kristofferson, he was spotted by pop singer/songwriter Paul Anka, who recommended the young performer to Buddah Records. His first album featured his song "The City of New Orleans," covered in 1973 by ARLO GUTHRIE for a major pop hit, and "You Never Even Called Me by My Name," a major country hit two years later for David Allan Coe. This album led him to be called the next BOB DYLAN by many critics, such as his friend and fellow Chicagoan JOHN PRINE.

In 1975 Goodman moved to the Asylum label and continued to record for the label through 1980, achieving only limited success. During this period he helped revitalize the career of famed country mandolinist Jethro Burns, who had been living in semiretirement in Chicago. Burns toured and recorded with Goodman, leading to his first solo albums and later-day fame as a country-jazz mandolinist. In 1983 Goodman formed his own Red Pajamas label, but was already suffering from advanced leukemia, which would take his life on September 20, 1984. His posthumous reputation has grown through releases of live and previously unreleased studio material.

See also MANDOLIN.

"Goodnight, Irene" (c. 1930s) *song popularized by Lead Belly*

This waltz song was popularized by LEAD BELLY after he arrived in New York City in the mid-1930s. The singer/guitarist claimed to be the song's "composer," although—like many folk songs—it consists of several well-known "floating" verses (so-called because they "float" from song to song). (An earlier song written by black popular songwriter James Bland has a similar title, but is not related in melody or words.) The song became a major hit six months after Lead Belly's death when it was recorded by the folk-revival group the WEAVERS. It has since remained a favorite of folk performers.

Good Ol' Persons

The Good Ol' Persons were a mid-1980s San Francisco Bay–area based bluegrass/country band with a strong feminist twist, thanks to the strong lead vocals and original songs of guitarist Kathy Kallick and fiddler LAURIE LEWIS. The name is a play on "good ol' boys," here expanded in politically correct terms to include women. The cofounders—Kallick and Lewis—were what made this band special; they performed a combination of classic country material by the Carter Family and the Delmore Brothers among others, laced with their contemporary recastings of traditional country themes in their original songs. The band was also unusual in that it featured so many talented females as instrumentalists, including Lewis's fine fiddling (she was later replaced by Paul Shelasky and Kevin Wimmer, in succession) and Sally Van Meter's new-acoustic influenced DOBRO playing. Even after the band folded in the late 1980s, Kallick and Lewis remained closely aligned, recording a duo album in the early 1990s. They have since recorded as solo artists.

See also FIDDLE; GUITAR.

Graham, Davey (b. 1940) *guitarist*

Born on November 22, 1940, in Leicester, England, Graham became the most influential folk guitarist on the London scene in the late 1950s–early 1960s. Graham first played at the trendy Yellow Door Club in 1958, relocated to Paris in the early 1960s, and then moved to Tangiers, always absorbing a wide range of music. Returning to London, he became active in the nascent blues scene, working clubs frequented by Alexis Koerner—the founder of the British blues revival—and younger players such as JOHN RENBOURN and BERT JANSCH. While living in

London in 1964, American folkie Paul Simon learned Graham's fingerpicked instrumental "Angi," which Graham recorded in 1962, and Simon featured it on the Simon and Garfunkel album *Sounds of Silence.* Soon every acoustic guitarist was trying to learn it.

Graham was influenced by Indian raga, traditional British folk, and contemporary jazz. He developed many unique tunings to suit his modal-flavored instrumentals, many of which have become standards among acoustic guitarists. Graham recorded prolifically for the British pop label Decca in the 1960s, including a classic album accompanying singer SHIRLEY COLLINS. He then disappeared for a while but was lured out of retirement in the late 1980s by guitarist STEFAN GROSSMAN. Graham has recorded sporadically since, but it's no exaggeration to say that an entire generation of folk guitarists would not have developed without his influence.

Grant, Bill (b. 1930) and Delia Bell (b. 1930)
husband and wife performing duo
Billy Joe Grant was born and raised on a ranch near Hugo, Oklahoma, on May 9, 1930, and took up MANDOLIN playing in emulation of Bill Monroe. In the late 1950s, Grant befriended Bobby Bell, who introduced him to Delia Nowell (b. Bonham, Texas, April 16, 1930), who was playing GUITAR and singing at home. Bill and Delia began playing together and soon established a local following, thanks to appearances on radio and TV throughout the Oklahoma region. They later married.

While traveling through the area, Bill Monroe heard them perform and invited them to appear at his annual bluegrass festival held at Bean Blossom, Indiana, in 1969. This appearance helped broaden their popularity among bluegrass fans, and they decided to take to music making full time. They formed a backup band, the Kiamichi Mountain Boys, and Grant formed a record label to issue their material, also with the colorful Kiamichi name. Grant also established a major bluegrass festival in

his hometown of Hugo, which has become one of the biggest festivals west of the Mississippi.

In the late 1970s it looked like Delia Bell might establish a solo career. In 1978 she cut an album for County Records, featuring Grant in a supporting role. On it she recorded Grant's song "Roses in the Snow," which Emmylou Harris later covered as the title track for her influential 1980 bluegrass album. Through Harris Bell was signed to Warner Brothers, but her resulting 1983 solo album for the label was not a success. From this album Bell scored a minor country hit in a duet with John Anderson on "Flame in My Heart."

Meanwhile, the Grant-Bell duo continued to perform and record for various bluegrass labels, notably Rounder and Old Homestead. Grant has written a number of songs that have achieved popularity among bluegrass musicians, including "Rollin'," "Cheer of the Home Fires," and "Stairway to Heaven" (not to be confused with the Led Zeppelin song of the same name). A strong vocal duo who perform a mix of bluegrass standards and more contemporary country, Grant and Bell look back toward traditional country but also reflect modern trends. Since the mid-1990s the duo have hosted the Oklahoma Bluegrass Festival.

Graves, Buck/Uncle Josh (b. 1928) *Dobro*
player and comedian
Burckett K. Graves was born in Tellico Plains, Tennessee, on September 27, 1928. He was nine years old when he heard country musician Cliff Carlisle of the Carlisle Brothers playing an exotic instrument, the DOBRO. Carlisle's command of the instrument and his bluesy playing were immediately attractive to him, and he soon befriended the elder musician. However, Graves's first professional work was as a bass player, working with various country bands. By the early 1950s he had joined with the country/bluegrass duo, WILMA LEE AND STONEY COOPER, playing both bass and Dobro.

In 1957 the Coopers were invited to play on the *Grand Ole Opry.* Graves was quickly spotted by Flatt and Scruggs, and invited to join the band—as a bass player. However, within a month he was playing dobro with them. Emulating Scruggs's three-finger bluegrass banjo style on the dobro, Graves soon was playing lightning-fast solos that fit perfectly into the bluegrass instrumental style, while also offering bluesy accompaniments to Flatt's repertoire of songs. In addition to his instrumental skills, Graves played the comic foil to bass player Jake Tullock ("Cousin Jake") as the country-rube character "Uncle Josh."

In 1969, when Flatt and Scruggs disbanded, Graves initially stayed with the more traditional band led by Flatt. However, in 1971 he rejoined with Scruggs in the country-rock band the Earl Scruggs Revue, recording with them through 1974. At the same time, he played widely as a session musician on bluegrass and country recordings, including some of the best early records by Kris Kristofferson.

In 1974 Graves embarked on a solo career, while continuing to pursue both bluegrass and country session work. Through the 1970s and 1980s he recorded a number of solo albums in both bluegrass and jazz-oriented styles, with various musicians including guitarist Joe Maphis and fiddler Vassar Clements. Graves established himself as a regular presence in Nashville studios, on radio, and on TV. He continued to work throughout the 1990s, often in partnership with fiddler KENNY BAKER. However, Graves's health began to decline in the early 2000s; in 2001 and early 2002 he had two operations to amputate his legs. A benefit concert was held to help pay his medical bills in autumn 2001.

Greenbriar Boys, The

An influential group in the 1960s, the Greenbriar Boys were one of the first northern-based groups to establish themselves on the bluegrass circuit. The original group formed out of jam sessions held in Washington Square Park in New York City; the first lineup included Eric Weissberg on banjo and GUITAR, Bob Yellin on banjo, and singer/guitarist John Herald; Weissberg was soon replaced by MANDOLIN player RALPH RINZLER. They won first place at the prestigious Southern Fiddlers Convention held in Union Grove in 1960, and were soon touring. They often appeared with folksinger JOAN BAEZ, furthering their profile in the folk revival community, and recorded one album backing country vocalist Dian [James] in 1963. The group signed with Vanguard Records in 1962, although Rinzler retired by 1964 to focus on managing traditional performers such as Bill Monroe. Rinzler was replaced by mandolinist Frank Wakefield, who brought a jazz-influenced sound to the group. The group performed together until 1967, when Herald embarked on a solo career.

See also BANJO, FIVE-STRING; MANDOLIN.

Greene, Richard (b. 1942) *fiddle player*

Born in Beverly Hills, California, on November 9, 1942, Greene was raised in a musical family. He was a classically trained violinist who was named concertmaster of the Beverly Hills orchestra while still in high school. When he enrolled at the University of California at Berkeley, he was introduced to folk music and soon turned his attention to bluegrass, thanks to the influence of local fiddler Scotty Stoneman, son of legendary country star ERNEST STONEMAN.

Greene was hired by bluegrass legend Bill Monroe in the mid-1960s to play in his band, where he met another young musician who had his sights on a new, more progressive style of bluegrass, PETER ROWAN. Greene left Monroe to tour briefly with Jim Kweskin's Jug Band, which featured another Monroe alumnus, BILL KEITH, and then returned to California to form the rock band, Seatrain, with Andy Kulberg, formerly of the Blues Project; Rowan later joined the band as a vocalist/songwriter/guitarist.

In 1972, discouraged with the world of rock, Greene left Seatrain to work as a session musician in Southern California. He performed with Rowan, DAVID GRISMAN, Keith, and Clarence White in the group Muleskinner, one of the first progressive bluegrass "bands" (they actually performed together only once, for a TV special, and recorded one album, but never really stayed together as a band). A year later, he formed with Grisman the short-lived Great American Music Band, which featured blues guitarist TAJ MAHAL, performing a mixture of different music, and later in the 1970s he performed in the first incarnation of Grisman's Quintet.

Greene recorded sporadically through the 1980s as the leader of various loosely formed groups, including his own Greene String Quartet, which performed everything from classical material to jazz and pop. His combination of bluegrass, rock, and jazz elements into his playing style was quite influential on younger progressive bluegrass fiddlers in the 1970s and 1980s, and he continues to enjoy a loyal, if small, following. During the late 1980s and early 1990s he primarily worked with the Greene String Quartet, playing a mix of bluegrass, jazz, and classical-flavored originals. In the later 1990s he returned to playing bluegrass music, recording for the Rebel label.

See also FIDDLE.

Greenhill, Manny (1916–1996) *manager and promoter*

Manuel A. Greenhill was born in New York City on March 10, 1916. During the 1930s he worked as a union activist, and later befriended folk musicians such as PETE SEEGER. After serving in World War II, Greenhill worked as a newspaper advertisement salesman through the 1950s, settling in Boston. He became aware of the growing local folk scene there, helping to organize the Folksong Society, and in 1958 established Folklore Productions to produce concerts, beginning with folk-blues singer JOSH WHITE. A young singer/guitarist on the Boston scene named JOAN BAEZ caught his eye, and she became his first management client. Along with Baez, Greenhill remained politically active, participating in the antiwar and CIVIL RIGHTS movements. He also managed other acts, including DOC WATSON and REVEREND GARY DAVIS. In the mid-1970s he relocated his business to California, and began managing TAJ MAHAL. His son Mitchell became the prime mover in the business by the 1980s. Greenhill died after a long bout fighting cancer on April 14, 1996.

Griffith, Nanci (b. 1954) *singer and songwriter*

Griffith was born on July 16, 1954, in Seguin, Texas, a small town northeast of San Antonio. Educated as a schoolteacher, she was still teaching when she began issuing her music locally on her own label, beginning with *There's a Light Beyond These Woods* in 1978 (she called her label B.F. Deal). The folk label Philo Records picked up her recordings in the early to mid-1980s, where her haunting vocals and combination of original material and covers of other singer/songwriters made her a popular figure on the folk scene of the day. She was signed to MCA's country division in 1987, recording the LP *Lone Star State of Mind*, including her cover of "From a Distance," the Julie Gold ballad that was to be a hit for Bette Midler a few years later.

After a few commercially disappointing LPs aimed at the country market, MCA attempted to market her to a pop audience, moving her to the Los Angeles division of the label. At about this time, ironically, new country stars Kathy Mattea and Suzy Bogguss had hits covering Griffith's songs, Mattea with "Love at the Five and Dime" and Bogguss with "Outbound Plane." In 1993 Griffith abandoned the pop sheen of her previous two releases to record an entire collection of covers of folk-rock standards, as an homage to the singer/songwriters who influenced her most; the success of this collection inspired a second outing in 1997. Her production of new material slowed in the later 1990s, and she failed to find success among either country or more pop audiences. Some of her choices seemed odd, also, such as 1999's *Dust Bowl Symphony,* an attempt to wed her intimate songs with lush string accompaniments.

Grisman, David (b. 1945) *mandolin player*
David Grisman was born in Hackensack, New
Jersey, on March 17, 1945, and began his career as
a teenager performing in the New York area both
with traditional bluegrass musicians (Red Allen
and Don Stover) along with younger innovators
(BILL KEITH). He formed the New York Ramblers
in 1965 with banjoist Winnie Winston and Del and
Jerry McCoury on guitar/vocals and bass, respectively. Although the band did not issue an album
during its short period of existence, they achieved
a near-legendary status on both the FOLK-REVIVAL
and bluegrass circuits. During this period he
also played as an accompanist on sessions for
HAZEL DICKENS and ALICE GERRARD. Grisman
relocated to California in the late 1960s, joining
with eccentric guitarist/vocalist/songwriter PETER
ROWAN to form the folk-rock band Earth Opera,
and then moved on to the Great American Music
Band. In 1973 he was a member of Muleskinner, a
special band put together for a single album to
perform traditional and progressive bluegrass
featuring Rowan, guitarist Clarence White, fiddler
RICHARD GREENE, and banjoist Bill Keith. He also
did session work for many popular mid-1970s
singer/songwriters.

Grisman was invited to record a traditional
bluegrass album for Rounder Records in the mid-
1970s as a return to his roots performing this
music. At about the same time, in 1976, he formed
his first quintet to perform his jazz-influenced
compositions. The group's first album on the
California-based Kaleidoscope label almost single-
handedly launched what is now called "new
acoustic music." Grisman soon moved to A&M and
then Warner Brothers Records. He also recorded
with his idol, Stephane Grappelli, and his more
recent recordings show an even stronger jazz and
blues influence than previous work. At the same
time he continued to perform in traditional bluegrass settings, usually for one-time recording projects, and also formed an acoustic duo with head
Grateful Dead front man, Jerry Garcia, until his
death in 1995. Grisman founded the Acoustic Disc

label to issue his own and other acoustic-oriented
recordings in the early 1990s.

See also BANJO, FIVE-STRING; FIDDLE; GUITAR.

Grossman, Albert (1926–1986) *manager and
promoter*
Albert B. Grossman was born in Chicago, Illinois,
on May 21, 1926. He attended Roosevelt University
there, and began working for the Chicago Housing
Authority after graduation in 1947. With college
friend Les Brown, Grossman opened a new club, the
Gate of Horn, in 1956. Grossman was a savvy businessman and recognized the growing interest in
folk music; he hired BOB GIBSON and FRANK
HAMILTON to be house performers at the club, and
began to move into managing acts as well as booking them for the club. Grossman bought out Brown
by the end of the 1950s, and, using the club as a
power base, grew into a major folk promoter, managing ODETTA and the successful duo of Bob Gibson
and Bob Camp (later HAMILTON CAMP). Grossman
partnered with jazz promoter George Wein to
cofound and produce the first NEWPORT FOLK
FESTIVAL in 1959, which became a major launching
pad for folk performers.

In 1962 Wein and Grossman formed Production
and Management Associates in New York to manage folk acts. Grossman had envisioned a folk trio
consisting of two men and a female singer, and had
tried to convince various of his clients—including
Bob Gibson and CAROLYN HESTER—to form such a
group, to no avail. In 1962 he met singer Peter
Yarrow on the Greenwich Village scene and introduced him to Mary Travers, who in turn suggested
Noel "Paul" Stookey as a third member. Thus,
PETER, PAUL AND MARY was born, who became
major moneymakers for Grossman and also a
means to promote the songwriting skills of another
act he managed, BOB DYLAN.

Grossman gained fame as Dylan's manager, and
his mercurial temperament and unorthodox business dealings fed the rock rumor mill for decades.
Through Dylan he became the manager of the

Band, and also eventually represented Janis Joplin and the Paul Butterfield Blues Band. In the mid-1960s Grossman settled outside of Woodstock, New York, introducing Dylan to the area, and also opening a small home recording studio, which became the basis of his own label, Bearsville. Grossman continued to run the studio until his death in London on January 25, 1986.

Grossman, Stefan (b. 1945) *guitarist and teacher*

Born in New York City on April 16, 1945, Stefan Grossman was one of the most influential guitarists and teachers in the folk-blues revival. He was a mainstay on the Greenwich Village folk scene of the early 1960s, performing with various groups, including the short-lived Even Dozen Jug Band and early versions of the Fugs. An avid fan of the blues, he befriended Queens, New York–based guitarist REV. GARY DAVIS, and did much to promote his GUITAR style through instruction books and recordings. In 1967 Grossman relocated to England, where he signed with Transatlantic Records, a leading British FOLK-ROCK label. In the early 1970s he moved to Rome, Italy. In 1972 he formed Kicking Mule Records with producer Ed Denson to release recordings of both contemporary acoustic guitar players and performances by older blues musicians, notably Gary Davis. In the late 1970s he toured and recorded with British guitarist JOHN RENBOURN. He returned to the United States in the early 1980s, founding the Guitar Artistry label in partnership with Shanachie Records, and in the 1990s establishing Vestapol Videos to release classic performances by blues performers. Grossman continues to record, but rarely performs live.

guitar

The American guitar is a different instrument from its Spanish forebears. Its history has been shaped by a combination of technological advances along with new musical styles.

The common Spanish or "classical" guitar features a wide fingerboard, gut strings, a slotted peghead, and, most important, a fan-shaped bracing system under the instrument's wooden top, giving it a sweet sound; it dates back to the early years of the 19th century. However, the American guitar has its roots in a group of talented Viennese instrument builders who developed a new way of building guitars. Most notably, a German immigrant named Christian Friedrich Martin began making instruments in 1833 in New York City, moving six years later to Nazareth, Pennsylvania, where the company is still located.

Martin either developed or perfected a new form of bracing called an X-brace. This allowed for greater volume and eventually the introduction of steel strings (fan bracing will not support the increased tension that steel strings create on the face of a guitar). He also redesigned the guitar's body shape, exaggerating the lower bout (or half) of the instrument's body so that it was no longer symmetrical in appearance. By the late 1800s the Martin style had been copied by mass producers, and guitars were made by the hundreds that were available inexpensively through mail-order catalogs.

The guitar had found its way into the backwoods of American society as early as the 1860s, although banjos and fiddles still dominated the landscape. However, new trends in popular and folk songs toward melodies oriented around standard chord progressions favored the guitar—an instrument ideal for playing chords—rather than the fiddle (limited primarily to melody) and the banjo (not primarily oriented to playing chords, but rather combining melody with a percussive accompaniment). Many older songs that used to feature unusual scale notes, wandering melodies, and irregular forms were molded into a new style that featured regular, repeated verses, and simpler melodies suited to chord harmony accompaniment.

The second great innovation in the popularizing of the guitar occurred from the 1920s through the 1940s. As a band instrument, the guitar was hampered by its relative lack of carrying power, its ability to cut through other instruments. Steel strings

Carl Fischer Guitars

GUITAR No. G-550 $9.50

GUITAR No. G-560 $9.50

GUITAR No. G-570 $9.50

An Assortment of the Six Guitars Shown on this Page Sent Prepaid $50.00

No. G-550. Palm Tree Guitar shaded dark mahogany, ornamented with tropical design in colors. Decorated sound hole and back strip, black edging. Colored neck, cord and tassel.
Each..............$9.50

No. G-560. Castillian Guitar Beautifully shaded brown and amber walnut with neat white edging. Decorated with decalcomania of Spanish fan and design. Bone bridge, saddle and nut. Colored cord and tassel to match.
Each..............$9.50

No. G-570. Art Moderne Guitar, black and silver shading; modernistic design. Extra quality bridge. Bone saddle and nut. A pleasing and eye-arresting finish. Black and white cord and tassel included.
Each..............$9.50

GUITAR No. G-580 $9.50

GUITAR No. G-590 $9.50

GUITAR No. G-600 $9.50

An Assortment of the Six Guitars Shown on this Page Sent Prepaid $50.00

No. G-580. Crystaline Guitar in special black and silver lacquer. Ebonized pin bridge, bone nut and well made white celluloid guard plate. Red and black cord and tassel...each $9.50

No. G-590. Oriental Guitar shaded red mahogany. Decorated with Japanese effect decalcomania in gold and brilliant colors. Ornamented sound hole and back strip. Colored cord and tassel included. each $9.50

No. G-600. Minstrel Guitar finished in black dull ebony, lacquered with white edge and sound hole. Decalcomania of group of minstrels......................each $9.50

Mail-order guitars like these were readily available to aspiring musicians from the turn of the last century through the 1940s. (Courtesy BenCar Collection) helped, but didn't answer the problem entirely. Martin developed a new body style it labeled the "Dreadnought," after the great battleship. This squarer and larger-bodied instrument was an immediate success among country and bluegrass musicians. Meanwhile, rival guitar makers such as Gibson developed "Jumbo" bodied guitars, which were highly regarded by such cowboy stars as Gene Autry.

The guitar was also well suited to folk music because a fairly unskilled player could still accompany him or herself on the instrument, while those who cared to develop more complex styles could also take it into many different musical directions. Guitarists such as WOODY GUTHRIE were not particularly instrumental virtuosos, but they didn't need to be to effectively accompany themselves. At the other end of the spectrum, blues-influenced players such as LEAD BELLY were able to use the guitar (a twelve-string instrument in his case) for various different effects, from simple strumming to complicated, syncopated boogie-woogie influenced accompaniments.

The FOLK REVIVAL of the 1960s brought renewed interest in acoustic instruments, and Martin had its best sales year toward the end of the decade thanks to the popularity of folk-derived music. It seemed as though all an aspiring folksinger needed to get started was a beginner's guitar and some enthusiasm. Innovations—including built-in pickups to create acoustic-electric guitars (guitars that could be played acoustically but were easily amplified for playing in small clubs)—and new designs—including the popular Ovation fiberglass-backed guitar—brought more players into the fold. The guitar remains the most prevalent folk instrument.

See also BANJO, FIVE-STRING; FIDDLE.

Gully Jumpers

Paul Warmack was born and raised in Goodlettesville, a farming community north of Nashville, and was established in the city at least as early as 1921, when he opened an auto-repair shop there. Blessed with an Irish tenor voice, he began performing as early as May 1927 on radio station WSM. Warmack gathered a group of other local musicians—guitarist Bert Hutcherson, fiddler Charles Arrington, and banjo player Roy Hardison—to create his own band. The band made its *Grand Ole Opry* debut on June 30, 1927, under the generic name Paul Warmack and His Barn Dance Orchestra. By December the group had earned the more rural-sounding Gully Jumpers name and was off and running.

The band's most talented members were Warmack and Hutcherson. They performed separately as a duo on early-morning shows for WSM, earning the nickname the "Early Birds." Hutcherson was an influential guitarist, giving guitar lessons in Nashville, and performing on radio and at local events as a soloist. The band gained great popularity on the *Opry*, so not surprisingly they were among the groups recorded at the historic September-October 1928 sessions organized by Victor in Nashville. They recorded sentimental songs, featuring Warmack's warm vocals, as well as a number of instrumentals, including Oliver Stone's "Stone's Rag." (Oliver Stone was the lead fiddler for a rival group, the Possum Hunters; this fiddle tune became a country favorite, later revived by Western Swing king Bob Wills as "Lone Star Rag.")

In the early 1930s the Gully Jumpers *Opry* segment was so popular that the station charged significantly more for advertisements during their performance. Nonetheless, they never recorded again after 1928, and, although remaining on the *Opry* through the early 1960s, never had as wide a following as groups such as CHARLIE POOLE's North Carolina Ramblers or the SKILLET LICKERS. Warmack died in 1954, but the band continued on, drawing on musicians associated with various other *Opry* string bands.

See also FIDDLE; GUITAR.

Guthrie, Arlo (b. 1947) *singer and songwriter*

Born in Brooklyn, New York, on July 10, 1947, and son of folksinger/songwriter WOODY GUTHRIE, Arlo Guthrie has had a long career performing his own songs, beginning with the quirky half-spoken narrative "Alice's Restaurant," which launched his career in 1967. His first hit inspired a feature film in 1968, and Guthrie continued to record in a singer-songwriter style through the mid-1970s. He had a pop hit in 1972 with his cover of STEVE GOODMAN's song "City of New Orleans." In the mid-1970s Guthrie formed a band called Shenandoah to play country-rock, and also toured and recorded with PETE SEEGER. Dropped by major label Warner Brothers in 1981, Guthrie has since recorded on his own Rising Son label. He has given an annual Thanksgiving Day concert in New York for many decades.

Guthrie, Woody (1912–1967) *legendary singer and songwriter*

Woodrow Wilson Guthrie was born in Okemah, Oklahoma, on July 14, 1912. Guthrie's family were pioneers in Oklahoma when it was still part of the unsettled Indian Territory. His father ran a trading post and real estate office, prospering during the first Oklahoma oil boom. The elder Guthrie was also a part-time guitarist and banjo picker, and Guthrie's mother, Nora Belle Tanner, was a fine ballad singer. The young Guthrie grew up surrounded by music, including not only his family's singing and playing but also the music of Native Americans and African Americans, all of whom lived and worked in his hometown.

Guthrie's family life dissolved with the end of the real estate boom in the mid-1920s, when his father took to heavy drinking. His mother also began to show the symptoms of Huntington's chorea, a disease that would eventually lead to her institutionalization. His sister died in a fire started accidentally by his mother, who was slowly losing her coordination and her mental stability. By his early teens Woody had quit school and relocated to Texas, where he bummed around taking odd jobs and lived on and off with his father's half brother in the small town of Pampa. He received a few GUITAR lessons from his relative, and the two played locally. He married Mary Jennings and

took up work as a sign painter, while still singing at night.

In the 1930s the disastrous dust storms swept through upper Texas and Oklahoma, caused by years of poor land management. Thousands of family farmers were ruined and took to the road in search of better living conditions. Like many others, Woody also abandoned his home and traveled to California. There he began performing in 1937 as a cowboy act in a duo with Maxine Crissman known as "Lefty Lou." The two had a popular Los Angeles-based radio show performing the kind of western/cowboy material that was popular at that time thanks to the horsy escapades of actors/singers such as Gene Autry.

In 1940 he moved to New York City, where he encountered performers such as PETE SEEGER and other young members of the first FOLK REVIVAL. Their leftist political philosophy appealed to Guthrie, who had been radicalized by the suffering of rural Americans that he had experienced firsthand during the Depression. Guthrie's quick wit also appealed to them, and his ability to compose a song on almost any topic at the drop of the hat (often by fitting new words to time-honored traditional melodies) made him a favorite performer. He was hired by the WPA to memorialize the building of the Bonneville Dam in Colorado in 1941, writing a series of classic songs including "Roll On Columbia." He also recorded his famous set of *Dust Bowl Ballads* for RCA, as well as lengthy sessions organized by Alan Lomax for the Library of Congress. Although Guthrie's commercial recordings were not terribly successful at the time, they resurfaced in the 1950s and early 1960s during the next folk revival.

In the early 1940s Guthrie performed with a loose-knit group known as the Almanac Singers along with Seeger, Lee Hays, and Millard Lampell. He supplied the group with many of their popular songs, including "Union Maid," which encouraged workers to fight unfair management practices and unionize.

After serving in World War II, Guthrie settled in Brooklyn, New York with his new wife, a modern dancer named Marjorie Mazia. However, symptoms of Huntington's chorea were already manifesting themselves, making his behavior increasingly erratic. Guthrie continued to record and perform, often with CISCO HOUSTON, until the early 1950s when his health deteriorated to the point that he had to be hospitalized. By the early 1960s when he was a legend among younger singer/songwriters such as BOB DYLAN, he was confined to a hospital bed and unable to perform. Bedridden for more than a decade, Guthrie finally succumbed to Huntington's chorea on October 3, 1967. In 1968 at New York's Carnegie Hall and Los Angeles' Hollywood Bowl, two concerts in his honor were held, which was recorded and subsequently released on two records.

See also LOMAX, JOHN AND ALAN.

Hackberry Ramblers, The

The Hackberry Ramblers were one of the most popular Cajun bands of the 1930s. Founded by Lousiana-born fiddler Luderin Darbone—who was very much influenced by Texas-style WESTERN SWING—the group began broadcasting on local radio, and then signed to Decca. They were then signed to RCA's budget label, Bluebird, in 1935, by which time the lineup featured French-language vocalist Lennis Sonnier, English-language vocalist/guitarist Joe Werner, ACCORDION, and several backup guitarists. They began to record and perform in English around 1936 as the Riverside Ramblers when they earned the radio sponsorship of the Riverside brand of tires. They had a minor hit in 1937 with "Wondering" featuring vocalist Werner.

The group broke up during World War II but then reassembled to work locally through the 1950s. They recorded for various small labels, including the King subsidiary, Deluxe. A 1963 album for Arhoolie Records brought them to the attention of the FOLK-REVIVAL audience, and the Ramblers began playing folk festivals and colleges. They have continued to perform sporadically since, with various lineups.

See also FIDDLE; GUITAR.

Hale, Theron and Daughters

Fiddler Theron Hale was born in 1883 in rural Pikeville, Tennessee, 100 miles to the southeast of Nashville. His father and uncle were both noted gospel singers active in the Baptist church. Hale took up the FIDDLE and banjo from an early age, playing as an avocation. After attending religious school in Johnson City, Hale married and settled in his hometown, working as a farmer. For a brief period he moved his family to Iowa, but by 1915 had returned to Tennessee, settling in Nashville, where he initially worked on a dairy farm. When he first played on the *Grand Ole Opry*, he was working as a traveling salesman for a sewing machine company.

Hale's two daughters were both highly educated: Mamie Ruth was classically trained on the violin and would eventually teach at Vanderbilt, and pianist Elizabeth taught music in the Nashville schools. From childhood they had played with their father at home. Elizabeth later recalled that sometime in 1926 they were approached by George Hay, who was scouting for talent for the new *Opry* program. The family band—Ruth played a second, alto part to her father's lead, and both were accompanied by Elizabeth's piano—had a distinctive sound, much less ragged around the edges than many of their more rural contemporaries. This made them a successful addition to the *Opry*, where they were initially featured on a monthly basis from 1927 to 1929, and then as regulars every week until 1934, when the band broke up.

Theron Hale was also a talented banjo player, although he rarely played the instrument in public. He is said to have taught the instrument to his nephew, Homer Davenport, who later recorded and performed in and around Chattanooga in the 1920s and 1930s. Davenport played in a three-finger, picked style, which was quite a novelty for the time, and Hale may have also used this style. Hale's banjo was later inherited by SAM McGEE after his death.

By 1934 Mamie Ruth had married and left Nashville. Tiring of returning for the radio show, she dropped out of the band. Theron and Elizabeth tried to continue with other musicians, but no one could replace the close, harmonized fiddle part that Ruth had provided. Although the band ended, Theron continued to fiddle locally, working in the 1940s with guitarist Sam McGee. The duo made some local recordings in the early 1950s for use in teaching square dancing. He also operated a used piano business for a while. Theron died on January 29, 1954.

See also BANJO, FIVE-STRING; GUITAR; SQUARE DANCE.

Hamilton, Frank (b. 1934) *banjoist, guitarist, and teacher*

Born in New York City, Hamilton was raised in Los Angeles. As a teenager he became interested in folk music, and began hanging out on the local scene, where he met fellow musicians GUY CARAWAN and RAMBLIN' JACK ELLIOTT. The trio made a memorable trip to the South in the summer of 1953 to discover the roots of the music that they loved. Hamilton later settled in the Los Angeles area, where he began teaching GUITAR and performing. By 1956 Hamilton was living in Chicago, where promoter ALBERT GROSSMAN hired him as a regular performer for his new Gate of Horn folk club. A year later, Hamilton cofounded the Old Town School of Folk Music, teaching guitar and banjo. Among his students was a young Jim McGuinn, who went on to found the BYRDS.

Hamilton released a solo album in 1962, and that same year joined the WEAVERS as their banjo player, remaining with them through 1963. He then moved back to Los Angeles, opening a new guitar instruction school; among his students were future singer/songwriter Karla Bonoff. He began performing with his wife, Mary, focusing on children's material; by the 1990s the duo had settled in

Atlanta, Georgia. Hamilton issued his first new album of folk material in decades in 1999, and continues to perform in the Atlanta area.

Hardin, Tim (1941–1980) *singer and songwriter*

Born on December 23, 1941, in Eugene, Oregon, Hardin was a popular singer/songwriter in the mid-1960s who had a short, turbulent life. A regular on the Greenwich Village and Boston-area folk scenes in the early 1960s, Hardin was signed to the new Verve/Folkways label in 1966, recording three albums over the next two years. He is most famous for the songs he wrote, including classics "Reason to Believe" (covered in the 1970s by Rod Stewart), "If I Were a Carpenter" (a major pop hit for Bobby Darin) and "Misty Roses." However, by the end of the 1960s, his physical and mental health problems had taken their toll, augmented by a growing addiction to drugs. Hardin made his last recording in 1973, an album that did not feature a single original song. He died seven years later on December 29, 1980, in Los Angeles, California.

harmonica

The harmonica is a small, inexpensive musical instrument that folk players have made into a highly versatile and expressive one, used in many styles of music. Developed in the early 19th century and mass manufactured and distributed, a beginning player could buy a harmonica for as little as five cents and teach him or herself to play fairly quickly. Small enough to fit in a shirt pocket, it obviously was also one of the most easily portable instruments, ideal for the growing United States whose people seemed to be always on the go. At some point an enterprising harmonica player designed a small metal rack that could slip over the head and hold the instrument in place, freeing up the musician's hands so that he or she could play a GUITAR and harmonica at the same time.

One of the earliest virtuoso harmonica players was country musician DeFord Bailey, who was

Made of steel highly polished and nickel plated. No screws to cut into instrument. Easy to place on guitar and adjust to position. A favorite holder. Long in use. Very practical.

No. 5526.................................Each **$1.80**

PROFESSIONAL HARMONICA HOLDER

This holder will securely hold and enable the user to play all lengths, single side Harmonicas as well as Piano Chromatic Harmonicas, up to 8½" long, as well as numbers 4, 5 and 6, Polyphonias. Owing to the construction, the user can reach the highest and lowest notes with ease. Chromonica attachment, available at extra cost.

No. 5527. For harmonicas to 8½" long.

Each **$2.50**

No. 5528. For chromonica harmonica.

Each **$5.25**

ELTON HARMONICA HOLDER

Frame is made of nickel plated wire. Plate holding harmonica is made of brass, nickel plated. Fits the shape of the neck and is adjustable to any position.

No. 5520.................Dozen **$7.50**

ELTON GUITAR HARMONICA HOLDER

Highly polished nickel plated, quickly attached to any guitar by means of clamping screw. Has every adjustment necessary for any angle of harmonica.

No. 5522....................................Each **80c**

Harmonicas were heavily promoted through mail-order catalogs and advertisements like this one, showing various different holders used to allow a guitarist to play both instruments at the same time. (Courtesy BenCar Collection) featured on the *Grand Ole Opry* radio program almost from its beginnings. Unlike the rest of the *Opry* cast, Bailey was African American, and brought a strong, blues-influenced style to his playing. (The harmonica is a key instrument in urban blues styles.) He was famous for his imitation of freight train sounds in his "Pan American Blues," a signature solo piece that he performed on record and radio. Another early *Opry* star who played the harmonica was Dr. HUMPHREY BATE, a Nashville physician who also led a string band in the 1920s and early 1930s.

In the early days of the FOLK REVIVAL in the 1930s and 1940s, Sonny Terry was probably the most influential harmonica player. Coming to New York late in the 1930s, he appeared in Broadway shows and at nightclubs, often in partnership with blues guitarist Brownie McGhee. Terry's energetic harmonica playing and his vocal "whoops" and "hollers" made him a distinctive musician, influencing many others to take up the instrument.

However, most folk players did not reach the level of skill of people such as Bailey, Bate, or Terry. Just as he was an average guitarist, WOODY GUTHRIE played the harmonica with his guitar as an accompaniment, but didn't try to play anything particularly fancy, just puffing out the basic chords. Guthrie's use of the instrument was a direct influence on musicians who followed him, most notably BOB DYLAN. Although Dylan has gone through many stylistic phases in his career, he has never totally abandoned the harmonica, using it both in his acoustic and electric band settings. Dylan's use of the harmonica influenced countless others to take it up, and it remains one of the most popular folk instruments.

See also TERRY, SONNY, AND BROWNIE MCGHEE.

Harrell, Kelly (1889–1942) *singer and songwriter*

Born Crockett Kelly Harrell in Drapers Valley, Virginia, on September 13, 1889, Harrell was discovered when he was living and working as a mill hand in Fries, Virginia by legendary country producer Ralph Peer. He began recording in 1924, and continued through the rest of the decade, usually accompanied by FIDDLE (played by Posey Rorer, who also performed with banjoist Charlie Poole), GUITAR, and sometimes banjo, in the relaxed string band style of the upper South.

Harrell recorded many traditional songs, including the popular late 19th-century ballad "Charles Guiteau" about the assassin of President Garfield, as well as composing "Away Out on the Mountain," later covered by Jimmie Rodgers, and "The Story of the Mighty Mississippi," a hit for ERNEST STONEMAN. Like many other early country artists, Harrell received little or nothing in the way of royalties from these successes, and his career ended when the Depression knocked the wind out of country music recording. He returned to mill work in the 1930s, and died of a heart attack on July 9, 1942.

See also BANJO, FIVE-STRING.

Hartford, John (1937–2001) *performer and songwriter*

John Cowan Harford (he later added a *t* to his last name) was born in New York City on December 30, 1937, but raised in St. Louis, and was soon an active figure in the city's bluegrass scene, performing with artists Doug Dillard and BYRON BERLINE. An early love of the Mississippi River led to a brief career working as a deckhand on one of the last great steamboats, as well as part-time work as a local deejay. In 1965 he moved to Nashville in search of a country-music career.

Hartford signed with RCA Records in the mid-1960s, recording his highly personal songs, ranging from the comic "Old Fashioned Washing Machine" (in which he imitated the sound of an ancient washer on its last legs) to the wordy anthems "Gentle on My Mind" and "Natural to Be Gone." Hartford's big break came with the 1967 hit recording of his "Gentle on My Mind" by singer/guitarist Glen Campbell. Hartford subsequently moved to Los Angeles, where he wrote for both the Smothers Brothers and Glen Campbell TV programs, as well

John Hartford in the mid-1970s. (Courtesy the artist)

as recording his last album for RCA (*Iron Mountain Depot*), an early stab at country-rock, including a cover of the Beatles' "Hey Jude."

In 1970 he returned to Nashville and signed to Warner Bros., releasing his classic LP *Aeroplane.* Hartford established a band bringing together the most talented and progressive of Nashville's musicians, including Tut Taylor (DOBRO), NORMAN BLAKE (GUITAR), VASSAR CLEMENTS (FIDDLE), and Randy Scruggs (bass). However, Hartford soon dissolved his band and spent most of the 1970s and 1980s touring as a solo musician. Accompanying himself on banjo, guitar, and fiddle, Hartford rigged up a plywood board with a microphone to enable him to clog dance while singing and playing. His love of the Mississippi River was expressed most deeply in the concept LP *Mark Twang* released by Flying Fish Records in 1976, which earned him a Grammy. In the late 1980s

Hartford briefly re-signed to a major record label (MCA) and began performing with his son.

In the early 1990s he issued his recordings on his own colorfully named label, Small Dog A-Barkin'. In 2000 he performed on the soundtrack for the Coen Brothers' film *O Brother, Where Art Thou?*, and emceed a concert of traditional music at the Ryman Auditorium in Nashville that was featured in a documentary film by D. A. Pennebaker, *Down from the Mountain.* In the mid-1990s Hartford was diagnosed with cancer, which he had previously battled some 20 years earlier. Determined to continue to perform, he played concerts until about two months before his death on June 4, 2001.

Havens, Richie (b. 1941) *singer and songwriter*
Born Richard Pierce Havens on January 21, 1941, in Brooklyn, New York, Havens was one of the few African-American performers to come to prominence as a singer/songwriter during the 1960s FOLK REVIVAL. He moved to Greenwich Village when he was 20, and became an active performer on the scene, noted for his highly rhythmic GUITAR accompaniments and half-chanted vocals. Two albums on a small local label were followed by a contract with Verve/Forecast in 1967. An appearance at the 1969 Woodstock Festival—performing an impromptu version of "Motherless Child"—gave Havens's career a big boost, and his older albums suddenly began to sell. He had a top-20 pop hit with his cover of the Beatles' "Here Comes the Sun" in 1970 following his exposure in the Woodstock film. However, this popularity was short-lived, and Havens retired from recording and performing by the late 1970s. In 1987 he returned as a performer, mostly of his "classic" material, regularly touring on the folk-revival circuit.

Haywire Mac (1882–1957) *singer and songwriter*
Harry Kirby McClintock was born in Knoxville, Tennessee, on October 8, 1882 and raised in a middle-class home, where he learned to play GUITAR as a

youth. At age 14 he left home to join a traveling show, working his way to New Orleans. Longing to see the world, Mac was working as a mule driver two years later in the Philippines, delivering supplies to the American troops, and then, in 1899, working as a journalist's assistant in the Boxer Rebellion. From China he worked his way to Australia and then South Africa, where he again served as a mule driver in the Boer War. By 1902 he was in London, and then South America and the Caribbean, finally returning sometime around 1905 to San Francisco, where he lived for the rest of his life.

McClintock then worked as a railroad brakeman. Sympathizing with his fellow workers and left-leaning in his politics, he became an organizer for the Industrial Workers of the World (IWW) union. He wrote a rousing theme song for his fellow workers, "Hallelujah I'm a Bum," around the early teens. Still working as an amateur singer, he began to attract attention singing on the streets, leading, eventually, to his own daily radio show, which began broadcasting out of San Francisco in 1925. Three years later, he made his first recordings for Victor Records under the name of "Haywire Mac." He cut 41 sides over the next three years, including "Hallelujah I'm a Bum" and two follow-ups, and his best-known song, "The Big Rock Candy Mountain," along with cowboy and novelty numbers.

The Depression slowed Mac's recording career, but he made a strong comeback in 1938 for Decca, rerecording his earlier hits. That same year he moved to Hollywood to appear in a number of westerns with Gene Autry. He also built on his myth by writing stories, plays, and nonfiction pieces for various publications, including his popular column, "The Railroad Boomer," which appeared from 1943 to 1953 in a railroad-enthusiast publication. His homespun humor resembled Will Rogers and also WOODY GUTHRIE's newspaper work, and he achieved similar fame among folk-music and liberal readers.

In 1953 McClintock returned to San Francisco to host his own radio/TV show, *The Breakfast Hour.*

Two years later, he "retired," although he continued to perform until his death on April 24, 1957. However, McClintock's songs—and legend—lived on after his death. Burl Ives repopularized "The Big Rock Candy Mountain" as a children's song in the 1950s and 1960s, achieving a minor hit with it. McClintock's 1928 recording of the song was included on the soundtrack of the Coen Brothers film *O Brother, Where Art Thou?* in 2000, bringing renewed attention to the cowboy/hobo singer.

Herdman, Priscilla (b. c. 1950) *performer and songwriter*

Herdman was born in Eastchester, New York, to a musical household. Her older siblings, including sister Susan, played music, as did her mother, which influenced her to take up the GUITAR as a teenager. After attending the University of Iowa, she settled in New York in the early 1970s, beginning to perform at local coffeehouses. In 1976 she moved to Philadelphia, and a year later made her debut album, *The Water Lily,* for the independent Philo label; it was unusual because it focused primarily on the lyrics of an early 20th-century Australian folk poet named Henry Lawson, whose work inspired Herdman to create new musical settings. On her next album she turned to contemporary singer-songwriter material. Herdman continued to record her own songs and other contemporary folk material through the 1980s. Taking time out to give birth to her daughter in 1985, Herdman was inspired to write a series of children's songs that became her most successful recording, the 1988 album *Stardreamer: Nightsongs & Lullabies.* In 1989 it was selected as an American Library Association Notable Children's Recording and received the Parent's Choice Gold Seal Award. It was followed by the 1993 album *Daydreamer* and *Moondreamer* in 1998. Herdman has continued to perform and record as a solo artist through the 1990s and into the new century. She has also made regular tours and recordings with fellow folksingers Anne Hills and Cindy Mangsen.

Hester, Carolyn (b. 1937) *singer*

Born in Waco, Texas, Hester moved to New York in 1955 to pursue a career as an actress and singer. By then her parents were living in Lubbock, Texas, and when visiting them the young singer met producer Norman Petty, who ran a studio in nearby Clovis, New Mexico. Petty was famous for producing rocker Buddy Holly, and invited Hester to record her first album with him. Hester befriended Holly, and supposedly they recorded together for a second album, although these tapes have never been heard.

Back in New York, Hester recorded an album for the CLANCY BROTHERS Tradition label in 1960, and then signed with Columbia. At this time she was married to folksinger RICHARD FARIÑA, who introduced her to a new musician in town, BOB DYLAN. Dylan had been working as a HARMONICA player accompanying various performers in Greenwich Village, and Hester invited him to play on her Columbia sessions. John Hammond, who was producing these sessions, was introduced to the young singer/songwriter, and soon signed him to Columbia as well.

Hester and Fariña soon separated, but she remained active on the folk scene, cutting a second album for Columbia. However, she saw little success, and soon returned to working with Petty in his Clovis studios. This time he paired her with a young guitarist named Jimmy Gilmer, who had a 1963 hit with the Petty-produced "Sugar Shack" with his group, the Fireballs. It was an unusual pairing of a rock guitarist with a folk performer; nonetheless the duo produced some interesting early attempts at FOLK-ROCK, covering material by younger songwriters such as TOM PAXTON and MARK SPOELSTRA.

Hester then returned to Columbia for a couple of singles in the mid-1960s, but still success eluded her. Changing with the times, she formed a psychedelic folk-rock band, the Carolyn Hester Coalition, but the odd marriage of her folk-flavored vocals with improvised accompaniments failed to find an audience. In the early 1970s she wed jazz pianist/songwriter David Blume, and the two have worked together off and on over the following decades. Hester has continued to perform on occasion, and her Columbia recordings were reissued in the late 1990s, thanks to her early association with Dylan.

Hiatt, John (b. 1952) *guitarist, singer, and songwriter*

Born and raised in Indianapolis, Hiatt first began playing during his high school years with a local R&B band. In 1970 he moved to Nashville, and by mid-decade was signed by Epic Records, where he recorded two LPs, followed by two more for MCA; none sold well, although they helped establish his reputation. He worked for a while in Ry Cooder's backup band, but then went solo again by the mid-1980s, when he recorded a number of albums for Geffen. However, his increasing dependence on alcohol, plus his record's poor sales, put an end to his recording career for a while.

Hiatt returned magnificently with 1987's *Bring the Family*, accompanied by Cooder along with British punk-country singer Nick Lowe on bass and session drummer Jim Keltner. BONNIE RAITT scored her first comeback hit with a cover of Hiatt's bluesy rocker "Thing Called Love" from this album. Hiatt continued to record with various bands—notably the band he called the Goners featuring guitarist Sonny Landreth—as well as participating in a reunion with the Bring the Family group, now called Little Village.

Hiatt's work has veered from punk-tinged rock to the acoustic blues-influenced album *Crossing Muddy Waters* (2000). In 2001 he reunited with Sonny Landreth and the Goners and has recorded several albums with the group as well as touring.

Hickerson, Joe (b. 1935) *folklorist and performer*

Joseph Hickerson was born on October 20, 1935, in Highland Park, Illinois, to an educated, musical family. He became interested in folk music while attending Oberlin College, establishing the folk music club there in 1953. With a group of fellow students, he formed the group the Folksmiths, who made an album for Folkways in 1957. After that, Hickerson took a master's degree in folklore at Indiana University. In 1963 he was named Reference Librarian at the ARCHIVE OF AMERICAN FOLKSONG in the Library of Congress, and 11 years later became its director, serving until his retirement in 1998. He also was a cofounder of the Folksong Society of Greater Washington in 1964. Hickerson has performed thousands of times, although recorded less prolifically; his best-known recordings appeared in the mid-1970s on the small Folk Legacy label. He is known as a virtual encyclopedia of traditional folk songs, and lectures on folk music around the country.

Hi Flyers, The

During the 1930s Texas was a hotbed of swinging string ensembles usually founded to play sponsored shows on radio, and then hitting the local circuit of honky-tonks and dance halls. The Hi Flyers were one of the more distinctive and successful of these groups, who went through varied styles (and band members) during their approximately 15-year heyday.

The band, originally christened the "High Flyers," made its debut on Fort Worth radio in 1929, the brainchild of announcer Zack Hurt. The original group featured Kentucky fiddler Clifford Gross playing a mixture of popular and dance tunes, particularly waltzes. By 1932 the band was rechristened with the more concise "Hi Flyers" name, and was now led by guitarist Elmer Scarborough. Influenced by the success of Milton Brown and Bob Wills, Scarborough changed the band's emphasis to jazzy instrumentals and modern instrumentation. The band was still FIDDLE led, but new fiddler Pat Trotter was far more jazz-oriented than Gross. In 1936 Trotter and several others were hired away by an Amarillo radio station and were rechristened as the Sons of the West. Nonetheless, a year later, the Hi Flyers made their recording debut, featuring

Scarborough, fiddler Darrell Kirkpatrick, steel guitarist Billy Briggs, and Landon Beaver, a jazz-styled pianist, as the key players.

The band underwent a transition from 1937 to 1938, leaving Fort Worth and moving for a while to a smaller Texas station. After a brief period of inactivity, Scarborough reactivated the group, now operating out of Oklahoma City. From 1939 to 1941 this version of the band—featuring the jazzy electric GUITAR leads of Sheldon Bennett and pianist Beaver—made the group's most memorable and best-loved recordings. Their signature number, "Hi Flyer Stomp," became a classic of Western Swing recordings. They also added to the group Buster Ferguson, a smooth-voiced vocalist in order to compete with Wills's band, which featured the noted singer Tommy Duncan. Ferguson's vocals looked forward to the popular, postwar honky-tonk ballads of beer and betrayal.

The band members scattered during the World War II years, as various players were inducted into the services. Following the war, Scarborough once more tried to revive the group, working back in their original home base of Fort Worth, but this band lasted only about a year before the Hi Flyers were no more.

Highwoods Stringband, The

Originating in the Berkeley, California, old-time music community of the 1970s, the lineup of this group stabilized around 1973 after its future members relocated to Ithaca, New York. Mac Benford's hoarse vocals, the ragged-but-right sound of the twin fiddles played by Walt Koken and Bob Potts, and Doug Dorschug's Riley Puckett–influenced guitar runs made for a sound that was both contemporary and nostalgic. Their first LP, *Fire on the Mountain,* was recorded outside, in an attempt to capture the spontaneous sound of the band; their next two LPs, *Dance All Night* and *Radio Special #3,* were more professionally recorded. However, none of their albums captured the excitement of the band's live performances. The band influenced countless other outfits, amateur and professional, particularly the Plank Road Stringband, the Chicken Chokers, and the Tompkins County Horseflies.

After the band broke up, Benford recorded a solo banjo LP and briefly formed a new band, the Backwoods Band, in the style of Highwoods; Dorschug went to work as a record producer for June Appal Records; Koken recorded two solo banjo records for Rounder during the 1990s. The other band members faded from the performing scene.

See also FIDDLE.

Hill Billies (Al Hopkins and the Hill Billies)

Pianist Albert Green Hopkins led this influential early country string band during the 1920s. Key group members were fiddlers Charlie Bowman and Tony Alderman, Al's brother John on GUITAR, and Frank Wilson on Hawaiian guitar. The group was groundbreaking in many ways: although from rural western Virginia, they were performing in Washington, D.C., over major radio station WRC as early as 1925. They were signed by Okeh Records, and their first session was supervised by legendary producer Ralph Peer. When Peer asked Hopkins for the group's name, he is said to have replied, "Call the band anything you want. We are nothing but a bunch of hillbillies from North Carolina and Virginia anyway."

The Hill Billies were so popular that they landed a job in New York in 1927; within the next few years, they performed for President Calvin Coolidge and appeared in an early Vitaphone 15-minute "soundie" (short film). The band was also unusual in featuring piano accompaniment, played by leader Hopkins, as well as Hawaiian-styled slide guitar. Some of their sides were issued under the equally colorful name of the Buckle Busters. However, the Depression brought an end to the group's short ride of fame, and they returned to life in the mountains.

See also FIDDLE.

Hinojosa, Tish (b. 1955) *singer and songwriter*

Born Leticia Hinojosa on December 6, 1955, and raised in a working-class family in the multiethnic city of San Antonio, Hinojosa began playing GUITAR in high school, influenced as many others were at the time by the early 1970s soft-rock of JONI MITCHELL, JUDY COLLINS, JAMES TAYLOR, and BOB DYLAN. She began writing her own material soon after, and recorded a few singles in Spanish for the local market. Relocating to New Mexico, she issued her self-produced cassette *From Taos to Tennessee* in 1987, staking out her territory as a new-country artist with southwestern roots. Soon after, major label A&M picked her up, releasing an album called *Homeland* in 1989, produced by Los Lobos's sax player, Steve Berlin. A second LP was recorded, but was not released; in a management shuffle, Hinojosa was dropped from A&M.

Picked up by specialty label Rounder Records, Hinojosa released *Culture Swing,* a mostly acoustic album reflecting Mexican, Spanish, country, and even Caribbean sounds. Strangely enough, the smaller label was able to get her more attention than A&M, and she had a minor hit with her ode to migrant workers, "Something in the Rain." During the later 1990s Hinojosa veered between producing Spanish-language recordings, records for children, and her own material, failing to build on the critical success of *Culture Swing.* After a three-year recording hiatus, she returned in 2000 with *Sign of Truth,* with 12 new songs that she wrote or cowrote.

Holcomb, Roscoe (1913–1981) *banjoist, guitarist, and singer*

Born in Daisy, Kentucky, Roscoe lived and worked near Hazard, Kentucky, the center of Kentucky's coal mining region. His brother-in-law gave him a homemade banjo when he was 10, and he was soon playing for local dances. By his late teen years he was working in the mines and married to a religious woman who urged him to give up music as the devil's work. He abandoned playing for a while, but soon was back to making music as a sideline to his mining career.

By the late 1950s when folklorist John Cohen first heard him play and subsequently recorded him for his record, *Mountain Music of Kentucky,* Holcomb was working odd jobs around his home. Even after he was recorded by Cohen and began appearing at folk festivals, Holcomb continued to do hard labor, including paving work on many of the super highways that were then being put through the mountains. Holcomb never viewed music making as a "profession," although he was deadly serious about maintaining a high level of performance. Holcomb's high-pitched falsetto singing was perfectly suited to his repertoire of bluesy songs. He played the banjo in a two-finger, picked style, and used a similar style when picking the GUITAR (achieving a unique, banjolike style when playing this instrument). Holcomb's intensity as a performer was legendary; he lived the songs, sometimes crying during performances onstage, even if he was performing a song that he had already sung countless times before. Holcomb died on April 25, 1981.

See also BANJO, FIVE-STRING.

Holt, David (b. 1946) *banjoist and storyteller*

Born in Gatesville, Texas, on October 15, 1946, banjo player/storyteller David Holt was raised from his early teen years in Palisades, California. He played drums in local rock bands as a teen, as well as the traditional percussion instruments, the bones and spoons, which he learned to play from his father. A visit to Texas led to an encounter with classic cowboy singer/storyteller Carl T. Sprague, who taught Holt HARMONICA and encouraged his interest in traditional tales. Holt studied biology in college, and in the early 1970s settled in western North Carolina to seek out older traditional musicians. In 1975 he founded the Appalachian Music Program at Warren Wilson College in Swannanoa. He issued his first album on the local June Appal label in 1981

and became a professional performer at that same time.

Holt combines traditional banjo songs with his storytelling on both his recordings and in his stage shows, which are often constructed around single themes. His revival of traditional Appalachian folklore has led to regular appearances on the *Grand Ole Opry* and other country music shows. Holt hosted a seven-part series for Public Television called *Folkways,* and has also hosted the radio series *Riverwalk.* He established his own record label, Windy Audio, to release his recordings.

See also BANJO, FIVE-STRING.

Holy Modal Rounders

The Holy Modal Rounders were originally a duo, formed in New York City in the early 1960s by banjo player/vocalist Peter Stampfel and guitarist/vocalist Steve Weber. Stampfel was the more energetic of the pair, with a high, nasal voice and rough-hewn FIDDLE style that was perfectly suited to the material; Weber was quieter, playing a blues-influenced GUITAR and providing low harmony vocals. They recorded two albums for Prestige Records before the group began to grow, incorporating many of the same musicians who were playing with the FOLK-ROCK group the Fugs. Their later 1960s albums, with a growing cast of supporting characters, combined avant-garde noise with electrified fiddling, a musical marriage that went nowhere. They were reunited in the late 1970s by Rounder Records, the folk label named in their honor, but Weber soon moved to Portland, Oregon. Stampfel performed sporadically during the 1980s and 1990s with numerous "bands" (loose conglomerations of different musicians), sometimes using the name the Holy Modal Rounders, and sometimes using other names (such as the Bottlecaps). Against all odds, the duo reunited in the late 1990s and began performing in New York City at small folk clubs, reviving much of their mid-1960s repertoire.

See also BANJO, FIVE-STRING.

Holzman, Jac (b. 1932) *founder of Elektra Records*

Jac Holzman was born and raised in New York City, where he developed an interest in new recording technologies as a teenager. He attended St. John's College in Annapolis, Maryland, and there heard folk music for the first time. While a student, he befriended a young folk performer named Glenn Yarbrough, and in 1950 issued an album of Yarbrough's music. Soon after, he was back in New York's Greenwich Village, where he opened a record store and continued to build his new label, called Elektra Records. He was a savvy talent spotter, signing acts such as FRANK WARNER and JEAN RITCHIE to the young label. Elektra's first big success came in 1956, when Holzman came up with the idea of recording an album of "risqué" songs of the Renaissance with performer ED MCCURDY; the album sold beyond anyone's expectations. The label continued to grow, boosted in 1961 by Holzman's signing of new folk performers JUDY COLLINS and PHIL OCHS. In 1963 the label signed the Paul Butterfield Blues Band, its first electric band and a harbinger of its future.

In 1964 Holzman founded Nonesuch as a companion label to Elektra, first issuing low-cost classical releases but soon after beginning the famous "Explorer" series, one of the earliest labels devoted to world music recordings. By the later 1960s Elektra had moved into rock with the singing of the Doors, among other acts. The label was merged with Warner Brothers and Atlantic in 1970; Holzman continued to work for the firm as an executive thereafter.

"Home on the Range" (1910) *early classic cowboy song*

Cowboy or western songs were not well known until folklorist John Lomax published a book of these songs in 1910. He collected them from cowboys themselves, through writing to other folklorists, and through scanning western newspapers for cowboy-themed poems. One of these was "Home on the Range." Lomax's book was reissued in 1927, when the fad for cowboy performers was beginning to grow (thanks to early country artists such as Jimmie Rodgers), and it became the source for numerous recordings, and the song was soon widely popular. Although Lomax presented it as a "traditional" song, it turns out that it was in fact a composed piece, first published in 1873; the words were written by a Kansas doctor named Brewster M. Highley, and the music by a local musician named Dan Kelly. Sentimental songs of family and home are very popular among folk performers, and "Home on the Range" is undoubtedly the granddaddy of them all.

See also LOMAX, JOHN AND ALAN.

Hot Mud Family

Centering on the husband-wife team of Dave (FIDDLE, vocals) and Suzanne (GUITAR, vocals) Edmundson, along with banjoist Rick Good and bass player/vocalist/songwriter Tom "Harley" Campbell, Hot Mud Family was one of the few old-time bands to feature a female as a lead vocalist. Suzanne Edmundson also played a number of instruments, although she most often limited herself to guitar onstage. The group recorded a number of albums for Jimmie Skinner's Ohio-based Vetco label in the mid-1970s before moving on to the larger Flying Fish label. However, as the old-time revival fizzled out, so did the band (and the Edmundson's marriage), and by 1982 they had called it quits.

The group's repertoire focused on old-time fare and some straight honky-tonk country, thanks to Suzanne's affinity for country-weepers. Good was able to recreate the banjo and vocal style of legendary performer Uncle Dave Macon, which became a feature of their stage show. Campbell was a fine bass vocalist, and in the 1980s formed an acoustic-folk trio with fiddler Tom McCreesh and hammer-dulcimer player

Walt Michael. He is also the author of the fine bluegrass-gospel number, "The Man in the Middle," which has been covered by a number of 1980s-era newgrass bands.

See also BANJO, FIVE-STRING; DULCIMER (HAMMERED).

Hot Rize

Banjo player Pete Wernick formed the progressive bluegrass band Hot Rize in the late 1970s. Wernick began his career playing second banjo to TONY TRISCHKA in the all-instrumental, progressive COUNTRY COOKING band from Ithaca, New York in the mid-1970s. He then moved to Colorado and recorded a solo album, and then formed Hot Rize; its name is taken from a brand of flour made by the Martha White bakeries, Flatt and Scruggs's radio sponsors. The group recorded several albums through the 1980s, drawing on the traditional repertoire of country songs from the 1930s and 1940s, bluegrass standards, as well as their own compositions in a traditional style. The band's other members were MANDOLIN player/guitarist/lead vocalist Tim O'Brien, lead guitarist Charles Sawtelle, and bass player Nick Forster.

In the early 1980s Hot Rize introduced a new element to their live show, introducing themselves as another band entirely called Red Knuckles and the Trailblazers. This parody-country bar band specialized in the honky-tonk weepers of the 1950s and were both an homage to and a subtle satire of the best and worst in this style of music. As an altar-ego band, Red Knuckles made two separate albums from Hot Rize, and became almost as popular as the original group.

By the late 1980s O'Brien had moved to Nashville in search of a career as a singer/songwriter, and the band fizzled out. Wernick reemerged in 1993 with his second solo album, a collection of bluegrass-styled instrumentals along with original compositions recorded with a light-jazz trio (clarinet, vibes, and drums). Sawtelle died in the late 1990s after a long struggle with cancer.

Houston, Cisco (1918–1961) *guitarist and singer*
Houston was born Gilbert Vandine Houston in Wilmington, Delaware, on August, 18, 1918; his father was a sheet metal worker originally from North Carolina, and exposed his son to mountain songs and traditions. When Houston was two years old, the family relocated to Southern California, where Houston was raised. He showed talent for acting as a teenager, but his education ended when his father left the family in 1932, and Houston took to the road. About this time he took the name "Cisco" after the town of the same name in California.

Back in California by the mid-1930s, Houston befriended radio actor/activist Will Geer, who introduced him to singer WOODY GUTHRIE. Guthrie and Houston began performing together locally and on radio, and the two traveled to New York in 1939 in search of work. Houston enrolled in the merchant marine during World War II, and Guthrie soon followed. While stationed in New York before sailing, they continued to perform together, along with PETE SEEGER and other New York area folk performers.

After the war, Houston returned briefly to New York, coming in and out of the city as opportunities to perform arose, and also traveling back to Hollywood, where he landed a few minor roles in films. He also recorded as accompanist to Guthrie and as a solo performer for MOSES ASCH's new Folkways label. Houston appeared in the 1948 production of Marc Blitzstein's social-protest musical, *The Cradle Will Rock,* on Broadway. In the early 1950s he was back in California, and began hosting a syndicated television program, the *Gil Houston Show,* which was picked up by the Mutual Broadcasting System and broadcast on more than 500 stations at the height of its success. He also recorded for Decca during this period. However, Houston's left-leaning political past caught up with him, and his TV show was cancelled. For several years he did not record, although he continued to work when he could.

In 1959 the U.S. State Department sponsored a tour of folk musicians to India, which included Houston. When he returned, he was invited by

CBS-TV to narrate one of the first major network programs on the growing interest in folk music, which was broadcast in 1960. However, within a year, Houston was diagnosed with cancer, and he passed away in San Bernardino, California, on April 16, 1961.

Hurt, Mississippi John (1893–1966) *blues and folk performer*

Born John Smith Hurt on July 3, 1893, in Teoc, Mississippi, Hurt was a blues performer who enjoyed greater success upon his "rediscovery" in the 1960s than he had during his original, brief recording career in the late 1920s. A lifelong farmer,

Hurt's repertoire mixed traditional blues, play party songs, and folk ballads. His relaxed voice and gentle finger-picking on the GUITAR made him stand out from the more intense blues performers from his native state.

Hurt grew up in Avalon, Mississippi, a small town north of Greenwood. He began playing guitar at age 10, and was soon entertaining at house parties. By the early 1920s he was working with a white SQUARE DANCE fiddler. Hurt was recorded by the Okeh label in 1928, but these recordings saw little success at the time, and he returned to his life as a farmer. However, one of the songs, a version of "Frankie and Albert" was reissued on HARRY SMITH's influential 1952 set, *The Anthology of*

Mississippi John Hurt performs at an afternoon workshop at the 1963 Newport Folk Festival; Dave Van Ronk listens intently, while just behind Hurt, Brownie McGhee can also be seen. (Photo © John Byrne Cooke, http://www.cookephoto.com)

American Folk Music. This set introduced a number of important performers to the younger folk and blues revivalists. One of them, Tom Hoskins, began collecting Hurt's 78s, including the song "Avalon Blues." On it Hurt described his hometown of Avalon, Mississippi; Hoskins decided to travel there to see if he could find Hurt, and surprisingly he was still living there.

At first, Hurt's playing and singing were somewhat rusty, as might be expected, but he soon developed into an engaging performer. Signed to the FOLK-REVIVAL label Vanguard Records, he made a series of albums and became a popular performer on the college, small club, and folk festival circuits. He died on November 2, 1966, in Grenada, Mississippi.

See also FIDDLE.

Hutchings, Ashley (b. 1945) *bandleader, performer, and songwriter*

Ashley Hutchings was born in the Muswell Hill neighborhood of London on January 26, 1945, and has been a major force in the British FOLK-ROCK movement since the mid-1960s. Hutchings was a founding member of FAIRPORT CONVENTION in 1966, which combined American singer-songwriter material with traditional British folk songs and tunes in its repertoire. He left the group in 1969 to form STEELEYE SPAN to further explore British traditional music; in 1971 he left Steeleye Span to form the first of the many Albion bands.

The name "Albion Band" has been used by Ashley Hutchings since 1972 for a series of folk-rock groups that he has led. It was first used on SHIRLEY COLLINS's (then Hutchings's wife) 1971 album, *No Roses,* which Hutchings produced. Within a year a full touring band had formed, recording one album (which was not released until 1976), and then disbanded due to the cost of touring. Hutchings and Collins began working locally with an acoustic band they called the Etchingham Steam Band from 1973 to 1975, while waiting for the economy to improve. In 1975 a new Albion

Band arose, featuring singer/songwriter/melodeon player John Tams, guitarists Graeme Taylor and Simon Nicol, along with a large cast of supporting musicians. Between 1976 and 1979, the group appeared regularly on the London stage as accompanists/performers at London's National Theater. However, in 1979 the band splintered, with Hutchings and Nicol maintaining the Albion name and the rest of the crew taking a new identity under the name the Home Service.

The 1980s-era Albion band mostly focused on original material by Ashley Hutchings and other band materials, and new vocalist Cathy Lesurf, who remained with the group until 1987. Hutchings's songs tended to address folk and traditional themes, and the band also continued to play traditional English dance music. During the 1990s Hutchings led various outfits under different names. The Albion name was revived by a new "acoustic" group from 1993 to 1997. This lineup, once again featuring Simon Nicol with singer/songwriters Chris While and Julie Matthews, performed mostly original songs. In 1997 While and Matthews left to form a performing duo; Nicol returned to Fairport Convention full time; and the acoustic band folded. In 1998 Hutchings premiered a new Albion lineup.

All along, Hutchings has pursued independent projects, including various concept albums, drawing on many of the same musicians. Most notable among these are *Morris On* (1972), the first folk-rock album to celebrate the English Morris dance tradition, *Son of Morris On* (1975), *Kicking up the Sawdust* (1977), an album of English dance music featuring traditional performers accompanied by an electrified rhythm section, and various albums of music from dramatic productions. Hutchings also recorded *An Evening with Cecil Sharp* (1983), based on Hutchings's one-man show about the life and times of the great British folksong collector, and *Big Beat Combo* (1996), an exuberant collection of late 1950s and early 1960s rock instrumentals joined with traditional English dance tunes.

Hutchison, Frank (1897–1945) *blues and folk guitarist and singer*

Born on March 20, 1897 and raised in Logan County in the coal belt along the West Virginia–Kentucky border, Hutchison was exposed early on to blues music thanks to an influx of black laborers who came to the area to lay track for the railroads that serviced the coal mines. One worker who was particularly influential was Henry Vaughn, who, according to Hutchison-family legend, taught the boy the rudiments of playing slide-GUITAR using a knife to dampen the strings when Hutchison was eight years old. Another early influence was Bill Hunt, described by Hutchison as "a crippled Negro living back in the hills"; along with blues, Hunt was a repository of ragtime-era novelty songs, ballads, play-party songs, and other items popular in the hills around the turn of the last century. Hutchison absorbed much of this repertoire and was performing locally by the early 1920s. The tall, red-headed guitarist of Irish stock specialized in performing the blues, quite a novelty for a white musician at the time.

Okeh Records of New York heard about Hutchison and brought him to the big city to record two songs in late 1926: his most famous number "The Train That Carried My Girl from Town," featuring train-whistle sound effects performed on the guitar, and "Worried Blues." The success of this first recording led to more sessions in 1927, producing a series of blues-tinged recordings, including the traditional badman ballad "Stackalee," a reworking of the black ballad "John Henry" as "K.C. Blues," a song about the hard times in the coal mines ("Miner's Blues"), and even a half-spoken narrative record based on the sinking of the *Titanic* ("The Last Scene of the Titanic"). After 1927 Hutchison recorded sporadically through 1930, and told friends that he would have recorded more blues numbers if Okeh had let him (by the end of his recording career, the company was pushing him to record more mainstream country material for a white market, persuading him to work with a country fiddler). In 1930 the company stopped recording Hutchison, probably because of the onset of the Depression.

Sometime in the 1930s Hutchison gave up music making, which was always at best an avocation for him. He became a storekeeper and relocated to Columbus, Ohio, where he died on November 9, 1945.

Ian, Janis (b. 1951) *pianist, singer and songwriter*
Born Janis Eddy Fink on May 7, 1951, in New York
City, Ian began playing piano at an early age. She
began writing songs at age 12 and began performing
around New York, taking the stage name of Janis
Ian from her first and her brother's middle name.
She was signed to Verve/Forecast records in 1966,
and her first single—"Society's Child (Baby I've
Been Thinking)"—tackled the controversial topic
of interracial dating. An appearance on a TV documentary hosted by conductor Leonard Bernstein
launched Ian's career, although her follow-up
releases did not enjoy the same level of success or
controversy.

Ian briefly retired from performing in 1970, but
returned soon after transforming herself into a
singer/songwriter. In 1975 she had her biggest success with *Between the Lines,* with the hit single "At
Seventeen." However, again she was unable to follow this up with further hits, and by the early 1990s
she was living in Nashville and working as a songwriter. She returned to recording with her 1993
album *Breaking Silence,* which addressed her own
lesbianism. She has since recorded a mix of topical
and personal songs.

Ian and Sylvia

Ian Tyson (GUITAR, vocals; b. British Columbia,
Canada, September 23, 1933) and Sylvia Fricker
Tyson (vocals, bass; b. Chatham, Ontario, Canada,
September 19, 1940) began performing together in
1961 in their native Canada and later moved to New
York in search of a more sympathetic audience. The
married couple joined up with folk music's most
masterly manager, ALBERT GROSSMAN, who at the
time also handled BOB DYLAN and PETER, PAUL AND
MARY. He got Ian and Sylvia a contract with

*Sylvia Fricker and Ian Tyson (aka Ian and Sylvia) performing
at the 1963 Newport Folk Festival.* (Photo © John Byrne
Cooke, http://www.cookephoto.com)

Vanguard Records, and they had their first hit with Tyson's multilingual "Four Strong Winds," sung in English and French, a favorite of college students through the 1960s.

The duo was quite popular through the mid-1960s, helping to introduce new Canadian songwriters to the American market, including GORDON LIGHTFOOT and JONI MITCHELL. Increasingly interested in blending country music with their own form of folk-pop, they recorded an album entitled *Nashville* that featured a strange blend of country and improvisational jazz. They then formed a country-rock group called Great Speckled Bird, but its debut album, produced by seminal rocker Todd Rundgren, was a sales failure.

After the pair divorced in 1974, Ian hosted his own Canadian TV show, originally called *Nashville North,* while Sylvia pursued a solo career. During the 1990s Ian has recorded a couple of albums of western and cowboy-flavored songs, both his own compositions and covers of old standards.

"If I Had My Way (Samson and Delilah)"
(1961) *popular folk song*
Blind street singer the REVEREND GARY DAVIS created a moving version of this biblical story out of different traditional sources. His performance—punctuated by shouts of "Good God!" and virtuosic GUITAR work—made it one of his most memorable performances. Originally from North Carolina, he settled in New York City in the late 1940s, and became a well-known figure on the FOLK REVIVAL scene, thanks to concerts and recordings beginning in the mid-1950s. The folk revival group PETER, PAUL AND MARY recorded Davis's version of this song for their debut album and, unlike many other folk revival bands, gave him authorship credit to the song. (Many others would label songs from folk sources like Davis "traditional" and take an arranger's credit, denying their source any income from royalties.) Thanks to this credit, Davis was able to buy a more comfortable home in

Queens, New York. The song's success also led to further performing opportunities for him.

Incredible String Band, The
Combining childlike innocence in their lyrics with Celtic mysticism and a good dose of 1960s "flower power," the Incredible String Band were a unique ensemble in the British FOLK-ROCK movement. Formed originally by Scottish musicians Robin Williamson (b. November 24, 1943) and Clive Palmer to perform at Palmer's Incredible Folk Club, they soon enlisted a third member, Mike Heron (b. December 12, 1942), to record their debut album, a collection of quirky original songs. After its release, Palmer went to Afghanistan in search of new musical frontiers, and the group became a duo. Heron and Williamson both composed songs in a similar psychedelic-flavored style, and the two also mastered a range of instruments, including for-that-time exotic instruments from around the world, including sitars and tabla. The band reached their greatest success with the 1968 album *The Hangman's Beautiful Daughter,* which featured their innovative version of the traditional Bahamian folksong, "We Bid You Goodnight." The duo expanded to include various other musicians, and they even appeared at 1969's Woodstock Festival, but by the early 1970s the steam was beginning to run out of the collaboration. Since the ending of the band, Williamson has continued to perform, primarily playing Celtic harps and singing his own compositions, while Heron has turned to singer/songwriter–flavored rock.

Irish Rovers, The
The Irish Rovers, despite their name, are actually a Canadian group. Inspired by the success of the CLANCY BROTHERS, brothers George (GUITAR), Joe (ACCORDION), and Will (guitar, banjo) Millar decided to form their own group, bringing in vocalist Jimmy Ferguson and Wilcil McDowell (accordion).

They signed with Decca, and in 1967 had a hit with the Irish-flavored song "The Unicorn," which was actually written by American songwriter Shel Silverstein. They continued to have hits primarily in their native Canada, while also appearing on a regular TV show on Canadian television from 1971 to 1974. In 1980 they scored another fluke hit, this time on the American country charts, with "Wasn't That a Party?" Later editions of the group have featured various different lineups. The band lost a key member, Jimmy Ferguson, when he died on October 8, 1997. Nonetheless, the group soldiers on, mostly performing their "classic" (older) material.

See also BANJO, FIVE-STRING.

Irvine, Andy (b. 1942) *guitarist and songwriter*

Born in London, England, on June 14, 1942, Irvine first performed as a child actor. During the brief skiffle craze in the mid-1950s, he took up GUITAR, and soon began performing traditional music. He moved to Dublin to pursue an interest in Irish music and culture in the early 1960s. In 1966 he was a founding member of the group Sweeney's Men, which recorded for Transatlantic. Two years later, he traveled to Eastern Europe, learning local musical traditions, and returning to England around 1970. In 1972 he joined the original lineup of PLANXTY, the influential Irish revival band, remaining with the group until it folded in 1975. Over the next year he toured with guitarist/songwriter PAUL BRADY, and then from 1978 to 1983 performed with a reunited version of Planxty. During the later 1980s and 1990s, he recorded several solo albums, featuring both traditional songs and ballads and his own compositions. From 1986 to 1989, and again from 1993 on, Irvine has also performed with the group Patrick Street.

Ives, Burl (1909–1995) *actor and singer*

Born on June 14, 1909 in Jasper County, Illinois, Ives first heard traditional songs and tunes from his parents. He left home as a teenager, seeking work as an actor and singer; by 1937 he had worked his way to New York City, and within a year was acting on Broadway and singing in local clubs. His 1940 hit version of the traditional song "Wayfaring Stranger" led to a job hosting a radio program of the same name on the CBS network. After World War II, he began recording, first for the small Stinson label, then for Decca, scoring a pop hit in 1948 with "Blue Tail Fly." He then signed with Columbia, and more hits followed. In 1951 his recording of the folksong "On Top of Old Smokey" made the top 10 on the pop charts, and a year later he returned to the Decca label for more albums and singles. Unlike some other folksingers such as PETE SEEGER, Ives cooperated with the House Un-American Activities Committee (HUAC) hearings, and so his career was unaffected by his association with leftwing causes in the 1930s and 1940s. Ives also began to enjoy success in the movies, notably playing Big Daddy in the 1958 film of Tennessee Williams's *Cat on a Hot Tin Roof* (although his Oscar that year for best supporting actor came for his role in another film, *The Big Country*).

In the early 1960s Ives turned to recording country-flavored music, scoring top pop and country hits with "A Little Bitty Tear" in 1961 and "Funny Way of Laughin' " a year later, which earned him a Grammy Award. He mostly focused on acting through the balance of the decade, then returned to recording topical folk music in the later 1960s. Ives recorded more sporadically over the next years, in country, gospel, and children's music styles. He retired from performing in 1979, and died on April 14, 1995, in Anacortes, Washington.

Jackson, Aunt Molly (1880–1960) *singer*

The daughter of a coal miner, Mary Magdalene Garland was born in Clay County, Kentucky. As a professional midwife, she worked with many mining families, and her own life was affected by many personal tragedies, including serious injuries to her father and brother and the deaths of another brother, her husband, and son. She was first jailed for union activities when she was 10 years old, and by 1936 was run out of her mountain home by vigilantes. She was befriended by folklorist Alan Lomax and novelist John Steinbeck, who helped organize concerts in New York and Washington to raise money for miners' causes. In the 1940s she was recorded by Lomax for the Library of Congress.

Jackson took the powerful vocal style of mountain singing and wed it to topical subjects. Her most famous song is "I Am a Union Woman (Join the CIO)," which became a battle cry for unions in many different industries. Many of her songs were tinged with a bluesy undertone, reflecting not only the many tragedies in her life but also a defiance of fate. Although Jackson was idolized by urban listeners, she recorded only one commercial record, and was not well known by country performers. Jackson died on September 1, 1960. Her half-sister Sarah Ogan Gunning and half-brother Jim Garland continued to perform topical songs on the folk circuit through the 1960s and 1970s.

See also LOMAX, JOHN AND ALAN.

Jansch, Bert (b. 1943) *guitarist and songwriter*

Born on November 3, 1943, in Glasgow, Scotland, Jansch has had a long career on the British folk scene, both as a solo artist and as a member of the influential folk-jazz-rock group PENTANGLE. By the early 1960s Jansch was playing GUITAR and performing his own songs in small London clubs. He was signed to the folk label Transatlantic in 1965, recording his first album in one sitting using a borrowed guitar. He soon began playing duets with fellow fingerpicking guitarist JOHN RENBOURN, and the two released the influential instrumental album *Bert & John* in 1966. Grouping with singer Jaqui McShee, bassist Danny Thompson, and percussionist Tony Cox, the quintet formed the FOLK-ROCK group Pentangle, which had an initial run from 1967 to 1971. The group innovatively mixed traditional British songs and ballads with original compositions and showed the influence of jazz as well as world music. Meanwhile, Jansch continued to record solo albums focusing on his own guitar work.

After the first Pentangle lineup disbanded, Jansch reverted to a solo act, recording in a singer/songwriter style through the mid-1970s, and then returning to more guitar-instrumental work toward the end of the decade. Since then, he has continued to record and perform, although with less overall impact than in his initial career, and has also performed with various versions of Pentangle, usually involved McShee, and usually playing in a more folk-rock style than the original group.

Jarrell, Tommy (1901–1985) *fiddle player*

Born Thomas Jefferson Jarrell in Round Peak, North Carolina, on March 1, 1901, Jarrell came from a musical family; his father, Ben, was a fine fiddler well known in the Galax, Virginia–Mt. Airy, North Carolina, region. In 1927 Ben recorded as a member of Da Costa Woltz's Southern Broadcasters, a local string band. In addition to admiring his father's fiddling, Tommy learned from older fiddlers in the area, including two Civil War veterans, Pet McKinney and Zack Paine, and banjoist Charlie Lowe who was also associated with his father.

Tommy was "discovered" in the 1960s after years of working as a manual laborer in the mountains and performing locally. On many of these recordings, Tommy was accompanied by another banjo player, FRED COCKERHAM. While Tommy also played a simple style of old-time banjo, Fred also doubled on FIDDLE, but his fiddling was strongly influenced by more modern players such as FIDDLIN' ARTHUR SMITH, and so had a jazzier feel to it.

When the old-time revival blossomed in the 1970s, Tommy became a role model to many young aspiring musicians. He opened his home to hundreds of players, appeared regularly at festivals, and recorded widely. Besides his excellent fiddle playing, Tommy was a talented singer, whose expressive vocals added much to his performances. He died on January 28, 1985. Tommy's son, B. F. (for Benjamin Franklin, named for his grandfather), has performed as a bluegrass fiddler, carrying the family's musical tradition into a third generation.

See also BANJO, FIVE-STRING.

Jenkins, Reverend Andrew (1885–1956)
singer and songwriter

Andrew Jenkins was born partially blind in Jenkinsburg, Georgia, on November 26, 1885. Little is known of Jenkins's early life, although he apparently mastered a number of musical instruments by his early 20s, including GUITAR, MANDOLIN, banjo, and HARMONICA. He became a Holiness minister in Atlanta in 1910, and nine years later married his second wife, who came from a musically talented family. By this time he had lost his sight entirely. Jenkins and family became regular performers on Atlanta's Station WSB from the time it opened in 1922 (they were among the very earliest country performers on radio) and then recorded for a number of years.

Jenkins composed much of their material, including many songs that have entered the country tradition, such as "God Put a Rainbow in the Clouds" and "Billy the Kid." His most popular composition was "The Death of Floyd Collins," which was based on the true story of a young man who was exploring the caverns near Mammoth Cave in 1925 when he tragically died in a cave-in. When it was recorded by early country star Vernon Dalhart, it became one of the most popular of all country 78s, long after the actual event was forgotten. Jenkins did not record after the 1920s; he died in 1956.

See also BANJO, FIVE-STRING.

Jenkins and Sherrill

DeWitt "Snuffy" Jenkins, (banjo, GUITAR, vocal; b. Harris, North Carolina, October 27, 1908–April 30, 1990) started playing banjo to accompany his brother Verl, a fiddler. The two added a guitarist-cousin to their duo and became the Jenkins String Band, broadcasting on radio out of Charlotte beginning in 1934. Two years later, Snuffy joined the successful group led by J. E. MAINER, the Mountaineers, recording with them through 1938 and performing over station WIS in Columbia, South Carolina.

Mainer took a more lucrative radio job elsewhere in 1939, leaving his backup group to fend for themselves. Announcer Byron Parker, who went by the moniker "The Old Hired Hand," took over the band's leadership that year, and a new player, Homer Lee "Pappy" Sherrill (fiddle, vocal; b. Sherrill's Ford, near Hickory, North Carolina, March 23, 1915–November 30, 2001), joined the band. Sherrill had played fiddle since age seven, making his radio debut six years later, and had since worked with a number of popular local groups.

Under Parker's leadership, the group was renamed the WIS Hillbillies. With varied membership, they continued to perform over the radio and made recordings in 1940 and 1946. In 1948 Parker died, and Jenkins and Sherrill took over the band, which they named the Hired Hands in Parker's memory. Along with ex-medicine show comedian Julian "Greasy" Medlin, the group expanded its range to country comedy, and the hillbilly characters of "Snuffy" (Sherrill) and "Pappy" (Jenkins) were born.

The group continued to work on WIS radio and then television through the 1950s. With the FOLK REVIVAL of the early 1960s, they were "discovered" and recorded by Harry Oster on his Folk Lyric label. This led to engagements at folk and bluegrass festivals and further recordings in the early 1970s for Rounder. Although the band continued to work through the 1980s, Snuffy's health began to deteriorate, and vocalist/guitarist Harold Lucas, along with his son banjoist Randy, took over as leaders of the band. A final Old Homestead album was issued in 1989, but it was a sad reflection of the duo's earlier work.

See also BANJO, FIVE-STRING; FIDDLE.

Jim and Jesse

James Monroe McReynolds ("Jim"; vocal, GUITAR; b. February 13, 1927–December 31, 2002), and Jesse Lester McReynolds (vocal, MANDOLIN; b. July 9, 1929) were born in Coeburn, Virginia. Their musical pedigree is impressive: their fiddling grandfather led the Bull Mountain Moonshiners, who recorded in 1928 for RCA. The young boys first performed over local radio in 1947, as well as making some recordings, signing with Capitol in the early 1950s. Their career was briefly interrupted when Jesse was drafted to serve in the Korean conflict, but picked up steam after his discharge in 1954. They returned to radio work, this time on Knoxville's famous *Tennessee Barn Dance* program, leading their group the Virginia Boys. Signing with Epic Records in 1962, they had a series of chart successes beginning

with 1964's "Cotton Mill Man," followed by their biggest chart hit "Diesel On My Tail." These recordings prominently featured the traditional harmonizing of the brothers, along with Jesse's distinctive mandolin playing.

Through the 1970s, 1980s, and 1990s, Jim and Jesse rode the crest of the bluegrass revival, performing at festivals throughout the United States and the world. In 1994 the brothers became members of the *Grand Ole Opry,* and began adding band backing—including electric guitar, bass, and drums—from the house band to their numbers. This backup is reflected on their most recent recordings for the small Pinecastle label. The duo continued to perform until Jim's death at the end of 2002.

Johnson Mountain Boys, The

The Johnson Mountain Boys were formed in reaction to the great popularity of "progressive" bluegrass in the late 1970s. They wished to return the music to its earlier roots, and emulated bands like the Stanley Brothers, Bill Monroe, and Flatt and Scruggs in their dress, music, and stage presentation. The band featured guitarist Dudley Connell on lead vocals, supported by David McLaughlin on MANDOLIN, Eddie Stubbs on FIDDLE, Richard Underwood on banjo, and Marshall Wilborn on bass. As the band became more mature through the 1980s, they let their own personalities flavor the music more, as well as showing off to good effect their instrumental and vocal virtuosity. Although they officially disbanded in 1988, they have come out of retirement occasionally to perform again. Stubbs remains active as a popular bluegrass-country music DJ in the Washington, D.C., area.

See also BANJO, FIVE-STRING.

Johnstons, The

The Irish vocal group the Johnstons was another family act in the style of the CLANCY BROTHERS, initially consisting of siblings Adrienne, Luci, and Michael Johnston. Originally from the Boyne River valley, the siblings settled in Dublin in the early 1960s and began working local folk clubs. They scored their first hit with their British number one pop cover of EWAN MACCOLL's contemporary ballad "The Traveling People." In Dublin they hired multi-instrumentalist MICK MOLONEY, who brought in another talented instrumentalist, PAUL BRADY, to join the group in 1967 (at the same time, brother Michael dropped out). This was the most successful lineup, thanks to the added punch brought to the band by Moloney's and Brady's instrumental work. Both were also talented vocalists and Brady was beginning his songwriting career. The group moved to recording more contemporary material, and settled in London. Luci left in 1969, and Moloney followed three years later; the remaining duo of Adrienne and Paul Brady soldiered on until 1974. Adrienne was killed in somewhat mysterious circumstances in 1975. Moloney and Brady have gone on to distinguished careers in Irish traditional music, although Brady has turned his attention primarily to songwriting since the early 1980s.

Jones, Bessie (1902–1984) *singer*

Bessie Jones was born in Smithville, Georgia, on the Georgia Sea Islands, on February 8, 1902. Originally a large plantation, the Sea Islands were captured by Union troops in the early years of the Civil War, and the remaining slave population remained there afterward as free farmers. Much of the African culture, including the Gullah language, was maintained there, and a rich tradition of harmony singing also survived. Jones was a key practitioner of this style, first recorded in the 1950s by visiting folklorists, including Alan Lomax. She formed the Georgia Sea Island Singers in the early 1960s, who traveled widely performing at folk festivals and at clubs and on college campuses, spreading this unique unaccompanied singing style around the country. Many of her most popular albums were aimed at children, as the traditional singing games and dances from the Sea Islands were uniquely suited to young listeners. A collection of her songs, stories, and children's games was published in 1981 called *Step It Down,* which was coauthored by folklorist/song collector Bess Lomax Hawes. Jones died in Brunswick, Georgia, on her beloved Sea Islands, on September 4, 1984.

See also LOMAX, JOHN AND ALAN.

![musical notation with letter k]

Kahn, Si (b. 1944) *activist and singer*

Si Kahn was born on April 23, 1944, in Boston, Massachusetts. His father was a rabbi and activist, the head of the national Hillel organization. Kahn's family moved from Boston to a small Pennsylvania town and then, in 1959, to Washington, D.C., where

Si Kahn in the late 1970s (Courtesy Flying Fish Records)

he discovered the Library of Congress's ARCHIVE OF AMERICAN FOLK SONG. Returning to Boston to attend Harvard College, Kahn was exposed to more folk music in the vibrant scene around Harvard Square's Club 47, and heard social-protest music when he traveled south in the mid-1960s to participate in the growing CIVIL RIGHTS MOVEMENT. Kahn began writing his own protest songs, and in the early 1970s signed to record an album for the progressive Appalachian cooperative recording label, June Appal. On this record he worked for the first time with hammer dulcimer player John McCutcheon; the two would later collaborate on songs. In 1979 Kahn signed with Chicago-based Flying Fish label, and recorded six albums for them through 1991. A children's record, produced by CATHY FINK, was released in 1993. He has continued to record and tour through the 1990s and the early 21st century.

See also DULCIMER (HAMMERED).

Kazee, Buell (1900–1976) *banjoist and singer*

Buell Kazee was born in Burton Fork, Kentucky, on August 29, 1900. Unlike many other mountain musicians, Kazee was college educated, eventually becoming an ordained minister. His banjo playing was fairly restrained, as were his vocals, but he did record many classics of the American folk repertoire from 1926 to 1930, including the folk ballad "Wagonner's Lad." He also recorded two series of humorous skits, one recounting a typical backwoods election day and the other called

"A Mountain Boy Makes His First Record," which played up his rural roots. Perhaps because Kazee was more educated, his singing style was fairly simple, without much of the ornamentation or intensity that marked other mountain performers. Kazee's relaxed vocals and clear enunciation were two factors that made his records popular, particularly among other folk music collectors. An ordained Missionary Baptist minister, Kazee abandoned his "career" as an entertainer when the Depression led his record label, Brunswick, to close down.

Kazee was "rediscovered" during the FOLK REVIVAL years, and made an album for Folkways Records that showed that his style was little changed over the decades. He also occasionally performed at folk festivals. He died on August 31, 1976.

See also BANJO, FIVE-STRING.

Keen, Robert Earl (b. 1956) *singer and songwriter*

Born in Houston, Texas, on January 11, 1956, Keen is the son of an attorney and oil speculator, and grew up in upper-middle-class luxury in Houston. His parents had a large collection of folk and country recordings, including Marty Robbins's *Gunfighter* album, which inspired the teenage Keen to begin writing narrative poems. While attending Texas A&M University in the mid-1970s, he met Lyle Lovett, and began setting his poems to music. Both Lovett and Keen went to Nashville in the early 1980s, but only Lovett found major label interest. Keen worked menial jobs while he recorded a series of albums for the country-folk label Sugar Hill.

Not to be dissuaded, Keen returned to his native Texas, where he had a strong cult following. His career was given a significant boost when the Highwaymen (aka Johnny Cash, Willie Nelson, Waylon Jennings, and Kris Kristofferson) selected his "The Road Goes on Forever" as the title cut for their third album. In 1996 he was signed to Arista Texas, a new label trying to cash in on the "Alt-Texas" country phenomenon. He recorded several albums, including a song cycle called *Walking*

Distance in 1998. He has continued to record and tour in the early 2000s.

Keith, Bill (b. 1939) *banjoist*

Born William Bradford Keith in Brockton, Massachusetts—a suburb of Boston—on December 20, 1939, Keith first took up tenor banjo to play Dixieland style music during his high school years, but he was soon sucked into the vibrant folk music revival scene of the Boston area. While attending Amherst College, he befriended another young folk musician, Jim Rooney, and the pair soon began performing as a duo. Influenced by PETE SEEGER, he switched to five-string banjo and learned to pick in what was then called "Scruggs style" (after bluegrass banjoist Earl Scruggs), learning the rudiments from Seeger's book. In the early 1960s Keith and Rooney were active figures in the Boston folk music scene. They recorded a locally produced album in 1962 that was picked up by the national folk/jazz label Prestige. Keith briefly played with bluegrass legend Bill Monroe in 1963; Monroe was impressed with his innovative banjo picking, and recorded his arrangement of "Sailor's Hornpipe." Soon after, Keith gave up bluegrass to play with JIM KWESKIN's Jug Band, a 1960s FOLK-REVIVAL group, and then took up pedal steel guitar, reuniting with Rooney to record as the Blue Velvet Band, featuring fiddler Greene and banjoist Eric Weissberg, on an album of country standards.

Keith returned as a banjo player in 1972 when DAVID GRISMAN formed the group MULESKINNER to perform on a television program along with Bill Monroe; the band recorded an album that was highly influential on the progressive bluegrassers of the 1970s. Since then, Keith has recorded more sporadically, issuing a couple of solo albums in the 1980s and 1990s.

See also BANJO, FIVE-STRING.

Kentucky Colonels, The

Clarence, Eric, and Roland White were born in rural Lewiston, Maine, but the family relocated to California in 1954. There, the brothers began performing and even had a local TV show, billed as the *Three Little Country Boys*. By 1958 banjoist Billy Ray Latham had joined the group, now simply known as the Country Boys. Five years later the group was known as the Kentucky Colonels, featuring the final lineup of Clarence and Roland White, Latham, and Roger Bush, sometimes along with fiddler Bobby Sloan; the group was now based in the Los Angeles area. Later, Scotty Stoneman (son of the legendary ERNEST STONEMAN, an early country music star) performed with the band, playing a highly ornamented, flashy, show-style FIDDLE.

Clarence White's life was changed when he heard guitarist DOC WATSON perform at a California folk club, the Ash Grove. Watson had developed a unique style of flatpicking fiddle tunes, with his signature piece being a flashy "Black Mountain Rag." White quickly learned the piece, and adapted the flatpicking style to other traditional tunes and ballads. His lightning-fast picking was featured on the Colonels' third album, *Appalachian Swing*, an all-instrumental outing.

The group folded by 1967–68, when Clarence became increasingly interested in country-rock. He performed on the Byrds's legendary *Sweetheart of the Rodeo* album, and soon after joined the second incarnation of the group, remaining with them through 1972. When mandolinist DAVID GRISMAN and fiddler Richard Greene were asked to form a bluegrass band to perform on a TV show with Bill Monroe, they enlisted White and singer/guitarist PETER ROWAN to form MULESKINNER. The band recorded one album that was highly influential on the development of newgrass later in the decade.

By 1973 White was again performing with his brother Roland in a more traditional bluegrass setting. Sadly, while they were touring, he was struck down by a drunk driver and killed. Roland White soon joined forces with Alan Munde to form COUNTRY GAZETTE, a band that went through many incarnations through the mid-1980s; more

recently, he has been performing with the NASHVILLE BLUEGRASS BAND. Billy Ray Latham and Roger Bush performed in a number of FOLK-ROCK ensembles, including Dillard and Clark and one of the many later versions of The Flying Burrito Brothers.

See also BANJO, FIVE-STRING; MANDOLIN.

Kessinger, Clark W. (1896–1975) *fiddle player*

Kessinger was born in South Hills, West Virginia, in the Kanawha River valley, on July 27, 1896. The region is known for its many talented fiddlers, including Ed Haley, Burl Hammonds, and Franklin George. Having learned the FIDDLE as a youngster, Kessinger went professional sometime after World War I, often accompanied by his nephew, Luke (b. Luches K., Kanawha County, West Virginia, August 21, 1906–May 6, 1944). After working local radio in West Virginia, they were heard by a scout from Brunswick Records, who signed them to the label and named them the Kessinger Brothers. They recorded extensively from 1928 to 1930, and many of their instrumentals sold well for the dime store label.

Kessinger's recording career was ended by the Great Depression, which slowed much recording of country musicians (and indeed crippled the entire recording industry). He continued to play fiddle conventions and to perform on radio and at dances, but made his primary living by painting houses. He played less frequently after Luke died prematurely in 1944, although he continued to perform occasionally.

In the early 1960s he was "discovered" by folklorist/record label owner Ken Davidson, who championed the music of West Virginia on his small Kanawha label. Kessinger began performing again, taking prizes at major fiddler's conventions, including Galax and Union Grove. He eventually recorded four albums for Kanawha and one for Rounder. Kessinger remained active until a stroke in 1971 left him unable to perform; he died four years later, on June 4, 1975.

Kincaid, Bradley (1895–1989) *guitarist and singer*

William Bradley Kincaid was born in Point Leavell, a small town in the backwoods of Kentucky, on July 31, 1895, and was already playing music as a young child. His father was a talented singer and musician, who traded a hunting dog for a GUITAR for his young son. Traditional songs, ballads, and hymns were performed by all the members of his immediate family, and Kincaid could remember performing the minstrel-show song "Liza Up in the 'Simmon Tree" when he was just three years old!

Educational opportunities were scarce in rural America when Kincaid was young. However, a school in Berea, Kentucky, was dedicated to educating mountain youth, as well as preserving the traditional arts and crafts of the Appalachians. Kincaid enrolled at the school at age 19, entering at the sixth grade level, and, except for two years during World War I, remained there until he earned his high school degree. In the late 1920s he relocated to Chicago to attend the YMCA college.

It was through the YMCA that Kincaid had his first radio job as a member of a vocal harmony quartet performing on Chicago's largest radio station, WLS. At that time WLS was also home to the *National Barn Dance.* When the station manager heard that Kincaid knew many traditional folk songs, he invited him to appear on the program to present his traditional repertoire. Kincaid's appearance was an immediate success, and he became a show regular in 1928. WLS was owned and operated by Sears, Roebuck Co., who were immediately flooded by requests for copies of Kincaid's songs. At Sears' urging, Kincaid compiled a series of songbooks, mostly drawing on his memories of the songs that were popular in his youth. At the same time, Sears arranged for his first recording sessions with the Gennett company in the late 1920s. Kincaid continued to record for a number of different labels through the late 1930s.

From the late 1920s through the mid-1950s, Kincaid performed on a variety of radio stations, including Nashville's famous *Grand Ole Opry* program from 1944 to 1949. He also had a touring show. Kincaid bought his own radio station in 1949 so he could continue performing out of his retirement home of Springfield, Ohio. When he "retired" in 1954, he bought a local music store, and soon was performing again. He made recordings in the early 1960s and 1970s, and continued to perform until an automobile accident slowed him down in the mid-1980s. He died on September 23, 1989.

Kingston Trio, The (1956–1967)

The most successful of all the FOLK-REVIVAL groups, the Kingston Trio was formed by three college students, Dave Guard (1934–91), Bob Shane (b. 1934), and Nick Reynolds (b. 1933) in 1957. Shane and Reynolds knew each other from their native Honolulu, and when they first joined with Guard they played Hawaiian and other novelty numbers for frat parties. The group began playing Calypso music—which was then popular thanks to HARRY BELAFONTE's hit recordings—and thus took the name the Kingston Trio after the Bahamian town. Self-taught as musicians and vocalists, the group began to attract local notice, eventually getting bookings at San Francisco's popular Purple Onion club in early 1957 as an opening act; by midyear they were booked for an extended run as the featured performers. This led to a contract with the West Coast–based Capitol label.

The trio was soon booked at upscale clubs around the country while they worked up material for their first album. This initial release yielded a number one pop hit, "Tom Dooley," an old Appalachian folk song that they reworked with a jazzy accompaniment and tight harmony arrangement. Their version was attacked by folk purists, but nonetheless did much to popularize folk music to a wider audience. They landed TV appearances on all of the major variety shows and toured extensively. By 1960 the trio's recordings accounted for 20 percent of Capitol's total sales volume.

Disappointed with the group's more commercial turn, Guard—who had the strongest background in folk music—left in 1961, and was replaced by John Stewart (b. 1939; Stewart was later a singer/songwriter with some success during the mid-1970s). After some initial success, the new group was overshadowed by developments in folk music—the ascent of BOB DYLAN and more politically motivated groups such as PETER, PAUL AND MARY—and the British Invasion on the pop charts. They were dropped by Capitol in 1964 and disbanded three years later. In 1972 Shane formed a "new" Kingston Trio, which, with varying personnel, has performed on the oldies circuit for the last 30-plus years.

Kirkpatrick, John (b. 1947) *accordionist and songwriter*

John Kirkpatrick was born in Chiswick, a suburb of London, England, on August 8, 1947. He began performing as an accompanist for traditional English Morris dancing—a form of ritual dance that has enjoyed a revival of interest since the turn of the 20th century. Playing ACCORDION and concertina, Kirkpatrick attracted the attention of producer/bandleader ASHLEY HUTCHINGS, who asked him to participate in an album of FOLK-ROCK arrangements of Morris dance tunes called *Morris On,* which was released in 1971; at the same time, Kirkpatrick's first solo album was released on the Trailer label. Hutchings and Kirkpatrick then collaborated on *Rattlebone and Ploughjack,* a recording focusing on a variety of English dance music. The two would work together on various projects through the early 1980s, including theatrical productions and performances with Hutching's Albion Band. Kirkpatrick also formed a duo with his then-wife, oboe/hammer dulcimer player Sue Harris, and the two recorded and toured together.

In the late 1970s through mid-1980s, Kirkpatrick often performed in a trio with MARTIN CARTHY and trumpeter Howard Evans; this led to the formation of a band, Brass Monkey, which was active in the mid-to-late 1980s (and revived in the late 1990s). Kirkpatrick also toured with folk-rock guitarist Richard Thompson, playing on many of his 1980s

and early 1990s recordings. All the while, he pursued a solo career as a performer. In the mid-1990s he formed his own folk-rock group, the John Kirkpatrick Band, featuring guitarist Graeme Taylor and other musicians who had been associated with the Albion Band in the past. Kirkpatrick has also composed a number of tunes and songs in a traditional style, many of which have become favorites among folk revivalists.

See also GUITAR; DULCIMER (HAMMERED).

klezmer music

The music of Eastern European, Yiddish-speaking Jewish musicians has enjoyed a revival among folk performers since the mid-1970s. Known as klezmer music—from the Hebrew words *klei zemer,* meaning musical instruments—it is a style made up of many elements, from the gypsy music of Eastern Europe to the jazz and pop sounds of 1920s–1930s America. The original klezmer bands were probably made up of strings, particularly FIDDLES, cellos, and the tsimbl (a stringed zither that is a relative of the American hammered dulcimer). Later, when Jews were forcibly enlisted into local military brigades, they were introduced to brass instruments, FLUTES, clarinets, and other instruments found in military bands. These instruments had worked their way into klezmer ensembles by the early 20th century.

The repertoire of the klezmer band was a diverse mix of Yiddish dance music and song and music from the surrounding cultures. The most common dance was the *frelekh* (which means "lively"). Most dance music was played as part of the wedding ceremony. Besides dance music, the other major instrumental tradition is the *doina.* These pieces are played in a nonrhythmic, singing style, imitating the chanting of the cantor in the synagogue. The instrument's voice soars up and down the scale, exploring different nuances and textures. The *doina* has its roots in Romanian gypsy music.

Many klezmer musicians came to the United States during the great waves of Jewish immigration beginning in the 1880s, as Jews were driven out of

Eastern Europe through mass relocations, loss of land or businesses, and programs of mass extermination. When they arrived in the United States, many found employment in dance bands, and incorporated the sound of jazz and swing music into their playing. Perhaps most famous was the clarinetist/bandleader Dave Tarras, who lived long enough to inspire the first generation of klezmer revivalists. The vibrant Yiddish theater in New York's Lower East Side also nurtured many singing stars, and provided new songs and tunes for the klezmer to perform.

The mid-1970s klezmer revival began with bands such as the Klezmer Conservatory Band in Boston, the Klezmorim in California, and Kapelye in New York City. These groups inspired dozens more, some very traditional, others blending avant-garde, jazz, and rock influences into their style.

See also DULCIMER (HAMMERED).

Koerner, "Spider" John (1938–2002)
producer and songwriter

Spider John Koerner was born and raised in Rochester, New York, and enrolled at the University of Minnesota to study engineering. Recordings of BURL IVES and JOSH WHITE influenced him to take up the GUITAR. After a short stint in the Marine Corps, Koerner settled in San Francisco in the mid-1950s, and then returned to Minnesota in 1959. On the local scene, he met two other blues enthusiasts, HARMONICA player Tony "Little Sun" Glover and 12 string guitarist/vocalist Dave "Snaker" Ray (August 17, 1943–November 28, 2002). The trio began performing at local parties and clubs, and released their first album in 1963 on a small local label. The larger Elektra label bought the rights to this record, and subsequently the trio recorded and toured on the folk-blues revival circuit through the mid-1960s. Koerner began writing his own songs, which were highlighted on the 1969 release, *Running, Jumping, Standing Still,* and he then opened his own studio. One of his early discoveries was blues guitarist/

singer Bonnie Raitt, who recorded her debut 1972 album at Koerner's studio. Koerner also self-released several albums of his own material in the early 1970s.

In 1972, after a final Koerner, Ray, and Glover reunion, Koerner left the music scene, eventually relocating to Denmark. He did not return to recording and performing until the mid-1980s. Since then he has performed and recorded for small folk labels, both as a solo performer and with his old band mates. Ray died of cancer in November 2002.

Kottke, Leo (b. 1945) *guitarist*

Born in Athens, Georgia, on September 11, 1945, Kottke began playing GUITAR at age 11. He discovered such blues performers as Mississippi John Hurt and LEAD BELLY as a teenager, and began emulating their finger-style guitar playing, on both six- and 12-string guitars. Settling in 1969 in the Twin Cities area after a brief stint in the navy and at college, Kottke began playing local coffeehouses, and recorded his debut album for a local label. An uncomfortable singer, Kottke modeled his playing after his idol JOHN FAHEY; when he sent Fahey a copy of his initial album, Fahey invited him to record an instrumental record for his Takoma label. The result, *6 and 12 String Guitar,* issued in 1971, became an instant classic among fingerpicking guitarists. Rather improbably, Kottke was signed to the major label, Capitol, which encouraged him to sing as well as play, and he achieved some commercial success in the early 1970s on record and on tour. From 1976 to 1983 he recorded for Chrysalis, and then moved to the smaller Private Music label. However, troubles with his picking hand led him to cut back considerably on recording and performing from the mid-1980s, although he remains a favorite cult figure. In 2002 Kottke reemerged on a duet album, *Clone,* with Mike Gordon, the bass player for the popular jam-rock band Phish, which helped introduced Kottke to a new audience.

Kweskin, Jim (b. 1940) *performer and singer*
Born on July 18, 1940, Kweskin attended Boston College, where he became involved in the local folk scene. He began playing with bass player Fritz Richmond in a loose-knit band called the Hoppers, playing blues, jazz, pop, and folk material. Richmond left to join the army, and Kweskin performed as a solo act in the Boston area, except for a brief period in the early 1960s when he relocated to San Francisco. On his return in 1962, he began working the club scene again, encountering blues guitarist Geoff Muldaur, among others. Kweskin was approached by the owner of Vanguard Records to record a band album in late 1962, and he enlisted Richmond, Muldaur, and banjo and HARMONICA player Mel Lyman to form his first Jug Band. The group was an immediate hit, thanks to their playful combination of standards and folk tunes. While performing in New York, they met fiddler/vocalist Maria D'Amato, who soon joined the group and married Muldaur. In 1964 Lyman was replaced by banjo player Bill Keith. The band was signed to major label Reprise in 1966, making a final album featuring new member Richard Greene. Kweskin then announced he was breaking up the band, and he joined a mysterious commune run by Mel Lyman. He recorded a few more albums, but then disappeared from the scene for a while.

Kweskin returned to the folk scene as a solo performer in the late 1970s, although by then his earlier work was more or less forgotten. He continued to record and perform sporadically over the next two decades. In early 2000 Kweskin revived his band with fiddler/vocalist Samoa Wilson for touring and recording; his first new album in many years, *Now and Again,* appeared in early 2003.

See also MULDAUR, GEOFF AND MANA.

La Farge, Peter (1931–1965) *performer and songwriter*

Of Native American heritage, Peter La Farge was born in Fountain, Colorado. He was raised on the Tewa reservation until age eight, when he was adopted by writer Oliver La Farge. By age 14 La Farge was singing on local radio and competing in rodeos. Through his interest in Native American and western culture, he began to learn traditional folk songs, mentored by guitarist/singer CISCO HOUSTON. La Farge served in the Korean conflict in the early 1950s, and then returned to performing on the rodeo circuit. However, in 1956 he lost a leg while competing and decided to study acting, first in Chicago, and then moving to New York, looking for work. There he began performing in Greenwich Village.

La Farge became a close friend of several folk performers, including a young BOB DYLAN when he arrived in the city in 1961. Elder statesman PETE SEEGER also took La Farge under his wing, encouraging him in his songwriting. La Farge recorded one album for Columbia in 1962, but then was dropped by the label; the remainder of his recordings appeared on Folkways. Johnny Cash, also on Columbia, heard La Farge's song "The Ballad of Ira Hayes" and was so impressed he built a concept album called *Bitter Tears* on the plight of Native Americans, including many La Farge compositions. Cash's recording of the song was a number-three country hit, despite its antiwar message.

Thanks to that success, La Farge was signed to MGM Records in 1965 to record a country album, but his health began to fail before he could complete it. He was found dead in his New York City apartment on October 27, 1965; his death was officially reported as a stroke, but rumor had it that he committed suicide.

Lavin, Christine (b. 1952) *songwriter*

Born January 2, 1952, Lavin is one of a group of female songwriters of the 1980s who tackled women's issues—particularly troubled relationships with men—head on. She first performed in Greenwich Village in the late 1970s and early 1980s, with her first album, a live recording, appearing in 1981. Many of her songs take a humorous view of the problems of keeping a relationship together in the modern world, including "If You Need Space, Move to Utah" from her second recording, 1983's *Husbands and Wives.* 1984's "Don't Ever Call Your Sweetheart by His Name" ironically focuses on the changing cast of characters in her love life. One of her most popular tongue-in-cheek odes to modern romance is "Sensitive New Age Guys." Her song "Ameba Bop" is the basis for a children's book of the same name released in 2003, and offers a humorous take on protozoan biology. Lavin has also written social-protest songs, notably the anti-Bush anthem "Like Father, Like Son," composed for the 2004 Republican National Convention. To date, she has released 16 solo albums.

From 1990 to 1997 Lavin had a side project with the group Four Bitchin' Babes. She was a founding member along with Patty Larkin, Sally Fingerett,

Christine Lavin at the Philadelphia Folk Festival, early 1980s
(Photo © Larry Sandberg)

and Megon McDonough, specializing in humorous material on feminist issues. The group had various members during Lavin's tenure, and continues to tour and record now that she has left to focus on her solo career.

Lawson, Doyle (b. 1944) *mandolin player and singer*

Born Doyle Wayne Lawson in Kingsport, Tennessee, on April 20, 1944, Lawson's father was a gospel singer who encouraged his young son to sing and play music. The family relocated to Sneedville, Tennessee, when Doyle was nine, and there he befriended a neighbor, JIMMY MARTIN, the great bluegrass guitarist/vocalist. Lawson's first love was the MANDOLIN, but he also learned GUITAR and five-string banjo, and it was as a banjo player that he first worked professionally, joining Martin and his Sunny Mountain Boys in 1963. After working with Martin for seven months, he relocated to Louisville, Kentucky, where he worked with various bands. In 1966 he joined with J. D. CROWE, working as a

guitarist with Crowe's Kentucky Mountain Boys, and singing tenor harmonies; he remained with Crowe through 1971.

In 1971 he joined the second incarnation of the COUNTRY GENTLEMEN, led by original member Charlie Waller. Lawson finally got to play mandolin, and helped establish the new version of this venerable band as one of the best on the bluegrass circuit throughout the late 1970s. In 1977 he also recorded his first mandolin solo record, supported by many other well-known names in blue and newgrass, including JERRY DOUGLAS, KENNY BAKER, and Crowe.

In 1979 Lawson formed the first version of his own band, Quicksilver. Unique among progressive bluegrass bands, they decided to alternately issue secular and gospel albums; surprisingly, the gospel albums were far more popular, and the group became known for their a cappella renditions of traditional and newly written gospel songs.

In 1982 Rounder Records organized a kind of bluegrass "super session," enlisting Lawson, Crowe, guitarist/vocalist TONY RICE, fiddler Bobby Hicks, and bassist Todd Phillips to rerecord classic bluegrass songs. Issued as *The Bluegrass Album*, it was a very successful offering, and was subsequently followed up by several more albums and tours through the 1990s.

Throughout the 1980s and 1990s Quicksilver went through various personnel lineups while maintaining its mix of gospel and bluegrass material. Lawson's imaginative mandolin playing and strong tenor lead has made him one of the most distinctive voices in the bluegrass revival. And his love of gospel hymns has set him apart from many others, and won him an audience beyond the limits of bluegrass.

See also BANJO, FIVE-STRING; FIDDLE.

Lead Belly (Huddie Ledbetter) (1888–1949) *influential blues guitarist and songwriter*

Huddie Ledbetter was born on a plantation near Mooringsport, Louisiana, on January 15, 1888. His father was a sharecropper, meaning he rented his land and paid for supplies to the land owner; share-cropping was in a sense a continuation of slavery, because the black farmers had little chance of making enough profit to buy their own farms. Nonetheless, Huddie's father was able to purchase a farm in Harrison County, Texas, when Huddie was about five years old. He briefly attended school between the ages of eight and 12, and then went to work on his father's farm. He learned to play a number of instruments as a child, including button ACCORDION and, when he was about 15, obtained his first GUITAR. A year later, he moved to Shreveport, Louisiana, on his own, supporting himself by playing for parties, dances, and on the streets. He worked as a traveling musician until he was about 20, when an illness forced him to return home to his family. There he married, and then settled in Dallas, Texas, around 1910.

Around 1912 Ledbetter met Blind Lemon Jefferson, another blues musician, and the two paired up as a team. At about the same time, Huddie switched to 12-string guitar, perhaps because of its greater volume or as a contrast to Jefferson's six-string. The two traveled around the region, playing wherever they could. Ledbetter had his first brush with the law in 1915, when he was convicted of carrying a pistol and sentenced to 30 days on the chain gang; he escaped, moving to Bowie County, Texas, where he farmed under the name of Walter Boyd, while continuing to play for dances and parties. At one party in December 1917, he was embroiled in a fight and ended up murdering one man and assaulting another; this led to two convictions, with a minimum term of seven years. In prison he was nicknamed Lead Belly because of his physical stamina and ability to work long hours on the chain gang.

Lead Belly was a popular entertainer, even in prison, and news of his singing and songwriting abilities soon spread. In 1924 he wrote a song requesting a pardon from Texas governor Pat Neff, and played it for him; a year later, Neff pardoned the singer. On his release, Lead Belly first settled in Houston, but then returned to his original home-town of Mooringsport. There, in 1930, he was convicted of knifing a man and sentenced to six to 10 years in Louisiana's notorious Angola Prison Farm. The farm was famous—and dreaded—among the local population for its inhuman conditions.

In July 1933 folklorists John A. and Alan Lomax arrived at Angola, hoping to discover traditional singers. Lead Belly was a natural for them, and they recorded him initially that year and more extensively a year later. Lead Belly again wrote a song requesting his pardon, this time addressed to Louisiana governor O. K. Allen, but his sentence was soon completed. Soon after, Lead Belly was employed by the Lomaxes as a chauffeur for their field trips, and they brought him north to appear at some lecture-demonstrations they were giving on folk music. The Lomaxes also arranged for his first recordings to be made, for the budget label ARC, in early 1935, although only a few were issued at the time. A year later, the Lomaxes published *Negro Folk Songs Sung by Lead Belly*, and the singer moved to New York to better capitalize on his newfound fame. He began performing in local clubs and at concerts, mostly promoted by the folk music community, and was befriended by WOODY GUTHRIE, PETE SEEGER, and other folk performers. However, another stabbing incident occurred in 1939, leading to an eight-month prison term for the singer.

Over the next few years, Lead Belly recorded for a number of labels, including one session with the Golden Gate Quartet for RCA Victor in 1940, and a series of less formal sessions for MOSES ASCH from 1941 to 1944. From 1944 to 1946 he lived on the West Coast, recording for Capitol. He then returned to New York; in 1948 jazz scholar Frederic Ramsey Jr. obtained an early tape recorder and recorded lengthy sessions of Lead Belly singing and discussing his life and music. These were issued in 1952 in their entirety on Folkways Records as *Lead Belly's Last Sessions*.

Lead Belly's health began to fail in 1948, and while touring France in early 1949 he was diagnosed with Lou Gehrig's disease (ALS). He returned home to New York, but by the year's end passed away on December 6, 1949. Ironically, soon after, Pete Seeger and the WEAVERS had a major hit with Lead Belly's song "GOODNIGHT, IRENE," which led to renewed interest in his songs and recordings. The growing FOLK REVIVAL of the later 1950s and 1960s led to reissues of his recordings, and many guitarists emulating his style.

See also LOMAX, JOHN AND ALAN.

Ledford, Lily May (1917–1985) banjoist and fiddler

Born in tiny Pilot, Kentucky, on March 17, 1917, Ledford began performing on a homemade banjo with a groundhog hide for a tone head when she was seven. She took up the FIDDLE at age 11, and by the time she was 17 was fiddling for tips at the local train station. A local businessman arranged for her to travel north, where she won a talent contest in 1936 and a place on the influential WLS National Barn Dance. Producer John Lair encouraged the youngster to switch to banjo, adapt her wardrobe to stereotypical mountain garb, and perform the older traditional songs of her youth.

A year after Ledford came to Chicago, Lair moved to Kentucky to produce the new Renfro Valley Barn Dance radio program, taking most of his major performers with him. He had the brainstorm of creating an all-women's band in a backwoods mold. He christened the group the Coon Creek Girls, featuring Ledford on fiddle and banjo, her sister Rosa Charlotte "Rosie" (1915–76) on guitar, mandolinist Esther "Violet" Koehler, and fiddler/bass player Evelyn "Daisy" Lange. The group was an immediate sensation, becoming one of the most popular acts on the new program. By 1939 Lily's sister Minnie Lena (1922–87), known as "Black-Eyed Susan," joined the act, which was now a family trio since Koehler and Lange had both quit, and the group continued to perform with various personnel for another 18 years.

Ledford was married to Glenn Pennington for 22 years from 1945 to 1967; son J. P. led the pop group Exile in the 1970s, scoring a major hit with 1978's "Kiss You All Over," and then switched to a country

sound in the 1980s with hits "She's a Miracle" and "Woke up in Love." Ledford herself returned to performing in the 1970s on the old-time music circuit, reintroducing her theme song, the traditional mountain song "Banjo Picking Girl." She performed sporadically through the end of the decade. She died on July 14, 1985.

See also BANJO, FIVE-STRING.

Leventhal, Harold (b. 1919) music promoter and manager

Harold Leventhal was born in New York City. In the late 1930s Leventhal worked as a song plugger for Irving Berlin Music, hoping to encourage popular singers to perform songs owned by the company. He also participated in various left-wing and progressive causes, a lifelong passion for him. After World War II he became aware of the growing folk scene in New York City, and particularly admired a new group he heard at the Village Vanguard, the WEAVERS. Because of his sympathies for their politics and also his connections with the music business, he became their manager. From that connection, he began a long association with PETE SEEGER, whom he continues to manage, and in 1954 was hired by WOODY GUTHRIE's family to handle his recordings and music. Leventhal was one of the few promoters in the 1950s and early 1960s who defied the blacklist, and without his efforts Seeger undoubtedly would not have been able to continue his career through this difficult period.

Leventhal became a major folk promoter in New York City in the late 1950s and 1960s, producing the legendary memorial concerts following Guthrie's death, among many other programs. He also entered film production with ARLO GUTHRIE's film Alice's Restaurant in 1969, and has produced Guthrie's annual Carnegie Hall Thanksgiving Day concert for more than three decades. Leventhal has also produced theatrical shows and the documentary film on the Weavers, Wasn't That a Time? Into his 80s, Leventhal has continued to manage Seeger and the Guthrie family interests. With Dave Marsh, he edited a collection of Guthrie's unpublished writings and drawings, titled *Pastures of Plenty,* in 1990. In 2002 he was honored with a Folk Alliance Lifetime Achievement Award.

Lewis, Laurie (b. 1950) *singer and songwriter*

Born in Long Beach, California, on September 28, 1950, Lewis was first introduced to bluegrass music in 1965 through the early progressive band, the DILLARDS. In 1973 she formed her first band, the Phantoms of the Opry, playing bass, and later was fiddler for the GOOD OL' PERSONS from 1975 to 1977. Through the rest of the 1970s, she worked as a studio musician for a number of Bay-area folkies, including feminist singer/songwriter Holly Near, besides running her own instrument repair shop.

In 1983 Lewis formed a new backup band, the Grant Street Stringband, issuing her first solo album with this group three years later. A number of her original compositions were recorded by new country artists, including "Love Chooses You," which was covered by Kathy Mattea. Legendary country singer Patsy Montana recorded her "The Cowgirl's Song," which was selected as the official theme song of the Cowgirl Hall of Fame. Lewis's albums featured her new-styled honky-tonk singing on her own country-folk ballads, along with her bluegrass-flavored fiddling. In 1988 she was a member of the all-female Blue Rose band along with CATHY FINK and other "all-star" women musicians, and she also has continued to perform as a duet with Kathy Kallick, another Good Ol' Person alumna. In the early 1990s Lewis began doing session work in Nashville for a number of new country acts. In 1994 Lewis was involved in a bad automobile accident while touring with Grant Street, but luckily recovered and continued to record and tour through the decade's end.

Lewis Family, The

Roy "Pop" Lewis Sr. (b. Pickens, South Carolina, September 22, 1905) and his wife, Pauline, are the sires of the Lewis family dynasty. Their four sons—Wallace (b. Lincoln County, Georgia, July 6, 1928), Talmadge, Esley, and "Little Roy" (b. February 24, 1942)—were the original group members, beginning to perform locally in the late 1940s as the Lewis Brothers. Eventually, father Roy Sr. joined in on bass, and Esley and Talmadge retired, and various Lewis daughters joined the act. The group first recorded for the tiny Sullivan label in 1951, and then joined up with legendary country promoter/record executive Don Pierce. Pierce would bring them to his Starday label in 1957, where they would continue to record through 1970. They have since recorded primarily for Christian-oriented labels.

In 1954 the family launched a live bluegrass/gospel TV show, broadcast out of Augusta, Georgia, which continued on the air for 38 years, making it probably the longest running gospel show. In 1990 they began a tradition of a family homecoming bluegrass festival that they sponsor in their hometown of Lincolntown.

Lightfoot, Gordon (b. 1938) *singer and songwriter*

Gordon Lightfoot was born in the small town of Orillia, in the province of Ontario, Canada, on November 17, 1938. He was raised in the back country north of Toronto, and by his teen years was working in local rock and pop bands. In search of a musical career he traveled to Los Angeles in 1958, studying at a small college. There he heard folk performers such as PETE SEEGER and began writing his own songs. Returning to Canada in the early 1960s, Lightfoot began performing at Toronto area coffeehouses. He recorded for a small local label, but these releases saw very little distribution. However, the popular folk duo IAN & SYLVIA heard his songs, and they had hits with his "For Lovin' Me" and "Early Morning Rain"; PETER, PAUL AND MARY also covered "Rain," and this led to their agent, ALBERT GROSSMAN, signing Lightfoot.

Lightfoot had his greatest period of success in the early to mid-1970s, scoring a top 20 pop hit with "If You Could Read My Mind" in 1971 and a number one record, "Sundown," in 1974. His laid-back vocals, and soft pop-rock accompaniment, made him an attractive performer for mainstream radio. After the 1970s, however, Lightfoot was less active, although he did stage a comeback as a performer in the 1990s. Lightfoot suffered from an abdominal hemorrhage in 2002, which left him in a coma for several weeks, but miraculously returned to recording, releasing a new album in 2004.

Lilly Brothers

Everett (b. Charles Everett, July 1, 1924) and B (b. Mitchell Burt, December 15, 1921) were born and raised in rural Clear Creek, West Virginia, where they heard traditional mountain music from birth. They were also exposed to the popular brother acts of the 1930s, particularly the Blue Sky Boys and the Monroe Brothers, through recordings and radio. Emulating the sound and style of these acts, B took up GUITAR and Everett MANDOLIN and they made their professional debut on *The Old Farm Hour* broadcast out of Charleston in the late 1930s. They continued to work as a duet and in various groups through the mid-1940s on various radio stations in the South.

In 1945 they were hired by a major radio station, WNOX out of Knoxville, Tennessee, to play on a show hosted by Lynn Davis and Molly O'Day. Three years later, they moved up in the country world by joining WWVA's *Wheeling* [West Virginia] *Jamboree,* where they first met a young Texas-born FIDDLE player, Benjamin "Tex" Logan, who would later work with them when they were based in Boston.

After two years with the Jamboree, the brothers quit in a financial dispute and for a while gave up their act. Everett joined the new Flatt and Scruggs group in 1951, recording and touring with them as mandolinist and harmony singer for about a year. A call from old friend Tex Logan, who had relocated to Boston, where he was working with a young banjo player named Don Stover, convinced the brothers to reunite and move to the northern city in 1952. The group eventually became the house band at a club that catered to both country and bluegrass fans as well as to young college students who made up the core of the FOLK-REVIVAL audience. Albums on the folk labels Folkways and Prestige International helped broaden their audience base and made them one of the most influential groups in the first bluegrass revival.

The Lilly Brothers continued to perform with Stover and Logan through early 1970 in Boston, making them one of the most stable lineups in bluegrass history. In 1970 Everett's son died in a car crash, and he decided to leave Boston. From that point on the band would reunite on occasion for tours and recordings throughout the late 1970s. In the 1980s Everett worked primarily with another son, Mark, in a band called Clear Creek Crossin'; B retired from music making.

Lloyd, A. L. (1908–1982) *performer and author*

Albert Lancaster Lloyd, known as "Bert," was born on February 29, 1908, in London, England. Lloyd was orphaned by the age of 15, and so shipped out to Australia to work as a sheep farmer. He became interested in traditional music there and began collecting songs during the 1920s as well as singing. He returned to England in the early 1930s and became involved in folk music and radical politics. He eventually was hired by the BBC to work on documentaries, and then he worked as a journalist.

Lloyd became prominent as a folk music performer during the 1950s. Along with EWAN MACCOLL, he was probably the best-known performer of English songs and ballads, recording prolifically for many labels, including the British Topic label, and in the United States Riverside, Tradition, Prestige, and other labels. Lloyd was made artistic director of Topic Records in the mid-1950s and brought many young folk performers to the label, as well as providing documentary notes for many of the label's albums. In 1967 he published the landmark book *Folk Song in England,* which remains one of the most important studies of traditional British song.

Lloyd's unique falsetto singing style, with his trademark vibrato, makes him instantly recognizable as a performer, and many others on the British FOLK-REVIVAL scene emulated his work. He also set tunes to many traditional song texts, or assembled songs from various texts, which have become the standard versions for the following generations of performers.

Lomax, John (1867–1948) and Alan
(1915–2002) *father and son folklorists*

Born in Goodman, Mississippi, on September 23, 1867, John Avery Lomax was fascinated with the local songs and legends that he heard from his neighbors, family, and friends. When he entered Harvard, he met folklorist George Lyman Kittredge, a noted Shakespeare scholar and collector of folk ballads who encouraged his students to go out among the people and collect their songs. Lomax published his first collection of what he called "cowboy songs" in 1910, with an introduction by naturalist/politician Theodore Roosevelt. This became the source for many so-called cowboy recording stars from the 1930s on, introducing songs that have become veritable chestnuts, such as "Home on the Range."

After working for a while in banking and as a dean at the University of Texas, Lomax took again to the road in 1933, bringing along one of the first portable recording machines (it recorded on discs and was powered off the battery of his car); his 18-year-old son, Alan (January 15, 1915–July 19, 2002) accompanied him. One of their most famous stops was to the notorious state prison farm in Angola, Louisiana, where they discovered a talented guitarist named Huddie Ledbetter, later famous as LEAD BELLY. Ledbetter became the Lomaxes' driver, and was later brought to New York to become one of the stars of the first FOLK REVIVAL. Meanwhile, the Lomaxes published several more collections, including 1934's *American Ballads and Folk Songs,* 1941's *Our Singing Country,* and 1947's *Folk Song, U.S.A.* The two became directors of the Library of Congress's ARCHIVE OF AMERICAN FOLK SONG in 1937; Alan Lomax also became active in producing radio programs and recordings of traditional folk musicians beginning in the late 1940s. The elder Lomax starred in his own radio series, *The Ballad Hunter,* shortly before his death on January 26, 1948. In the late 1950s Alan was among the first to take stereo equipment into the field, producing two large series of recordings of traditional country and blues music from the South, issued by Atlantic and Prestige Records.

From the mid-1960s on Alan Lomax became increasingly involved in the study of what he called "cantometrics," an attempt to study the links between traditional music from around the world. Working out of Columbia University, he became more active in the academic field rather than in popular folklore. In the early 1990s he produced a series of programs on world music and dance for public television, and also has written his memoirs of recording blues musicians in the South in the 1930s, 1940s, and 1950s. Later in the decade, the Lomax Archives arranged for Rounder Records to issue his complete recordings; already dozens of CDs have appeared, with more to come.

Lulu Belle and Scotty *radio personalities*

Lulu Belle (b. Myrtle Eleanor Cooper, Boone, North Carolina, December 23, 1913–February 8, 1999) began performing as a soloist in her teen years, successfully auditioning for a role with the popular *National Barn Dance* radio show out of Chicago when she was 19. She first performed country comedy bits (playing a backwoods hayseed in the manner of Minnie Pearl) with popular entertainer Red Foley, and then the station paired her with another newcomer, Scott Wiseman (Scott Greene Wiseman, November 8, 1909–January 31, 1981), nicknamed

"Skyland Scotty." Their radio partnership blossomed into a romance, and the duo married.

Lulu Belle and Scotty became one of the most popular acts on the *Barn Dance,* and thanks to their considerable exposure, recorded prolifically for many different labels. They performed a mix of traditional and more recent compositions, leaning toward sentimental and heart songs, many composed by Wiseman to suit the duo's romantic image; their best-remembered song was "Remember Me." From the late 1940s to their retirement from performing in 1958, they expanded on their radio work to host a local, Chicago-area musical-variety television program.

In the late 1950s, sensing the onslaught of rock and roll, the duo retired to North Carolina, where Lulu Belle became a successful local politician and Scotty took up teaching. After Scotty's death, Lulu Belle remarried and took the name Lulu Belle Wiseman Stamey.

Lunn, Robert (1912–1966) *singer and guitarist*

Robert Rainey Lunn was born in Franklin, Tennessee, on November 28, 1912, and began performing as a teenager in vaudeville, and then worked during the early 1930s over radio. Besides singing and playing the GUITAR, he also did imitations and worked as a ventriloquist. In late 1933 Lunn came to Nashville, where he began performing at the posh Hermitage Hotel. His signature number was a "Talking Blues." Although he became most closely associated with this song, it probably was originated by an earlier singer/comedian named Chris Bouchillon, who recorded a "Talking Blues" in 1926 for Columbia; it was a strong seller, leading to several followups. Lunn was heard by a WSM executive and invited to perform on the *Grand Ole Opry* in early 1934.

Lunn joined the *Opry* in March 1934, remaining with the show for 28 years (with a break for service in World War II). Despite the popularity of his act he rarely recorded, perhaps because most of his material was fairly similar. However, his regular radio appearances were quite influential on other country performers, most notably WOODY GUTHRIE, who transformed the talking blues into an effective, and often ironic, form of commentary on social conditions during the Depression and World War II years. He retired from the *Opry* in 1958, and died on March 8, 1966.

Lunny, Donal   See BOTHY BAND and PLANXTY.

Lunsford, Bascom Lamar (1882–1973)
banjoist and folklorist

Bascom Lamar Lunsford was born in Mars Hill, North Carolina (a small town north of Asheville), on March 21, 1882. Although he learned to play banjo and FIDDLE as a child, Lunsford did not initially pursue a career in music. His first job was as a rural fruit tree salesman, and he traveled throughout the Appalachians selling his product. Along the way he became interested in the traditional songs, dances, and tales that he heard. He returned to school to study folklore and law, eventually becoming a full-time lawyer and an amateur folklorist. In 1928 he was instrumental in starting what was officially known as the Mountain Dance and Folk Festival in Asheville. He also made a few commercial recordings in the 1920s, but like BUELL KAZEE he never pursued a professional performing career.

In the 1930s Lunsford became a close friend of Scotty Wiseman, one half of the famous mountain-music team of LULU BELLE AND SCOTTY. He wrote the original lyrics for "Good Old Mountain Dew," which Scotty set to music, which has since become a favorite of the folk music revival. Also in the 1930s he began recording for the Library of Congress, becoming an important informant for folklorists John and Alan Lomax, and he also helped in the founding of the National Folk Festival.

After World War II Lunsford recorded sporadically for FOLK-REVIVAL labels, and continued to perform in the Asheville area. He used the banjo as a simple, but effective accompaniment to his repertoire, which was made up mostly of traditional ballads, 19th-century play party and folk songs, and more recently composed compositions. He died on September 4, 1973.

See also BANJO, FIVE-STRING; LOMAX, JOHN AND ALAN.

Luther, Frank (1899–1980) *performer*

Frank Luther Crow was born in Larkin, Kansas, on August 4, 1899. Educated in music in college, Luther performed with several local popular vocal quartets of the mid-1920s, including the DeReszke Singers (for whom he provided piano accompaniment) and the Revellers, who were minor midwestern radio stars. He came to New York in 1928, where he joined up with fellow Kansas native CARSON J. ROBISON, and the duo recorded many pop, novelty, and countrified songs for the urban market, often under the names of Bud and Joe Billings. With Robison, Luther took songwriting credit for his adaptations of traditional humorous and cowboy numbers, including "Barnacle Bill the Sailor" and "Home on the Range," both of which existed long before the duo "wrote" them. Luther also recorded as a solo artist, picking up on the cowboy fad in the 1930s.

In the mid-1930s he formed a radio trio with his wife, Zora Layman (1900–61), a fiddler who had previously worked with Robison; the duo were sometimes accompanied by Ray Whitley (a singing cowboy star of the era). Layman also recorded as a solo artist; her "Seven Years with the Wrong Man" was an early abused-wife saga that was phenomenally popular. By the decade's end, Luther was writing and performing children's material with his wife, and the two became popular children's artists on record; although they divorced in 1940, they continued to perform together for another eight years. In the 1950s he moved into record production before finally retiring from the music business. He died on November 16, 1980.

See also FIDDLE.

MacArthur, Margaret (b. 1928) *harpist and artist*

Margaret MacArthur was born in Chicago, Illinois, on May 7, 1928, and raised in Arizona and the Missouri Ozarks. In 1948 she moved to southern Vermont when she was married, and began collecting and performing local folk songs and ballads. Her first record appeared on Folkways in 1962, with MacArthur accompanying herself on an unusual harp-zither (known as the MacArthur Harp because she is one of the few people who still play it) and Appalachian dulcimer. She did not record again for another 10 years, this time with her children, notably Dan (GUITAR), Gary (FIDDLE and MANDOLIN), and Megan (bass). She worked as an Artist-in-the-Schools throughout Vermont, teaching and collecting traditional songs and folklore. She continued to record for various labels through the 1970s, 1980s, and 1990s. In 1985 she was named a "New England Living Art Treasure" by the University of Massachusetts, Amherst. She has also produced a book/cassette on how to play the MacArthur Harp.

See also DULCIMER (APPALACHIAN).

MacColl, Ewan (1915–1989) *songwriter and performer*

Born James Miller in Auchterarder, Scotland, MacColl was raised near the industrial town of Manchester, England. His Scottish parents sang traditional ballads and songs that MacColl heard from his youth. At age 15 he decided to pursue a career in theater, and changed his name to Ewan MacColl, after a 19th-century Scottish poet. He became active in politically oriented street theater in the early 1930s, and continued to act and write through the 1940s. After World War II, MacColl settled in London, and began performing folk songs in local clubs. In 1953 he founded one of the first clubs devoted to traditional song in Britain, called the Ballad and Blues Club, and later in the decade founded an important home for young songwriters, called the Singers Club, and the Critics Group as a performing outlet for them. MacColl also began a prolific recording career in the mid-1950s. He also collaborated with A. L. LLOYD on a series of Radio Ballads for the BBC in the late 1950s and early 1960s, which featured MacColl's original songs.

Late in the 1950s PEGGY SEEGER came to London and met MacColl; the two were soon romantically involved and eventually married. Seeger would often perform as his accompanist, and the two recorded many albums together from the 1960s until MacColl's death. He wrote the song "The First Time Ever I Saw Your Face" for Seeger, which became a major pop hit for Roberta Flack in 1972. Because of his leftist politics, MacColl was often denied entry to the United States, but he was a regular performer in London for many decades and helped encourage many younger performers, including FRANKIE ARMSTRONG, Maddy Prior (later of STEELEYE SPAN), and even Elvis Costello, at the beginning of their careers. MacColl and Seeger's children often performed with them beginning in the mid-1980s, and daughter Kirsty MacColl (1959–2000) became a popular new-wave artist in the late 1980s and 1990s.

Mainer, J. E. (1898–1971) *performer*

Joseph Emmett Mainer (b. Weaverville, North Carolina, July 20, 1898) and his younger brother, banjo player Wade (b. April 21, 1907), were both cotton mill workers who began working semiprofessionally in the late 1920s as musicians. In 1934 they were hired by station WBT out of Charlotte, North Carolina, and formed their first band, a quartet originally known as the Crazy Mountaineers. A year later, they were signed to Bluebird, and made their first recordings, including their 1935 hit, "Maple on the Hill."

The Mountaineers existed in various forms through the 1930s. At times Wade and J. E. would split, each leading his own Mountaineers, while at other times they came back together. Wade formed his own group, the Sons of the Mountaineers, in 1937, scoring a hit with "Sparkling Blue Eyes" two years later.

After a period of inactivity during World War II, both brothers turned up again in the late 1940s as recording stars on the King label. Toward the end of the decade, folklorist Alan Lomax "discovered" Mainer's band, recording them for two large projects he was producing at that time, *The Sounds of the South* series (issued by Atlantic Records in the late 1950s) and a similar series for the Prestige label. This led to renewed interest in the group, and some bookings on the FOLK REVIVAL and bluegrass circuits. Later in the 1960s, Wade was leading a more bluegrass-oriented outfit, while J. E. was in semiretirement, working repairing fiddles. J. E. died on June 12, 1971.

See also LOMAX, JOHN AND ALAN.

Makem, Tommy   See CLANCY BROTHERS, THE.

mandolin

The mandolin, originally of Neapolitan origin, has become a key voice in folk, bluegrass, and country music. Its odyssey into traditional music is a typical American story of experimentation and innovation.

The eight-stringed instrument, tuned like a FIDDLE, originally was made with a bowl-shaped back, like a lute. In the late 19th century, American musical instrument designer Orville Gibson came up with a new idea: a carved-body instrument, to emulate the design of the great violins. The back of the instrument had a slight arch, but sat more comfortably against the player's body. Gibson came up with two basic designs, one a pear-shaped instrument with a sweet sound that he called his

Gibson A-4 mandolin, c. early 1920s (Courtesy George Gruhn)

"A" series, and the other a more fancy design with scrolls and points that he called the "Florentine" or "F" models. Mandolin clubs sprang up on college campuses and in small towns, many organized by the Gibson Company, while just after World War I an inexpensive "Army and Navy" model was introduced specifically for sale at military bases. Other makes—notably mass-marketers Lyon and Healy—entered the fray, and soon instruments were readily available inexpensively.

The first popularity of the mandolin came in the so-called brother acts of the 1930s, although there had been a couple of mandolin players in earlier string bands. The sweet-voiced instrument, perfect for playing short melodic fills, became a favorite after it was popularized by duos like the Blue Sky Boys. Then, in the mid-1930s, a new brother act with a much higher-powered sound hit the radio, the Monroe Brothers. Bill Monroe played a Gibson F-5, the fanciest of the Florentine models introduced in the 1920s, which had a biting sound; his melodic parts were intricate, high-powered, and flashy. After the brothers broke up, Bill formed his first Blue Grass Boys, and became the pioneer of bluegrass style mandolin. Woody Guthrie, while by no means a virtuoso player, could pick out SQUARE DANCE tunes on the mandolin, a legacy of his younger days playing for dances in the Southwest.

The mandolin enjoyed a further resurgence in popularity in the 1970s, when a group of ex-bluegrass players took the instrument into the realm of a blend of new-acoustic and jazz music. DAVID GRISMAN pioneered what he called "Dawg music," performing in a quintet with two mandolins; soon others were forming similar outfits. Earlier pickers such as "TINY" MOORE (who had played for Bob Wills) and Jethro Burns (one half of the famed Homer and Jethro comedy act) gained new popularity as masters of a jazz-flavored style of picking. The instrument, which was rarely heard on country recordings outside of bluegrass records, enjoyed new popularity thanks to session work by Grisman and others. Most recently, Sam Bush (an original

member of New Grass Revival) has been Nashville's busiest session picker.

Martin, Benny (1928–2001) *legendary fiddler*

Benjamin Edward Martin was born in Sparta, Tennessee, on May 8, 1928. He was already enamored of country music as a youngster, religiously listening to Knoxville's *Mid-Day Merry Go Round* radio program, which featured such stars as Charlie Monroe and MOLLY O'DAY. At age 13 he traveled to Nashville and began his professional career as a member of the backup band for Big Jeff and Tootsie. Tootsie was the owner of the legendary Tootsie's Bar in downtown Nashville, and became a kind of surrogate mother to the young fiddler. Benny appeared on radio with the duo, and recorded with them beginning in 1944; in 1946, he cut his first solo record, "Me and My Fiddle." He also began to work the *Grand Ole Opry*. Sometime during this period, Martin gained his nickname "The Roarin' Tiger," supposedly bestowed on him by Hank Williams Sr.

After meeting the young fiddler at the *Opry,* legendary bluegrass bandleader Bill Monroe hired him to join his group in 1947. Two years later, Martin left Monroe to join with Flatt and Scruggs, remaining with the band on and off for the next four years. He appeared on the classic instrumentals that the band recorded in 1952–53, including "Dear Old Dixie" and "Flint Hill Special." In 1954 Martin joined Johnny and Jack's road show, accompanying them and Kitty Wells. He also signed with Mercury Records as a solo act, and scored hits with his own songs, including "Ice Cold Love" and "Lover of the Town," the latter featuring his impressive lead GUITAR work.

In the later 1950s Martin's popularity faded, as did many country acts, in the face of the onslaught of rock and roll. Nonetheless, Martin continued to score vocal hits through the mid-1960s, now recording for the Starday label. Martin was less active from the late 1960s through the late 1970s. However, with a new generation of bluegrass fans arising, and the reissue of many classic recordings that featured Martin's fiddling, he returned to performing both on his own and as a studio musician in the 1980s and 1990s, particularly working with JOHN HARTFORD. Unfortunately, Martin suffered from a rare disease that affected his vision and speech in his later decades that limited his ability to tour. He died on March 13, 2001.

See also FIDDLE.

Martin, Jimmy (b. 1927) *singer*

James Henry Martin was born in Sneedville, Tennessee, on August 10, 1927. His career began on the radio in 1948; a year later, he was invited to join Bill Monroe's Bluegrass Boys as lead vocalist to replace MAC WISEMAN. Martin performed with Monroe on classic recordings until 1953.

In 1954 Martin, mandolinist/vocalist Bobby Osborne, and his banjo-playing brother Sonny performed as the Osborne Brothers band for a year; two years later, Martin formed the first of his Sunny Mountain Boys, performing on both the *Grand Ole Opry* and the *Louisiana Hayride* radio programs. Martin was the first of the pure bluegrass stars to cross over, attempting to create what he called "good 'n country music," a kind of less hard-driving, more vocally oriented bluegrass music. This led to mid-1960s hits with songs such as "Widow Maker" and "Sunny Side of the Mountain," which became his theme song. Martin's career was given a gigantic boost when he was invited to perform on the Nitty Gritty Dirt Band's landmark 1971 recording, *Will the Circle Be Unbroken*. Martin formed his own label in the 1990s and has continued to perform on the bluegrass circuit into the 21st century.

See also BANJO, FIVE-STRING; MANDOLIN.

McAuliffe, Leon (1917–1988) *guitarist and vocalist*

William Leon McAuliffe was born in Houston, Texas, on January 3, 1917. Influenced by Bob Dunn, who played lap steel GUITAR with Milton Brown's band, he took up the instrument. He became famous in 1935, when he joined Bob Wills's band, the Texas Playboys. His recording of "Steel Guitar Rag" in 1936 was a major success, further spreading the sound and popularity of the instrument. His electrified steel guitar lines, often in duet with electric guitarist Eldon Shamblin, helped mold Wills's sound throughout the 1930s. McAuliffe also sang lead vocals on many of the more bluesy numbers. Wills's joyful shouts of "Take it away, Leon!" are heard on many of these classic recordings.

McAuliffe spent the World War II years in the navy, but returned in 1946 to form his own band, known as the Cimarron Boys. His 1949 recording of his own composition "Panhandle Rag" became a much-imitated standard in the Western Swing repertoire. He continued to lead bands and record through the early 1960s. By the late 1960s he owned two small radio stations around Rogers, Arkansas, but the mid-1970s Western Swing revival brought him out of retirement as a leader of the Original Texas Playboys, featuring many players from Wills's bands. The band was active for about a decade, until age and ill-health caught up with many of the members. McAuliffe died of heart disease on August 20, 1988.

McCoury, Del (b. 1939) *guitarist and banjoist*

Delano Floyd McCoury was born in Bakersville, North Carolina, on February 1, 1939, and was raised in a musical family; his mother was an amateur singer/guitarist. The family relocated from North Carolina to rural southeastern Pennsylvania soon after his birth. When he was a teenager, McCoury heard a recording of Flatt & Scruggs and decided to take up the banjo. In the late 1950s he was playing banjo in the Baltimore area.

From 1963 to 1964, McCoury was lead singer with Bill Monroe's band. Although hired as a banjo player, he ended up playing GUITAR after BILL KEITH came on board. McCoury's distinctive mountain-flavored vocals returned Monroe's sound to his Kentucky roots. In 1964 McCoury relocated to

California, where he formed the Golden State Boys, but by 1968 was back in Pennsylvania leading his Dixie Pals.

The band became a family affair in 1981, when son Ronnie joined on MANDOLIN, followed eight years later by Rob on banjo. In 1989 McCoury recorded with DAVID GRISMAN on his bluegrass album, *Home Is Where the Heart Is,* and subsequently toured with Grisman to promote the album. In 1992 McCoury left Pennsylvania for Nashville. Thanks to a series of albums released on Rounder Records beginning in the early 1990s, McCoury established a strong following in the bluegrass community.

In 1999 McCoury's band accompanied Steve Earle on his bluegrass-flavored album of originals, *The Mountain,* and Del sang tenor vocals to the raspy-throated singer/songwriter. McCoury's band subsequently toured with Earle. McCoury is also a talented songwriter, and his songs have been covered by many other bluegrass groups. The rock group Phish recorded his "The Beauty of My Dreams," which helped bring him a new group of fans. In 2000 the group was signed to the Hollywood label.

See also BANJO, FIVE-STRING.

McCurdy, Ed (1918–2000) *singer and songwriter*

Born in Willow Hill, Pennsylvania, Edward McCurdy began his career working as a gospel singer on the radio, eventually landing in Oklahoma City. In 1946 he relocated to Canada to continue his radio career, and began singing traditional Canadian songs. He released his first album in 1950, the same year he wrote the folk classic "Last Night I Had the Strangest Dream," a song reflecting the anxieties of war in the nuclear age.

McCurdy moved to New York in 1954 to continue his singing career, and signed with a new folk label, Elektra Records. The owner of Elektra, JAC HOLZMAN, came up with the idea of recording an album of slightly risqué songs of the Elizabethan era with McCurdy; the result was the 1956 album *When Dalliance Was in Flower.* The album sold well beyond anyone's wildest expectations, and, because of its slightly off-color content, was very popular on college campuses. McCurdy issued several more albums of this material through the 1950s.

Although McCurdy's career slowed in the early 1960s, his song "Strangest Dream" became very popular in the new era of social-protest anthems. The CHAD MITCHELL TRIO had a solid hit with it, and Simon & Garfunkel, PETE SEEGER, and dozens more covered it. McCurdy's last album of original material, issued in 1967, featured the song. He eventually returned to Canada, where he retired. McCurdy died on March 23, 2000.

McDonald, Country Joe (b. 1942) *singer and songwriter*

Born in Washington, D.C., on January 1, 1942, but raised in El Monte, a suburb of Los Angeles, California, Country Joe McDonald is best known for leading the 1960s social-protest rock band the Fish, although he has had a long career also as a singer/songwriter. He played in local bands through his high school years, and then enlisted in the navy for four years, where he first heard folk music. On his return he began performing his own songs in small Los Angeles area clubs. An early opponent of the Vietnam War, he became disillusioned with Los Angeles's commercialism and moved north to Berkeley, California, in the mid-1960s, then the center of the growing peace and hippie movements. There, with guitarist Barry Melton, he formed the group Country Joe and the Fish, in 1966. The band's performance of Joe's "I Feel Like I'm Fixin' to Die Rag," opening with the rousing "Fish Cheer," was a highlight of 1969's Woodstock rock festival. The band broke up officially in 1971.

Meanwhile, growing disillusioned with the rock scene, Country Joe issued his first solo album, *Thinking of Woody Guthrie,* in early 1970. He continued to record prolifically through the 1970s, a mix of his own social-protest material, folk standards, and country-rock songs. He has recorded only sporadically since then, although he continues to perform on occasion for social causes.

McEuen, John (b. 1945) *banjoist*

Born in Long Beach, California, on December 19, 1945, John was first exposed to rock and roll and R&B through his older brother Bill, who was a local deejay and concert promoter. While still in high school, John formed a folk band with a couple of friends, originally taking the name the Illegitimate Jug Band (because they didn't have a jug player!) This group evolved into the Nitty Gritty Dirt Band, and brother Bill soon became their manager. McEuen primarily played bluegrass-styled banjo in the group, although he also played GUITAR, MANDOLIN, and sometimes even FIDDLE.

After leaving the Dirt Band in the late 1980s, McEuen produced a couple of solo albums in a style that melds bluegrass with Irish traditional music, old-time country, and jazz, similar to other performers in the progressive bluegrass/newgrass styles, such as TONY TRISCHKA. He also produced and hosted a special on the music of the old West for TNN. Throughout the 1990s he has continued to record, mostly in a progressive bluegrass style. In 2000 he reunited with Nitty Gritty Dirt Band singer Jimmy Ibbotson for a duet album, *Stories and Songs.*

See also BANJO, FIVE-STRING.

McGarrigle, Kate and Anna *singers/ songwriters*

Kate (b. 1944) and Anna (b. 1946) McGarrigle are singers/songwriters from Montreal, Canada, raised in a bilingual (French and English) household. They were raised in the small Quebec village of Saint-Sauveur-des-Monts, and both were encouraged to play piano and sing from an early age. While attending college at McGill University, the sisters became active in the local folk scene. They also began writing their own songs; Anna's song "Heart

Like a Wheel" was a major success for singer/songwriter Linda Ronstadt in 1974, leading the sisters to be signed as a recording duo to Warner Brothers Records a year later. Several albums followed through the mid-1970s, and then their recording work slowed. The McGarrigles have written and sung in both French and English, and have often combined traditional instrumentation and folklike melodies and themes in their original compositions. They rarely tour, but have continued to record with various family members and friends over the following decades. Kate's children with her ex-husband singer/songwriter Loudon Wainwright III are both performers; son Rufus is a well-known songwriter and performer, and daughter Martha has also been performing her own material. In 1994 the McGarrigle sisters were awarded the Order of Canada for their work promoting Canadian music and culture.

McGee, Dennis   See ARDOIN FAMILY.

McGee, Sam (1894–1975) *guitarist and* Grand Ole Opry *performer*

Samuel Fleming McGee, born in Franklin, Tennessee, on May 1, 1894, came from a musical, farming family; his father was a fiddler, and Sam and his brother, Kirk, were playing music early on in the family band. The brothers were discovered by Uncle Dave Macon in 1924; Sam was 30 years old at the time and working as a blacksmith. Soon the two brothers were touring with the flamboyant banjoist, with Sam playing GUITAR and Kirk playing FIDDLE. They became members of the *Grand Ole Opry* in 1926 and made their first solo recordings at the time, including Sam's unusual fingerpicked guitar instrumental, "Franklin Blues," showing the influence of black blues guitarists. Macon and the McGees were joined by fiddler Mazy Todd in a 1927 recording session as the FRUIT JAR DRINKERS, recording some of the most high-spirited string band music of the era.

Although both McGees continued to perform with Uncle Dave through the 1930s, they also joined a more modern performer, FIDDLIN' ARTHUR SMITH, early in the decade to form the Dixieliners. Kirk switched to banjo in this group that featured Smith's more modern, jazz-influenced fiddling and his smooth vocals. The group disbanded by the decade's end, but would reunite in the 1960s to record and perform at folk festivals.

In the 1940s the McGee Brothers joined Bill Monroe's new band, the Blue Grass Boys, joining Monroe's traveling tent shows. During the 1950s they continued to perform on the *Opry*, often as members of a revived Fruit Jar Drinkers featuring various other *Opry* old-timers. The 1960s FOLK REVIVAL brought them an entirely new audience of young, urban pickers; MIKE SEEGER produced two albums of the McGees with Arthur Smith as well as a solo album by Sam in the early 1970s.

Sam McGee continued to perform on the *Opry* until his death in a farming accident on August 21, 1975. At that time, his brother, Kirk, also pretty much retired from playing.

See also BANJO, FIVE-STRING; TERRY, SONNY, AND BROWNIE MCGHEE.

McGuinn, Roger   See BYRDS, THE.

McLean, Don (b. 1945) *singer and songwriter*
Born in New Rochelle, New York, McLean's first love was Buddy Holly and rock and roll. As a teenager, he discovered PETE SEEGER and folk music, and, after briefly attending college, took up performing in folk clubs up and down the northeast United States. He began working with Seeger on the sloop *Clearwater*, a re-creation of a 19th-century river boat designed to bring attention to the need for cleaning up the Hudson River. This led to his first recording contract with a small label in 1970. Perry Como picked up McLean's song "And I Love Her So" from this album, scoring a hit, so larger label United Artists signed the singer/songwriter.

McLean became a major star in 1971–72 with the release of his epic song, "American Pie," which told the story of the death of Buddy Holly and the end of the first phase of rock and roll. His follow-up song, a soft folk-ballad about the trials of Vincent van Gogh called simply "Vincent," was also a hit. However, McLean's pop career was short-lived, and his follow-up albums of both his own materials and covers of folk and traditional songs did not fare well. He had another brief period of success in 1981, when he released a cover of Roy Orbison's "Crying," but since has performed a mix of covers and his own songs on both records and tour, mostly for his dedicated fans.

Miller, Buddy and Julie *guitarist and songwriters*
Steve "Buddy" Miller was born in Princeton, New Jersey. He began playing rock music as a teenager, performing locally in his own band in the early 1970s. By the mid-1970s he had moved to Austin, Texas, and became interested in the "new country" movement centered in that city. He joined a local country-rock band, Partners in Crime, which also included a local singer, Julie. Born in small-town Waxahachie, Texas, Julie settled in Austin just as the new folk-country-rock-blues style was developing there. Buddy and Julie were married in 1981, and began looking for work as performers and songwriters, working through the 1980s in music centers New York and Los Angeles. During this period Buddy was guitarist for country-pop singer Jim Lauderdale, while Julie recorded four contemporary Christian albums.

In 1993 the couple settled in Nashville, just as the alt-country movement was growing. Julie's songs and Buddy's GUITAR-playing skills attracted the attention of Emmylou Harris. Buddy was soon a member of her early 1990s touring band, Spyboy, and Harris also covered Julie's song "All My Tears." Buddy released his first solo album, *Your Love and Other Lies*, soon after the couple settled in Nashville; from that point forward the two have collaborated on a series of albums, although they have been either issued as Buddy or Julie "solo" discs. In 1997 they both issued solo albums, his second (*Poison Love*) and her first (*Blue Pony*). Both received strong reviews from critics. Julie followed up in 1999 with *Broken Things,* an album of all original songs, with the exception of the traditional ballad "Two Soldiers," recorded as a duet with Emmylou Harris. A critical and artistic success, it featured several songs that are destined to be new-country classics, including "I Know Why the River Runs," later covered by Lee Ann Womack. Buddy followed with his next solo album, *Cruel Moon,* featuring the hard-country romp "Does My Ring Burn Your Fingers," also covered by Womack. In 2001 they released their first true duo album, featuring a more hard-rocking sound than some of their earlier efforts.

Miller, Emmett (1903–1962) *singer*

Emmett Dewey Miller was born in Macon, Georgia, on February 2, 1903. Miller began his performing career as a teenager, performing with traveling minstrel troupes. By the early 1920s he was settled in New York, where he began appearing in local vaudeville theaters, often working with Cliff Edwards (aka Ukulele Ike). Through Edwards, he got his first opportunity to record in 1924, cutting his first hit, "Anytime." From the start, Miller's unique singing style was featured on his recordings; he would suddenly break from his normal voice into a crying falsetto. Miller's falsetto yodel also became a vocal trademark for Hank Williams.

In August 1925 Miller was appearing in Asheville, North Carolina, where he again had the opportunity to record. His "Lovesick Blues" was recorded here, complete with his warbling yodels. On a later trip to the city in 1927, Miller met the Callahan Brothers, who learned "St. Louis Blues" from him, which was among their first recordings. Miller may also have encountered and influenced Jimmie Rodgers in Asheville, although there is some question if the two ever met or if Rodgers simply heard Miller's recordings. Although he continued to tour the South, Miller spent the balance of the 1920s back in New York. In 1928 he rerecorded his early hits, and also cut for the first time "St. Louis Blues" and "I Ain't Got Nobody." He cut a total of 28 sides during 1928–29, including blackface minstrel dialogues, reflecting his long experience in MINSTREL TRAVELING SHOWS.

Miller remained committed to vaudeville and traveling shows through the 1930s and 1940s, making his last recordings in 1936. Meanwhile, many country artists were emulating his style. However, Miller was forgotten as a performer, and died in obscurity on March 29, 1962.

minstrel/traveling shows

Classic minstrel shows—in which white entertainers performed in blackface—are a rich source of folk music traditions, including musical instruments (banjo, FIDDLE), humor, skits, and songs. Although often criticized as degrading to blacks (for good reason), the shows were tremendously popular in the 19th century, and eventually embraced black entertainers as well as white. They served as models for touring and tent shows that later regularly crisscrossed the South.

The classic minstrel era is usually defined as running from the late 1840s through the 1880s, when minstrelsy gave way to other forms of entertainment. Originally, individual performers such as banjo player J. W. Sweeney toured with traveling circuses or other informal entertainments. Early performers such as George Washington Dixon and Thomas "Jim Crow" Dartmouth Rice developed their own specialties, as well as a group of stock characters, including the archetypal backwoods slave ("Jim Crow") and the uptown Dandy ("Old Zip Coon").

As instrumentalists began to pair up with dancers or comedians, they developed individual acts that could be integrated into an evening of song and dance. In 1843 in New York City, four

The Ethiopian Serenaders, a typical early minstrel performing group. Note the banjo players (center), the two endmen (bones on left, tambourine on right), and—an unusual feature—the melodeon player (fourth from left). (Courtesy David A. Jasen)

early performers decided to stage an evening's entertainment: violinist Dan Emmett, banjo player Billy Whitlock, bones player Frank Brower, and tambourinist Dick Pelham. They called themselves the Virginia Minstrels, and they were an immediate phenomenon, touring Britain and the United States and developing the typical cast and format for the minstrel show.

Minstrel troupes—large and small—toured throughout the country, bringing a new musical instrument—the five-string banjo—and repertoire of jokes, songs, and dances to the hinterlands. Banjo tunes that are still collected from traditional players today, such as "Boatman's Dance," and fiddle tunes including "Turkey in the Straw," among dozens of others, all can be traced to the minstrel repertoire. Sketches in which the country rube outwits the city slicker—such as the comic dialogue of "Arkansas Traveller"—also are derived from similar minstrel routines.

Blacks were not the only figures caricatured in minstrelsy. America was being flooded with new ethnic populations beginning with the immigration of Germans, Slavs, and Irish in the mid-19th century. The Irish came to escape the crushing poverty—and the infamous potato famine—and soon became a new working class, often maligned in the popular press. Irish step dancers also became popular entertainers, and step dancing undoubtedly influenced the growth of traditional Appalachian flat foot or clog dancing and also African-American tap dance styles. Several dance styles imitating animal movements—such as the buck and wing—had African sources, and themselves became part of the folk repertoire.

Many songs that are considered "folk" or "traditional" today were in fact minstrel songs. STEPHEN FOSTER was the most famous composer in the genre, contributing "Camptown Races," "Oh! Susanna," and dozens more to the folk repertoire.

James Bland, an African-American songwriter of the later 19th century, also composed sentimental songs in the Foster vein, notably "Carry Me Back to Old Virginny," another classic of the era. Moreover, sentimental popular songs—first introduced on the minstrel and then traveling show stages—entered the repertoire of folk singers, sometimes preserved for decades later. Early collectors often mistakenly labeled this music as "folk song," not realizing that it was merely the (by then forgotten—at least among city dwellers) popular music of a previous era.

Although the minstrel shows "died" in the later 19th century, their format of humorous skits, dazzling instrumental solos, dances, and sentimental numbers lived in numerous tent and traveling shows. So-called medicine shows—usually selling some remedy of dubious quality and usefulness—often employed individual or groups of musicians, dancers, and comedians to hawk their wares. Musicians themselves soon realized that, for a small investment in equipment, they could mount their own touring shows. During the later 1940s, Bill Monroe sponsored several successful tent shows of his own, which featured not only musical performances but also a traveling baseball team, which would challenge locals to a game.

See also BANJO, FIVE-STRING.

Mitchell, Joni (b. 1943) *singer, songwriter, and guitarist*

Born Roberta Joan Anderson in Fort Macleod, Alberta, Canada, on November 7, 1943, Mitchell has had a long and varied career that has taken her far beyond her singer-songwriter roots. She learned to play piano as a child, and then took up GUITAR as a teenager and began to sing traditional folk songs and write her own compositions. In 1965, she moved to Toronto, where she met singer/guitarist Chuck Mitchell on the local folk scene; they were soon married and performing together as an IAN AND SYLVIA style duo. They moved to Detroit, Michigan, in 1966, but soon separated, and Mitchell began performing on the local scene. Her songs soon attracted attention, and by 1967 she was signed to Reprise Records. In 1968 JUDY COLLINS had a major hit with Mitchell's "Both Sides Now," which brought her wide attention. Mitchell's second album, *Clouds,* reached the top 40 propelled by interest in the song.

The balance of Mitchell's career took her far away from her folk roots. In 1971 she released *Blue,* an acclaimed, starkly produced album that focused on confessional songs about her life and loves. By the mid-1970s, working with musician/arranger Tom Scott, Mitchell began recording in a more pop-jazz style, scoring a hit with "You Turn Me On (I'm a Radio)" in 1974. Her increased interest in jazz led her to collaborate late in the decade with legendary composer/bandleader/bassist Charles Mingus; they collaborated on the 1979 album *Mingus,* which was released shortly after Mingus passed away from ALS (Lou Gehrig's disease).

The 1980s and 1990s saw a more variable output from Mitchell, mostly in a pop-rock vein, although she flirted with various styles, including electronica. Much of this work was produced by Larry Klein, who was married to Mitchell between 1984 and 1994, but continued to work with her even after their marriage ended. Her most recent albums have featured lush orchestral accompaniments. On them, Mitchell's once quavering soprano has been reduced to a more husky baritone, due to years of cigarette smoking.

Molloy, Matt   See BOTHY BAND and CHIEFTAINS, THE.

Moloney, Mick (b. 1944) *performer and record producer*

Born in Limerick, Ireland, on November 15, 1944, Mick Moloney was first exposed to folk music as a college student in Dublin in the early 1960s. On the scene was also instrumentalist Donal Lunny (later a founder of PLANXTY and the BOTHY BAND) and Brian Bolger, and the trio formed the Emmet Folk Group, emulating the style of the popular trios of the day, such as the CLANCY BROTHERS. In 1966 Moloney's instrumental skills brought him to the attention of the popular vocal group the JOHNSTONS, who invited him to join the band as a singer/accompanist; also in the group was instrumentalist PAUL BRADY. In 1971 the group toured the United States, and Moloney met and befriended folklorist KENNETH S. GOLDSTEIN, who invited him to study at the University of Pennsylvania.

Moloney came to the United States and became an active performer and record producer, working with both older traditional musicians (notably Philadelphia fiddler Eugene O'Donnell) and many younger players on the scene. He earned his Ph.D. in folklore in 1992, and has since become a major promoter, producer, and performer, arranging tours, appearing on television and radio, and producing countless records.

See also FIDDLE.

Moonshine Kate (1909–1994) *performer*
Banjo and GUITAR player Rosa Lee "Moonshine Kate" Carson (b. Atlanta, Georgia) is best known as the accompanist to her father, Fiddlin' John Carson. Serving as a foil to her father on a number of classic country-comedy recordings, Kate established the character of a sassy, wisecracking mountain woman, setting the stage for the next generation of female country comics. Additionally, Kate made some excellent solo recordings from 1924 to 1935, with her slow, drawling, blues-influenced vocals forecasting the honky-tonk singers of the 1950s. Her best-known recording was of the topical ballad "Little Mary Phagan," retelling the story of the 1913 murder of an innocent factory girl, supposedly at the hands of her employer, Leo Frank. She also recorded the sentimental "heart songs" that were a favorite part of many singer's repertoires, including "The Poor Girl's Story" and "The Lone Child." She even covered Jimmie Rodgers's "T for Texas," complete with yodeling and fancy guitar runs, forecasting the popularity of the yodeling cowgirls of the mid-1930s and 1940s.

See also BANJO, FIVE-STRING.

Moore, Christy (b. 1945) *Irish folk artist*
Born on May 7, 1945, Christy Moore sang in school choir, and learned to play piano as a child. Initially attracted to rock and roll as a teen, he was then exposed to folk music after hearing recordings of the popular CLANCY BROTHERS and meeting fellow musician DONAL LUNNY, who would become a long-time collaborator with Moore. After graduating from college, he worked in a Dublin bank, while also performing on the local folk scene. He befriended the famed bagpipe player WILLIE CLANCY in 1964, and the two played locally over the next few years. In 1966 he moved to London, where he continued to perform.

In 1971 Moore was back in Dublin and signed to the small Tara label. He asked Lunny to play on and produce his album, and Lunny and Moore assembled a group of musicians who would become the core of a new band called PLANXTY. The resulting album, 1972's *Prosperous*, became one of the most influential works in the new Irish folk movement. Moore remained with the group for two years, and then returned to solo recording and performing. In the early 1980s he formed Moving Hearts, also featuring Lunny and a group of talented musicians, who mixed Irish traditional themes, melodies, and instruments with more contemporary sounds. Moore left the group in 1983 to briefly rejoin a reunited Planxty, but then returned to solo performing. A songwriter as well as a performer, Moore's songs such as "Ordinary Man," "City to Chicago," and 1996's "North and South of the River" (coauthored with Bono and the Edge of U2) have gained some popularity on the revival scene. His brother performs as a singer-songwriter under the name of Luka Bloom.

Moore, "Tiny" (1920–1987) *mandolinist*
Billie Moore was born in rural Hamilton County, Texas, on May 12, 1920. He was raised in Port Arthur, Texas, and initially studied violin. He began playing MANDOLIN after hearing Leo Raley, then mandolinist for Cliff Bruner's Western Wanderers. Raley was perhaps the first mandolinist to play an

amplified instrument, inspiring Tiny to also take up an electrified instrument. Moore joined the band of Western Swing pioneer Bob Wills in 1946, staying with him during his stay in Southern California through the early 1950s. Working with Wills, he played a single-note style inspired by jazz guitarist Charlie Christian. Around 1952 Moore purchased a five-string electric mandolin from pioneering maker Paul Bigsby. Unlike other mandolins, the strings were not doubled, and the instrument included an extra bass string. The sound Moore got was closer to an electric GUITAR than a traditional mandolin, and it became his trademark.

After working with Wills, Moore remained in Southern California, opening his own music store and playing occasionally. In the 1970s avid Bob Wills's fan Merle Haggard brought Moore out of semiretirement for his Bob Wills's tribute album. Moore subsequently joined Haggard's touring band. In 1979 Moore paired with Jethro Burns (one-half of the legendary country duo Homer & Jethro) for an album of jazz-flavored instrumentals; this brought him renewed attention, and he subsequently recorded a solo album. Moore remained active until his death on December 15, 1987.

Morris Brothers, The

Zeke (b. Claude Zeke Edward Morris, May 9, 1916–August 5, 1999) and Wiley Elder (b. Wiley Andrew Morris, February 1, 1919–September 22, 1990) were born in rural Old Fort, North Carolina. Brother Zeke first worked professionally as a guitarist and vocalist with J. E. MAINER's Mountaineers, a nostalgic country string band of the mid-1930s. He participated in the band's 1935 recording sessions, singing lead on the country best-seller, "Maple on the Hill," later a bluegrass favorite. A year later, he left the band with Mainer's brother Wade to form a vocal duo, and then in 1937 his brother, Wiley, joined them to make a trio. Wiley also played GUITAR, so Zeke switched to MANDOLIN.

Later in 1937, Mainer left and was replaced by fiddler Homer "Pappy" Sherrill, and the trio became the Smiling Rangers, broadcasting out of Raleigh, North Carolina. In 1938–39 the brothers recorded with Sherrill for Victor budget label Bluebird, with their most popular number being "Let Me Be Your Salty Dog." From 1939 to 1944 the Morrises were working out of Asheville, North Carolina. During this period the Morrises also worked with Charlie Monroe's band.

Briefly separating in 1944–45, the Morrises were reunited by Victor country producer Eli Oberstein, who oversaw their last classic-period recordings in 1945. They recut "Let Me Be Your Salty Dog" as "Salty Dog Blues," and also recorded "Tragic Romance," which was later covered by bluegrass groups in the years to come. However, this was pretty much the end of their professional careers. In 1964 the brothers appeared at the NEWPORT FOLK FESTIVAL, having been "rediscovered" during the FOLK REVIVAL of the early 1960s. In 1972 the Morrises were lured out of retirement by the bluegrass-revival label, Rounder Records, recording with old friend Homer Sherrill.

Muldaur, Geoff and Maria
performers
Together and separately, Geoff and Maria Muldaur have had long careers on the folk-blues revival scene, beginning in the early 1960s. Geoff Muldaur was born in 1945 in Pelham, New York, and began to record and perform in the early 1960s in the Boston area. He met JIM KWESKIN there and was invited by Kweskin to join his new jug band. Fiddler Maria D'Amato (b. New York City, September 12, 1943) was an active participant in New York's Greenwich Village folk scene. In 1964 she performed as part of the Even Dozen Jug Band, which brought together a motley group of New York folkies for one album. When the Kweskin band performed in the Village soon after, D'Amato was smitten with Muldaur and was soon his wife and a member of the group.

Maria D'Amato and Geoff Muldaur performing with the Jim Kweskin Jug Band at Club 47 in July 1964 (Photo © John Byrne Cooke, http://www.cookephoto.com)

After the Kweskin Jug Band ended in 1968, the Muldaurs recorded two albums as a duo featuring Maria's silky vocals and Geoff's inventive GUITAR and band arrangements. They were also active on the Woodstock scene, and were invited by blues HARMONICA player Paul Butterfield to join his new group, Better Days, in 1971. However, the couple divorced in 1972, and Maria went solo with Geoff remaining in the Butterfield band, although the band folded by 1974. Both Muldaurs recorded as solo artists, with Maria achieving the greatest success in 1974 with "Midnight at the Oasis," a top-10 hit from her debut solo album. Since then, both have recorded sporadically, with Maria performing gospel, blues, and jazz, and Geoff making a mini-comeback in the late 1990s and early 21st century with performances and recordings.

See also FIDDLE.

Muleskinner

One of the first revival bluegrass "supergroups," Muleskinner lasted only long enough to appear on a single TV special and make one album, but was quite influential on the growth of progressive bluegrass. All of the group's members had originally performed in bluegrass bands: PETER ROWAN, RICHARD GREENE, and BILL KEITH were early 1960s alumni of Bill Monroe's band; Clarence White had been a founding member of the KENTUCKY COLONELS; and

DAVID GRISMAN was a founding member of the New York Ramblers, and had performed with RED ALLEN and DEL MCCOURY, as well. In the mid-to-late 1960s and early 1970s they had all pursued different musical directions, with Keith joining JIM KWESKIN's Jug Band, White playing lead GUITAR for the BYRDS, Greene fiddling with the rock-jazz fusion band Seatrain, and Grisman and Rowan forming the progressive rock band Earth Opera. Muleskinner was their first return to their bluegrass roots.

The band was formed at the invitation of a California public television station that had booked Bill Monroe's Blue Grass Boys and wanted to have a young band as a second act to provide a "fathers and sons" angle to the show. Their performance was so successful that they were given a one-record deal with Warner Brothers; this album was reissued several times through the 1970s and 1980s, influencing subsequent generations of bluegrass pickers. Besides reworkings of traditional material, it featured the first appearance on record of a David Grisman original composition as well as Rowan's unique original songs. (His "Blue Mule" is a retelling of the traditional "Molly and Tenbrooks" story, this time with Molly beating her opponent by flying up into outer space!) The album also introduced Clarence White's excellent acoustic-guitar picking to an entire new generation (his earlier bluegrass recordings were virtually unavailable at the time). Although the band never toured, band members (with the exception of White, who was tragically killed in a hit-and-run accident soon after) have reunited from time to time.

Murphy, Jimmy (1925–1981) *performer*

Jimmy Murphy was born in Republic, Alabama, on October 11, 1925, the son of a coal miner. He was exposed early on to the music of the *Grand Ole Opry* and classic blues performers such as Blind Boy Fuller and LEAD BELLY through 78 recordings. He learned to play the GUITAR from local musician Bee Coleman, who showed him an open E tuning that was ideally suited to the blues (Coleman's father recorded country blues under the name Dutch Coleman in the late 1920s and returned to recording in the 1950s, now focusing on gospel material). Murphy first performed on radio in Birmingham, and then, after finishing school, joined his father as an apprentice bricklayer. Sometime around 1950, he arrived in Knoxville, where he eventually ended up as a featured performer on *Midday Merry-Go-Round* on the local radio station. About the same time, he was introduced to Chet Atkins, who arranged for his first recordings for RCA.

Murphy's recordings were unique among postwar records in that they just featured his bluesy guitar with the accompaniment of Anita Carter on bass and background vocals. They also were made up of his own compositions, which had unusual themes (aging, wayward children) and imagery. For instance, his song "Electricity" is a fast-moving blues with lyrics that compare the power of God's love to the invisible force of electrification.

Murphy's 1951–52 recordings for RCA were unsuccessful, and he did not return to the studio until 1955, when he recorded some new compositions in a rockabilly style for Columbia. However, these records also failed in the marketplace, and although Murphy continued to perform on radio and in local appearances, his recordings were more sporadic through the late 1950s and 1960s.

Musicologist Richard K. Spottswood rediscovered Murphy in 1976, when he was assembling a set of recordings for the Smithsonian Institution in honor of the bicentennial. He arranged for the recordings that were issued by bluegrass revival label Sugar Hill in 1978 that brought Murphy back into the limelight. These sensitively produced sessions (produced by Ricky Skaggs) introduced a new generation to Murphy's dry vocals, hot guitar licks, and unique songs. Characteristically, Murphy disappeared again after making his comeback. He died on June 1, 1981.

Nashville Bluegrass Band, The

One of the most popular of the revival bluegrass bands, the original group was centered on the vocals of Pat Enright (GUITAR) and Alan O'Bryant (banjo). Specializing in performing straight-ahead bluegrass, they were augmented by the Bill Monroe-influenced MANDOLIN playing of Mike Compton. The final original band member was bassist Mark Hembree. Soon after they formed, fiddler Stuart Duncan joined, making the group a quintet.

In 1988 a touring accident left bass player Hembree injured; he and Compton left the band soon after. Compton was replaced by legendary mandolinist Roland White, of the KENTUCKY COLONELS and, more recently, COUNTRY GAZETTE; the new bass player was Gene Libea. During the 1990s the band's reputation grew, while individual band members—particularly Stuart Duncan—became in-demand session players for mainstream country acts. The band won several International Bluegrass Music Association honors, and their albums have been nominated for several Grammys. In early 2000 Roland White retired from the band, and Mike Marshall returned to fill his shoes. They continue to record and tour in the new century.

See also BANJO, FIVE-STRING.

Nesmith, Michael (b. 1942) *songwriter and member of the Monkees*

Michael Nesmith was born in Houston, Texas, on December 30, 1942. The son of a secretary who invented Liquid Paper, and thus earned a small for-

tune, Nesmith learned to play the GUITAR after serving a stint in the air force in the early 1960s. After a successful audition, he gained a position as the only star of the Monkees TV show who actually played his instrument and wrote songs. For the group's first album, he supplied the countryesque "Last Train to Clarksville." Although Nesmith continued to provide country-rock originals for the group, he was dismayed by the hype surrounding them, and left soon after the TV show was canceled.

Nesmith's fame as a songwriter steadily grew in the late 1960s. His "Different Drum" was covered by Linda Ronstadt as a member of the Stone Poneys and was a 1967 hit; the Nitty Gritty Dirt Band had a minor hit with his "Some of Shelley's Blues," and mainstream vocalist Andy Williams had a big hit with his early 1970s composition "Joanne." Meanwhile, Nesmith formed a series of loose-knit country rock bands, called the First (or Second) National Band, often in partnership with steel guitarist Red Rhodes. In the mid-1970s Nesmith became increasingly interested in experimentation with video, suggesting the original idea for MTV and becoming one of the first and most inventive creators of music videos through his company, Pacific Arts. He more or less retired as a performer, although he continues to occasionally produce new material in a style that is distinctly his own.

New Christy Minstrels, The

One of the most popular groups of the 1960s FOLK REVIVAL, the New Christy Minstrels was the brainchild of Los Angeles–based singer/guitarist Randy Sparks. Like many solo folk performers, he was influenced by the success of the KINGSTON TRIO to form a folk trio in 1961, enlisting Nick Woods and his wife, Jackie Wilson, and they performed in local clubs. Sparks also was impressed with the success of choral arrangements of folk music made by mainstream groups—notably Mitch Miller's studio vocal ensembles and felt that wedding the folk-trio sound with a large vocal force would be equally successful. He drew on several existing local groups to form a 10-voiced ensemble, naming it after the 19th-century minstrel troupe formed by E. P. Christy. Sparks was the guiding force, choosing the material and costumes, and pressing the group to present a clean, well-scrubbed face to the public. (Sparks also co-owned the band with two music business managers; the rest of the group members were on salary.)

The group was signed to major label Columbia, and their 1962 debut album was an unexpected hit, winning a Grammy and selling well based on their upbeat version of WOODY GUTHRIE's "This Land Is Your Land." This led to the group being signed as regulars on the 1962–63 season of the popular TV variety show hosted by singer Andy Williams. Some original members left, and an existing folk duo of Barry Maguire and Barry Kane were brought on board; Maguire's strong lead vocals became a hallmark of hits like "Green, Green, Rocky Road" (cowritten by Sparks and Maguire, a number three hit in 1963) and "Saturday Night." Countless other folk groups were inspired to record and perform with large vocal ensembles thanks to the Christy's success.

Sparks left the group in May 1963, tiring of touring, but remained the behind-the-scenes manager/ controller. He put Maguire in the lead vocal spot and also hired a new singer, GENE CLARK, to fill his shoes. Other band members—most of whom were on salary—resented this move, and various members came and went over the coming months. By this time the clean-scrubbed image of the group was wearing thin, as many in the folk revival were

now enamored of the social-protest singers such as BOB DYLAN and PHIL OCHS. Sparks finally sold his share in the group at the end of 1964, and Maguire left in 1965 to pursue a solo career (enjoying a major hit with the Dylanesque protest song "Eve of Destruction" later that year). Various other band members had careers as pop performers, including Sparks's wife who joined with Gayle Caldwell to record and perform as Jackie & Gayle. The group, meanwhile, had a hit with their cover of "Chim Chim Che-ree" from the Disney film *Mary Poppins.*

The group's remaining managers were less interested in folk music than in keeping the cash flowing from appearances and recordings, so began to direct them toward performing more pop and novelty material. Most of the original members were gone by early 1966, replaced by future country star Kenny Rogers, future pop-rock singer Kim Carnes, and future actress Karen Black, among others. (Rogers left almost immediately with fellow group members Terry Williams and Thelma Lou Comacho to form the folk-pop trio the First Edition.) The group managed to continue to perform through 1971 before finally ending; various revival groups have toured over the following decades.

The 2002 film comedy *A Mighty Wind* features a group, the New Main Street Singers, that effectively satirizes the New Christy Minstrels sound and performing style.

See also MINSTREL/TRAVELING SHOW.

New Grass Revival

One of the most influential of the progressive bluegrass groups, the New Grass Revival was born out of an earlier group known as the Bluegrass Alliance, featuring hot guitarist DAN CRARY as its leader. When Crary left the band in 1970, he took the name with him; he was replaced by fiddler/MANDOLIN player Sam Bush (b. Bowling Green, Kentucky, April 15, 1952), who along with banjo player Courtney Johnson (b. Barren County, Kentucky, December 20, 1939–June 7, 1996), Curtis Burch on GUITAR and

DOBRO, and and Harry "Ebo Walker" Shelor (b. Louisville, Kentucky, October 19, 1941) on bass, brought a rock-and-roll sensibility to their performance of traditional instrumentals and songs. Walker was soon replaced by powerful singer John Cowan (b. Evansville, Indianapolis, August 24, 1952), who had previously performed in a rock-and-roll band exclusively. This first version of the band, which lasted through the early 1980s, helped popularize the new grass sound.

Burch and Johnson tired of the endless touring that is the life of a bluegrass outfit, and were replaced by progressive banjoist BÉLA FLECK and singer/guitarist Pat Flynn. Fleck brought a more jazz-influenced sound, particularly in his approach to harmonies and his sparse, melodic improvisations. The band scored their greatest success with 1988's *Hold to a Dream,* their sole LP to demonstrate much action on the country charts. However, they were quite a successful performing band, touring on the bluegrass, college-campus, and to some extent traditional country circuit.

The band fizzled out in the early 1990s. Bush continues to be a much in-demand session musician, while Fleck formed his jazz-country fusion band, the Flecktones, who have had some success both on the pop and country charts.

See also BANJO, FIVE-STRING; FIDDLE.

New Lost City Ramblers

MIKE SEEGER, the son of folklorist Charles Seeger and half brother of folk revivalist PETE SEEGER, was enamored of bluegrass and country music in the Washington, D.C., area, where he grew up. Yale-educated JOHN COHEN was active in the New York

Two-thirds of the New Lost City Ramblers accompany "Mother" Maybelle Carter at the Newport Folk Festival. Left to right: John Cohen, Maybelle, Tracy Schwartz. (Photo © John Byrne Cooke, http://www.cookephoto.com)

folk scene in the 1950s, while Tom Paley, a mathematician, was from the Boston area. They first started to play together in the late 1950s in New York's Greenwich Village. The trio's academic background is reflected in their approach to the music, particularly on their first few albums released by Folkways in the late 1950s and early 1960s. They often focused on a single theme—such as Prohibition or songs of the Depression—and presented the music with meticulous documentation, including information on their sources. Their appearance at the 1959 NEWPORT FOLK FESTIVAL introduced them to the FOLK-REVIVAL audience and led to many years of popularity on the college and small folk-club circuit.

Paley left the group in 1963 to form another short-lived old-time band, the Old Reliable String Band, with New York–based musician Artie Rose; he then relocated to England, where he recorded a duet album with Mike Seeger's sister Peggy. In the late 1960s he formed the New Deal String Band with British musicians Janet Kerr on FIDDLE and Joe Locker on banjo, and in the late 1970s he recorded a solo album.

To replace Paley, Seeger brought in his friend Tracy Schwartz, who brought a more modern sound to the group. Schwartz's background in bluegrass widened the group's repertoire to include recreations of 1950s-era country recordings as well as the older styles they had previously performed. The band recorded an all-instrumental album, perhaps the first to emphasize this side of the old-time music tradition, as well as accompanying legendary country performer COUSIN EMMY on a 1967 recording.

By the early 1970s the Ramblers were performing only sporadically together. Seeger was pursuing a solo career, and also performing with his then-wife, ALICE GERRARD, as a duo and in the bluegrass/country band the Strange Creek Singers, which also featured Tracy Schwartz. Cohen formed the Putnam String County Band with fiddler Jay and guitarist/vocalist Lynn Ungar and cellist Abby Newton, one of the early 1970s more innovative revival bands. Schwartz performed with Seeger in the Strange Creek Singers for a while, and then

began touring with his wife, Eloise, and eventually his children, as well, while pursuing an interest in CAJUN MUSIC.

Although the Ramblers never officially disbanded, they have only performed together on and off for more than two decades, mostly for special occasions such as reunions or at festivals. They issued their first new album of studio recordings in over a decade in 1998 for the Smithsonian/Folkways label (*There Ain't No Way Out*).

See also SEEGER, PEGGY.

Newman, Jimmy "C" (b. 1927) *Grand Ole Opry performer and singer*
Born in Big Mamou, Lousiana, on August 27, 1927, Newman is an authentic French-Louisianian. As a teen he began performing in the Lake Charles area and was already performing the mix of country and traditional Cajun dance numbers that would become his trademark. He recorded for several small local labels beginning in 1949 and quickly gained a strong regional following. Hired for the popular *Louisiana Hayride* radio program, he was quickly signed to Dot, where he had the rockin' country hit with "Cry, Cry, Cry" (1954). He was invited to join the *Grand Ole Opry* in 1956, and had his biggest country-pop hit a year later with "A Fallen Star." He remains a performing member of the *Opry*.

After a couple of hitless years, Newman returned to the country charts under the hands of producer Owen Bradley at Decca Records, beginning with 1961's "Alligator Man" (playing off his Cajun heritage) and the half-spoken record "Bayou Talk." In 1962 he recorded *Folk Songs of the Bayou Country* to appeal to the FOLK-REVIVAL audience; this featured many songs sung in his native Cajun French, and wonderful instrumentation by noted Cajun fiddler Rufus Thibodeaux and "Shorty" LeBlanc on ACCORDION. Unfortunately, most of Newman's later Decca recordings were pitched at the mainstream country audience, and much of his Cajun heritage was lost.

In the mid-1970s Newman returned to his roots with a new band called Cajun Country. Although no longer a strong chart presence, he continues to record and perform, mostly focusing on traditional material.

Newport (Rhode Island) Folk Festival

The Newport Folk Festival was an outgrowth of the earlier Newport Jazz Festival held annually in the resort town of Newport, Rhode Island. Promoter George Wein had great success with his jazz concerts and reasoned that folk music would also draw a young, college-educated crowd. The festival became an institution in the late 1950s/early 1960s FOLK REVIVAL, bringing together contemporary folk revivalists such as the NEW LOST CITY RAMBLERS, PETE SEEGER, and BOB DYLAN with "traditional" performers MISSISSIPPI JOHN HURT, ROSCOE HOLCOMB, and the STANLEY BROTHERS, among many others. The major folk label Vanguard released a series of live albums based on recordings made at these early festivals, spreading the word about the event as well as about the featured performers.

At the height of its popularity in 1965, Newport became the scene of one of the most famous confrontations in pop music history. Scheduled to perform at the festival were both Bob Dylan, who had begun experimenting with electric instruments and accompaniments, and the Paul Butterfield Blues Band, a group that already employed electric GUITAR, bass, and drum. Dylan enlisted the band to perform as his backup group for his main appearance on the Saturday evening concert. Many in the folk crowd, who viewed Dylan as their greatest new star, were shocked and dismayed when he played his set. Some blame the primitive amplification; others the lack of rehearsal; and still others the parochial view of the folk fans who hated to see Dylan "go electric." In the many versions of what occurred on that night, some reported that Dylan was roundly booed off the stage, and there are various (disputed) reports of festival organizers, including Alan Lomax and PETE SEEGER, trying to unplug the amplifiers from backstage and fighting with Dylan's manager, ALBERT GROSSMAN.

Ironically, after 1965 the rise of folk-rock and the success of pop groups like the Beatles led to the folk revival's receding in popularity. The festival went on, notably introducing singer songwriter James Taylor in 1969, but by 1971 Wein tired of promoting summer shows moved to New York, and the Newport Folk Festival ended.

In 1986 Wein revived the festival, working with his associate, Robert Jones. Modern folk-pop acts such as the Indigo Girls and Shawn Colvin made their first major appearances there in the early 1990s, and corporate sponsors—ranging from the quirky Ben & Jerry's Ice Cream to the Apple & Eve juice makers—have helped keep the festival financially afloat. However, the festival no longer plays the major role it enjoyed during the heyday of the folk revival.

See also LOMAX, JOHN AND ALAN.

Nickel Creek

Like many bluegrass groups, Nickel Creek is a family affair. Raised in Southern California, long a country music mecca, both the Watkins and Thiele families were local patrons at a Carlsbad pizzeria that featured the newgrass band Bluegrass Etc., associated with well-known fiddler BYRON BERLINE. The young guitarist/singer Shawn and fiddler Sara Watkins and MANDOLIN player Chris Thiele began studying with band members, and a local promoter, who recognized their talent—and young, well-scrubbed looks—and encouraged them to hit the road, taking along Chris's father, Scott, on bass. They hit the bluegrass trail, playing festivals big and small, while building an audience among the traditional music set. Meanwhile, they garnered awards, particularly Thiele, who became a noted mandolin player, and began sessioning in Nashville, recording his own solo albums and working with Dolly Parton. Signed to the Sugar Hill label in 1999, the band produced their debut album in 2000, which led to great media attention, and also a Grammy nomination. They followed up with a second album in 2002, which was equally successful.

Niles, John Jacob (1892–1980) *song collector and performer*

Born in Louisville, Kentucky, on April 28, 1892, John Jacob Niles was the son of a carpenter who also was known as a talented singer of traditional songs; his mother was a classically trained organist. When he was around 10 years old, he was given an Appalachian dulcimer by his father, who encouraged him to build his own instruments; eventually, Niles crafted several dulcimers of his own design. He began collecting local songs while still in high school, and on graduation took a job as a surveyor that enabled him to travel through the Kentucky mountains, furthering his song collecting. Niles left Kentucky to serve in World War I in 1918; while flying in the air corps, he was seriously injured in a plane crash, which left him unable to walk for several years. During his recovery, he studied music in Paris and then, in 1919, returned to the United States to continue his studies at the Cincinnati Conservatory of Music.

By the early 1920s Niles was living in New York. He formed a partnership with singer Marion Kirby, and the two began touring college campuses, singing folk songs. Niles began publishing songs from his earlier collecting trips in the later 1920s, continuing through the 1930s. He toured extensively in the United States and Europe. His classical-style arrangements and concert hall voice made him an attractive performer to audiences unfamiliar with the rougher folk styles. Niles was signed to RCA Victor in 1939 and recorded for the label over the next three decades achieving success with his songs such as "Black Is the Color of My True Love's Hair," and arrangements of traditional folk songs, including "You Got to Cross That Lonesome Valley," and "Froggy Went a'Courtin'."

Niles continued to perform through the early 1970s, when he retired to his native North Carolina. He died on May 1, 1980.

See also DULCIMER (APPALACHIAN).

O'Brien, Tim (b. 1954) *songwriter and bandleader*

Timothy Page O'Brien was born in Wheeling, West Virginia, on March 16, 1954. He first learned GUITAR at age 12, then mastered MANDOLIN and FIDDLE as well. By his late teens he was leading a local bluegrass band. At around age 20 he moved to Boulder, Colorado. In 1978 he was one of the founding members of the group HOT RIZE, formed by banjoist Peter Wernick. O'Brien remained with the band for its 12-year run, writing a number of their best-loved songs.

O'Brien launched a solo career in 1990, initially signed with mainstream label RCA. However, the album was abandoned by the label, so he moved to a smaller bluegrass label Sugar Hill. O'Brien formed a backing band, the Oh Boys, which featured well-known bluegrass bassist Mark Schatz. O'Brien has also recorded and performed with his sister, Molly He has recorded albums of his own songs, as well as a Grammy-nominated 1996 album of BOB DYLAN covers. He has continued to experiment, releasing in 1999 *The Crossing,* an album tracing the Celtic roots of bluegrass music, and an interesting, living-room album of duets recorded with multi-instrumentalist Darrell Scott on the independent Howdy Skies label in 2000.

See also BANJO, FIVE-STRING.

Ochs, Phil (1940–1976) *songwriter and performer*

Phil Ochs was born on December 19, 1940, in El Paso, Texas. He attended college at Ohio State University, where he studied journalism, and began writing songs commenting on current events. In 1962, a few months before graduation, he moved to New York's Greenwich Village, the center of the SINGER/SONGWRITER MOVEMENT of the early 1960s. A year later, he was signed to Elektra Records. More satirical than many of his contemporaries, Ochs wrote a number of classic songs, including "Draft Dodger Rag" (commenting on the Vietnam War) and "Love Me, I'm a Liberal." He also showed a more sensitive side on "There But for Fortune," which was covered successfully by PETER, PAUL, AND MARY, and many other folk acts. In 1967 Ochs signed with A&M Records and turned to composing more confessional, singer-songwriter–styled material. He surprised his fans in 1970, when he began performing a mix of rock and roll oldies and his own compositions, dressed in a gold lamé suit; a performance at Carnegie Hall at the time horrified his core group of fans (and was later released on the aptly titled album, *Gunfight at Carnegie Hall*). Ochs descended into a period of deep depression and alcohol abuse in the early 1970s. In 1975 he briefly came to the fore again, performing in support of the freedom movement in Chile and writing a few songs. However, on April 6, 1976, Ochs took his own life by hanging himself while visiting his sister.

O'Connor, Mark (b. 1961) *multi-instrumentalist*

O'Connor was born in Seattle, Washington, on August 5, 1961, and mastered a number of musical instruments by the age of 11; he first started playing classical GUITAR at age six, winning a flamenco competition four years later. He soon turned his attention to country music, quickly learning bluegrass guitar, MANDOLIN, banjo, and DOBRO. But his true capabilities were first revealed when he picked up the FIDDLE at age 11 (he was inspired to take up the instrument after seeing Doug Kershaw performing on Johnny Cash's TV show); 18 months after his first violin lesson, he won the Junior division of the National Old-Time Fiddler's Contest in Weiser, Idaho. He was signed to Rounder Records, a bluegrass label, soon after, and released his first album at age 12; he recorded five more albums for the label in the 1970s, including a solo guitar record that showed his capabilities as a flatpicker. Over the next decade, he won every major U.S. fiddle championship, winning the open competition at the National Festival four times before retiring undefeated.

Like many other contest winners, Mark's original style was very flashy, designed to bring a crowd to its feet. However, in his late teen years, he came under the influence of progressive bluegrass and acoustic-jazz musicians such as DAVID GRISMAN, whose group he joined in the early 1980s (as a guitarist!) His fiddling began to pick up a sweeter tone and a sophistication and subtlety that is not usually heard in championship fiddling circles. After a year with Grisman, O'Connor played briefly with the Dregs, the original country/grunge-rock fusion group, and also toured with Doc and Merle Watson, PETER ROWAN, and Jerry Douglas. In 1983 O'Connor relocated to Nashville, where he soon was working as a studio musician.

O'Connor's dexterity on a number of instruments, and his ability to quickly fashion an appropriate style for an accompaniment, led him to be a major session player, recording with country stars as well as pop-rock singers such as JAMES TAYLOR and Paul Simon. In the late 1980s he signed with Warner Brothers as a solo artist, producing the *New Nashville Cats* LP as an homage to his bluegrass roots with popular country stars Ricky Skaggs, Vince Gill, and Steve Wariner as his informal band mates.

As O'Connor's fame has grown, so have his musical ambitions, although he has been less successful outside of the pure country realm. He composed a violin concerto that was premiered by the Santa Fe and Nashville Symphony Orchestras in 1993, taking the solo chair himself. In 1995 he signed with Sony Records, continuing to produce an eclectic mix of albums featuring jazz, classical, and bluegrass-styled performances. In 1998 he issued an album of his own classical-flavored solos, *Midnight on the Water,* and three years later, *Hot Swing,* in honor of famed jazz fiddler Stephane Grappelli.

O'Day, Molly (1923–1987) *singer*

Lois LaVerne Williamson was born in McVeigh, Kentucky, on July 9, 1923, the daughter of a coal miner. Her family was all musically talented, and Molly listened to the *National Barn Dance* radio program out of Chicago as a child. In 1939 her older brother, Skeets, got a radio job in West Virginia and invited his then 16-year-old sister to be his vocalist, under the stage name of Mountain Fern. In 1940 she broke with her brother and joined Lynn Davis's group, the Forty-Niners, and a year later she married Davis. The two spent the World War II years working radio in West Virginia, Alabama, and Kentucky; it was in their last job, in Louisville, that Williamson gained the stage name of Molly O'Day. The duo's greatest success came in 1945, when they joined Knoxville's WNOX. A year later Molly was signed to Columbia and had a hit with "Tramp on the Street," her best-loved song. Molly's music was also spread through her popular songbooks, which she sold through her radio show and personal appearances throughout the South and Midwest.

As her career progressed O'Day showed a growing propensity for religious material, particularly songs that emphasized humanity's failures and the need to seek solace in God. In 1949 she was hospitalized, apparently following an emotional breakdown, and, following her release, she and her husband entered the Church of God. Although she continued to record through 1951, she was no longer interested in being an entertainer. In 1954 Lynn was ordained a minister, and for the next three decades the duo preached in small West Virginia coal mining towns. O'Day made some religious recordings for small labels in the 1960s. She died of cancer on January 25, 1987.

Odetta (b. 1930) *recording artist*
Born Odetta Felious on December 31, 1930, in Birmingham, Alabama, Odetta was raised in Los Angeles. She studied classical piano and was trained as an opera singer as a youngster. When she was a teenager, she began acting locally, and at age 19 was hired to perform in a touring company of *Finian's Rainbow*. She next performed in summer stock outside of San Francisco, then began singing folk music in local clubs. In 1953 Odetta made her first trip to New York to perform, and then returned the next year to play a yearlong engagement at San Francisco's Tin Angel. A live album recorded there was her first record release. She recorded a mix of folk standards, blues, and new compositions, all with her rather simple, classical-flavored GUITAR accompaniment. Odetta recorded for Riverside and Tradition in the 1950s, and then Vanguard and RCA in the 1960s. Her greatest success came during the FOLK REVIVAL years, when she was one of the few African Americans to enjoy considerable popularity with the white folk audience. After 1970, however, Odetta rarely recorded or performed until the later 1980s, and then again in the later 1990s and early 21st century.

Old and in the Way
Before founding the Grateful Dead, Jerry Garcia performed as a bluegrass banjo player in the San Francisco Bay area. When the Grateful Dead became successful, Garcia formed the informal group Old and in the Way to express his love for bluegrass music (the name comes from the words of a sentimental old-time song). He joined forces with DAVID GRISMAN on MANDOLIN and PETER ROWAN, who had previously played together in another one-off group, MULESKINNER. Fiddler VASSAR CLEMENTS was an alumnus of JOHN HARTFORD's early 1970s band and had played with many other folk revivalists, including DAVID BROMBERG. They recorded one album, released by the Dead's own Round label, featuring many Rowan originals that have since become newgrass standards: "Panama Red" and "Land of the Navajo," two of his mythic western ballads, being the best known. Garcia revived the band from time to time with various different personnel; he teamed up again with Grisman in 1993 to record an acoustic duo album for children, and then cut another album of old-time country standards.

See also BANJO, FIVE-STRING.

Osborne Brothers, The
MANDOLIN player Bobby (b. Robert Van Osborne, December 7, 1931) and banjo player Sonny (b. October 29, 1937) were born in rural Hyden, Kentucky (southwest of the coal mining center of Hazard). The two brothers performed together from childhood, and were already working professionally in the early 1950s when Bobby was drafted into the Korean conflict. Young Sonny was an accomplished banjo player at age 14 in 1952, so good that he was invited to join bluegrass legend Bill Monroe's band for touring and recording during that summer. When Bobby returned from Korea, the brothers began performing together as a duo in 1953 over local Knoxville radio. In 1954 they relocated to Michigan to perform and record with JIMMY MARTIN, another Monroe alumnus, including the classic sides "Chalk up Another One" and "20/20 Vision."

A year later they were in Dayton, Ohio, where they joined another bluegrass legend at the beginning of his career, RED ALLEN. The group signed with MGM Records in 1956, scoring with their cover of COUSIN EMMY's classic reworking of "Reuben/Train 45," renamed "Ruby." Their dramatic harmonies—Red on lead, Bobby, with his distinctive high tenor, and Sonny on baritone—highlighted on the a cappella introduction, made the single a standout. The use of drums on these recordings made them controversial among pure bluegrass fans, although they clearly fit in with the high-energy music that the brothers created. They also pioneered the use of twin harmony banjos, an innovation later copied by progressive bands such as COUNTRY COOKING.

After Allen left the group, the brothers began performing over the WWVA Jamboree radio program in Wheeling. In 1959 Sonny Birchfield took over the lead vocal chores. A year later the band was booked into Antioch College in Yellow Springs, Ohio, introducing bluegrass music to a young, educated audience. They were soon in demand on the college and folk festival circuit, while they still maintained strong ties to country music. In 1964 they were invited to join the *Grand Ole Opry,* one of the few bluegrass groups at that time on the *Opry* stage, and signed with Decca. Their mid-1960s recordings broke further barriers in instrumentation, including their use of piano on "Up This Hill and Down," electric bass on "The Kind of Woman I Got," and pedal steel on their big 1967 hit, "Rocky Top," which has become perhaps the most over-played song in all of bluegrass.

In 1976 the Osbornes left Decca for the more traditional bluegrass label CMH, and then began recording for Sugar Hill in the early 1980s; since the mid-1990s they have recorded for Pinecastle, a small bluegrass label.

See also BANJO, FIVE-STRING.

Parker, Linda (1912–1935) *singer*

Genevieve Elizabeth Meunich was born in Covington, Kentucky, across the river from Cincinnati, on January 18, 1912. She was raised in Hammond, Indiana, where she began singing popular songs as a teenager on radio and in clubs. John Lair, the enterprising producer of Chicago's WLS *National Barn Dance* radio show, discovered her there and gave her a new name, Linda Parker, and encouraged her to sing country songs and dress in a gingham sunbonnet and dress. She was made the featured singer of the show's house band, the Cumberland Ridge Runners. Although she was often pictured holding a banjo or GUITAR, Parker did not play either instrument.

From 1932 to her death from appendicitis three years later, Parker was a favorite act, dividing her repertoire between 19th-century weepers like "I'll Be All Smiles Tonight" and the occasional traditional song like "Single Girl." She sang in a clear, soothing style that reflected her pop music roots, and became a model for country radio stars through the 1930s. Her death at age 23 on August 12, 1935, cemented her appeal to Depression-era listeners; WLS stars Karl and Harty rewrote the old standard "Bury Me Beneath the Willow" in her honor to become "We Buried Her Beneath the Willow."

See also BANJO, FIVE-STRING.

Paton, Sandy (b. 1929) *song collector and record label owner*

Charles Alexander "Sandy" Paton was born in Jacksonville, Florida, on January 22, 1929. He was raised in Portsmouth, New Hampshire. At age 14 he went to western Kansas to work harvesting wheat for the summer, then briefly studied at the Corcoran Art School in Washington, D.C., and in Seattle. In the early 1950s he became interested in folk music through hearing recordings by BURL IVES and the WEAVERS. In 1954 he met PAUL CLAYTON, who introduced him to folklorist/record producer KENNETH GOLDSTEIN, furthering his interest in traditional music. Soon after, he was living and performing in Berkeley, California, where he met his future wife, Caroline. They wed and spent a year collecting folk songs in England and Scotland, before eventually settling in Chicago in the late 1950s, where Paton heard traditional performers Horton Barker and FRANK PROFFITT at the University of Chicago Folk Festival. He went to visit both at their homes, recording them, giving these initial tapes to MOSES ASCH to release on Folkways Records.

By this time Paton had moved to Vermont, where a friend, Lee Hagerty, suggested that they release some other tapes from his southern trip on their own. The Patons with Hagerty started Folk Legacy Records in 1961, modeled after Folkways in the presentation. (The recordings were placed in plain black covers with a wraparound printed jacket; each came with an annotated booklet giving the history of the performers and lyrics to the songs). The initial Folk Legacy releases focused on traditional performers of the United States and England, but by the early 1970s the Patons began recording folk revivalists, including GORDON BOK and MICHAEL COONEY. Informal sing-alongs held at their home studio were released featuring many of their friends and fellow performers under the general name of the Golden Ring. The label has continued to operate to the present, reissuing many of its earlier LPs on CD.

Paxton, Tom (b. 1937) *songwriter*

Tom Paxton was born in Chicago, Illinois, on October 31, 1937. His family moved to Bristow, Oklahoma, in 1948. In the summer of 1954, an aunt bought him his first GUITAR while he was on break from the University of Oklahoma in Norman, where he began writing songs. In 1960 he enlisted in the army reserves and was stationed at Fort Dix, New Jersey, not too far from New York City's Greenwich Village. He began hanging out at New York's folk clubs, and settled in Greenwich Village in September 1960 after his service was over. His early songs began appearing in folk music journals, notably *Sing Out!* and *Broadside,* and Paxton released his first album, recorded live at the Village's Gaslight Club, featuring his own songs.

Influenced by WOODY GUTHRIE, Paxton wrote children's songs such as "The Marvelous Toy" and "Goin' to the Zoo," but the song that established his fame—and is perhaps still his best-known composition—was "Ramblin' Boy." The song became the title of Paxton's first Elektra album in 1964, which also featured two more classics, "The Last Thing on My Mind" and "I Can't Help But Wonder Where I'm Bound." "The Last Thing" was an immediate success with a wide variety of performers, covered by folk, country, pop, and rock singers numerous times over the years.

Paxton's second album, *Ain't That News,* put him squarely in the topical singer-songwriter category, although its best remembered song is the light-hearted "Bottle of Wine." Swept up by the FOLK-ROCK and SINGER/SONGWRITER MOVEMENT of the later 1960s, Paxton's following albums became progressively more personal in content and more elaborately produced. In the early 1970s he briefly relocated to England and recorded for the pop label Reprise, but then moved back to the United States. He recorded through the 1970s and mid-1980s for Vanguard, Mountain Railroad, and other smaller folk labels, sometimes working with fellow 1960s folk veteran BOB GIBSON. Paxton also returned to composing in the two styles that had made him famous: topical, satirical material and children's songs. He continued to record for a number of labels through the 1990s and into the 21st century, appearing occasionally on folk music revival shows as well as performing for both children and adults.

Pentangle

Pentangle was a British folk-jazz fusion group of the 1960s born out of the collaboration of guitarists BERT JANSCH and JOHN RENBOURN. Both were interested in melding folk, blues, and jazz influences, so when they decided to add a rhythm section to their duets, they hired two ex-jazz players: bassist Danny Thompson and percussionist Tony Cox. From the folk world they enlisted singer Jacqui McShee. Unlike FAIRPORT CONVENTION, which drew on the instrumentation of rock, Pentangle offered a softer, more introspective mix of British traditional songs and ballads, along with jazz-tinged instrumentals. The group recorded three albums, released on major label Reprise in the United States, but they never really achieved great popularity beyond the folk movement. After folding in 1973, various forms of the group performed, usually led by Jansch and McShee and employing various folk-rock veterans.

Peter, Paul, and Mary

Probably the most successful of all the FOLK-REVIVAL trios, Peter, Paul, and Mary was formed by agent ALBERT GROSSMAN, who recognized the growing popularity of folk music in Greenwich Village. Grossman was particularly impressed by the chart success of the KINGSTON TRIO, and also the unique vocal blend of the WEAVERS, who featured one female singer (Ronnie Gilbert) among the four members. Grossman approached a young folksinger, Peter Yarrow (b. May 31, 1938, New York City), who was playing in Greenwich Village clubs, about forming a mixed trio.

Mary Travers was born in Louisville, Kentucky, on November 9, 1936, but her parents relocated to Greenwich Village, where she was raised amid the artists and nonconformists who peopled that New York neighborhood. She had been singing with a local group called the Song Swappers, who performed traditional and topical folk songs at local clubs. "Paul" (actually Noel) Stookey (b. November 30, 1937, in Baltimore, Maryland), had played in an R&B outfit in high school before settling in Greenwich Village, where he initially worked as a singer and comedian. He met Travers on the local scene, and the two began writing songs together.

Grossman and Yarrow initially approached Travers about joining their proposed new group, and she recommended Stookey for his abilities as an emcee. Grossman hired arranger Milton Okun, who had previously worked for the CHAD MITCHELL TRIO among others, and he helped craft the trio's distinctive vocal blend. Almost immediately upon their debut in Greenwich Village in 1961, the group was a smash. Their first album came a year later from Warner Bros. Records, producing hits with "Lemon Tree" and the top 10 "If I Had a Hammer" (written by PETE SEEGER and Lee Hays); the album also was honored with two Grammy Awards.

Grossman recognized that his popular group would be an excellent vehicle for promoting another one of his acts, songwriter BOB DYLAN. The group introduced Dylan's "Blowin' in the Wind" in 1963, which became a major hit, and helped make the song an anthem in the growing CIVIL RIGHTS MOVEMENT. They performed it at the famous March on Washington in August of that year when Martin Luther King Jr. delivered his "I Have a Dream" speech.

The coming of the Beatles in 1964 changed the pop music landscape, as did the growing popularity of singer/songwriters such as TOM PAXTON, GORDON LIGHTFOOT, and JONI MITCHELL, replacing the earlier interest in social-protest songs. The group adapted to the times, scoring a hit in 1965 with Lightfoot's "For Lovin' Me" and a major hit in 1969 with "Leavin' on a Jet Plane," written by a (then-new) songwriter, JOHN DENVER. They also had a hit in 1967 with Stookey's satiric "I Dig Rock 'n' Roll Music," on which the group mimicked the sounds of many of the popular pop-rock groups of the time. 1969's album *Peter, Paul, and Mommy*, reintroduced the group's 1963 hit, "Puff the Magic Dragon," and was among the first children's-oriented record by younger revivalists.

Throughout this period, the group was politically active, appearing at countless rallies and demonstrations in support of the civil rights, anti–Vietnam War, and peace movements. They vigorously campaigned for Senator Eugene McCarthy in his unsuccessful bid for the Democratic presidential nomination in 1968. Unlike many of the other commercial folk groups who avoided politics, Peter, Paul, and Mary has always had a political message.

The group disbanded in 1970 to pursue solo projects. Travers attempted to become a pop singer/songwriter; Yarrow wrote political songs and recorded; and Stookey experimented with jazz and Christian-themed music. A tentative reunion in 1978 led in the early 1980s to a decision to permanently reunite on a part-time basis. The group continues to perform for part of the year, while freely doing solo work. They have become a major attraction on public television; their 25th anniversary show was an enormous success, and in 2003 the network aired their 40th anniversary celebration.

Phillips, Bruce "U. Utah" (b. 1935) *songwriter and storyteller*

One of the last great songwriter/storytellers, Bruce Phillips was the son of union organizers who instilled in him progressive politics from an early age. His mother and father divorced when he was young, and Phillips was raised in Cleveland by his mother, who married a vaudeville house manager; in 1947 the family moved to Utah. Phillips began playing ukulele and GUITAR, learning the songs of such country legends as Jimmie Rodgers and Harry McClintock (HAYWIRE MAC).

After serving in Korea in the early 1950s, Phillips returned home and became a card-carrying member of the Industrial Workers of the World (IWW). Known as Wobblies, the IWW's members were among the most progressive and radical of all unions. At a meeting Phillips met activist Ammon Hennacy, active in the Catholic Workers' Movement, who introduced him to pacifism and anarchism. Phillips worked in the Utah State Archives by day, and played his guitar and sang his own songs in local clubs at night. In 1960 visiting folklorist KENNETH GOLDSTEIN heard him play and recorded his first album. However, Phillips didn't abandon his day job until nine years later, when—after an unsuccessful run for Senate as the candidate of the "Peace and Freedom" party—he left Utah and traveled to New York.

Phillips's greatest popularity came in the late 1960s through the mid-1970s, thanks to a series of albums on Philo Records. He was a favorite in folk clubs and festivals because of his humorous stories (most famously an anecdote called "Moose Turd Pie") and his songs of rambling ("Starlight on the Rails") and social consciousness ("Room for the Poor"). Phillips continued to record and perform through the late 1980s, when he lost the facility to play the guitar due to disease. In 1995 alternative-rocker Ani DiFranco, a longtime fan, recorded Phillips telling a number of stories and then created rhythmic accompaniments for them; the result, *the past didn't go anywhere,* was released in 1996 on her own Righteous Babe label. That same year, Phillips announced his "retirement," although he has continued to record with various accompanists.

Pickard Family, The

Led by multi-instrumentalist Obed "Dad" Pickard and his wife, Leila May, the group began broadcasting over the *Grand Ole Opry* in 1926 and then moved to more than 40 other radio stations in a long history of performing. Dad specialized in the sentimental ballads of the late 19th century that had been popular in suburban parlors and then spread to the country, such as "Poor Kitty Wells," evergreen classics like "She'll Be Comin' 'Round the Mountain," and cowboy standards like "Bury Me Not on the Lone Prairie." The group eventually worked in major cities such as Detroit, New York, and Philadelphia, spreading the country music style into urban areas, plus publishing many popular songbooks that became the basis for many artists' performing repertoires. They recorded about 40 sides during the height of the country music craze from 1927 to 1930. By the late 1930s the Pickards (like the Carter Family) were broadcasting over the powerful border radio stations out of Mexico. In 1940 the family moved to California, making a few appearances in budget films, and then starred on a live television variety program out of Los Angeles from 1949 to 1954.

Planxty

Among the most popular of the Irish revival bands of the 1970s, Planxty combined energetic arrangements, instrumental virtuosity, and vocal harmonies. The group had its beginnings in 1972 when singer CHRISTY MOORE decided to record a solo album, and invited several local musicians to accompany him: singer/MANDOLIN and bouzouki player Andy Irvine; bouzouki player DONAL LUNNY; and Irish bagpiper Liam O'Flynn. The group's sound was so compelling they continued to play, taking the name Planxty. The group's first three albums were very popular both in Ireland and the United States, where they helped fuel the Irish music revival. The original lineup lasted only a little more than a year; Lunny left in 1973 to form the BOTHY BAND, and was replaced by singer/fiddler/bouzouki player Johnny Moynihan. By the end of 1974, Moore left, replaced by singer/guitarist PAUL BRADY. In 1975 the first run of the band ended.

Four years later, with the Bothy Band closing down, the original foursome reunited, adding Bothy Band FLUTE player Matt Malloy (although he stayed only for about a year). This lineup recorded and performed through 1983, and then finally called it a day.

Poole, Charlie (1892–1931) *vocalist and banjoist*

Born Charles Cleveland Poole in rural Randolph County, North Carolina, on March 22, 1892, Poole developed a unique banjo style based on the traditional styles around him. Poole worked most of his life in the textile mills, as did many other contemporary country musicians. He was working in the small textile town of Spray, North Carolina, when he began his performing career. He first formed a duo with fiddler Posey Rorer, originally a coal miner from Tennessee who was injured in a mining accident and so had taken to working in the mills. They were joined by guitarist Norman Woodlieff to form the first version of what would become the North Carolina Ramblers. In 1925 the trio got jobs in Passaic, New Jersey, working for a car manufacturer, which brought them north. Poole went to New York and arranged for them to record for Columbia Records, where they made their first recordings in 1925, which were immediately successful. The first record issued by the Ramblers was "Don't Let Your Deal Go Down," a blues-influenced song that remained in print for years and became Poole's signature number.

The band had a unique style, centering on Poole's wry, uninflected vocal style, and intricate, chordal work on the banjo. Poole sang a combination of sentimental heart songs and comic novelty numbers, many originating in the late 19th and early 20th centuries. Unlike other string bands, the North Carolina Ramblers were a subdued group, focusing on Poole's banjo and vocals accompanied by discreet GUITAR and FIDDLE. Poole's versions of many songs, including "Jay Gould's Daughter," "Ramblin' Blues," "Hungry Hash House," and "If I Lose (Let Me Lose)," have become standards in the old-time country repertoire. Poole made jazz-influenced recordings of old-time numbers, such as his "Goodbye Liza Jane," which would indirectly influ-

ence such artists as Western Swing fiddler Bob Wills, who also adopted old-time fiddle tunes to a new, jazz-and-blues influenced style.

The band went through several personnel changes in its short life; West Virginia guitarist Roy Harvey replaced Woodlieff on their second Columbia session in 1926, and fiddler Rorer left the band in 1928, to be replaced by Lonnie Austin and, two years later, by Odell Smith. Like many recording units of the day, the band was not a fixed ensemble, but probably had a set of floating members who would come together for specific recording dates or local jobs.

In 1929 Poole decided to enlarge the Ramblers to include many of the other musicians who had been performing with them. However, producer Frank Walker at Columbia was unwilling to change the successful Ramblers formula. Instead, the group went to the budget Paramount label, recording under the name of the Highlanders. This group featured a much richer ensemble sound, including piano played by Roy Harvey's sister, Lucy Terry, and the twin fiddles of Austin and Smith. They also made a series of comic-novelty dialogue recordings, entitled "A Trip to New York," perhaps to answer the popularity of the SKILLET LICKERS's series of miniplaylets.

Charlie Poole and his North Carolina ramblers from a mid-1920s record catalog (Courtesy BenCar Collection)

In 1931 Poole was so popular that he was invited to Hollywood to provide background music for the movies. However, he died of a massive heart attack on May 21, 1931, before he could make the trip west. When County Records, a New York old-time revival label of the 1970s, began reissuing these sides, they found a new and enthusiastic audience.

See also BANJO, FIVE-STRING.

Prine, John (b. 1946) *guitarist and songwriter*

Prine's family was from Kentucky, but moved to Maywood, Illinois, a western suburb of Chicago, before his birth on October 10, 1946. He began playing GUITAR as a teenager, inspired by his grandfather, who had worked as an accompanist for country star Merle Travis. After serving in the army in the early 1960s, Prine began performing in Chicago at local clubs. There he met another promising singer/songwriter, STEVE GOODMAN, and the two became leading lights of the Chicago FOLK REVIVAL. He was signed to Atlantic Records and released his debut album in 1971, which included the antiwar song "Sam Stone," told from the point of view of a drug-addicted Vietnam veteran. Prine's songs became favorites among folk and pop performers, notably "Paradise," about the coal mining industry (popularized by the Everly Brothers) and "Angel from Montgomery" (sung by Bonnie Raitt). Prine moved to Asylum Records in the late 1970s, and then formed his own label in the 1980s. He made a comeback in 1991 with *The Missing Years,* which featured duets with Bruce Springsteen, Tom Petty, and Bonnie Raitt. Prine continues to record and perform his mix of social-protest and satiric songs.

Proffitt, Frank (1913–1965) *singer, guitarist, and banjoist*

Proffitt was born in Laurel Bloomery, Tennessee, on the Tennessee–West Virginia–North Carolina border, in January 1913, but his family soon moved southeast to Reese, North Carolina. His father was a farmer who made traditional-style banjos, fabricating the rims and necks out of solid wood, with an animal skin head inset into the wooden body of the instrument. His father also sang traditional songs and ballads, which Frank heard from an early age. In 1932 Frank married Bessie Hicks, from a noted storytelling family of the region, and settled on his own farm in the colorfully named Pork Britches Valley. The Hicks had been "discovered" in the mid-1930s by folklorists Anne and Frank Warner, who asked the family if they knew other traditional musicians. Frank's in-laws recommended that the Warners visit him, and they began notating his songs during the early 1940s, eventually collecting more than 120 local songs. One of these songs, a ballad about a love affair gone wrong between locals Tom Dula and his beloved Laurie Foster, would change Proffitt's life.

The Warners were active on the folk circuit in the 1950s and began performing the ballad of "Tom Dula." A young FOLK-REVIVAL group called the KINGSTON TRIO heard the Warners' version and issued it as a single in late 1958 under the title "Tom Dooley"; within a year it had sold more than a million copies. A local newspaper tracked down Proffitt, and he was invited to appear at the first University of Chicago folk festival in 1961. This led to a flurry of concerts on the folk circuit through the mid-1960s; two albums were released during this period. Proffitt also continued the family tradition of banjo making, and his soft-voiced, traditional wooden banjos became much sought after and copied by other makers. He died on November 24, 1965.

See also BANJO, FIVE-STRING.

progressive bluegrass

The mid-1970s bluegrass revival spawned a number of groups that used traditional bluegrass instrumentation but were influenced by other types of music, from swing and jazz to rock and progressive music. Known at the time as either "progressive" or "newgrass" bands (the newgrass name coming from the popular group NEW GRASS REVIVAL), these bands were met with some hostility from traditionalists while they greatly helped expand the bluegrass style and the market for bluegrass music. Many of the newgrass pioneers returned to playing more traditional bluegrass styles in later years.

Undoubtedly the most important group to the growth of progressive bluegrass was the New Grass Revival. While there had been groups in the 1960s that sought to stretch the bluegrass repertoire (the COUNTRY GENTLEMEN, the GREENBRIAR BOYS, and the Charles River Valley Boys, to name a few) by drawing on a wider range of musical influences, the New Grass Revival was the first to try to introduce the energy of rock and roll as well as pop and rock songs into their repertoire. Their use of electric bass and electrified banjo and FIDDLE was distressing to bluegrass traditionalists.

Another important early progressive band was COUNTRY COOKING. The original instrumentals by band members TONY TRISCHKA and Peter Wernick were based on jazz harmonies and unusual rhythms. Trischka also produced a number of even more far-out solo albums in the 1970s, beginning with his *Bluegrass Light,* which took the banjo far beyond the usual bluegrass repertoire. The music was so experimental that some people mockingly called it "spacegrass," a name that stuck.

In the mid-1970s, mandolinist DAVID GRISMAN expanded progressive music to encompass acoustic jazz. This hybrid form of music—he called it Dawg Music—was often played in small ensembles featuring just MANDOLINS, fiddle, and GUITAR, but mainstream bluegrass bands were also influenced by Grisman's ventures into jazz and swing territories. This movement was called by some "jazzgrass," although it didn't last very long. Soon Grisman's lighter, swinging style of picking the mandolin was simply incorporated into mainstream progressive bluegrass, although he continues to produce his own quirky brand of music into the 1990s.

Like most progressive music, the best elements of progressive bluegrass—advanced harmonies and rhythms, electrified instruments, a broader range of songs—have all been incorporated into mainstream bands today. Meanwhile, artists such as Sam Bush (originally of New Grass Revival) and Trischka have returned to playing more traditionally oriented music, so that progressive and traditional bluegrass have met on a new common ground. While progressive bluegrass was undoubtedly an important trend in the expansion of bluegrass both as a style and in reaching a broader audience, it has not survived as a separate genre.

See also BANJO, FIVE-STRING.

Puckett, Riley (1894–1946) *guitarist and singer*
George Riley Puckett was born in Alpharetta, Georgia (northeast of Atlanta), on May 7, 1894. When he was three months old, a mistreated eye ailment led to his almost total blinding. Trained at the Macon School for the Blind, he first took up the banjo, and then switched to the GUITAR, quickly evolving a unique style featuring bass-note runs as bridges between chord changes. While doubtless other guitarists used bass runs previously, Puckett's runs were more elaborate and fully worked out than others who were recording at the time or immediately after.

When Georgia fiddler James Gideon Tanner was invited to record for Columbia Records in 1924, he took Puckett along as his accompanist to the New York sessions. Soon after, when Columbia urged Tanner to form a string band to cash in on the popularity of that format, Puckett and Tanner formed the SKILLET LICKERS. Puckett's vocals were an integral part of the band's popularity during its heyday from the mid-1920s through the mid-1930s. His fine baritone voice, with just a slight country inflection, made him immediately appealing not only to a country audience but also to the broader pop market. He made many solo recordings at the same time, working with Tanner's band, including the 1924 recording of "Rock All Our Babies to Sleep," on which Puckett yodels, thought to be the first country recording featuring this unique vocal style.

From 1934, when the Skillet Lickers folded, through 1941, Puckett primarily recorded for RCA Victor (he also briefly recorded for Decca in 1937), while performing on radio stations in Georgia and bordering states. His vocal style became increasingly smooth, showing the influence of such pop crooners as Bing Crosby. World War II brought an end to his recording career, and Puckett passed away on July 13, 1946.

See also BANJO, FIVE-STRING.

Reagon, Bernice See Sweet Honey in the Rock.

recording

The recording of folk music has a long history, dating back to the birth of the phonograph itself. Early cylinder recorders, which captured sound on cylinders made out of wax, were used by pioneering folklorists such as Frances Densmore (to collect Native American music), Percy Grainger (collecting British folk song), and Robert Gordon (collecting American folk song). The early commercial recording companies also occasionally issued folk music (or folk-style music).

The phonograph record industry took off with the introduction of disc records in the late teens, which offered better sound and were more durable than the earlier cylinders. However, disc recording equipment was considerably more bulky than cylinder machines, and it took awhile for portable equipment to be developed for use in field work. The discovery of the market for country music in 1923 with the recordings of Georgia musician Fiddlin' John Carson persuaded many of the commercial labels to set up temporary studios in southern towns such as Atlanta and Dallas to record local talent. The Victor sessions held in 1927 in Bristol, Tennessee/Virginia were particularly productive, as both the Carter Family and singer Jimmie Rodgers made their first recordings there.

In 1933 folklorists John and Alan Lomax had a special portable disc-recording machine built into the truck of their car and set out on a trip down South to record traditional performers, primarily in southern prisons. They were able to record many performers who would later establish themselves as folk or blues musicians, including Lead Belly, Muddy Waters, Bascom Lamar Lunsford, and countless others. In the early 1940s Alan Lomax began working with the commercial record labels to reissue earlier recordings by country performers who reflected the folk tradition.

The urban FOLK REVIVAL of the mid-1930s to 1940s led to the establishment of the first record labels catering to this new market. In New York City a sound engineer named Moses Asch began recording local folk performers, including Pete Seeger, Woody Guthrie, and Lead Belly initially for his Asch and Disc labels. Other specialty labels like Musicraft and Keynote also issued folk-oriented material.

The real boom in folk recording came after World War II with two new developments: the invention of the tape recorder, which made it easier to record outside the studio, and possible to record longer performances than the earlier discs, which were limited to three or five minutes; and the coming of the LP, which enabled these longer performances to be issued economically. Asch recognized the new opportunity early, establishing the Folkways Records label in 1949 to document the new folk music. He was able to inexpensively produce albums by operating his own small studio and employing many folklorists who made "field recordings" using relatively inexpensive tape recorders. Eventually, folklorists such as JOHN COHEN, MIKE SEEGER, KENNETH GOLDSTEIN, Frederic Ramsey Jr., Art Rosenbaum, and many more would make their field recordings available to Asch to issue on LP. (In 1986 the Folkways collection was acquired by the Smithsonian Institution, which continues to issue new recordings on CD and preserve the more than 2,000 LPs issued by Asch).

A second generation of folk labels developed in the 1950s with a more commercial orientation than Folkways. JAC HOLZMAN formed the Elektra label and had initial success with such folk revivalists as OSCAR BRAND and JUDY COLLINS. The Solomon Brothers founded Vanguard, originally to offer high-quality classical recordings, but quickly began recording folk and blues performers, scoring a major success in the early 1960s with JOAN BAEZ. The CLANCY BROTHERS formed their own label, Tradition, in the mid-1950s to issue their own recordings and traditional Irish performers.

In the early 1960s several important new labels were founded. CHRIS STRACHWITZ, an Austrian immigrant who had developed an interest in the blues music of the Southwest, founded Arhoolie Records, which has become one of the most important labels dedicated to blues, CAJUN, and TEX-MEX MUSIC. Sandy and Caroline Paton founded Folk Legacy Records to feature both their field recordings and recordings of their folk revival friends, including GORDON BOK and MICHAEL COONEY. Several record collectors founded reissue labels to feature 78 recordings of folk styles, including Dave Freeman, who started County Records for old-time music, and Nick Perls, who founded Yazoo with a similar mission for blues.

The 1970s saw the establishment of several important new labels. Rounder Records was founded in Boston as a cooperative, and has grown to feature a wide array of musical styles, from traditional folk to country, bluegrass, rock, and jazz. Philo Records in Vermont was founded to feature singer-songwriters such as ROSALIE SORRELS and U. Utah Phillips. Flying Fish was founded in Chicago to document the local folk/blues scenes. Eventually, both Philo and Flying Fish were purchased by Rounder.

The LP and following CD eras, along with the boom in inexpensive home recording equipment, has enabled almost anyone to have his or her own "label." Many folk artists issue their own recordings as a means of promoting themselves and also as something to sell at live events. Artists often graduate from their own labels to more traditional outfits; singer/songwriter NANCI GRIFFITH first issued her own records on her playfully named B. F. Deal label, which were later reissued on Philo when she signed with them. Others choose to issue their own recordings so they don't have to deal with even the minimal commercial pressure of the folk labels; in his later career JOHN HARTFORD formed his own label, Small Dog A-Barkin', so he could record himself and his friends as he saw fit.

The coming of the Web and Internet file trading promises to make even more music available to the consumer. Large archives, such as the Smithsonian/Folkways collection, have been quickly making all of their holdings available in digital formats. The ability to hear folk, world, and other noncommercial music will undoubtedly continue to grow over the coming decades.

Red Clay Ramblers, The

Founded in Chapel Hill, North Carolina, in 1973, the original band members—centering on fiddler Bill Hicks, banjo player Tommy Thompson, and MANDOLIN player Jim Watson—were interested in pursuing the vocal-music side of the old-time tradition; other local bands, such as the Fuzzy Mountain Stringband (of which Hicks had been a member) and the Hollow Rock Stringband (of which Thompson had been a member) were instrumentally oriented. The group recorded their first album with guest artist Fiddlin' Al McCandless, who is more bluegrass oriented in his style than the rest of the band. While finishing these recordings, pianist

The Red Clay Ramblers in their early 1980s lineup: Jack Herrick (bass, trumpet), Tommy Thompson (banjo), Clay Buckner (fiddle), Mike Craver (piano), and Jim Watson (mandolin) (Courtesy Flying Fish Records)

Mike Craver joined the group, and they experimented with adding ragtime and blues to the mix. With the addition of trumpeter Jack Herrick in 1975, the group's best lineup was completed.

The Ramblers made a series of innovative records from the mid-1970s through the early 1980s. Thompson and Craver wrote some amusing novelty songs in the manner of country-jazz, including "The Ace," which tells of a blind date gone seriously wrong, and "Merchant's Lunch," playing off the country clichés of roadside diners and big-rig truckers. Vocalists Thompson, Craver, and Watson also did much to revive the repertoire of the Carter Family, recording a trio album in homage to the earlier group.

In the 1980s the band went through several personnel changes, while increasingly working with playwright/filmmaker Sam Shepard, scoring his play *A Lie of the Mind* and the film *Far North*. During the mid-1990s they worked with comic mimes Bill Irwin and David Shiner in their Broadway production *Fool Moon*.

In 1994 last original member Tommy Thompson left the band after being diagnosed with Alzheimer's disease; he subsequently died from complications of the disease. Herrick is the last of the classic 1970s-era ensemble left. After an eight-year hiatus from recording, the band returned with a new album, *Yonder*, on their own label in 2001.

See also BANJO, FIVE-STRING.

Redpath, Jean (b. 1937) *ballad singer*

Redpath was born on April 28, 1937, to a farming family outside of Edinburgh, Scotland; her father was an amateur musician, playing hammer dulcimer, and her mother sang Scottish songs and ballads. Her daughter took a great interest in these songs, so when she attended college she entered the School of Scottish Studies, specifically to study folklore. In 1961, she relocated to New York, where she began performing as a ballad singer. She recorded for a number of folk labels, gaining her greatest success in the mid-1970s thanks to a series of records on Philo Records, including several albums of songs by Scottish poet Robert Burns. Between 1974 and 1987, she was regularly featured on Public Radio's popular program, *A Prairie Home Companion*. In 1987, she was made an M.B.E. (Member of the British Empire) by the Queen. She continues to record and perform.

See also DULCIMER (HAMMERED).

Reed, Blind Alfred (1880–1956) *singer and fiddler*

The West Virginia coal miner and fiddler Blind Alfred Reed, born on June 15, 1880, was discovered by country producer Ralph Peer at the legendary 1927 sessions held in Bristol, Virginia, which also produced the Carter Family's and Jimmie Rodgers's first recordings. Reed recorded for Victor, playing fairly simple FIDDLE parts to accompany his own clearly sung vocals, usually performed with discreet guitar accompaniment. Reed had a clear, powerful voice, and his songs often tackled topical issues in a humorous way, making them immediately popular.

Many of his songs commented on the troubles he believes women bring to men, although it's not always clear just how serious the fiddler is in songs like "We Just Got to Have Them, That's All," which traces all the way back to the Garden of Eden the problems he believes women have created for their mates. Reed capitalized on his biggest hit, "Why Do You Bob Your Hair Girls," a semiserious indictment of the craze for short hair, with a second number ("Bob Hair Number 2") where he continues to take a

fundamentalist approach to the question of coiffure ("Short hair belongs to men," the song warns).

Perhaps Reed's greatest song is the poignant "How Can a Poor Man Stand Such Times and Live?" In a straightforward style Reed outlines how rural Americans are exploited by middlemen and entrepreneurs while they benefit little from their labor. The repeated chorus line (and title of the song) says it all; Reed does not embellish or force the message, but lets the song speak for itself. Perhaps only Fiddlin' John Carson's "Taxes on the Farmer Feeds Them All" comes close in its simple eloquence as a great social-protest song of the era. Reed did not record after 1929, remaining a local entertainer until his death on January 17, 1956.

Reed, Ola Belle (1916–2002) *music promoter and songwriter*

Born in Lansing, North Carolina, on August 17, 1916, Reed was one of 13 children of a musical schoolteacher named Arthur Campbell. He played FIDDLE, banjo, GUITAR, and organ, and formed his own traditional band six years before her birth, so she was raised with old-time music all around her. Her grandfather was also a fiddler, as well as a Baptist preacher. Both her mother and grandmother sang ballads and songs. The Reeds lived on the North Carolina–Virginia border, an area rich in old-time music (the famous Galax Fiddlers' Convention was held close by).

In the 1930s the family relocated to Baltimore, where Reed learned guitar and banjo, and began writing her own songs. She and younger brother Alex formed a band following World War II that played in an older, traditional country style. They become popular favorites, first on radio out of mid-Maryland and then out of their central Pennsylvania general store, Campbell's Corner.

Ola Belle and Alex were also important promoters of country music in Pennsylvania and Maryland. In 1951, along with Bud Reed, Ola Belle's husband, they founded New River Ranch, a music venue operating out of Maryland. They moved in

1960 to West Grove, Pennsylvania, where they remained for the next quarter-century producing concerts. Alex and Ola Belle were also talented songwriters, claiming to have written more than 200 songs. Some of Ola Belle's songs have become popular among traditional and new country performers, including "High on a Mountain."

During the 1970s Ola Belle gained new popularity thanks to a series of albums on Rounder and Folkways Records. She often toured and performed with her son, Dave. By the mid-1980s, however, she was confined to her home, and in 1988 a benefit concert was held in Washington, D.C., to help her pay medical bills. In 1986 she was awarded a National Heritage Fellowship by the National Endowment for the Arts. She continued to live in retirement in Maryland, until her death on August 16, 2002.

See also BANJO, FIVE-STRING.

Renbourn, John (b. 1944) guitarist

John Renbourn was born in Torquay, England. Like many in his generation, Renbourn was first introduced to folk music through the British skiffle movement in the mid-1950s. From there he became interested in blues and jazz, and began playing in London clubs after moving to the city in the early 1960s. He studied classical guitar from 1964 to 1966, and also began collaborating with fellow club guitarist BERT JANSCH. They recorded two albums of duets, and this led them to form a group, PENTANGLE, in 1967, to further explore the connections between folk blues and jazz. Even while Pentangle was performing, Renbourn continued to record as a solo artist, returning to his love of medieval and classical-inspired music with *Sir John a lot of Merry England* (1968) and the classic *The Lady and the Unicorn*. After Pentangle disbanded, Renbourn performed as a solo artist in the 1970s, also in the mid-1970s as a duet partner with blues guitarist STEFAN GROSSMAN. In the 1980s and 1990s he continued both as a soloist and in various ensembles, sometimes called the John Renbourn Group and sometimes Ship of Fools.

Reneau, George (c. 1901–1933) singer and guitarist

Born in Jefferson County, Tennessee, around 1901, Reneau was a blind street musician, born in the Smokies. When he was a teenager, his family relocated to Knoxville, where he learned the GUITAR and began playing on street corners. He was heard by a scout for Vocalion Records, who brought him to New York to record. Initially, Reneau was used strictly as an accompanist, working with pop singer

John Renbourn at the Philadelphia Folk Festival, early 1980s (Photo © Larry Sandberg)

Gene Austin. They were billed as the Blue Ridge Duo for these country recordings, including several blues-flavored songs, "Lonesome Road Blues" and "Blue Ridge Blues." Austin and Reneau recorded for both Vocalion and Edison.

In early 1925 Vocalion finally recorded Reneau singing and accompanying himself, and the results were several hits including versions of Vernon Dalhart's "The Prisoner's Song" and the well-known country songs "Jesse James" and "Wild Bill Jones." In 1927 Vocalion paired him with Lester McFarland (one-half of the popular duo Mac and Bob), issuing these recordings under a variety of names, including the Lonesome Pine Twins and the Collins and Cramer Brothers. These recordings were available through the early 1930s on a variety of dime-store labels.

The Depression ended Reneau's recording career, as it did for many other country performers. He returned to singing on the streets, where he apparently contracted pneumonia and died in late 1933.

Reno, Don (1927–1984) *banjoist*

Born Donald Wesley Reno in Spartanburg, South Carolina, on February 21, 1927, Reno learned to play banjo as a teenager, playing in the new "three-finger" (picked) style that would come to be called "bluegrass banjo." Originally playing with the MORRIS BROTHERS, Reno was almost hired by Bill Monroe to take the banjo spot in his Blue Grass Boys band in 1943; unfortunately, he was drafted and Earl Scruggs got the job. However, when Scruggs left the band with Lester Flatt to form their own group, Reno came on board, performing with Monroe in 1948 for about a year; he then met guitarist/vocalist Red Smiley (b. Arthur Lee S., May 17 1925–January 2, 1972), and the two performed with a couple of other bands before forming their own group in 1951, the Tennessee Cutups. His unique banjo style, including picking single-string melodies in the style of tenor banjo players of the 1930s, made him an immediate standout. In 1955 Reno joined Arthur "Guitar Boogie" Smith in recording the original version of what was then called "Feuding Banjos" (and is now better known as "Dueling Banjos"), with Smith playing tenor and Reno playing five-string.

The Reno and Smiley group was one of the most respected in bluegrass, slightly more progressive than Monroe and Flatt and Scruggs in their outlook, and certainly very prolific. However, Smiley's health began to deteriorate in the early 1960s, and by 1968 he had to leave the band (he died in 1972); Reno then formed a new Cutups with vocalist/guitarist Bill Harrell, and they worked together until 1978. Reno continued to perform until his death on October 16, 1984, often accompanied by his sons Ronnie on GUITAR, Dale on MANDOLIN, and Don Wayne on banjo.

See also BANJO, FIVE-STRING.

"Reuben James" (c. 1941) *folk standard written by Woody Guthrie*

When the United States was attacked at Pearl Harbor, suddenly the folk movement, which had previously been antiwar, was mobilized in the fight against fascism. WOODY GUTHRIE eagerly joined the fight, writing dozens of songs inspired by events in the war. One was inspired by the Nazi torpedoing of a U.S. ship, the *Reuben James,* in October 1941. Guthrie's original song featured a long list of the men killed on the boat, because he felt it gave an accurate picture of the diverse population of the United States serving in the fight against Hitler. Working with PETE SEEGER, Millard Lampell, and other New York–based folksingers, he fleshed out the story of the song, and finally created the memorable chorus, asking "What were their names?" rather than listing them all. The song was recorded by the Almanac Singers (predecessors of the WEAVERS) in early 1942 and became a folk standard long after the events were forgotten.

Reynolds, Malvina (1900–1978) *songwriter and activist*

Malvina Milder was born to Jewish immigrant parents in San Francisco on August 23, 1900. She attended college hoping to teach, but due to her left-wing politics was unable to get a job on graduation in the mid-1930s. She began writing a column for *The Daily Worker,* and through her political activities came into contact with folksingers, including PETE SEEGER. This inspired her to begin writing her own songs. Her first recognition as a songwriter came when HARRY BELAFONTE recorded her song "Turn Around." However, Seeger had the greatest success with her songs, earning a minor pop hit in 1964 with her critique of suburban sprawl, "Little Boxes." A year later, the British folk-pop group the Searchers had a hit with her antinuclear war song, "What Have They Done to the Rain?" Reynolds recorded on her own, but was only a modestly gifted performer. Most of her recordings were issued on her own label. She died on March 17, 1978.

Tony Rice in the late 1970s (Courtesy Rounder Records)

Rice, Tony (b. 1951) *guitarist and vocalist*

Born in Danville, Virginia, on June 8, 1951, Rice got his start as a guitarist and vocalist in the Bluegrass Alliance and banjoist J. D. Crowe's influential early-1970s progressive band, the New South. Rice's GUITAR work was heavily influenced by Doc Watson and Clarence White, although his skills soon outstripped those of his mentors. He recorded progressive bluegrass with DAVID GRISMAN on his 1975 *Rounder Album* and then joined in the formation of Grisman's first quintet, dedicated to performing the mandolinist's jazz-influenced compositions. Rice soon struck out on his own, forming his Tony Rice Unit to perform progressive string music of his own composition.

In the 1980s he alternated between recording instrumental and vocal LPs. His vocal LPs tended to feature material from singer/songwriters from both FOLK-ROCK and new country movements, such as BOB DYLAN, Rodney Crowell, GORDON LIGHTFOOT, Norman Blake, Mary-Chapin Carpenter, and JAMES TAYLOR. He also recorded an LP of duets with Ricky Skaggs in 1980, in the manner of the brother acts of the 1930s and 1940s. During the later 1990s Rice lost some of his vocal capabilities, but continued to perform as a guitarist in both bluegrass and jazz/new age styles. Rice has also worked with various all-star bluegrass bands, and cut two bluegrass albums with his brother Larry, along with Chris Hillman and Herb Pedersen, in the late 1990s.

See also BANJO, FIVE-STRING; MANDOLIN.

Riddle, Almeda (1898–1986) *singer*

Born Almeda James on November 21, 1898, and raised in rural Cleburne County, Arkansas, where she spent her entire life, Riddle learned a rich repertoire of traditional ballads, children's songs, and religious songs from her family, particularly her father, J. L. James, a descendant of the famous outlaw James Brothers, and a timber merchant of Irish descent who worked as an amateur singing teacher as well as playing the FIDDLE. Almeda could remember him singing every morning and evening from his large collection of songbooks; because he could read music, he would often form small singing classes, teaching a 10-day class in sight-singing. Almeda began collecting what she called "ballets" from a young age, including her father's version of the classic English ballad "The House Carpenter." Her mother's brother, Uncle John Wilkerson, was also a strong influence, although he sang many "silly songs" that Almeda's mother objected to his performing, including "Froggie Went a-Courtin'," with its unusual nonsense-word chorus, which Almeda performed for the rest of her life.

In 1916 Almeda married H. P. Riddle, who was himself a fine singer. The two would often sing together after supper. They lived together happily for a decade in Heber Springs, Arkansas, when a cyclone hit the town, taking the life of Almeda's husband and youngest child, and seriously injuring the other children. Almeda spent four months in the hospital recovering, and then returned to live on her father's farm with the remains of her family.

Riddle was never a professional performer and probably would have lived and died in obscurity if she had not been "discovered" by folklorist Alan Lomax when he was amassing a series of albums for Atlantic Records in 1959, issued as the *Southern Folk Heritage* series. Riddle's clear-as-a-bell singing and wide repertoire of unusual versions of well-known songs made her the hit of this series, leading to a solo album issued by Vanguard Records in 1966 along with appearances at folk festivals. In the 1970s she recorded two albums for Rounder Records, as well as a few recordings for smaller labels. Her chilling version of "The Old Churchyard" is one of the greatest recordings of solo singing on record. She died in June 1986.

See also LOMAX, JOHN AND ALAN.

Riders in the Sky

The Riders are a cowboy-comedy act that pays homage to the classic stars of cowboy music as well as satirizing the conventions of cowboy films and radio of the 1940s and 1950s. Guitarist/lead vocalist Douglas B. Green, their leader, was formerly the aural historian at the Country Music Foundation and a leading scholar who has written widely on the history of country music; Woody Paul (b. Paul Woodrow Chisman) was a nuclear engineer with a degree from MIT before he took up cowboy fiddling. Fred LaBour (aka "Too Slim") completes the band, playing bass. The band began as a genuine attempt to revive the goofy charm of early cowboy acts; the threesome appeared in the classic rhinestone-encrusted cowboy gear, and their stage show attempted to recreate the nostalgic charm of the early cowboy acts. They are popular as performers, with their own radio program, *Riders Radio Theater,* broadcast over National Public Radio, and even briefly their own network Saturday morning kiddie show. They appear regularly on the *Grand Ole Opry* and Country Music Television.

Rinzler, Ralph (1934–1994) *music collector and performer*

Ralph Carter Rinzler was born on July 20, 1934. In the early 1950s he attended Swarthmore College, where he became interested in folk music. Like many folk revivalists of the time, he was inspired by HARRY SMITH's *Anthology of American Folk Music* and PETE SEEGER's *How to Play the 5-String Banjo* instruction book to begin playing old-time music. In 1958 he joined the GREENBRIAR BOYS, one of the first second-generation bluegrass bands. In the early 1960s Rinzler encouraged TOM ASHLEY to return to performing. Through Ashley, he met and recorded DOC WATSON, and soon was managing Watson along with bluegrass MANDOLIN player Bill Monroe. He was also an early champion of CAJUN MUSIC, doing important fieldwork in the region from 1964 to 1967, and helping to bring the BALFA BROTHERS north.

Rinzler was hired by the NEWPORT FOLK FESTIVAL Foundation to do fieldwork to find traditional performers to appear at the annual festival; in 1967 he oversaw the creation of the Smithsonian Institution's

Festival of American Folklife, and remained its director thereafter. Rinzler worked at the Smithsonian over the next decades, arranging for the purchase of MOSES ASCH's Folkways Records in 1986. Rinzler died on July 15, 1994, and the Folkways collection, along with his own collection of recordings and papers, was incorporated in 1998 into the newly created Ralph Rinzler Folklife Archives and Collections at the Center for Folklife and Cultural Heritage, named in his honor. He was awarded a posthumous Lifetime Achievement Award by the Folk Alliance in 2001.

See also BANJO, FIVE-STRING.

Ritchie, Jean (b. 1922) *singer*

The Ritchie family were among the first settlers in the Cumberland Mountain region in the late 1700s. Many were known locally as fine ballad singers and musicians, including Ritchie's father, Balis, a

Riders in the Sky, c. 1980. Left to right: Fred LaBour, Cowboy Doug, and Woody Paul (Courtesy Rounder Records)

Jean Ritchie in the early 1980s (Courtesy Greenhays Records)

schoolteacher, and her mother, Abigail Hall. They had settled in Viper, Kentucky (southeast of the coal mining town of Hazard), where Ritchie was born on December 8, 1922. The relatives all gathered together and played various instruments, including FIDDLE, banjo, GUITAR, and the three-stringed dulcimer, which became Ritchie's favorite. As a youngster she became deeply interested in the traditional songs passed along by her family, beginning a lifetime of collecting.

Unlike other mountain children, Ritchie was fortunate to be able to attend college at the University of Kentucky, completing a B.A. degree in the mid-1940s. After graduation she moved to New York and soon won a Fulbright scholarship to study British balladry in England. On her return to Kentucky in the mid-1950s, she became active in the beginnings of the folk music revival, as well as publishing a collection of songbooks based on her family's song repertoire.

Ritchie was most popular in the late 1950s and early 1960s, when she recorded for mainstream labels Riverside and Elektra as well as Folkways Records. She appeared at the NEWPORT FOLK FESTIVAL for several years, as well as most other major festivals. After the folk boom died down in the late 1960s, Ritchie switched her emphasis to her own material, including topical songs addressing the damage done to the Kentucky landscape by strip mining. She continued to record sporadically for larger labels, often saddled with unsympathetic accompanists who played in a soft-rock style, clearly not suited to her back-home presentation.

In the early 1980s, along with husband, George Pickow, Ritchie formed the Greenhays label to issue her own recordings along with other folk revivalists. By the end of the decade, however, she was little heard or seen on the folk circuit.

See also BANJO, FIVE-STRING.

Roberts, "Fiddlin' " Doc (1897–1978) *fiddler*

Doc Phil Roberts was born in Madison County, Kentucky, on April 26, 1897. He came from a farm family that had settled in the mountains of Kentucky sometime before the Civil War. His older brother, Liebert, was a fine FIDDLE player, and Doc began learning tunes from Liebert and other regional fiddlers from the age of seven. One of the prime sources for both brothers was an African-American fiddler named Owen Walker; Roberts commented about Walker, "He was the fiddlingest colored man that was ever around Kentucky."

Roberts briefly attended school in Berea as a young teenager, then wed a local girl in 1913. They would eventually have 11 children, and Roberts set about supporting them by growing tobacco and corn as a sharecropper on land owned by his mother. A neighbor, Dennis Taylor, recognized Roberts's fiddling talents and arranged for him to make a trip to nearby Richmond, Indiana, where the studios of Gennett Records were located. Along with singer Welby Toomey and guitarist Edgar Boaz, Roberts made his first recordings in October 1925.

Over the next few years, Roberts's recordings were released on Gennett and a variety of subsidiary labels, under many different names. He is best remembered for his partnership with singer/guitarist Asa Martin, with whom he began recording in September 1927. The record company executives realized that vocal numbers sold better than fiddle tunes; so while Doc was still allowed to record his unique repertoire of material, the addition of Martin's vocals on other tracks were a decided plus. Martin provided the lead vocals on several best-selling records for Doc, including "When the Roses Bloom Again for the Bootlegger" and "The Virginia Moonshiner." In 1928 country radio star BRADLEY KINCAID brought Roberts to the popular *National Barn Dance* radio show out of Chicago.

Roberts continued to record through 1934, although he continued to appear on local radio occasionally. He was "rediscovered" by folklorists Archie Green and Norm Cohen in the late 1960s, and subsequently was visited by other old-time fiddle enthusiasts who wished to learn more about him and his music. He died on August 4, 1978.

Roberts, John and Tony Barrand
folksingers

English folksingers John Roberts and Tony Barrand met while studying psychology at Cornell University in 1968. Inspired by the COPPER FAMILY, they began singing together, with Barrand taking the tenor (melody) parts and Roberts the bass. Roberts also began playing a number of instruments, including concertina. They recorded their first album for the small Swallowtail label in 1971, and then moved to the (slightly larger) Front Hall label in the mid-1970s. Many of their recordings were focused on themes, such as songs of Christmas (with Steve Woodruff and Fred Breunig), or songs of the supernatural. Barrand also became a major figure in the Morris Dance revival, a form of traditional, ritual English dancing. The duo performed together through the early 1980s, and then made a reunion album in the early 1990s, but have generally been less active in the last two decades.

Robertson, Eck (1887–1975) *performer and songwriter*

Alexander Campbell Robertson was born in Amarillo, Texas, on November 20, 1887. Raised in the farm country of West Texas, Robertson began fiddling as a youngster, playing for socials and dances locally. By the time he reached his teenage years, he was already traveling around the state, competing in fiddlers' conventions. He is said to have dressed in full cowboy gear, and later claimed to be the first country performer to adopt this outfit. In 1922 Robertson and a local fiddler, Henry Gilliland, who was 39 years his senior, traveled to Virginia to appear at a Civil War veterans's reunion; they eventually worked their way up to New York City, where they made some recordings for Victor, including Robertson's legendary solo recording of "Sally Goodin." Robertson returned to Texas soon after and made only one further recording in 1929, accompanied by members of his family.

Through the 1930s and 1940s Robertson performed locally in Texas, both on radio and at fiddlers' conventions. The old-time music revival brought new attention to his early recordings, beginning with HARRY SMITH's legendary reissue of early recordings on his *Anthology of American Folk Music,* a six-record set issued by Folkways Records in 1952. It featured Robertson's "Brilliancy Medley," which has become a staple for bluegrass bands. Robertson was "rediscovered" in the early 1960s, and appeared at a number of folk festivals as well as making some final recordings for folklorist MIKE SEEGER, revealing that he was still a fine musician in the Texas style. He died on February 17, 1975.

Robeson, Paul (1898–1976) *singer*

Born in Princeton, New Jersey, on April 9, 1898, Robeson was the son of a minister and a school-teacher. He attended Rutgers University, where he excelled at athletics, becoming only the second African American to be named an All-American football player. He also excelled in academics, leading him to be only the third African American ever admitted to Columbia University's law school, where he earned his degree in 1923. However, while at Columbia, Robeson became interested in acting and singing, and soon appeared in numerous Broadway shows and revues. He made his concert recital debut in 1925, and made his first recordings a year later. Robeson sang a mix of traditional spirituals ("Go Down, Moses," "Jacob's Ladder"), political songs ("Joe Hill," "No More Auction Block"), and his signature piece, "Ol' Man River," from *Show Boat* (1927). Robeson made his first European tour in the late 1920s, remaining for two years.

Robeson became increasingly involved in left-wing politics and the folk movement in the 1930s. Working with composer EARL ROBINSON, he premiered *Ballads for Americans,* an antifascist, progressive suite of songs that Robeson performed on a radio broadcast in 1939 (and subsequently recorded). He became an activist for pacifism, traveling to Russia and attending numerous meetings. Robeson performed at the infamous 1949 concert in Peekskill, New York, along with PETE SEEGER and others, which ended with local citizens attacking the concertgoers and performers, angered by their (supposed) "Communist" sympathies. In 1950 Robeson's passport was revoked by the State Department, meaning he could no longer travel abroad, and his career virtually ended until the late 1950s. Free to travel again, Robeson renounced the United States and moved to London, giving a dramatic farewell concert at New York's Carnegie Hall. He returned to the United States in 1963 in failing health, and did not perform again. He died in Philadelphia on January 23, 1976.

Robinson, Earl (1910–1991) *composer*

Earl Hawley Robinson was born in Seattle, Washington, on July 2, 1910. His mother encouraged his interest in music, and he began playing piano at an early age. From 1928 to 1933 he attended the University of Seattle and studied music, and then embarked on a trip to China, working his way on a steamer. In 1934 he settled in New York City, seeking a career as a musician and immersing himself in left-wing and radical causes. In 1936 he composed "I Dreamed I Saw Joe Hill Last Night," with lyrics by Alfred Hayes, which has become a folk standard, popularized by PETE SEEGER among others. Robinson also led a workers' chorus affiliated with the Communist party, performing folk and world material. In 1939, with lyricist John Latouche, he composed "Ballad for Americans," which was premiered on national radio on November 5 by PAUL ROBESON. The ballad-opera was greatly successful and was hailed as a statement of patriotism. Its great success led him to receive a Guggenheim Fellowship and an invitation to perform for Eleanor Roosevelt.

In the mid-1940s Robinson moved to Hollywood to compose for films; he was also active in the Los Angeles folk movement, helping to form a branch of People's Songs (the New York–based organization dedicated to folk music and radical politics). However, in the early 1950s Robinson was blacklisted and unable to find work for a while. He returned to New York in 1957 to teach for the next decade, then returned to Los Angeles, where he resumed composing for television. In the 1980s he retired to his native Seattle, where he was killed in an automobile accident in 1991.

Robison, Carson J. (1890–1957) *singer and songwriter*

Carson J. Robison was born in Oswego, Kansas, on August 4, 1890. He began his career performing country songs in his hometown, eventually moving on to Kansas City, where he worked on local radio. In 1924 he made his first recordings for Victor, as a novelty whistler. In the same year he teamed with popular country singer Vernon Dalhart as his accompanist and occasional accompanying vocalist. Robison provided Dalhart with some of his hit songs, beginning with numbers on hot topics of the day, such as the Scopes Trial. After breaking up with Dalhart in 1927, Robison joined forces with another city-bred vocalist, FRANK LUTHER, and later led a series of western-oriented bands in the 1930s and 1940s.

Robison wrote hundreds of songs, including the country-nostalgia numbers "Blue Ridge Mountain Home" and "Left My Gal in the Mountains," the ever-popular comic novelty "Life Gets Tee-Jus, Don't It" (as well as the sequel "More and More Tee-Jus, Ain't It" and another humorous monologue, "Settin' By the Fire"), and the oft-covered slightly blue "Barnacle Bill the Sailor." In his later career Robison kept up with changing trends, recording with backup by his own Pleasant Valley Boys in a for-then modern-country style. He even recorded a humorous rockabilly song shortly before his death, "Rockin' and Rollin' with Grandmaw." He died on March 24, 1957.

Rogers, Sally (b. 1954) *children's songwriter*
Born in New York City on September 19, 1954, but raised primarily in rural Michigan, Rogers began singing and playing GUITAR as a preteen. After attending the University of Michigan, she began touring and recording her own songs, often working with her husband, Howie Bursen. Since the late 1980s Rogers has made a name for herself as a socially conscious songwriter writing for children; her 1992 album, *What Can One Little Person Do,* was a landmark for combining both her activism and her love of children's music. She has lived in Connecticut since the mid-1980s, and was named "Connecticut State Troubadour" for the year of 1997.

Rogers, Stan (1949–1983) *singer and songwriter*
Stan Rogers was born in Hamilton, Ontario, on November 29, 1949. Fascinated with local lure and legend, he began writing songs, recording his first (and still best-remembered) album in 1977. Called *Fogarty's Cove,* it included the title track, "45 Years," and "Barrett's Privateers," all folk-styled compositions by Rogers. He was accompanied by his younger brother, Garnet, a skillful guitarist. Rogers's insistence on developing a contemporary Canadian folk music made him beloved in his native country, and also a popular performer on the U.S. folk music circuit. While touring the United States in spring 1983, Rogers tragically died in the Cincinnati airport in a fire on board an Air Canada passenger flight. His brother, Garnet, who had previously worked solely as his accompanist, began a solo career, which in some ways built on the elder singer's legacy.

Rooftop Singers
Another one of the 1960s folk trios, the Rooftop Singers achieved instant success with their recording of "Walk Right In" in 1963, based on a 78 recorded by Memphis jugband leader Gus Cannon in the 1920s. The group centered on banjo player Erik Darling (b. September 25, 1933, Baltimore, Maryland), who had replaced PETE SEEGER in the WEAVERS after working with another revival group, the Tarriers in the 1950s. Lead vocalist Lynne Taylor had previously sung jazz with Benny Goodman and Buddy Rich, but became interested in folk music through club hopping in New York City's Greenwich Village. Darling invited friend and guitarist Bill Swanoe to round out the group. The group was formed specifically to record "Walk Right In" as a single for folk label Vanguard, without any plans to continue performing. However, the song shot to number one on the pop charts, and was followed by a well-received debut at the Newport Folk Festival. The group toured and recorded for the next four and a half years, with singer Taylor replaced by Mindy Stuart in 1965. The group folded in 1968.

See also NEWPORT (RHODE ISLAND) FOLK FESTIVAL.

Rooney, Jim (b. 1938) *record producer and musician*

Born in Boston, Massachusetts, on January 28, 1938, Rooney became involved in folk music while attending Harvard, where he met banjoist BILL KEITH. The two began performing together in 1960, about the time that Rooney became manager of the important Boston-area folk club Club 47. From 1967 to 1969, he ran the NEWPORT FOLK FESTIVAL, an important institution in the folk revival.

Along with Keith, in 1969 Rooney recorded a one-off country album, called the Blue Velvet Band. The record also featured fiddler RICHARD GREENE, then a member of the rock group Seatrain, and Eric Weissberg, soon to be famous for recording the theme for the movie *Deliverance*. A year later, Rooney moved to Woodstock, New York, to help manager ALBERT GROSSMAN establish his Bearsville studios and record label. Rooney was involved with recordings made there by the Band, Todd Rundgren, Bonnie Raitt, and many other early 1970s folk-rock artists. He was also a prime mover in the informal Mud Acres record and its follow-ups recorded in the 1970s by a group of Woodstock-based folk performers, including HAPPY AND ARTIE TRAUM and Maria Muldaur.

In 1976 Rooney relocated to Nashville, where he formed a partnership with producer/recording studio owner "Cowboy" Jack Clement. The duo formed a music publishing company, and Rooney began doing engineering work in Clement's studio. In the early 1980s Rooney became a well-known producer, working with singer-songwriters, particularly Texan NANCI GRIFFITH, as well as JOHN PRINE, JERRY JEFF WALKER, IRIS DEMENT, PETER ROWAN, TOWNES VAN ZANDT, and many others. Rooney has also recorded on his own, primarily for smaller independent labels.

See also BANJO, FIVE-STRING; MULDAUR, GEOFF AND MARIA.

Rosenbaum, Art (b. 1938) *recording artist and author*

Born in Ogdensburg, New York, on December 6, 1938, Rosenbaum first made an impression on the revival scene in the mid-1960s, when his roots-styled banjo playing was featured on an Elektra Records anthology of banjo music; because this label catered to city folks (and even folk-rockers), these recordings helped introduce old-time banjo playing to a new audience. He also recorded and produced a fine collection called *Fine Times at Our House* for Folkways Records, featuring fiddler John "Dick" Summers, which became a favorite among young old-time revivalists. In 1968 he authored a banjo instruction book that emphasized mountain styles.

In the early 1970s Rosenbaum relocated to Iowa, where he was teaching painting. He recorded a duo album with bluegrass-styled fiddler Al Murphy that was released by the tiny Meadowlands label, followed by two solo albums for the folk-instructional label Kicking Mule. In the late 1970s he relocated again to Athens, Georgia, where he began recording blues, religious music, and old-time string band music. These field recordings were issued by Flyright Records (a British label) and Folkways. He also authored a book on Georgia's traditional music, illustrated with his own drawings and paintings of musicians along with his wife's photographs. In 2003 he issued a new CD of his music, the first in many years.

See also BANJO, FIVE-STRING.

Rouse Brothers *songwriters and performers*

Ervin (September 18, 1917–July 8, 1981), Gordon (b. Gordon Ernest, July 4, 1914–May 17, 1995), and Earl B. (November 1, 1911–February 1983) Rouse were born in Craven County, North Carolina, where their father farmed tobacco. There were 15 siblings, with eight becoming musicians of some sort. Ervin learned to fiddle from his mother and was already performing in vaudeville at age five. Already a seasoned performer by age 11, Ervin hit the RKO circuit, developing trick fiddling techniques like playing the instrument between his legs or behind his head. His brother Gordon worked with him as a guitarist.

Gordon and Ervin settled in the Jacksonville, Florida, area during the 1920s. However, their work took them as far north as New York, where they played at the famous Village Barn and also broadcast over the radio. They also worked in a Miami nightclub. The brothers first recorded in June 1936 for ARC; they were joined at this time by another sibling, Earl B. In 1938, riding on the inaugural run on a new train from Miami to New York, Ervin was inspired to compose "The Orange Blossom Special." Although they were not the first to record it, Ervin fortunately copyrighted the piece immediately. The piece has become a standard among bluegrass and contest fiddlers. Ervin was a prolific songwriter, and he tried his best to score another hit by penning more train songs. His next big hit, however, was a sentimental tearjerker, "Sweeter Than the Flowers," first recorded by Moon Mullican in 1948, which became a number three country hit.

The brothers career slowed in the 1950s, while both Ervin and Gordon apparently battled mental illness and alcoholism. "Rediscovered" in 1965 by Johnny Cash, Ervin returned to Nashville briefly, but was unable to relaunch his career. He spent his declining years in Florida, eventually dying in 1981 following a decade of health problems.

See also FIDDLE.

Rowan, Peter (b. 1942) *songwriter and performer*

Born in Wayland, Massachusetts, on July 4, 1942, Rowan was a product of the teeming FOLK-ROCK movement of the greater Boston area. Boston hosted a crowd of nascent rockers and social-protest singers, but also had a strong tradition of supporting bluegrass and country acts. Rowan was impressed with the energy of bluegrass music, and relocated to Nashville to meet the father of the music, Bill Monroe. By the mid-1960s he was writing with Monroe (the classic "Walls of Time") and recording as a member of the Blue Grass Boys, along with young fiddler RICHARD GREENE. Rowan ultimately was frustrated by Monroe's strict traditionalist approach and returned to Boston to form the eclectic rock band Earth

Opera, with mandolinist DAVID GRISMAN, also an ex-bluegrass musician.

In the late 1960s Greene invited Rowan to join the progressive California rock band Seatrain, and so he relocated to California. After Seatrain reorganized in 1972, Rowan formed several short-lived bluegrass bands, including 1972's MULESKINNER and OLD AND IN THE WAY. Both bands performed traditional bluegrass numbers and Rowan's bluegrass-styled original songs, including "Blue Mule" (which took the story of Tenbrooks and Molly, a Monroe classic, into outer space!) and the classic update of a badman ballad, "Panama Red." In the mid-1970s he joined his two brothers, calling themselves the Rowans, and they recorded two folk-rock albums for Asylum Records that gained the group a cult following if not great commercial success.

By the end of the 1970s, Rowan was performing as a soloist leading his own Green Grass Gringos band, featuring floating membership including traditional bluegrass fiddler Tex Logan, progressive fiddler Richard Greene, and Tex-Mex ACCORDION whiz Flaco Jiminez. Rowan continued to work with various accompanists over the next decades, recording both his own compositions and more traditional bluegrass songs. Rowan's intense and expressive high-tenor lead vocals were perfectly suited to his songs that wed new age sensibilities to classic stories of the Southwest. Rowan created a new mythical cowboy past, all within his unique sensibilities.

See also MANDOLIN.

Rush, Tom (b. 1941) *singer and songwriter*

Born in Portsmouth, New Hampshire, on February 8, 1941, Rush attended Harvard University in the late 1950s–early 1960s, where he was exposed to folk music in Boston's vibrant club scene. He was already touring and recording (for the small label Prestige) when he graduated in 1963, playing acoustic blues. He soon signed with the larger Elektra label, continuing to record blues. But then in 1968 he issued the landmark album, *The Circle Game,* with the title track composed by

Tom Rush performing at Boston's famous Club 47, a center of the folk scene in that city, in 1963. (Photo © John Byrne Cooke, http://www.cookephoto.com)

the then little-known songwriter JONI MITCHELL. The album also featured songs by Jackson Browne and Rush himself. Rush moved to Columbia Records in 1970, but his career as a singer/songwriter soon faded. Since the early 1980s he has mostly worked in the Boston area, where he remains popular, releasing several live recordings on his own label.

Sainte-Marie, Buffy (b. 1941) *singer and songwriter*

Born on Piapot Reserve in Saskatchewan, Canada, on February 20, 1941, Sainte-Marie was born to Cree Indian parents, although she was adopted and raised by a white Canadian family. Exposed to folk music as a teenager, she began writing her own songs. British FOLK-ROCK star Donovan had a hit with her "Universal Soldier," and she was signed to Vanguard Records. She wrote both social-protest songs drawing on her Native American heritage ("Now That the Buffalo's Gone" and "My Country 'Tis of Thy People You're Dying" being among the best known), but also wrote more conventional pop-flavored songs, such as "Until It's Time for You to Go" (which became a hit in a cover version by Elvis Presley in the mid-1970s).

Like many other successful folk revivalists of the 1960s, Sainte-Marie turned to a more folk-rock style in the late 1960s and early 1970s, recording with Ry Cooder and Neil Young's backup band, Crazy Horse. Her later career included a long-running engagement performing children's music on the popular PBS series *Sesame Street*, and also writing for films.

"Salty Dog Blues" (1927) *the first hit for the Allen Brothers*

This song helped popularize the ragtime-blues style among folk performers. It was so popular that the ALLEN BROTHERS recorded it twice, and many of their other songs were clearly based on it. The song was derived from a traditional folk-blues that was widely performed in the South; LEAD BELLY recorded his own version of it as "You Salty Dog."

Sandburg, Carl (1878–1967) *poet and singer of traditional songs*

Carl August Sandburg was born in Galesburg, Illinois, on January 6, 1878. His parents were Swedish immigrants, and his father worked as a blacksmith for the railroads. When he was 19, Sandburg left home to bum around the country, riding the railroads with the hoboes, where he first heard traditional American songs. He then served in the Spanish-American War, and on his return home, entered college, eventually graduating in 1902. He worked in a number of jobs, while beginning to write and publish poetry in midwestern newspapers. By 1908 he was active in socialist politics in Milwaukee, where he had settled and married, and was beginning to focus on his poetry writing. In 1914 he moved to Chicago, and two years later published *Chicago Poems*, which established him as a major voice of the midwestern experience. Many of these poems employed regional slang and dialect and reflected on the hard life of midwestern farmers and workers, a trend that would continue in his work throughout the 1920s and 1930s.

In the early 1920s Sandburg became a popular lecturer, traveling around the country to read his poetry. As a part of these readings, he began performing traditional American songs to his own guitar accompaniment. His singing was well received, and Sandburg made his first recordings in 1926. A year late Sandburg's collection *American Songbag* was published; it was one of the earliest collections of traditional American folk songs, and became a standard songbook for folk revivalists from the 1930s on, remaining in print for decades. Sandburg recorded and performed folk music through the 1960s, while also writing prolifically, including a well-regarded multivolume biography of his boyhood hero, Abraham Lincoln. Sandburg died on July 22, 1967.

Savoy, Marc (b. 1940) *Cajun music performer*
Marc Savoy was born in Eunice, Louisiana, on October 1, 1940. A master ACCORDION maker and player in the Cajun style, Savoy, and his wife, Ann, have been prime movers in preserving Cajun culture. Savoy originally played accordion with the famed BALFA BROTHERS, while he also began making traditional styled single and double row accordions. In 1978 he formed a partnership with Michael Doucet (of BEAUSOLEIL) to form the Savoy-Doucet Cajun Band, featuring his wife, Ann, on vocals and GUITAR, to play traditional CAJUN MUSIC with acoustic instruments. Savoy received the Heritage Award from the National Endowment for the Arts in 1992, and authored the book *Cajun Music: A Reflection of a People.*

Schwarz, Tracy See NEW LOST CITY RAMBLERS, THE.

Scott, Tommy (b. 1917) *medicine show performer*
Thomas Lee Scott was born in Toccoa, Georgia, on June 24, 1917. He took his first job with a traveling medicine show when he was 13 years old, working for "Doc" M. F. Chamberlain, who developed and sold "Herb-O-Lac" patent medicine. In 1933 Scott formed his Peanut Band, broadcasting out of a small South Carolina radio station. He portrayed "Peanut," a blackface character both on the road and radio. Three years later, Chamberlain gave the recipe for "Herb-O-Lac" to the young performer, and Scott became the owner/manager of the show. By the late 1930s Scott had joined Charlie Monroe in his original Kentucky Pardners band, broadcasting out of North Carolina. His patent medicine was now being sold under the name of "Manoree." However, the two had a falling out over splitting the profits, and by about 1940 Scott was back on his own selling "Herb-O-Lac."

In 1940 Scott moved to Kentucky, where he met future comedy star Stringbean; the two formed a comic duo of Stringbean and Peanut, which lasted about a year. In 1941 Scott briefly joined the *Grand Ole Opry,* appearing as a ventriloquist. Later that year, he was back on the road, now paired with country performer Curly Sechler, working the radio for yet another herbal remedy, "Vim Herb." From 1943 to 1947 he began to broadcast over the powerful Mexican border radio stations, and also found a national sponsor in the American Tobacco Company.

In the later 1940s Scott headed to Hollywood to look for work in cowboy films; he befriended a number of minor-league cowboy stars of the day, including "Colonel" Tim McCoy and Sunset "Kit" Carson, who would continue to travel with him during the 1950s and 1960s in his road shows. From the late 1940s he has traveled throughout the country with his *Medicine Show,* which has featured various performers. His wife, Frankie, frequently appeared as "Clarabelle, the Gal From the Mountains," performing magic tricks and comedy. Scott's traveling show was on the road as recently as the late 1990s.

See also MINSTREL/TRAVELING SHOWS.

Seeger, Mike (b. 1933) *performer and music collector*
The son of ethnomusicologist Charles Seeger and composer Ruth Crawford Seeger, and half brother of folk revivalist PETE SEEGER, Mike Seeger was born

in New York City, on August 15, 1933, but raised in the Washington, D.C., area. Seeger began performing as a bluegrass-styled banjo player in the mid-1950s. He produced for Folkways Records one of the first albums of bluegrass music in 1957. About the same time, he formed the NEW LOST CITY RAMBLERS with Tom Paley and JOHN COHEN, a band dedicated to performing the old-time music of the 1920s and 1930s in almost literal, note-for-note recreations.

Seeger made his first solo LP in 1962 (*Old-Time Country Music,* Folkways). By using an Ampex multitrack tape machine, he was able to play all of the parts, creating in effect his own string band. The sound of the album was not much different from the style of the Ramblers at that time. Perhaps most interesting was his recreation of both Monroe Brothers on the tune "Rollin' On."

In this same period, he began making a series of field trips to the South. One of the first artists he "discovered" was blues guitarist ELIZABETH "Libba" COTTON, who had worked as a maid for the Seeger family. It turned out that she was a talented GUITAR player in the country-blues style, as well as a skilled songwriter. (Her "Freight Train" became one of the hits of the FOLK REVIVAL.) Seeger also sought out performers of the 1920s and 1930s who had stopped recording; one of his most important finds was banjoist Doc Boggs. Seeger was also a champion of the autoharp, introducing the country-picking of Maybelle Carter and other important autoharp players to a new audience. His anthology *Mountain Music on the Autoharp* introduced several fine players, including Kilby Snow.

Seeger recorded a second solo album in 1965 for Vanguard, a more low-keyed affair than his first, while continuing to perform with the Ramblers through 1968. Although the Ramblers never officially "disbanded," they were less active from 1968 onward. Seeger made two excellent solo albums for Mercury in the mid-1970s, *Music from True Vine,* and *The Second Annual Farewell Reunion,* which featured Seeger performing with traditional performers and revivalists.

In the early 1970s Seeger formed with Ramblers bandmate Tracy Schwartz, then-wife, ALICE GERRARD, HAZEL DICKENS, and bluegrass banjo player Lamar Grier a bluegrass-country group called the Strange Creek Singers. This short-lived band played an amalgam of country and bluegrass sounds. Seeger also performed as a duo with Gerrard, recording an album for Greenhays Records, and with his sister, PEGGY SEEGER. (The two made a 1968 duo recording for British Argo records, and also performed songs from their mother's collections of children's songs for Rounder Records.)

Through the 1980s and 1990s Seeger continued to perform as a soloist and sometimes member of the New Lost City Ramblers. He continued his fieldwork, producing the videotape *Talkin' Feet* in the late 1980s, a documentary on traditional flat-foot

Mike Seeger plays the autoharp at the Philadelphia Folk Festival, c. 1980. (Photo © Larry Sandberg)

dancing of the upper South. An anthology of his 1950s–1960s–era field recordings was issued by Smithsonian/Folkways in 1998.

See also BANJO, FIVE-STRING.

Seeger, Peggy (b. 1935) *singer and songwriter*

Born Margaret Seeger in New York City on June 17, 1935, Peggy Seeger was raised in a musical household, along with her brother, Mike. She began playing banjo and GUITAR as a youngster, and at age 20 traveled to Europe to collect folk songs; that same year, her first album appeared on Folkways. In England she met singer EWAN MACCOLL, whom she wed in 1958. She primarily recorded as an accompanist for MacColl until his death in 1989, but also appeared on her own records. Like MacColl, she became involved in producing "radio plays," documentaries about English working people, helping to compose and perform the songs for them. Her best-known song is the women's liberation anthem "I'm Gonna Be an Engineer," which she wrote in the mid-1970s. After MacColl's death, Seeger has continued to record and perform, returning to live in the United States in late 1994.

See also BANJO, FIVE-STRING; SEEGER, MIKE; SEEGER, PETE.

Seeger, Pete (b. 1919) *singer, songwriter, author, and activist*

Son of musicologist Charles Seeger, Pete Seeger was born in New York City, on May 3, 1919. After attending Harvard for a few semesters, Seeger left school in 1938 to accompany folklorist Alan Lomax on a field trip to the South. It was there he heard banjoist Pete Steele, who impressed him not only with his energetic banjo playing but also his repertoire of traditional songs about coal mining, and his own compositions, including "Pay Day at Coal Creek." He settled in New York in 1940, forming the Almanac Singers, one of the first FOLK-REVIVAL groups, with singers Lee Hays and

Millard Lampell; WOODY GUTHRIE joined the fold in 1941. They recorded topical songs on unionism and pacifism (before the United States entered World War II), and antifascist anthems (while the United States was at war with Germany). Seeger enlisted in the army during the war, and the group disbanded.

After the war, Seeger again became involved with progressive musicians in the New York area, helping to found People's Songs, as well as the folk journal *Sing Out!* in 1950. In 1948 Seeger self-published the first edition of his book *How to Play the Five-String Banjo,* which not only gave detailed instruction in his distinctive frailing style but also introduced bluegrass picking to urban players, highlighting the contributions of Earl Scruggs. In 1949, along with Hays, Fred Hellerman, and Ronnie Gilbert, he formed the WEAVERS. They attracted the attention of Decca Records with their energetic reworkings of world folk songs, and had major pop hits with their arrangements of the African folk song "Wimoweh" (featuring Seeger's high tenor vocals and strummed banjo) and LEAD BELLY's "GOODNIGHT, IRENE." The Weavers were the model for all of the folk-revival groups of the early 1960s, including the KINGSTON Trio, The Tarriers, PETER, PAUL, AND MARY, and dozens more. Despite their great initial success on the charts, the band's members were attacked by anticommunist politicians and groups who were suspicious of their earlier leftist activities. Unable to get work, the group folded in 1952, but then reunited triumphantly in 1955. Seeger left permanently in 1958 and was replaced by Erik Darling.

During the 1950s Seeger began recording for the small specialty label Folkways. His first solo album, *Darling Corey,* featured mountain folk songs that Seeger had learned during his field trip with Lomax and from other traditional sources. He also recorded in the mid-1950s the seminal *Goofing Off Suite,* in which he adapted classical, jazz, and pop tunes to the five-string banjo. Toward the end of the 1950s he recorded a series of folk ballads (*America's*

Favorite Ballads, five albums) as well as traditional industrial ballads.

In the early 1960s Seeger became increasingly involved with political causes, and began performing more contemporary material. He also began writing his own songs, although he had previously written the folk classic "If I Had a Hammer" in the early 1950s with his Weavers' mate Lee Hays. In the 1960s he set the words of Ecclesiastes to music, producing a hit for the BYRDS with "Turn, Turn, Turn"; he also wrote the hits "Where Have All the Flowers Gone?" and "Bells of Rhymney." His song "Waist Deep in the Big Muddy" got him into trouble again with the censors, because it criticized President Lyndon Johnson's war efforts in Vietnam.

By the late 1960s Seeger was increasingly playing the 12-string guitar rather than the banjo, emulating the style of LEAD BELLY. Although he continued to perform in the 1970s (often in partnership with ARLO GUTHRIE) and 1980s to today, increasing hearing problems have limited his performance schedule since the early 1990s.

See also BANJO, FIVE-STRING; LOMAX, JOHN AND ALAN.

Seldom Scene

Seldom Scene was born out of one of Washington's longest-lived and most popular bluegrass outfits, the COUNTRY GENTLEMEN, centering primarily on high-tenor vocalist and MANDOLIN player John Duffey. With the smooth lead vocals of John Starling, the band from the start focused more on contemporary country and FOLK-ROCK songs than on traditional bluegrass fare. Named the "Seldom Scene" because they began their lives as an informal band playing at Washington's legendary Red Fox Inn, by the mid-1970s they had amassed a huge following, particularly among younger bluegrass fans.

The group was not only progressive in their song selection, they also featured some of the finest bluegrass players around. Mike Auldridge was the first of many second-generation DOBRO players who transformed the instrument from primarily a background instrument used for special effects to one capable of taking solos. Similarly, Starling was an energetic lead guitarist, whose single-note leads influenced the next generation of new acoustic pickers. The band was rounded out by bassist/vocalist Tom Gray.

The original band began to run out of steam by the late 1970s, with Starling making an abortive attempt at a career as a soloist in the early 1980s; he was replaced by singer/songwriter Phil Rosenthal. A smoother voiced singer, Rosenthal led a more pop-oriented band, and for a while it looked like the group might achieve wider commercial success. However, Rosenthal in turn left in 1986 and was replaced for a while by Lou Reid, and when bassist Gray left, his shoes were filled by T. Michael Coleman on electric bass (who had previously worked with DOC and Merle WATSON), giving them an even more contemporary sound. In 1993 Reid was replaced for a year by original member John Starling, pleasing fans of the 1970s-era group.

In 1995 it looked like the band was doomed when Auldridge, Coleman, and new lead singer Mondi Klein left to form the band Chesapeake. However, the determined Duffey and Eldridge brought on board former Johnson Mountain Boys lead singer Dudley Connell along with dobro player Fred Travers and bass player Ronnie Simpkins to form yet another new lineup. Sadly, however, within a year Duffey died of a heart attack. Although disheartened, the band decided to soldier on, bringing back lead singer Lou Reid to replace Duffey. In 2000 they issued a new album, showing that the spirit of the original band remained pretty much intact, combining bluegrass instrumentation with contemporary songs.

shape-note singing

Shape-note singing refers to a method of teaching music to nonmusically literate singers, employed in the late 18th and early 19th centuries by traveling "singing masters." Originally based in New England,

and then spreading to the South and West, these itinerant teachers came to towns, mostly at the invitation of the local church, to teach the local choirs how to sing. They employed special songbooks that drew on a repertoire of well-known folk and hymn tunes that the congregation would presumably know. The parts were notated using different shapes for the various scale tones (triangles, squares, diamonds, etc.) and were often limited to a five-note (pentatonic) scale, which was common to folk and hymn tunes. The harmonies were also simplified, based on common intervals such as fourths and fifths, giving the music a distinct archaic sound. By singing the tones associated with the shapes, the congregation could quickly learn new songs and new harmonies.

Although shape-note singing soon died out in the cities, where more sophisticated congregations learned to read music properly, it lingered in rural areas. Annual conventions were held with the purpose of singing an entire songbook in a single day and evening (this was accomplished by rapidly "reading" each hymn). This helped singers remember the repertoire and also encouraged them to broaden the number of songs they performed throughout the year. These events also involved communal socializing, and often a large community-prepared meal would be served about halfway through the day.

Even in churches that did not employ shape-note singing, the harmonies from these hymnals could be heard, so that an older style of singing was unintentionally preserved. When bluegrass groups began incorporating gospel music into their repertoires, they naturally drew on the rich shape-note singing tradition. Many bluegrass singers were raised performing in their local church choirs, and so their vocal styles and harmonies often recall the tonalities of this earlier style. This is particularly true of the more traditionally oriented groups, such as the Stanley Brothers, although more modern bands ranging from the RED CLAY RAMBLERS to the NASHVILLE BLUEGRASS BAND have made this style of singing a part of their performances.

Shocked, Michelle (b. 1962) *singer and songwriter*

Michelle Karen Johnston, aka Michelle Shocked, was born on February 24, 1962, in Dallas, Texas. She first performed on the Austin club scene in the early 1980s, then briefly lived in San Francisco and Amsterdam before returning to her native Texas in 1986. A year later, she was singing at an informal session at the Kerrville Folk Festival when English record producer Pete Lawrence heard her perform; he issued recordings made informally at the festival as *The Texas Campfire Tapes* in the same year. This led to a major label signing with Mercury Records, and her first studio album, *Short Sharp Shocked*, a year later, focusing primarily on her talents as a singer/songwriter. *Captain Swing* was an attempt to modernize Western Swing for a new audience; this produced the minor hit "The Greener Side." Her 1992 album, *Arkansas Traveler*, took as its theme the unusual idea of writing new lyrics to traditional FIDDLE tunes, featuring many fine acoustic pickers, with mixed results.

After that release, Shocked hoped to record an album with the pop group Tony! Toni! Tone!, and when that idea was rejected, a gospel album. She was then dropped by her label, and has since recorded for a series of small, independent labels, turning mostly to more "alternative" styles rather than pursuing her explorations of folk and country.

Silber, Irwin   See *SING OUT!* MAGAZINE.

Silly Wizard

Centering on the talented Cunningham brothers (Phil on ACCORDION, keyboards, and whistle and John on FIDDLE and vocals) and singer/banjo player Andy Stewart, Silly Wizard was an influential

Scottish music revival band of the 1980s. When John Cunningham was just 14 years old, the original band formed, with guitarists Gordon Jones and Bob Thomas, and singer Maddy Taylor. Taylor soon left, and Andy Stewart, John's younger brother, Phil, and Martin Hadden (bass, GUITAR, vocals) came on board. The band achieved success with their first album, 1978's *Caledonia's Hardy Sons,* and the follow-up, *So Many Partings,* from a year later. They continued to record and tour through the late 1980s, when they made their final album, *Live Wizardy.* John Cunningham died in 2003, but his brother and Stewart have continued to perform as solo artists, and in collaboration with other artists, since the band broke up.

singer/songwriter movement

The singer/songwriter movement grew out of the social-protest movement of the 1960s. BOB DYLAN had shown that a talented songwriter could also perform his own songs, often in a more effective way than the more "professional" folk groups such as PETER, PAUL, AND MARY. This influenced others to begin performing their own songs, including TOM PAXTON, TOM RUSH, and JONI MITCHELL. Turning away from songs that commented directly on current events, these singers—particularly Mitchell—began writing songs reflecting the ups and downs of their own personal lives. Mitchell's strong introspection reached its height with the starkly produced album *Blue,* issued in 1971. Another popular songwriter who drew on his life experiences and emerged at this time was JAMES TAYLOR, who enjoyed an enormously popular hit with his 1970 album, *Sweet Baby James.*

While the singer/songwriter movement mostly influenced pop singers, it fed back into the folk movement itself. Younger folk musicians who specialized in their own songs were now beginning to write about a broader range of topics, influenced by the singer-songwriters. Often, topical subjects, such as women's liberation, were expressed through personal stories, so that the social-protest and singer/songwriter trends were blended together in the work of female singers such as Holly Near. In the mid-1980s singer/songwriters such as Suzanne Vega tackled varied topics, such as child abuse (in Vega's hit "Luka"), again using personal experience to illuminate larger issues.

Sing Out! magazine *leading publication of the folk music scene*

Sing Out! has been the leading voice of the folk music movement in America for more than five decades. The magazine grew out of the demise of an earlier organization, People's Songs. Founded in 1946, People's Songs was dedicated to spreading folk music through concerts, local organizations (mostly in major cities, including New York, Chicago, and Los Angeles), and song sheets, books, and newsletters. It was a left-leaning organization, encouraging the use of folk and topical songs for progressive causes, notably union rallies. Many of the singers associated with People's Songs participated in Henry Wallace's unsuccessful campaign for the presidency in 1948; Wallace was widely attacked for his progressive views, cementing many people's opinions that folksingers were dangerous "liberals." A summer 1949 concert organized by the related booking agency, People's Artists, in Peekskill, New York, ended with an angry mob attacking performers PETE SEEGER, PAUL ROBESON, and others. People's Songs folded in 1949 due to financial and political difficulties.

People's Artists struggled on. Many felt the continued need for a magazine/newsletter to spread the organization's message and new songs. *Sing Out!* was started in 1950 as a less political, more song-oriented monthly publication to fill this need. By late 1951, Irwin Silber—a strongly opinionated, but organized and dedicated member of the People's Songs/Artists movement—took over as the journal's editor, a position he held until 1967. Silber was a member of the Communist Party in the 1930s and 1940s, and brought to the magazine a strongly liberal, progressive voice. When People's Artists finally folded due to financial difficulties in 1956, the magazine temporarily suspended publication. In 1957 the magazine was incorporated as a separate identity, and, a year later, Folkways Records owner MOSES ASCH invested in it, hiring Silber to work for Folkways, in essence underwriting Silber's work as *Sing Out!*'s editor. In 1960 Asch and Silber partnered in establishing Oak Publications to publish folk music collections and instruction books.

The folk song revival turned out to be the saving grace for the small, underfunded publication.

Cover of Sing Out! *magazine from 1972 showing Happy and Artie Traum* (Courtesy BenCar Collection)

Having survived for years with just a few hundred subscribers, the sudden interest in folk music—and the need for young singers to learn both traditional and newly composed songs—led to a huge jump in circulation. By 1964, at the height of the revival, *Sing Out!* boasted 15,000 subscribers and was able to begin publishing in a larger format on a bimonthly basis. Universally recognized as the "voice" of the folk movement, *Sing Out!*—through editorials by Silber—commented on the growing commercialization of folk music and expressed concerns that it was losing its political edge. Silber's most famous piece came after BOB DYLAN's appearance at the 1965 NEWPORT FOLK FESTIVAL (when Dylan "went electric," alienating his original folk fans). Silber wrote an "Open Letter" to Dylan, questioning his motivations, and chastising him for abandoning his original audience.

Success, however, brought problems. Younger readers were put off by Silber's denunciation of the "commercial" FOLK-ROCK that for many was a natural and welcome extension of the earlier folk movement. The magazine's ownership was restructured in 1966 in the form of a cooperative, with an Advisory Board and Silber serving as equal owners. Growing dissatisfaction with Silber's aggressive politics led to his being removed as sole editor in 1967, and ultimately leaving the magazine a year later. Folksong revivalist Happy Traum became de facto editor, but the declining interest in folk music led advertising and subscription revenues to drop.

The magazine appeared poised to close when a new editor, Bob Norman, came on board in the early 1970s. Norman was more attuned to the less-political end of the folk revival, and introduced "teach-ins" in the magazine for banjo, GUITAR, and other popular instruments. Songs continued to be published, but there was far less emphasis on political action than in the past. After Norman left the magazine in the later 1970s, it went through a bumpy period again, with expenses from its New York offices eating away at its always small profits. The magazine again nearly failed when folk music fan/writer Mark Moss convinced the board to let him try to revive it. Relocating its offices to rural Bethlehem, Pennsylvania, Moss was able to cut costs while building on Norman's legacy of a less politically oriented publication. He embraced an even wider swath of music, from world music to singer-songwriter to new acoustic styles. Moss also brought in new writers and enhanced the magazine's coverage of news and events. Although less cutting-edge than it was in the 1960s, the magazine has found a loyal audience and appears to be financially stronger than it has ever been.

See also BANJO, FIVE-STRING; TRAUM, HAPPY AND ARTIE.

Skillet Lickers, The

James Gideon "Gid" Tanner (1885–1960) was the elder statesman of the band, a famous solo performer on his own who made FIDDLE recordings for Columbia in 1924 accompanied by blind guitarist/vocalist RILEY PUCKETT. Tanner sang in a comic, high falsetto voice, and his fiddle playing was in the rough, often loose rhythmic style typical of his generation of Georgia fiddlers. The Columbia label urged Tanner to form a band because of the increasing popularity of string bands, and so he invited younger Georgia fiddler Clayton McMichen (1900–1970) to join with him and Puckett, along with banjoist Land Norris (who can just barely be heard on their recordings).

Influenced by the jazz and pop music of the 1920s, McMichen was intent on making the Skillet Lickers a more modern band. As the band gained in popularity, Tanner's role was often reduced to just occasional falsetto vocals; McMichen took the fiddle lead and introduced a second fiddler, another young Georgian named Lowe Stokes, to play harmony. Sometimes McMichen, Stokes, and Tanner all played, forecasting the harmony fiddles of later bluegrass recordings. Unlike other string bands, the banjo was always kept discreetly in the background, perhaps reflecting McMichen's

feeling that the instrument was old-fashioned and not suited to his more modern, hard-driving music. Puckett was the lead vocalist of the band; his rich baritone voice was perfectly suited to the sentimental and old-time dance songs that the group performed.

McMichen left the band in the early 1930s, and the great days of the original Skillet Lickers ended. Tanner continued to use the name with various supporting musicians, including his son Gordon on fiddle. McMichen formed his Georgia Wildcats, a band that recorded pop and jazz as well as country, forecasting the Western Swing movement of later in the decade. He relocated to Kentucky, where he continued to perform until the early 1950s, when he retired from music making, although he made one appearance during the FOLK REVIVAL days of the 1960s at the NEWPORT FOLK FESTIVAL.

The Skillet Lickers served as a model for several old-time revival bands, most notably the HIGHWOODS STRINGBAND, who adopted their twin-lead fiddle sound and raucous performance style. In turn, many others emulated the Highwoods sound, so that the Skillet Lickers style lived on through the 1990s.

See also BANJO, FIVE-STRING.

Sky, Patrick (b. 1940) *singer and songwriter*

Patrick Sky was born in Liveoak, Georgia, on October 2, 1940, but raised in rural Lousiana. He began playing GUITAR and singing as a teenager, but did not begin performing professionally until after attending college and serving in the army. He moved to New York City's Greenwich Village, then the center of the FOLK REVIVAL, and began performing in the local clubs. BUFFY SAINTE-MARIE had a hit with his song "Many a Mile," leading to Sky's earning a contract with her record label, Vanguard. Sky recorded several albums of his own songs, moving from social protest to more personal subjects. He surprised—and shocked—many fans with the satiric 1971 album, *Songs That Made America Famous*, which was so scurrilous that Sky was unable to find any label willing to release it, so he put it out himself in 1973. In the mid-1970s Sky developed an interest in traditional Irish BAGPIPES and traveled to Ireland to learn from piper Seamus Ennis. He formed a record label, Innisfree, to release traditional Irish musicians, with a subsidiary, Green Linnet, for revivalists. His last album as a singer/guitarist was issued in 1985.

Skyline

Skyline was an early 1980s New York–based bluegrass band led by banjo whiz TONY TRISCHKA and his then-wife, DeDe Wyland, with support from guitarist Danny Weiss, MANDOLIN player Barry Mitterhoff, and electric bass player Larry Cohen.

Both Weiss and Wyland were smooth vocalists who combined folky leanings with a love for the newer countryesque songs created in the 1970s and 1980s. Trischka and Mitterhoff (a founding member of New Jersey's Bottle Hill Boys), were both enmeshed in progressive, far-out picking, so that the group's accompaniments were often skittish and disjointed, seemingly at odds with the pop-country flavorings of the songs. Cohen's electric bass playing was often innovative, and he was responsible for many of the group's progressive arrangements. Wyland left in 1988 and was replaced briefly by Rachel Kalem. The group disbanded in the early 1990s. Mitterhoff, Weiss, and Cohen have continued to perform together as a trio under the name of Silk City through the 1990s.

See also BANJO, FIVE-STRING.

Skyline in the late 1970s. Left to right: Larry Cohen, Tony Trischka, DeDe Wyland, Danny Weiss, and Barry Miterhoff (Courtesy Flying Fish Records)

Smeck, Roy (1900–1994) *multi-instrumentalist and performer*

Roy Smeck was born in Reading, Pennsylvania, on February 6, 1900, but raised in New York City. From an early age, he had mastered several different string instruments, including GUITAR and tenor banjo. He worked on the RKO (Radio Keith Orpheum) circuit in New York, as well as appearing in early Vitaphone shorts produced by Warner Bros. to promote the idea of talking pictures. He melded a number of influences in his playing, including the jazz single-note picking of guitarist Eddie Lang, the Hawaiian slide work of early recording star Sol Hoopii, and the high-energy tenor banjo work of jazz/novelty musician Harry Reiser.

Besides his solo recordings, Smeck worked as an accompanist on slide and regular guitar for country performers Vernon Dalhart and CARSON ROBISON, as well as sessioning with jazz and dance bands. He led his own group, the Vita Trio, through the 1930s, usually playing slide guitar on instrumental versions of pop numbers. Smeck also issued a seemingly endless stream of instruction books, so-called five-minute methods for guitar, Hawaiian style-playing, ukulele, and tenor banjo, which were sold through mail-order houses and music shops, influencing countless musicians.

Smeck continued to produce recordings into the 1960s, often playing ukulele on heavily produced sessions for Kapp, ABC-Paramount, and other labels. In the mid-1970s blues reissue label Yazoo inspired a new round of Smeck-mania by reissuing some of his classic 78 recordings, wowing another generation of bluegrass, blues, and jazz pickers. Smeck died on April 5, 1994.

See also BANJO, FIVE-STRING.

Smith, Fiddlin' Arthur (1898–1971) *fiddler*

Born in Bold Springs, Tennessee, on April 10, 1898, Smith was a railroad worker and talented amateur fiddler. In the early 1930s he partnered with Sam and Kirk McGee to play traditional and jazz-influenced instrumentals. They broadcast regularly on Nashville's WSM radio station and recorded prolifically, often featuring Smith's smooth vocals on contemporary pop songs. Smith also worked with the Delmore Brothers in a group called the Dixieliners around this time. One of their best-selling recordings is the oft-covered "More Pretty Girls Than One" issued in 1936.

After World War II, Smith relocated to the West Coast, where he worked in various low-budget westerns and accompanied many country artists on tour and record. In the early 1960s, thanks to the FOLK REVIVAL, the McGee Brothers were rediscovered and recorded again with Smith, issuing two albums on the Folkways label produced by MIKE SEEGER. They also appeared at folk and bluegrass festivals. Smith died on February 28, 1971.

See also SAM MCGEE.

Smith, Harry (1923–1991) *anthology producer and music collector*

Harry Everett Smith was born on May 29, 1923 in Anacortes, Washington. Both his parents sang folk songs, and his father's purchase of CARL SANDBURG's *American Songbag* influenced the young Smith to search for recordings of traditional performers. Smith studied anthropology at the University of Washington in Seattle, and began searching for folk recordings in secondhand shops. After World War II, he settled in Berkeley, by chance renting an apartment in the same building as ballad scholar Bernard Bronson, and the two began swapping material. After the war, many older 78s were dumped on the market, and Smith eagerly purchased blues, folk, and jazz recordings.

In the early 1950s Smith approached small record label owner MOSES ASCH about selling his collection. Asch suggested instead that Smith produce an anthology of these recordings for his Folkways label. Smith immediately took to the task, assembling three two-album sets, with an elaborately illustrated booklet designed and created by Smith to annotate the selections. Rather than focusing on single styles of music or breaking down the collection by racial lines, Smith instead created a kind of American "playlist," linking the songs loosely by topic, and moving easily from blues to old-time music to CAJUN MUSIC to traditional folk. His clever newspaper-style headline reductions of the content of each song and his brief notes helped introduce dozens of performers from the 1920s and 1930s to a new audience.

It is not an exaggeration to say that Smith's *Anthology of American Folk Music* was the single most important influence on the old-time, blues, and folk revivals. An entire generation of performers and collectors—including JOHN COHEN, RALPH RINZLER, MIKE SEEGER, Peter Stampfel of the HOLY MODAL ROUNDERS, and hundreds more—were inspired by the *Anthology* to search out older musicians. Older performers such as MISSISSIPPI JOHN HURT and TOM ASHLEY were "rediscovered" and had new careers thanks to their inclusion on this set. Asch kept the six-volume *Anthology* in print until his death and the sale of Folkways to the Smithsonian Institution; the entire collection was reissued in a lavish boxed CD set by Smithsonian/Folkways in 1997 and became a best seller and Grammy winner.

Smith's varied career included recording traditional Peyote ceremonies, making avant-garde films, and serving as a "Shaman-in-Residence" at the Naropa Institute in Colorado. Shortly before his death, he was awarded a lifetime achievement award at the Grammy ceremonies. He died on November 11, 1991.

Smith, Hobart (1897–1965) *multi-instrumentalist*
Hobart Smith was born on May 10, 1897, in Saltville, Virginia. He learned banjo, FIDDLE, GUITAR, and MANDOLIN from his father, beginning to play at age seven; by 1915 he was working at tent shows around his native Virginia, and also leading his own string band, gaining fame primarily as a banjo player. In 1918 he met fellow banjoist TOM ASHLEY, who became a close friend and also musical inspiration. While Smith held many jobs from farming to house painting, he was unusual in that he primarily made

his living playing music, working local dances and festivals. In 1936 he and his sister, Texas Gladden (a ballad singer whom Smith often accompanied on guitar), gave a command performance for Eleanor Roosevelt at the White Top, Virginia, folk festival. This led, in 1942, to Alan Lomax recording him for the Library of Congress, and also MOSES ASCH recording a commercial album of 78s for his Disc label. In 1959 Lomax made further recordings of Smith and Gladden while compiling his *Sounds of the South* albums for Atlantic Records. By this time, Smith was embraced by the folk and old-time music revival community and was regularly performing at colleges and festivals. He made a final album for Folk Legacy Records in the early 1960s, but sadly passed away on January 11, 1965, at the height of his newfound success.

See also BANJO, FIVE-STRING; LOMAX, JOHN AND ALAN.

"So Long, It's Been Good to Know You (Dusty Old Dust)" (1939) *Woody Guthrie song*
WOODY GUTHRIE wrote this song to tell the story of the Okies who fled from the ravages of the dust storms of the 1930s, seeking a better life in Southern California. The song became closely associated with him. Guthrie used a version of it, with different lyrics, as the theme song for his 1940 CBS radio series, *Pipe Smoking Time*. The WEAVERS covered it, with Guthrie supplying new lyrics again, and had a number two hit with it in early 1952.

Sorrels, Rosalie (b. 1933) *singer, songwriter, and folk song collector*
Born in Idaho and raised there and in Utah in several small towns, Sorrels first learned folk songs from her father, who both sang and played a few instruments by ear. She also heard music at the local church. In 1950 she married Jim Sorrels, an amateur guitarist who also worked for the phone company. Both became avid folk song collectors, and Jim often accompanied Rosalie's singing; the couple

later divorced. In 1961 she recorded her first album for Folkways Records, which led to a few performances at festivals and colleges. She returned in 1967 on the album *If I Could Be the Rain,* with a title song written by fellow Utah folksinger, BRUCE "U. UTAH" PHILLIPS. Sorrels also began to compose her own songs at this time. She continued to record and perform through the 1970s and 1980s, even making one album in the early 1970s for the commercial pop label Sire Records. In 1988 she suffered a stroke, but has managed to return to recording and occasional performing.

Speer Family, The

One of the first and longest-lived gospel singing families, the Speers performed from the mid-1920s to the mid-1960s in a style that harked back to traditional shape-note harmonies. The religious Speers got their start when bass vocalist George Thomas Speer wed the talented pianist and singer Lena Brock in 1920; enlisting the help of his sister and brother-in-law, Pearl and Logan Claborn, to sing alto and tenor, George formed a family gospel quartet. The group made their living selling songbooks in rural churches throughout the mid-South, performing the material so that their audience could hear it and then be inspired to buy the books.

By the late 1920s the arduous life of traveling musicians began to wear on the Claborns, and, meanwhile, the Speers themselves were beginning to produce talented singing offspring. The children were gradually brought on board to replace their aunt and uncle, eventually including eldest brother, Brock, followed by Ben, Rosa Nell, and Mary Tom. By the late 1930s Rosa Nell was showing talent on the piano, so her mother switched to the ACCORDION.

After World War II, with the growth of interest in gospel music in the country-music field, the Speer family finally settled down in Nashville. Their postwar recordings were highly influential, particularly noteworthy for the powerful vocals of Mother Speer on her signature song "I'm Building a Bridge." In the early 1950s the Speer daughters were settling down to form families, so Brock's wife was brought on board, as well as the first non-Speer members, who became honorary "Speer sisters." In 1954 the family landed a local TV gospel show, gaining further exposure. Until her death in 1967, Mom Speer remained the motivating force behind the group. Her powerful vocals, with just a hint of jazzy syncopation, gave the group its characteristic sound.

See also SHAPE-NOTE SINGING.

Spence, Bill (b. 1940) *dulcimer player and record label owner*

William Spence was born in August 1940 in Iowa City, Iowa. He formed his first folk group while a high school student. He attended the University of Iowa from 1958 to 1962, then served in the army until 1965. Spence then settled in upstate New York, working in the Television, Audio, and Graphic Design Department at the State University of New York in Albany until 1998 when he retired. At a folk festival in 1969, he heard hammer dulcimer player Howie Mitchell and was immediately hooked on the instrument; in 1970 he formed Fenning's All Star Band as an outgrowth of the Pick'n and Sing'n Gather'n, an open jam session for folk musicians organized by Spence and his wife, Andy. In 1973 he issued his first album, *The Hammered Dulcimer,* on his own Front Hall label. (Front Hall is a mail order record, instrument, and book business run by Spence and his wife.) The record was an unexpected best seller, selling more than 80,000 copies to date. Its popularity was boosted when the PBS show *Crockett's Victory Garden* adapted a medley from the record as its theme music. The Fenning's band was active until the early 1980s, achieving great popularity on the festival and folk club circuit. In 1977 Andy and Bill founded Old Songs, Inc., a not-for-profit corporation to present folk music and dance through concerts and educational events. Spence's last album of hammer dulcimer music appeared in 1992. Front Hall Records has grown beyond issuing Spence's own recordings to include recordings by other folk revivalists, including JOHN

ROBERTS, TONY BARRAND, and MICHAEL COONEY. Over the last decades, the Spences have operated the Front Hall business, while Bill Spence continues to lead workshops and classes for dulcimer players.

See also DULCIMER (HAMMERED).

Spoelstra, Mark (b. 1940) *folk-rock artist*

Mark Spolestra was born on June 30, 1940, in Kansas City, Missouri. His family soon relocated to California, where Spoelstra was raised. As a teenager, he began playing GUITAR, interested in traditional blues styles. He moved to New York City, then the center of the folk-blues revival, and began performing in Greenwich Village clubs. He was an early champion of the 12-string guitar, and recorded two albums featuring the instrument for Folkways in 1961. He then signed with larger label Elektra, and began recording a mix of blues, folk, and new singer/songwriter material. However, in 1966 he was drafted into the military, serving for two years. Spoelstra returned to recording in a FOLK-ROCK style in 1969 for Columbia, and continued to record and perform through the early 1970s, when he became a born-again Christian. He made an album of gospel-inspired songs in 1976, and then did not release any further recordings until 2001, when he returned with a second release focusing on traditional blues and his own compositions.

square dance

Traditional American square dancing evolved out of several European traditions. English country dancing was traditionally performed by couples in long lines (like the well-known Virginia Reel), although occasionally square-type sets were also used. The French quadrille—a more formal dance performed by four couples in a square formation—is generally credited as the model for American square dancing. Together with English and American dance tunes, and many figures borrowed from the English and French traditions, the square dance developed during the 19th century as a key form of social dancing.

Other popular 19th-century social dances—such as mazurkas, polkas, and waltzes—were probably also part of a typical dance evening that might include a mix of various styles of dance.

In the early decades of the 20th century, square dancing was heavily promoted through several different movements. The physical education movement, which became an important part of both elementary and secondary education, adopted the square dance as a relatively easy-to-perform style that encouraged not only physical development but also "social skills." Automobile magnate Henry Ford, who felt that modern jazz dance and music were corrupting influences on American youth, heavily promoted square dancing as a traditional American style that upheld conservative values of family and culture. Finally, the Western Square dance movement grew to formalize the rules for square dances, regularize dance styles, and institute competitions and graded instruction so that participants from any part of the country could easily dance together.

In New England the English long-line dances survived alongside square dances. These were known as contra dances (from the French *contre,* meaning "facing across" because the men face the women in long lines). The contra dance tradition was considerably looser than square dancing, and for that reason has been more attractive to folk revivalists and musicians since the early 1970s. While Western Square groups usually dance to records and perform the dances in a uniform way, contras are usually danced to live music and can vary in terms of figures and style.

Stanley, Roba (1910–1986) *guitarist and singer*

The daughter of country fiddler Rob Stanley (c. 1859–c. 1935), Roba was raised on a farm in North Georgia. She showed an early talent as a guitarist, borrowing her older brother's instrument while he worked in the fields. Her father soon invited her to accompany him at SQUARE DANCES. Their local performances drew the attention of Atlanta's radio station WSB, where she debuted with her father in early 1924. The novelty of a young female guitarist performing and singing traditional dance songs led to an offer to record from Okeh records. Roba made a series of recordings in 1924 and again in 1925. On her later date she was accompanied by HENRY WHITTER, one of the pioneering country guitarists. Impulsively marrying at age fifteen, Roba settled with her new husband in Florida; discouraged from performing, she retired from the music business. She died on June 8, 1986.

See also GUITAR.

Stanley Brothers and Ralph Stanley
performers
Carter Glen (August 27, 1925–December 1, 1966) and Ralph Edmond (b. February 25, 1927) Stanley were born and raised in rural McClure, Virginia, in the mountainous western region of the state, near the Kentucky border. Their mother was an old-time banjo player, and both sons began playing the banjo, learning such traditional songs as "Little Birdie" in the drop-thumb or clawhammer style. Carter switched to GUITAR after Ralph became proficient on banjo, and the duo began performing locally. Their first professional work came in 1946 with Roy Sykes and the Blue Ridge Boys; one year later, they left the band, along with mandolinist "Pee Wee" (Darrell) Lambert, to form the Clinch Mountain Boys. It was about this time that they heard the legendary performances of Bill Monroe's Blue Grass Boys, and Ralph adopted the finger-picking style of Earl Scruggs to his banjo playing. The Stanleys' band was hired to perform over the radio in Bristol, Tennessee, and made its first recordings for the tiny Rich-R-Tone label out of Johnson City.

In 1949 they relocated to take a radio job in Raleigh, North Carolina, where they were heard by Columbia talent scout Art Satherly, who signed them to that label. The Stanleys recorded for Columbia for three years, featuring their breathtaking traditional harmonies on traditional mountain ballads and Carter Stanley's compositions in a traditional vein, including the classic "White Dove" and "A Vision of Mother." In 1952 guitarist/vocalist George Shuffler joined the group, a talented flatpicker who would be featured prominently as a soloist in the band for the next decade.

Carter briefly took a job as lead vocalist for Bill Monroe's band in 1952, recording the lead vocals on Monroe's own "Uncle Pen" and the honky-tonk song "Sugar Coated Love." The brothers reunited in 1953, signing to Mercury, remaining with the label through 1958, and then recording for King/Starday until Carter's death. By this time, they had solidified their sound around lead guitar and banjo, with Ralph's licks limited to a fairly small repertoire. Carter's expressive lead vocals were perfectly complemented either by Ralph's unearthly high mountain tenor or Shuffler's more modern-sounding harmonies.

In the late 1950s and early 1960s the market for bluegrass music was fairly small, so the Stanleys relocated to Florida for the winters, hosting a radio program as well as recording for smaller local labels. The FOLK REVIVAL of the 1960s helped revive the Stanleys' popularity, and they toured the revival circuit and in Europe. Carter's life was cut short by alcoholism in 1966, and for a while it seemed as if the band would fold.

However, Ralph emerged as an important band leader by the decade's end. To fill Carter's shoes, he first enlisted vocalist Larry Sparks, who went on to be one of the 1970s most important progressive bluegrass performers, and then the more traditionally oriented Roy Lee Centers, who sounded eerily like Carter. The band signed with Rebel Records, and were popular both on the revival and traditional bluegrass circuits. Centers's murder in 1974 was another blow to Stanley, but he was soon followed by two high school age musicians whom the elder banjo player had discovered—mandolinist Ricky Skaggs and guitarist Keith Whitley—helping to launch their careers in bluegrass and later the new traditional Nashville music.

From the 1970s to the 1990s the Stanley band centered on Ralph's banjo, the showy fiddling of

Curly Ray Cline, and the bass playing of Jack Cooke, usually augmented by a young guitarist/vocalist and mandolinist. Despite the variability in the talents of the lead vocalists, the sound of Stanley's music remains unchanged. Ralph Stanley's career was given a major boost by the 2000 release of *O Brother, Where Art Thou?* In the film's soundtrack, Stanley is prominently featured singing an a cappella version of the song "O Death," which earned him a Grammy award.

See also BANJO, FIVE-STRING; FIDDLE; GUITAR; MANDOLIN.

Steeleye Span

ASHLEY HUTCHINGS, one of the founders of FAIRPORT CONVENTION, formed Steeleye Span to further explore his interest in setting traditional British ballads and songs to contemporary, rock-flavored accompaniments. The original band consisted of two former folk duos—Tim Hart and Maddy Prior and Gay and Terry Woods—with Hutchings, and no drummer (although their first studio album featured session drummers). The Woods dropped out almost immediately and were replaced by longtime folk guitarist MARTIN CARTHY and fiddler Peter Knight. Like Fairport, the group was marked by the excellent lead vocal work by a female singer, in this case Maddy Prior. Prior's vocals combined a traditional quality in tone and ornamentation with the strength needed to head an electrified band. This lineup lasted until 1971, when Carthy and Hutchings left.

The 1971–76 Steeleye Span lineup was the most commercially successful of all, perhaps thanks to the addition of guitarist Bob Johnston and bass player Rick Kemp, both of whom came out of rock bands, and, in 1973, a full-time drummer. They even managed a top five U.S. hit in 1975 with their arrangement of the traditional song "All 'Round My Hat." However, Johnston and Knight left the band to form a duo in 1977, and a caretaker lineup with Martin Carthy and JOHN KIRKPATRICK completed the band's last album and final tour dates in 1978.

Like many other long-lived British FOLK-ROCK bands, the group has reassembled with its 1971–76 lineup (more or less) many times over the years, beginning in 1986. Meanwhile, Prior has had a long solo career as a singer, sometimes working in conjunction with Kemp, whom she married.

Stewart, John   See KINGSTON TRIO, THE.

Stoneman, Ernest "Pop" (1893–1968) *recording artist and performer*

One of the first country artists to record, Ernest Stoneman was also one of the longest to remain on the scene, returning as the leader of the Stoneman Family Band in the 1950s and 1960s until his death.

Born on May 25, 1893, to a musical family in Monarat, Virginia, Stoneman was a carpenter by trade and a musician by vocation. By his twenties he could play the GUITAR, autoharp, mouth harp (or HARMONICA), and Jew's harp. He contacted Okeh recording executive and pioneering country music producer Ralph Peer in 1924 and made some test recordings that were eventually released early the next year, including the first recording of "The Sinking of the Titanic." Stoneman continued to record throughout the 1920s for numerous labels, both as a soloist and as leader of a string band, The Blue Ridge Corn Shuckers, featuring fiddler Uncle Eck Dunford.

With the coming of the Depression, the recording industry was severely crippled and Stoneman's initial career ended. He worked in a munitions factory during World War II, settling outside of Washington, D.C., and did not return to active performing until the first FOLK REVIVAL of the early 1950s. Stoneman had 13 children, many talented musically, and so he formed a family band that began performing in the Washington area, with sons Scotty (FIDDLE), Jim (bass), and Van (guitar), and daughters Donna (MANDOLIN) and Roni (banjo), plus Pop leading the brood on guitar and autoharp. They recorded for various labels, but their most important and influential album came out in 1957 on the Folkways label, introducing their sound to the urban folk revival audience. In 1962 they were made members of the *Grand Ole Opry,* and continued to perform throughout the 1960s for both country and folk revival audiences. They also appeared on many TV variety programs.

After Pop Stoneman's death, the group adopted a more bluegrass-oriented sound. Son Scotty left the band first and won fame on the West Coast as a bluegrass fiddler, particularly for his work with the progressive bluegrass band the KENTUCKY COLONELS in the early 1960s; daughter Roni became a talented comedian, appearing as a regular on the popular *Hee Haw* TV program. Stoneman died on June 14, 1968.

See also BANJO, FIVE-STRING.

Story, Carl (1916–1995) *bandleader and guitarist*
Carl Moore Story was born in Lenoir, North Carolina, on May 29, 1916. He was the son of an old-time fiddler who played local dances, and indeed FIDDLE was his first instrument, which he took up at age nine. Influenced by recordings of North Carolina string bands like CHARLIE POOLE's North Carolina Ramblers, Story soon took up GUITAR and began singing. When he was about 25 years old, he moved to Lynchburg, Virginia, where he began his radio career. In 1935 he briefly returned home, joining banjo player Johnnie Whisnant, who was then only 14 years old. The two got radio work in Spartanburg, South Carolina, first with an existing band called the Lonesome Mountaineers. The band broke up, and the duo formed their own group, the similarly named Rambling Mountaineers. The band lasted through the early 1940s, working out of several Carolina towns, when World War II decimated its membership. Story briefly joined Bill Monroe's band as a fiddle player, but then was himself drawn into the war, enlisting in the navy in 1943.

After the war Carl formed a new Rambling Mountaineers, first working out of Asheville and then Knoxville, Tennessee, where he broadcast until 1951 and then again from 1953 to 1957. In 1947 he

signed with Mercury Records, making his first recordings, and then in 1953 moved to Columbia, where he remained for two years. His bands of this period had various personnel, but he did not have the typical bluegrass lineup because he had no full-time banjo player. Instead, he focused on his own guitar work and on strong lead MANDOLIN, often handled by Red Rector.

In 1957 Story formed his first true bluegrass band with fiddler Tater Tate and the Brewster Brothers. This band recorded for Starday and led to a second career for Story on the bluegrass circuit. From 1957 to 1960 he had his own local TV show out of Asheville, and then continued the tradition during much of the 1960s out of Charlotte, North Carolina. Story continued to lead bands with various personnel, enjoying his greatest success during the bluegrass revival of the 1960s and 1970s. The group focused on bluegrass gospel, cutting several fine sacred albums. Story worked the bluegrass festival circuit and recorded until his death on March 30, 1995.

See also BANJO, FIVE-STRING.

Strachwitz, Chris (b. 1931) *record label owner*
Chris Strachwitz was born in Germany in 1931. When he was 16, in 1947, his family moved to Southern California, where he was exposed to folk music, blues, and Tex Mex sounds. He served in the army from 1954 to 1956, and then completed his education in Berkeley. He worked as a teacher, while collecting blues records as a hobby; to support himself and build his collection, he started a mail order record sevice, the International Blues Record Club, which brought him into contact with British blues collectors such as Paul Oliver. One of Strachwitz's favorite artists was Lightnin' Hopkins, so in 1959 he traveled to Texas in search of him. Hopkins would not record for him initially because Strachwitz couldn't afford to pay him as much as the commercial labels that typically paid $100 a song to blues performers like Hopkins. Armed with a list of names from Paul Oliver, Strachwitz began combing Texas and the South for blues performers to record.

He founded a record label, Arhoolie Records, named for the traditional southern field hollers known as "arwhoolies," as a means of issuing the tapes he was making. Among his early discoveries was Texas blues musician Mance Lipscomb (the first Arhoolie album featured his performances) and, in 1964, Cajun performer CLIFTON CHENIER.

Strachwitz was lucky when a local band led by COUNTRY JOE MCDONALD wanted to record McDonald's song "I Feel Like I'm Fixin' to Die Rag" for inclusion in the Berkeley publication, *Rag Baby;* Strachwitz agreed to record it free of charge in return for the publishing rights. He also took publishing rights for blues performers he recorded, including Fred McDowell. In 1969 he scored two major coups when McDonald's "Feel Like I'm Fixin' to Die" was used in the *Woodstock* film, and the Rolling Stones recorded McDowell's "You Gotta Move." The profits were plowed back into recording traditional music.

The label grew through the 1960s and 1970s, focusing primarily on Strachwitz's musical loves of blues, CAJUN MUSIC, and—beginning in the 1970s—TEX-MEX MUSIC. Strachwitz also partnered with filmmaker Les Blank to make documentaries on several important blues and Cajun performers. In 1976 he opened a record store/mail order service called Down Home Music, which became an important source for hard-to-find recordings from Europe and the United States in all genres of music. In 1995 he formed the Arhoolie Foundation to preserve, document, and provide educational resources on traditional music. Strachwitz was awarded a Lifetime Achievement award by the Association for Recorded Sound Collections (ARSC) in 2004.

Stripling Brothers, The

Charles Nevins "Charlie" (August 8, 1896–January 19, 1966) and Ira Lee (June 5, 1898–March 1967) Stripling were born near Kennedy, in Pickens County, Alabama. Charlie started fiddling at about the age of 18, and his brother took up the GUITAR soon after. The two became popular at local fid-

dlers' conventions. In 1926 Charlie took second place at the Dixie Fiddlers' Convention sponsored by industrialist/SQUARE DANCE enthusiast Henry Ford. By then the brothers had their own radio show out of Birmingham.

In 1928 they made their first recordings in Birmingham, cutting two numbers; one, "The Lost Child," is said to be the source for the popular bluegrass instrumental "Black Mountain Rag." Their next session was held a year and a half later in Chicago, producing 16 sides, including Charlie's own showpiece, "The Kennedy Rag." The traditional tune "Wolves A-Howlin' " was also cut at these sessions, and later this unusual local tune became a favorite of old-time revival fiddlers. This was the brothers' last recording before the Depression slowed the music business. However, in 1934 and 1936 they recorded once more, this time for Decca, first in New York and then, their last session, in New Orleans. Their total output was 40 instrumentals and two vocal numbers.

By the end of the 1930s, Ira had retired and Charlie had formed a band with his two sons, Lee and Robert, mostly performing locally. His two sons served in World War II, and then Lee settled in Seattle and Robert went to Alabama; neither pursued musical careers at the time. Charlie continued to fiddle until arthritis ended his career in 1958.

The brothers' work was introduced to the old-time music revival in 1971 when a compilation of their best recordings was reissued by County Records. This led to some renewed interest in their work, and many of their tunes were revived by young bands. In 1999 Charlie's son Lee was encouraged to take up fiddling again, and a year later reunited with his brother. The two have performed in the Seattle area and toured in spring 2001.

See also FIDDLE.

Sullivan Family, The

The Sullivans are a long-lived bluegrass gospel group. Enoch (b. September 18, 1933) and Emmett Sullivan (July 23, 1936–April 10, 1993) were born in

Saint Stephens, Alabama, near the Mississippi border. Their father was a revivalist preacher, and their uncle, J. B., was a banjo player who led local bands. Raised religiously, they were early fans of bluegrass music, listening regularly to Bill Monroe on the *Grand Ole Opry.* Guitarist Margie Brewster (b. Winnsboro, Los Angeles, January 22, 1933) also loved traditional country sounds, being an avid listener of the *Louisiana Hayride.* She was also an early convert to evangelical religion, beginning to travel the circuit as an assistant to a local female evangelist named Hazel Chain when she was a teenager. In 1949 she met Enoch at a revival in rural Alabama, and the couple married and settled in Enoch's hometown of St. Stephens.

After briefly working on the radio out of Mississippi, the two, along with Enoch's brother, Emmett, began broadcasting closer to home in 1950, working out of Jackson and then Thomasville, Alabama, broadcasting an early morning 15-minute gospel show every day. Around this time, they met Walter Bailes of the BAILES BROTHERS, who operated the gospel label Loyal Records. They began recording for Bailes, and their records became popular among the country-gospel audience. The group featured the robust lead singing of Margie Sullivan, who was influenced by big-voiced country singers such as MOLLY O'DAY.

The Sullivans entered the bluegrass world via their admiration for Bill Monroe. They befriended Monroe, who admired their harmony vocals, and he invited them to appear at his Bean Blossom Bluegrass festival in 1968. They have since performed on both bluegrass and gospel circuits. The band has included, from time to time, other family members, including their cousin Jerry, along with outside musicians. One young picker from Mississippi named Marty Stuart played with them

during 1969–70 before joining Lester Flatt. Stuart has remained close to the family and has produced several albums by Jerry and his daughter Tammy Sullivan. In 1989 the family began publishing *Bluegrass Gospel News* as a way of promoting the music and its performers.

Sweet Honey in the Rock

Sweet Honey in the Rock was formed out of a vocal workshop led by civil rights activist/singer BERNICE Johnson REAGON (b. October 4, 1942) in Washington, D.C., in the early 1970s. Reagon first came to prominence as an activist during the early 1960s CIVIL RIGHTS MOVEMENT in Albany, Georgia, where she worked as both a songleader and organizer. Eventually, she settled in Washington, D.C., where she began teaching a cappella singing at the local Black Repertory Theater school. The group grew out of these classes.

The a cappella vocal group began creating its own material, commenting on racism, sexism, and other contemporary issues. Drawing on traditional gospel harmonies, the group developed a unique combination of African rhythms and vocal styles combined with African-American religious and secular music. First recording in 1976, the group became a major presence in the folk, women's music, and protest music arenas through the mid-1980s. In addition to albums for adults, they have recorded several children's albums, to bring their message to younger listeners.

Reagon documented the group's birth and development in the book *We Who Believe in Freedom: Sweet Honey in the Rock Still on the Journey,* published in 1993. Although Reagon no longer tours with the group, she continues to have an influence on their repertoire and direction.

Taj Mahal (b. 1942)

Henry St. Clair Fredericks (aka Taj Mahal) was born in New York City on May 17, 1942; his father was a jazz pianist of Jamaican heritage, while his mother's family hailed from South Carolina. The family relocated to Springfield, Massachusetts, when he was fairly young, and Fredericks began showing interest in music as a teenager, teaching himself piano, GUITAR, and HARMONICA. He attended college at the University of Massachusetts, Amherst, and began appearing at folk clubs in Boston. After graduation in the mid-1960s, he moved to Santa Monica, California, where he began playing at coffeehouses, taking the stage name of Taj Mahal. He met fellow blues fan and guitarist Ry Cooder in California, and the two formed a band called Rising Sons; the group earned a recording contract, but never completed their first album before disbanding.

Mahal issued his first solo album in 1968. Mahal was one of the few young African-American guitarists to play acoustic blues, making him a novelty on both the folk/blues revival scene and in the blues rock arena. His first few albums were devoted primarily to traditional blues, but then he began exploring a wider range of African heritage music. In the late 1960s–early 1970s he lived briefly in Spain while touring Africa and Europe as a performer. In 1971 Mahal provided the soundtrack for the movie *Sounder,* and also took a small acting role in it. In the mid-1970s Mahal continued to expand his repertoire to include reggae, salsa, and calypso styles.

Mahal spent most of the 1980s living in Hawaii, studying the native music traditions there, while dropping out of the performing/recording scene. He returned with a new album in 1987 showcasing his new musical love, followed by a series of children's albums. In 1991 his score for *Mule Bone,* a play by Langston Hughes and Zora Neale Hurston, earned him a Grammy nomination (he would win a Grammy six years later for the album *Señor Blues*). He also recorded with a number of world music performers, including duets with African kora master Toumani Diabate, as well as Indian and Hawaiian musicians.

Tashian, Barry and Holly

Barry Tashian (b. August 5, 1945) was lead guitarist and founder of the Boston-based group the Remains, which actually opened for the Beatles on their last tour in 1966. He then moved to California, briefly working with Gram Parsons in the original Flying Burrito Brothers and then spent most of the 1980s as lead guitarist for Emmylou Harris's Hot Band. Holly (b. January 8, 1946) is a classically trained violinist who met her future husband while the two were still in high school. They began working together in the 1970s as members of the New England–based country band, the Outskirts.

The duo first began performing together in the mid-1980s. They were initially more popular in Europe than at home, releasing an album in Germany in 1989. Their success abroad led to a recording contract with bluegrass label Rounder in the United States. The title track of their second U.S. release, "Straw into Gold," reached number 11 on the short-lived Americana chart (this chart was designed to track the sales of "alt-country" artists such as NANCI GRIFFITH and Lyle Lovett). They have continued to tour through the 1990s, primarily on the bluegrass and folk circuits. Tashian has also led several Remains reunion tours.

Taylor, James (b. 1948) *singer and songwriter*

James Taylor was born on March 12, 1948, in Boston, Massachusetts. His father was a university professor who moved the family to Chapel Hill, North Carolina, when Taylor was young. The family continued to summer on Martha's Vineyard, where the teenage Taylor met guitarist Danny Kortchmar, and the two began playing together. Troubled by depression, Taylor committed himself to a mental hospital in 1965; on his release, he moved to New York, rejoining Kortchmar in a band they called the Flying Machine. The group made a demo tape including several Taylor originals, but it went unissued until after he became famous.

In 1968 Taylor left New York for London, where he was "discovered" by Peter Asher, who had been a member of the pop duo Peter & Gordon. More important, he was the brother of Jane Asher, the then-girlfriend of Paul McCartney. Peter wanted to become a record producer, and McCartney and the other Beatles had just established Apple Records, so Asher signed Taylor to the label, producing his first album. This first album made little impression, and Taylor returned to America. In 1970 he reunited with Asher to record his breakthrough album, *Sweet Baby James,* which produced many chart hits, including the autobiographical "Fire and Rain."

Taylor is more of a singer-songwriter than a pure folk performer, although his finger-style acoustic GUITAR work is derived from folk and blues models, and the subject matter of some of his best-loved songs—a soft, gentle nostalgia for the South—recall typical folk topics. Throughout the 1970s he continued to record and tour, achieving several hits, often with covers of earlier rock material ("How Sweet It Is" in 1975, originally cut by Marvin Gaye;

"Every Day" in 1981, originally a Buddy Holly hit). Since the 1980s, Taylor has been a regular touring performer, often appearing on PBS in live concerts during fund-raising periods, and recording albums every two to four years.

Taylor, Tut (b. 1923) *multi-instrumentalist*

Robert Taylor was born in Milledgeville, Georgia, on November 20, 1923. A talented musician who could play a variety of instruments by his early teens, Taylor began his career as an instrument builder. In the 1960s FOLK REVIVAL he toured with a number of semipopular folk bands, including the Folkswingers and the more bluegrass-oriented Dixie Gentlemen. He joined up with fiddler Vassar Clements, and the duo became the nucleus of JOHN HARTFORD's backup band in 1969, remaining with him for a couple of years. His tasteful playing with Hartford helped reintroduce the *dobro* to a new generation of pickers. He recorded two solo albums for Rounder Records in 1973 and 1977 and became a popular figure on the bluegrass circuit. In the 1980s Taylor turned his back on performing to focus on instrument building and repair; his music shop has become a mecca for traditional musicians in the Nashville area.

Terry, Sonny (c. 1911–1986), and Brownie McGhee (1914–1996)

Terrell Saunders "Sonny" Terry gave his birthplace as Greenwood, Georgia, on October 24, 1912, but other sources give the place as "near Durham, North Carolina," and place his birth exactly a year earlier. His father was a subsistence farmer living about 20 miles northeast of Durham, and played the HARMONICA as a pastime. When Terry was five years old, he began experimenting with his father's instrument. He also began to lose his eyesight and was totally blind by his teen years. That, and the death of his father, led him to relocate to Durham to try to make a living as a street musician in the early 1930s.

In Durham he met blues guitarists Blind Boy Fuller and REV. GARY DAVIS, and washboard player "Bull City Red." They played together in various combinations on the streets of the city, busking for coins. They were discovered by J. B. Long, a talent scout for Okeh Records, who arranged for them to record in 1938–39; Terry also was brought to New York to appear at the famous "From Spirituals to Swing" concert at Carnegie Hall, held in 1939. Fuller was Terry's main partner, but he died in 1940, and Terry soon formed a partnership with a young guitarist named Walter "Brownie" McGhee.

McGhee was born in Knoxville, Tennessee, on November 30, 1914. His father played GUITAR and sang, and his uncle was a fiddler, and the two played for white and play dances throughout eastern Tennessee. Brownie learned guitar and banjo as a youth, and by age 14 was traveling with medicine and tent shows as a performer; however, a youthful bout of polio led him to be partially crippled, although a 1937 operation was able to restore most of his mobility. In the early 1930s McGhee returned to work on the family farm—by then located in

Sonny Terry and Brownie McGhee on stage at the Newport Folk Festival, 1963 (Photo © John Byrne Cooke, http://www.cookephoto.com)

Kingsport, Tennessee—but was soon on the road again, eventually reaching Durham, North Carolina, where he became a member of the Fuller-Davis-Terry circle. J. B. Long brought McGhee and Terry to Chicago after Fuller's death in 1940, and McGhee's first recording was a tribute record to Fuller, recorded under the name of "Blind Boy Fuller No. 2."

Long began promoting the duo, booking them for concerts on the growing folk scene. At one show in Washington, D.C., they met and befriended guitarist LEAD BELLY, and the three made their first recording together in 1942. Lead Belly encouraged them to move to New York, where they met folk performers PETE SEEGER, WOODY GUTHRIE, and others on the scene. Terry even landed a featured role in the 1946 Broadway musical production *Finian's Rainbow*, bringing him further fame. McGhee's smooth vocals and simplified guitar accompaniments were perfectly complemented by Terry's backwoods-style harmonica playing (and his occasional half-yodel, half-yelps that he interjected in their performances). Throughout the 1950s until the mid-1970s they recorded together as a duo (although sometimes breaking up due to disagreements about who should enjoy top billing), and their albums were issued on dozens of folk and popular labels. After the duo split, they recorded separately, although they never achieved the same success as solo artists that they enjoyed as a pair.

Terry died on March 11, 1986 in Mineola, New York, and McGhee died in Oakland, California, on February 23, 1996.

See also BANJO, FIVE-STRING.

Tex-Mex music

Tex-Mex music combines the country music of Texas with the Spanish influence of Mexican music. There are two strands in this musical style: long story-songs known as *corridos*, which often recount the legendary exploits of outlaws and murders, local or national events, or the tragic stories of star-crossed lovers; and the *conjunto* dance music. The best-known exponent of the Tex-Mex vocal style was singer Lydia Mendoza, who made recordings during the 1920s and 1930s and again on her "rediscovery" in the 1970s. Her fine voice, GUITAR technique, and large repertoire of songs made her a great star. Tex-Mex dance music is played in bands usually featuring ACCORDION, guitar, bass, and drums, with a strong vocal tradition. Among today's accordion masters, Flaco Jiminez is recognized as one of the greatest performers.

"This Land Is Your Land" (1940) *Woody Guthrie classic*

Songwriter WOODY GUTHRIE originally wrote this song in response to the great popularity of Irving Berlin's "God Bless America," which was a great hit on the eve of World War II. Guthrie was annoyed by Berlin's blind patriotism, particularly in the face of the suffering he had witnessed during the Depression years. The original song's refrain ended with "God Blessed America for Me"; Guthrie was speaking for the disenfranchised, the people shut out by signs of "private property" from enjoying the nation's wealth. After World War II, the song was popularized by the FOLK-REVIVAL group the WEAVERS, who omitted the more political verses. Ironically, today the song is regarded as a statement of pure patriotism, much like Berlin's "God Bless America," rather than as a critique of the failings of the American system.

Thompson, Ernest (1892–1961) *singer*

Born Ernest Errott Thompson in Forsyth County, North Carolina, Thompson went blind during childhood, and also apparently suffered vocal-chord damage in a fire, leading him to have a piercing, high tenor voice. He learned piano tuning at the North Carolina State School for the Blind, and also mastered a number of instruments, including GUITAR and HARMONICA.

Thompson recorded twice in 1924, once on his own in April, and the second time with his niece, Connie Faw Sides, in November. His first release was the most popular, featuring "The Wreck of the Southern Old 97," which had previously been recorded in a different version by Henry Whitter, and "Are You from Dixie?," a 1915 vaudeville number written in a "southern" style. Both were immensely popular in their day.

Thompson never recorded again, but frequently played in his native North Carolina, around the Winston-Salem area, throughout the 1940s. Like many other street musicians, he played a mix of traditional and popular songs, as well as hymns and other favorites. He sometimes worked with his niece and his sister, Agnes, in an informal string band. In 1943 he was photographed by the local paper entertaining a group of soldiers on leave on the city's streets; he is shown playing a 12-string GUITAR, with a harmonica and small tin cup (for tips) around his neck. He wears a bowler hat labeled "Blind."

Thompson, Joe, Nate, and Odell *musicians*

The African-American Thompson family has a long history of music making in the North Carolina Piedmont according to family lore, dating back to Robert Thompson, born in 1849, who was said to be a FIDDLE player. Robert's sons included three musicians, John Arch, who was a fiddler, Jacob A., and Walter E. Thompson. John Arch and his brothers were active playing for both white and black dances in the region around the family farm. Arch had several sons, among them Nate (February 16, 1916–December 22, 1997), a banjo player, and Joe (b. Cedar Grove Township, North Carolina, December 9, 1918), a fiddler. Joe began to learn fiddle at an early age, despite his father's resistance to allowing him to even touch his instrument. Instead, he made a homemade fiddle using the wires from a screen door to make strings, impressing his father with his determination.

Joe and Nate were active locally playing for dances from the 1930s through the end of World

War II. During this time, they were sometimes joined by their cousin, Odell (b. Walter O. T., August 9, 1911–April 28, 1994), a banjo player and guitarist who was the son of their uncle, Walter E. After the war, Joe worked in a furniture factory and ceased making music. However, in the 1970s folklorist Kip Lornell "discovered" Joe and encouraged him to begin playing again, usually with his cousin, Odell; Nate also recorded and performed on occasion with both Joe and Odell. This led to a series of tours and recordings until Odell's death in 1994. Joe Thompson continued to perform through the 1990s, although increasing age and ill health slowed him toward the end of the decade. A stroke in 2000 slowed him considerably, although he recovered and was able to return to performing.

See also BANJO, FIVE-STRING.

Thompson, Uncle Jimmy (1848–1931) *fiddler and performer*

Although born in rural Putnam County, Tennessee, in a small farming town between Nashville and Knoxville, James Donald Thompson's family moved to Texas sometime around his 10th birthday. Thompson learned to FIDDLE there, and then made his way back to Tennessee by the mid-1880s, when he settled near his birthplace, marrying and working on a farm. Sometime around the turn of the last century he returned to Texas, settling near the Oklahoma border, where he began to focus more on his fiddle playing. Jimmy's big moment of fame in his early career came in 1907, when he participated in a famed fiddler's convention and contest held in Dallas. It was said to attract nearly 100 of the time's greatest fiddlers, and Jimmy took first place.

Jimmy returned to Tennessee around 1912, settling outside of Nashville on a small farm. His first wife soon died of cancer, but he was reunited with other family members, including his young niece, a music teacher named Eva Thompson Jones. He also began performing locally with his younger son, who was a guitarist, and his son's wife, a banjo

player. In 1916 he remarried; he joined his new wife, Ella, in her home in Wilson County, Tennessee, near the town of Laguardo, on a small farm. "Aunt Ella," as she was known locally, was a buck dancer who often danced on the streets accompanied by her fiddling husband. In 1923 Jimmy returned to Texas for another fiddler's contest and again took first prize.

But it was Jimmy's appearance on Nashville radio on the night of November 28, 1925, accompanied by his niece, Mrs. Eva Thompson Jones, on the piano, which would change his life. He played the traditional tune "Tennessee Wagonner," which brought an incredible response from listeners across the country. This launched the WSM *Saturday Night Barn Dance*, which would become famous as the *Grand Ole Opry*. Thompson played for the full hour on the first *Barn Dance* broadcast and continued to be the featured artist for at least a month afterward. When word spread that old-time music was being performed on the air, the show's producer/host George D. Hay was flooded with similar acts, but continued to employ Thompson until 1928; his traditional backwoods FIDDLE style strongly appealed to the rural audience that the program hoped to reach. Although he worked most of his life as a farmer, Thompson had also performed locally at dances and fiddlers' contests and conventions. He recorded for Columbia in 1926 and again for Vocalion in 1930, before dying of pneumonia at the age of 83 on February 17, 1931.

See also BANJO, FIVE-STRING.

"(Hang Down Your Head) Tom Dooley" (1868, 1957) *hit for the Kingston Trio*

The KINGSTON TRIO had their first number one pop hit in 1957 with their version of this traditional folk ballad. The song is based on the story of the hanging of Thomas C. Dula for murdering his girlfriend in Wilkes County, North Carolina on May 6, 1868. Banjo playing songster FRANK PROFFITT taught the song to folklorist/performer FRANK WARNER in the

1930s. Warner, in turn, recorded it in the early 1950s, changing "Dula" to the more easy to pronounce "Dooley" and smoothing out the lyrics and melody. It was Warner's version that the trio learned and enhanced with their pop-styled harmonies. The great success of this recording inspired countless other folk trios, although folk purists were upset by the pop arrangement and slick sound of the Kingston Trio's recording.

See also BANJO, FIVE-STRING.

Traum, Happy (b. 1939) and Artie (b. 1943)

Happy and Artie Traum were both born in New York City at the dawn of the first FOLK REVIVAL. They were exposed to folk music early on through attending jam sessions in Greenwich Village's Washington Square, a hotbed for folk players in the 1950s. Happy studied with blues guitarist Brownie McGhee, and then in the early 1960s joined the New World Singers, a topical folk group who recorded a solo album in 1964. He also began authoring a series of influential GUITAR instruction books, which helped generations of folk players get started on the instrument. In 1968 Happy became editor of the folk music magazine *Sing Out!*, a position he held through the early 1970s.

Artie followed in his brother's footsteps, learning the basics of blues guitar from him, but developing into a more accomplished lead guitarist. He was a member of the short-lived True Endeavor Jug Band in the mid-1960s, and then in a series of FOLK-ROCK bands; by the late 1960s he was composing his own songs, including the score for the independent film *Greetings* (which marked the debut of director Brian De Palma).

The brothers first worked together in the late 1960s, playing as an acoustic duo at folk festivals and in their new hometown of Woodstock, New York. After Capitol Records enjoyed success with the debut album by The Band (another Woodstock-based group), they signed the Traums to a contract, resulting in two albums. The Traums became the center of musical activity in the Woodstock area, and pulled together several informal jam sessions, including such local performers as Maria Muldaur, John Sebastian, Bill Keith, and others, for a series of albums playfully titled *Mud Acres* in the 1970s and 1980s. At the same time, Happy Traum began a business called Homespun Tapes to teach various folk instruments, which has developed into a major provider of instructional material for folk and rock musicians.

Since the 1980s Happy and Artie have performed primarily as individuals; Artie has recorded a variety of albums, featuring both his own songs and acoustic and electric guitar instrumentals. Happy returned to playing more traditional-oriented folk material. The brothers did reunite in 1993 for an album, *Test of Time,* but then returned to solo work.

See also MULDAUR, GEOFF AND MARIA; TERRY, SONNY AND BROWNIE MCGHEE.

Trischka, Tony (b. 1949) bluegrass banjoist

Born Anthony Cattel Trischka in Syracuse, New York, on January 16, 1949, Trischka originally reached prominence as a member of COUNTRY COOKING, an all-instrumental band that was famous for the twin banjos of Trischka and Peter Wernick. When the band dissolved in the early 1970s, Trischka released his first solo album, *Bluegrass Light,* a kind of Sun-Ra-meets-Earl Scruggs outing. Although not exactly easy listening, the album opened up the potential for playing a wider melodic and harmonic range on bluegrass-style banjo. During this same period, Trischka also performed with the eclectic band, Breakfast Special, a more spacey incarnation of the earlier Country Cooking.

After a few more avant-garde solo albums, Trischka returned to the fold on the half-traditional, half-modern album *Banjoland* from the late 1970s. He even played in traditional Scruggs style, announcing that the far-out players were not adverse to honoring bluegrass roots. In the early 1980s he formed the band Skyline, which featured an odd wedding of contemporary country songs with his own toned-down original instrumentals.

After Skyline's demise in the mid-1980s, Trischka performed as a solo artist and as part of Rounder Records banjo tours, featuring BÉLA FLECK, BILL KEITH, and other bluegrass pickers. While his picking still reflects the influences of jazz, avant-garde, and rock and roll styles, his repertoire increasingly draws on traditional sources, and even his own compositions stick closer to bluegrass roots. During the mid-through-late 1990s, he presented "History of the Banjo" concerts, in which he played everything from minstrel-era pieces to his own progressive instrumentals. In 1999 he introduced his latest jazz-fusion outfit, the Tony Trischka Band.

See also BANJO, FIVE-STRING.

v :||

Van Ronk, Dave (1936–2002) *guitarist*

Born in Brooklyn, New York, on June 30, 1936, Dave Van Ronk was raised in a middle-class family. As a teen, he began playing jazz GUITAR, and was working local clubs on his graduation from high school. In 1957 he was hired to work as an accompanist to folk-blues singer ODETTA, and he became interested in blues music. A duet album with blues researcher Sam Charters was issued a year later.

By 1959 Van Ronk was recognized as the leading blues revival musician on the New York scene. He recorded several albums between then and the mid-1960s, moving from Folkways to Prestige and finally to Mercury. Van Ronk also became a godfather to the next generation of folk performers, including young guitarist/singer BOB DYLAN (he recorded Dylan's "He Was A Friend of Mine" on one of his first albums). By the mid-1960s Van Ronk was recording with full jazz band accompaniment.

By the early 1970s Van Ronk had become a fixture of the folk scene, playing festivals and small clubs, but rarely recording; rather, his earlier albums were endlessly reissued. In 1976 he returned to the studio for the album *Sunday Street*, which brought him renewed attention from the folk community. An album of original, autobiographical songs was issued in 1985, *Going Back to Brooklyn*.

Van Ronk began recording again more prolifically in the 1990s (including several live albums), as well as performing as a solo artist and on FOLK-REVIVAL shows with groups such as PETER, PAUL, AND MARY. He continued to perform until shortly before his death, due to complications of surgery for colon

Dave Van Ronk belts it out at the 1963 Newport Folk Festival. (Photo © John Byrne Cooke, http://www.cooke photo.com)

cancer, on February 10, 2002. His autobiography *The Mayor of Macdougal Street,* appeared in 2005, which was edited and completed by Elijah Wald.

Van Zandt, Townes (1944–1997) *folksinger*

Van Zandt was born in Fort Worth, Texas, on March 7, 1944. His father was an oil worker who moved from state to state, so the young singer was raised in various western states. He briefly attended the University of Colorado, dropping out to become, in his own words, "a folksinger." He returned to Texas in 1966, playing a variety of small clubs. Van Zandt signed with Poppy Records in 1969, producing a series of albums over the next few years.

In 1976 Van Zandt finally moved to Nashville at the insistence of his manager, and signed to Tomato Records to produce a few more albums before again dropping into obscurity. Van Zandt's best-known song is "Pancho and Lefty," covered by Willie Nelson and Merle Haggard on their duet album of the same title, as well as Hoyt Axton and Emmylou Harris.

After almost a decade of inactivity on record, Van Zandt returned to the studio in 1987 for the specialty bluegrass label Sugar Hill. Van Zandt toured and recorded sporadically until his death; in 1990 he toured with the retro-rock group the Cowboy Junkies. He released his last two albums in 1994, a live disc (actually recorded in 1985) and a studio recording made in Ireland. He died suddenly on January 1, 1997, and following his death two more albums of previously unreleased material appeared.

"Waist Deep in the Big Muddy" (1966)
controversial song written by Pete Seeger

PETE SEEGER wrote this antiwar song and recorded it for his album *Waist Deep in the Big Muddy and Other Love Songs* in 1966, based on his growing dissatisfaction with the Johnson administration's escalation of the war in Vietnam. On September 10, 1967, the Smothers Brothers invited him to perform the song on their nationally broadcast variety program, breaking the "blacklist" of Seeger who had not appeared on nationwide television since he refused to name names in 1954 before the House Un-American Activities Committee. However, CBS, the Brothers' network, would not let him perform the song. Many viewers protested and eventually, in February 1968, Seeger was invited to return to the show and sing the song.

Walker, Jerry Jeff (b. 1942) *singer and songwriter*

Coming from a musical family, Walker's grandparents played in an upstate New York SQUARE DANCE band and his mother and aunt performed in a local tight-harmony trio reminiscent of the Andrews Sisters. Born and raised in Oneonta, New York, Walker spent most of his high school years playing basketball, although he quit school when he was 16 to wander around the country, eventually ending up as a street singer in New Orleans. He returned home to finish his schooling, and became interested in the folk revival music of PETE SEEGER and WOODY GUTHRIE, as well as the reissued recordings of Jimmie Rodgers.

Walker performed on the folk coffeehouse circuit in the East and Midwest through the mid-1960s. In the late 1960s Walker's big break came in the form of a radio appearance on alternative New York radio station WBAI. He performed his self-penned ballad, "Mr. Bojangles," inspired by a cellmate he met one night in Texas while sleeping off a drinking spree. The song was popularized over the station, and in 1971 was a big hit for the Nitty Gritty Dirt Band. It also earned Walker his first recording contract with Atlantic.

His first recordings were far from successful, and by the mid-1970s Walker was back in Austin. His homemade recordings were issued in 1973 by MCA Records, introducing a brief period of chart success. His second album from this period featured a cover of GUY CLARK's "LA Freeway," which was a minor hit for him.

Walker continued to record and perform through the 1970s, gaining a reputation for high living and erratic performances. Since then, Walker's career has mostly been limited to club dates around Austin and occasional tours. His performances, however, continue to be unpredictable. Since the mid-1990s his recordings have appeared on his own Tried & True label. During the later 1990s, Walker's birth month of March has become the occasion for a big celebration in Austin, with Walker performing several concerts. In 1999 he published his autobiography.

Ward, Wade (1892–1971) *banjoist*

Born Benjamin Wade Ward in Saddle Creek, Virginia (near Independence, in the southwest corner of the state), on October 15, 1892, Ward came from a Scotch-Irish family that had settled in the area at least as early as 1840. Wade's family moved when he was 10 to a farm known as Peach Bottom Creek, which was Ward's home for the remaining 69 years of his life. His father, Enoch, was a FIDDLE player, but he had already stopped playing when his youngest son was born, and his mother knew many of the traditional mountain ballads and songs; however, it was Wade's elder brother, David Crockett Ward (known as Crockett), 20 years his senior, who was the key musical influence on his life. Crockett was a fine fiddle player and began teaching his younger brother the rudiments of banjo and fiddle playing when he was an early teen.

Although professionally a farmer all of his life, Ward began performing as a part-time musician from an early age. First, he worked with his elder brother playing for dances, festivals, and other special occasions. When he was in his 20s, Ward began a life-long association with a local auction house; his job was to attract customers with his music. He formed his first band to play at local land auctions with the team of fiddler Van Edwards and his GUITAR-picking son, Earl. The guitar was a relatively new instrument in the region, and it changed the style of music playing from the old-time modal dance music to one more suited to modern chord harmonies. Ward also changed, switching from the older style clawhammer banjo style he had learned from his brother to a three-finger picked style most closely associated with popular recording artist CHARLIE POOLE.

In the early 1920s Ward's elder brother, Crockett, left the family farm to work in nearby Galax as a carpenter. By the early 1930s Crockett's son, Fields Ward, was an accomplished guitarist and vocalist, and along with Wade, they began playing as a trio. Local fiddler "Uncle" Eck Dunford teamed with the group to form what would be known as the Bog Trotters Band; fifth member, Doc Davis on autoharp, was a friend of Dunford's who joined the group in the mid-1930s. The group was "discovered" by noted folklorist John Lomax and his son, Alan, and recorded for the Library of Congress in 1937; for the next few years, they were prominent not only in their home region but also in the budding FOLK REVIVAL, because Alan featured them on his radio broadcasts promoting traditional folk music.

The band continued to play informally through the early 1950s, when Fields left the region for a job in Maryland. At the same time, Crockett suffered a stroke and did not play the fiddle again. In the mid-1950s folklorists interested in the Bog Trotters Band came into the region, including MIKE SEEGER and the team of Jane Rigg, Eric Davidson, and Paul Newman. The latter group was most instrumental in recording Ward through the mid-1960s; he was now primarily working with local fiddler Glen Smith. Ward continued to record, perform, and appear at festivals until his death in 1971. Fields Ward has recorded as a singer/guitarist sporadically during the 1970s for various folk labels.

See also BANJO, FIVE-STRING; LOMAX, JOHN AND ALAN.

Warner, Frank (1903–1978) *song collector and performer*

Frank Warner was born in Selma, Alabama, on April 5, 1903. Raised in Tennessee and North Carolina, he heard folk songs as a child, and began performing while attending Duke University. He took a graduate degree in Social Welfare at Columbia University, and then worked for the YMCA for 10 years. In 1935 he married Anne Locker, and the two began performing together as well as traveling through the United States and Canada collecting folk songs. One musician they encountered in the 1930s was banjo player FRANK PROFFITT, who taught Warner a local song about a convicted murderer, Tom Dula. In 1952 Warner recorded his own interpretation of the song as "Hang Down Your Head, Tom Dooley," which, six years later, would be adapted by the KINGSTON TRIO and become a major pop hit and sparked the folk song revival. The Warners continued to perform throughout the 1970s, by this time joined by their two children, Gerrett and Jeff, and also published collections of the songs they found. Several CDs of their recordings have also been issued under the general name *Music from the Anne and Frank Warner Collection*. Warner died in February 1978.

See also "(HANG DOWN YOUR HEAD) TOM DOOLEY."

Watson, Doc (b. 1923) *guitarist*

Coming from a musical family and blind from birth, Arthel Lane "Doc" Watson (b. Deep Gap, North Carolina, March 2, 1923) early on showed capabilities on a number of instruments. Inspired by his idol Merle Travis, he began playing FIDDLE tunes and elaborate melody fills on the GUITAR. By the late 1950s he was working in a local band playing electric lead guitar on rockabilly, country, and pop songs.

Folklorist RALPH RINZLER discovered Watson while recording old-time banjo player Clarence "TOM" ASHLEY. Watson was brought north and soon began performing and recording with his son, Merle (February 8, 1949–October 23, 1985), on second guitar. He became a major star on the FOLK-REVIVAL circuit, recording with JEAN RITCHIE and also as a duet with bluegrass mandolinist Bill Monroe, although these recordings were never legally released until 1993.

Watson's big break came when he was included on the sessions for *Will the Circle Be Unbroken?*, the Nitty Gritty Dirt Band's homage to country music legends. Watson's vocals were prominently featured, as well as his legendary flatpicking. He was immediately signed to the Poppy label, where he recorded two Grammy-winning LPs that suffered from far more cluttered productions than his earlier work for folk label Vanguard Records.

Although Watson remains active as a performer, the death of his son, Merle, from a farm accident in

Doc Watson in the mid-1960s (Courtesy Vanguard Records)

the mid-1980s devastated him and he went into semiretirement. He has continued to perform, often with Merle's son Richard as an accompanist.

See also BANJO, FIVE-STRING; MANDOLIN.

Watson, Gene (b. 1943) *singer and songwriter*

Born in Palestine, Texas, on October 11, 1943, Watson was raised in Paris, Texas. At age 16 he made his first recordings for Uni Records in a teen-pop style. Four years later, he moved to Houston in search of a musical career, singing at night at the Dynasty Club while working as an auto-body repairman by day. After a regional hit with 1975's "Love in the Afternoon," he was picked up by Capitol Records.

He continued to record in a solid honky-tonk mold for several labels, scoring hits with 1979's "Farewell Party" (his backup band was renamed the Farewell Party Band in honor of this number three country hit), the honky-tonk anthem "Should I Go Home (Or Should I Go Crazy)" from a year later, and particularly 1981's "Fourteen Carat Mind," his sole number one country hit. He has continued to record through the 1980s and 1990s with moderate success, but his unwillingness to change his style to bow to contemporary tastes has made him mostly a cult figure on the edges of mainstream country.

Weavers, The

The most influential and among the first of the FOLK-REVIVAL groups, the Weavers were a model for countless others who followed in their harmony singing, banjo and GUITAR strumming footsteps, including the KINGSTON TRIO. The group also introduced talented singer/songwriter PETE SEEGER, who would have a long, distinguished career on his own.

In the early 1940s Seeger and Lee Hays (1914–81) were among many folk musicians living in a loosely formed commune known as Almanac House in a loft-apartment in New York City's Greenwich Village. They formed a group known as the Almanac Singers to perform social protest songs, primarily at union meetings and rallies; members came and went, and included such friends/fellow musicians as WOODY GUTHRIE, LEAD BELLY, JOSH WHITE, and many others. They recorded 78 rpm albums in 1941, and by late in the year were appearing on network radio. The group turned to singing antifascist material, which made them more acceptable to a mainstream audience in the early years of World War II. However, by mid-1942 Seeger and other members left or were drafted, and the group ended.

After the war Seeger and Hays assembled a new, more organized performance group. They enlisted guitarist Fred Hellerman (b. New York, May 13, 1927) and singer Ronnie Gilbert. Hays selected the name the Weavers after the play of the same name

by left-leaning author Gerhart Hauptmann. The group was an instant success on their formal debut at New York's Village Vanguard club in late 1949, and were signed to Decca Records.

At Decca, arranger Gordon Jenkins—who had previously arranged for big band singers—wrapped the Weavers' folk sound in a smooth, pop accompaniment. This led to several hits, beginning with the traditional "On Top of Old Smokey" and extending through Lead Belly's "GOODNIGHT, IRENE" (released six months after the singer's death, and a number one hit), Woody Guthrie's "SO LONG, IT'S BEEN GOOD TO KNOW YOU," as well as early examples of world music material, including the African song "WIMOWEH" and the Israeli/Hebrew "Tzena, Tzena."

However, the growing anticommunist fervor in the United States brought new attention to the group member's prewar activities as singers for labor and civil rights rallies. This led to them being effectively blacklisted in 1952. Seeger went solo, but had difficulty obtaining work on his own, while the others temporarily retired from performing. The group's manager, Harold Leventhal, however, sensed that their popularity remained strong, so he rented Carnegie Hall for a well-publicized reunion concert at Christmastime in 1955. Its great success led the group to re-form, although Seeger soon returned to solo work. In its later incarnation, banjo players Erik Darling (later of the ROOFTOP SINGERS), Frank Hamilton, and Bernie Krause all "filled" Seeger's shoes. The group finally disbanded in 1963.

In 1981 the group reassembled for a 25th anniversary concert at New York's Carnegie Hall, although by then Hays was seriously ill. A year later, a documentary film, *Wasn't That a Time,* was released about the reunion and the group's distinguished career.

See also BANJO, FIVE-STRING.

Welch, Gillian (b. 1967) *singer and songwriter*

Welch was born in New York City on October 2, 1967, to parents who wrote music for the *Carol Burnett Show,* and she was raised in Los Angeles. While attending the Berklee School of Music in Boston, she met guitarist David Rawlings, who has become her performing partner. They moved to Nashville in 1992. In 1995 Emmylou Harris included Welch's song "Orphan Girl" on her *Wrecking Ball* album, which significantly boosted Welch's career. In 1996 she released her first album, *Revival,* full of vivid images of people and places that were drawn from the folk-country repertory. She followed in 1998 with *Hell Among the Yearlings,* a somewhat less focused collection.

Welch's producer, T-Bone Burnett, brought her to the attention of the Coen brothers when he was preparing the soundtrack for their southern epic, *O Brother, Where Art Thou?* She sang on several songs with Harris, and the album surprised nearly everyone by selling more than a million copies. Welch made another movie appearance in 2001, singing the traditional ballad "The Wind and Rain" for an independent film about a woman folklorist, *Songcatcher.* She also released her third album, *Time (The Revelator).* While still drawing on older folk themes, this album also featured more personal songs, showing the influence of confessional singer/songwriters like Neil Young.

Western Swing

Western Swing is a unique combination of string band music with jazz styles. It was born in the Texas-Oklahoma region in the late 1920s. There musicians were influenced by blues and jazz recordings, as well as early pop crooners, to form an amalgam of traditional country sounds with a swinging accompaniment.

The band credited with creating this sound was the Light Crust Doughboys in 1931–32, featuring fiddler Bob Wills and vocalist Milton Brown. Soon Wills and Brown formed their own bands. Although Brown's band was in many ways hotter than Wills's, it was short-lived (Brown died in the mid-1930s following an automobile accident); meanwhile, Wills's band mushroomed into a full jazz ensemble, with a large horn section and the crooning vocals of Tommy Duncan. The band's instrumentation also included smooth steel GUITAR, ragtime-influenced piano, and often twin harmony fiddling (Wills's fiddling was fairly primitive and he usually took a backseat to the more modern string men he employed). Wills's repertoire was made up of popular songs, blues, traditional FIDDLE tunes (often jazzed up), and big-band standards.

A second wave of Western Swing came in the late 1940s in Southern California, where many western musicians had settled after the war to appear in the countless cowpoke films that the lesser Hollywood studios (particularly Republic) were busily churning out. Wills's postwar band returned to the stripped-down sound of his original unit, now featuring electric guitar, steel guitar, and even electric MANDOLIN (played by TINY MOORE), with various vocalists (Wills had fired Duncan in 1948 in a fit of anger). Another popular California-based band was led by Spade Cooley.

The 1950s and 1960s were lean times for the music. But then, in the early 1970s, new, young bands began playing the music, such as Asleep at the Wheel, introducing a new generation to the Western Swing sound. Meanwhile, country superstar Merle Haggard recorded an entire album in homage to Wills's music, and then brought the star out of retirement for his famous last session in 1973. Many reissues of early recordings have made even the lesser-known bands famous once again.

"Which Side Are You On?" (1931) *miner anthem*

Coal miners in Harlan County, Kentucky, fought a long and bloody battle with mine owners to establish their rights to unionize, culminating in a long strike in 1931. A miner's wife, Florence Reece, wrote this stirring anthem after her home was invaded by the local sheriff, J. H. Blair, and his men, who were searching for her union-supporting husband. The song is set to a traditional tune, and became a stirring anthem for miners. In the 1940s the New York City–based folk group the Almanac Singers (a predecessor of the WEAVERS) recorded the song, introducing it into the FOLK-REVIVAL repertory. AUNT MOLLY JACKSON wrote the similar "I Am A Union Woman" using the same melody.

White, Josh (1908–1969) *guitarist and performer*

Joshua Daniel White was born on February 11, 1908, in Greenville, South Carolina. His father was a Baptist minister, and the young White was naturally exposed to gospel music from an early age. By his teens he was working as a companion to blind blues performers, while also building his own skills as a guitarist. By the mid-1930s he had landed in Chicago, where he became a prolific and popular recording artist, playing blues and party music.

In the early 1940s White came to New York and was quickly embraced by the folk music community. His appearances at such popular clubs as Café Society led to bookings on Broadway and radio. White began performing the kind of social-protest/topical material that appealed to New York audiences, including "Strange Fruit" (later closely associated with jazz singer Billie Holiday) and "Jim Crow Train." He also had hits with novelty numbers such as "One Meat Ball." White recorded prolifically for folk and major labels and became popular in the 1950s touring Europe. Unlike other folk performers, he voluntarily appeared before the House Un-American Activities Committee, so he was not blacklisted during the anticommunist days of the 1950s. White's clear voice and simple guitar style also endeared him to an audience that was not accustomed to the rougher stylings of some other blues musicians.

White's career moved into cabaret and club performing in the 1960s. Some on the folk scene felt he had gone too "pop," and his earlier roots as a blues performer were forgotten. He died on September 5, 1969, in Manhasset, New York. White's son, Josh White Jr. (b. New York City, November 30, 1940), has continued to play his father's music.

See also GUITAR.

Whites, The

The Whites are a family band that has gone through many changes in style in their nearly 30-year existence, from bluegrass group to mainstream country to gospel. Father Buck was Oklahoma-born and Texas-raised, playing both honky-tonk styled piano and bluegrass/WESTERN SWING on MANDOLIN, becoming something of a legend in the area; his claim to fame as a recording artist in the 1950s was that he was the pianist on the session that produced Slim Willet's "Don't Let the Stars Get in Your Eyes" in 1952. He retired to take a job as a pipefitter in Arkansas, but took up music again when his two daughters, Sharon and Cheryl, began playing GUITARs and singing as preteens. Along with wife, Pat Goza White, they formed The Whites as a bluegrass group in 1966. Five years later, Buck retired from his day job, and the family relocated to Nashville in search of success.

They made their first recording in 1972 for the bluegrass/country label County Records as Buck White and the Down Home Folks, a fairly straightforward recording in the progressive bluegrass style that was popular at the time. Buck also made some recordings on his own as a mandolinist in the mid-1970s, thanks to a renewal of interest in the instrument created by the jazz-tinged recordings of DAVID GRISMAN. The trio moved into a solid country direction with their 1978 album, *Poor Folks Pleasures,* issued by the more pop-oriented division of County, Sugar Hill. They toured with Emmylou Harris a year later, where Sharon met her future husband, Ricky Skaggs, who was then serving as Harris's musical director.

The Whites had their greatest chart success in the early through mid-1980s, beginning with 1981's rerecording of "Send Me the Pillow You Dream On." Most of their hits were remakes of 1950s weepers, prominently featuring Sharon's lead vocals with Buck and Cheryl limited pretty much to harmonizing. In 1982 they enjoyed their greatest chart success, actually making the country top 10 with "Holding My Baby Tonight." In 1984 the group joined the *Grand Ole Opry,* and four years later switched directions slightly by cutting an all-gospel album. The group has focused on gospel material through the 1990s.

Whitter, Henry (1892–1941) *multi-instrumentalist*

William Henry Whitter was born near Fries, Virginia, on April 6, 1892. A mill worker, Whitter was also a multi-instrumentalist who was most skilled as a HARMONICA player, but also played FIDDLE, organ, piano, and GUITAR. Not a particularly talented singer, he made some test recordings for the General Phonograph Corporation in 1923 (who owned the Okeh label) which were considered to be so bad that they were thought to be unreleasable. However, when FIDDLIN' JOHN CARSON scored a hit with "Little Old Log Cabin in the Lane," also released by Okeh, the company reconsidered and issued Whitter's recordings, including "The Wreck of the Old 97," in 1924. This record was covered by Vernon Dalhart, whose version became the first million-selling country hit.

Whitter's best recordings were made as one-half of the team of Grayson and Whitter. George Bannon Grayson was a blind fiddler/vocalist, and the duo made some fine recordings between 1927 and 1929, including several songs that have entered the bluegrass repertoire, most notably the instrumental "Lee Highway Blues." The Depression ended their recording career, although the duo continued to work together until Grayson was killed in an automobile accident in the mid-1930s. Whitter also recorded as an accompanist to the female fiddle player Roba Stanley, and led band recordings under the name of the Virginia Breakdowners. He died on November 17, 1941.

Williams, Lucinda (b. 1953) *singer and songwriter*

The daughter of a college professor/poet, Williams was born in Lake Charles, Louisiana, on January 26, 1953. Raised in a number of southern university towns, she began as a blues and country singer, covering songs by traditional country artists such as her namesake, Hank Williams. She recorded two albums for Folkways Records in the late 1970s, the first all traditional material, the second all her own songs, which gained some attention. She began focusing on her own brand of semiconfessional singer/songwriter material, relocating by the mid-1980s to Los Angeles, where she recorded her first pop-styled album for the punk-rock label Rough Trade in 1989. In the early 1990s she switched to Chameleon/Elektra, who rereleased her *Rough Trade* album as well as a new recording, *Sweet Old World,* in 1992.

Between 1992 and 1998, Williams went through a period of label hopping, making various attempts to record a follow-up to her previous album. She finally came through in 1998 with *Car Wheels on a Gravel Road,* which had a more produced feeling than her previous recordings. Its roots-rock sound was well received in the music press, and Williams won new fans among the "alternative-country" crowd. In 2001 she released *Essence,* a more personal, and starker, recording, again winning praise from the music press.

"Wimoweh" (1939/1952) *classic song*

This popular song has a long and tangled history. It was originally written by a South African singer named Solomon Linda and recorded as "Mbube" in 1939. This record was a big hit in Africa, so big that the local Decca affiliate sent a copy to the U.S. office hoping to interest them in releasing it. It just so happened that working at Decca at that time as a consultant was folklorist Alan Lomax, who heard the record and gave it to singer PETE SEEGER. Seeger heard the chorus words as "Wimoweh," and adapted the song into English, and sang it for his fellow members of the WEAVERS who worked out an elaborate harmonized vocal arrangement. Their recording hit the top 15 of the pop charts in 1952, making the song a folk standard. The group took composing credit under the composite name "Paul Campbell," not giving any credit to Linda. The KINGSTON TRIO revived it in 1959, adding themselves to the authorship line.

But the story doesn't end there. A New York doowop group, the Tokens, heard the Weavers' recording and began riffing on the song. In 1961 they sang it at an audition for pop producers Hugo (Peretti) and Luigi (Creatore) at RCA Records. Hugo and Luigi employed George Weiss as a songwriter, and the trio created new lyrics and renamed the piece "The Lion Sleeps Tonight"; by year's end it was a number one pop hit. The lucrative songwriting credit was taken by the producers and Weiss, bypassing both the Weavers and Solomon Linda.

The song was again revived in the 1990s as part of the score of the hit Broadway musical *The Lion King*. Through this entire process, the song's originator, Solomon Linda, received little compensation, and died nearly penniless.

See also LOMAX, JOHN AND ALAN.

Wise, Chubby (1915–1996) *fiddler*

Robert Russell Wise was born in Lake City, Florida, on October 2, 1915. Although he started out as a GUITAR player, Wise mastered the FIDDLE by his teen years, working the active country music club scene around Jacksonville, Florida. He befriended the ROUSE BROTHERS there, particularly fiddler Ervin, composer of the famed fiddle tune "Orange Blossom Special." In 1938 he began playing professionally with a local band, the Jubilee Hillbillies, and then was invited by Bill Monroe to join his band in Nashville in the early 1940s.

Wise is best remembered for his recordings with the classic Monroe band of 1946–48, featuring Lester Flatt and Earl Scruggs. Wise's WESTERN SWING–influenced fiddle was the perfect complement to the high-energy of Monroe's MANDOLIN and Scruggs's banjo. Because these recordings established the standard instrumentation and sound of bluegrass bands for years to come, Wise's fiddling became the model for his peers and future generation of bluegrass players. During this period, he also partnered with singer Clyde Moody, a

Monroe alumnus himself, co-composing and recording the popular "Shenandoah Waltz" with him in 1946. Through 1950 he alternated between working for Monroe and with Moody.

In the early 1950s Wise worked with a number of bluegrass bands, including Flatt and Scruggs. However, in 1954 he began a long association with popular country singer Hank Snow, which lasted until 1970. During this period, Wise continued to session with others, and recorded occasionally on his own. Wise then went solo, working out of Texas through the mid-1980s, when he returned to his native Florida. Wise continued to record in bluegrass and Western Swing styles until shortly before his death following a massive heart attack on January 6, 1996.

See also BANJO, FIVE-STRING.

Wiseman, Mac (b. 1925) *bluegrass performer*

Malcolm B. Wiseman was born in Cremora, Virginia, on May 23, 1925. Raised in the Shenandoah Valley, he was surrounded by old-time country music. He studied classical music at the Shenandoah Conservatory in Dayton, and then worked as an announcer at a small radio station out of Harrisburg, Pennsylvania. His first break as a singer came performing with MOLLY O'DAY after World War II. In the late 1940s he briefly joined Lester Flatt and Earl Scruggs, who had just left Bill Monroe's band. In 1950 Wiseman joined Monroe as lead vocalist, working for him for about a year.

A year later, Wiseman was signed as a solo act to Dot Records; six years later, he was hired as a house producer for the company, running their country-music division through the early 1960s. Wiseman's first hit recordings were the sentimental "Tis Sweet to Be Remembered" and "Shackles and Chains," both accompanied by a hybrid country/bluegrass band, featuring two fiddlers playing in harmony (something Wiseman borrowed from the popular WESTERN SWING style). In 1959 he had his biggest hit with the weeper "Jimmy Brown the Newsboy."

In the 1960s Wiseman continued to record in a traditional country vein, even though the Nashville sound was beginning to encroach on his (and most other) recordings. He left Dot for Capitol in the early 1960s, followed by a stint with MGM and then RCA. When Lester Flatt split from Earl Scruggs (because Scruggs wanted to record more popular music) in 1969, Wiseman teamed up with his old friend, recording a number of traditional bluegrass albums, first for RCA and then CMH. This return to bluegrass won him new friends on the traditional music circuit.

After Flatt died, Wiseman remained a popular touring attraction, returning to performing straight country, although he recorded only rarely. In 1986, when MCA revived the Dot label, he returned for an album in the style of his late 1950s recordings. Wiseman continued to be active through the 1990s on the bluegrass circuit. He was inducted into the Bluegrass Hall of Fame in 1993. In 1998 he issued a trio album with DOC WATSON and DEL MCCOURY. In 2000 he issued a similar recording with Bobby Osborne and Jim Silvers, who were cleverly marketed as "The Three Tenors of Bluegrass."

Young, Izzy (b. 1928) *businessman and concert promoter*

Israel Goodman Young was born on March 26, 1928, in New York's Lower East Side to an immigrant Jewish family. The family moved to the Bronx while he was young, and Izzy became involved in New York's growing folk music and dance scene beginning in the mid-1940s. In the early 1950s he met several key players on the scene, including folklorist/record producer KENNETH S. GOLDSTEIN. Employed in the family bakery business, as a sideline Young issued a mail order catalog of folk music and dance books in 1955; two years later, he rented a vacant storefront in Greenwich Village and opened the Folklore Center.

Young's center became the crossroads, meeting place, and hangout for New York's growing folk music scene. Young soon began promoting concerts along with selling books, instruments, and records, presenting PEGGY SEEGER in her first New York appearance. In early 1959 he became a regular columnist for *SING OUT!* MAGAZINE, the national voice of the folk revival, further solidifying his reputation as a major player. In 1960 he helped JOHN COHEN and RALPH RINZLER form Friends of Old Time Music, dedicated to presenting traditional performers (as opposed to folk revivalists). He also famously produced BOB DYLAN's first major New York solo concert on November 4, 1961, at the 200-seat Recital Hall at Carnegie Hall.

Young remained active as a businessman/concert promoter through the 1960s and early 1970s. In 1973 he relocated to Sweden, convinced the socialist state would be a better place politically and socially to promote traditional music.

zydeco music   See CAJUN MUSIC.

Appendixes

Appendix I

Chronology of Major Events in Folk Music

1826

July 4 Birth of Stephen Foster, noted American songwriter.

1830

May 21 Minstrel performer Thomas D. Rice appears for the first time as "Jim Crow," a stereotype black character.

1833

November 6 Christian Frederick Martin, guitar maker from Neukirchen, Saxony, arrives in America, opening his first guitar musical instrument company in New York City in early 1834; Martin would become the best-known American maker of acoustic guitars. Five years later, he moves the business to rural Nazareth, Pennsylvania, where the company continues to operate.

1843

April 24 The Virginia Minstrels give their first performance in New York City, launching the minstrel show craze, and helping to popularize the five-string banjo.

1845

First documented banjo made by Baltimore maker William Boucher, considered to be the first great maker of early banjos.

1848

February 25 First copyrighted version of "Oh! Susanna" by Stephen Foster is published; 19 more versions will appear over the next three years.

1855

Briggs' Banjo Instructor published shortly after the death of its author, Thomas F. Briggs, the first banjo instruction book to document the downstroke (frailing/rapping) style of playing; three more instruction books by other authors followed five years later.

1867

Slave Songs of the United States by William Francis Allen, Charles Pickard Ware, and Lucy McKim Garrison, is published, the first collection of African-American traditional songs to appear in this country.

1868

May 1 Thomas C. Dula is hanged for murdering his girlfriend in Wilkes County, North Carolina; his story is told in the popular folk ballad "Tom Dooley."

1872

The popular Fisk Jubilee Singers, who perform African-American spirituals, publish their first songbook.

1880

Banjo designer A. C. Fairbanks and teacher William A. Cole establish their banjo making business in Boston. Over the coming years, Fairbanks would design the classic American open-back banjos the "Electric," "Tubaphone," and "Whyte Lady" models, still widely treasured (and copied) for old-time music styles.

1883

First edition of *Complete American Banjo School* by S. S. Stewart of Philadelphia, well-known teacher, banjo maker, and banjo enthusiast. Stewart would manufacture hundreds of banjos over the coming two and a half decades.

1894

Orville Gibson makes his first musical instrument, in his home in Kalamazoo, Michigan. He designs two new body styles for flat-backed mandolins, and soon investors are interested in his work. In 1902 the Gibson company is incorporated, but Orville is forced out of the business within a year.

1909

Songs of the Workers is published by the Industrial Workers of the World (IWW); it becomes known as the "little red songbook" and remains in print for decades. Many classic protest songs appear in it.

1910

Cowboy Songs by John Lomax is published, the first collection of traditional songs from the West to gain widespread attention.

Howard Odum's collection of blues lyrics is published in the *Journal of American Folklore,* one of the first academic journals to recognize the importance of this musical style.

1914

"St. Louis Blues" by W. C. Handy is published, the first hit of the urban blues movement.

1917

Folk Songs from the Southern Appalachians by Cecil Sharp and Olive Dame Campbell is published, based on Sharp's field work in the mountains. It is the first book to show the survival of English traditional ballads and songs in the American South.

1922

The F5 mandolin is introduced by Gibson, its fanciest and best instrument to date. This instrument becomes the favorite of Bill Monroe, and thus a "must have" for any bluegrass mandolin player.

1925

Gibson introduces the Mastertone model banjo, equipped with a resonator and special tone ring. This instrument becomes the standard for bluegrass players from the 1940s to today.

1927

American Songbag, a collection of traditional folksongs gathered by Carl Sandburg, is published.

1928

July 1 Archive of American Folk Song established at the Library of Congress with Robert Gordon as its first director.

First Mountain Dance and Folk Festival held in Asheville, North Carolina, organized by banjoist and lawyer Bascom Lamar Lunsford.

1933

July While visiting Angola prison to record black inmates, John and Alan Lomax discover the 12-string guitarist/singer/songwriter Lead Belly, who would become a major figure in the folk revival.

1934

John and Alan Lomax's influential collection, *American Ballads and Folk Songs,* is published.

1939

May "Woody Sez," a column by folksinger Woody Guthrie, appears for the first time in *People's World,* a left-leaning publication

December 23 John Hammond presents From Spirituals to Swing, a concert at New York's Carnegie Hall, intended to illustrate the folk roots of jazz. Performers including Sonny Terry and Big Bill Broonzy.

1940

March 3 Will Geer sponsors a "Grapes of Wrath" evening at the Forrest Theater, featuring performers Aunt Molly Jackson, Burl Ives, Woody Guthrie, and Pete Seeger, among others.

Late March Alan Lomax records Woody Guthrie's songs and stories for the Library of Congress over a three-day period.

April 26, May 3 Woody Guthrie records his *Dust Bowl Ballads* for RCA Records in New York.

1941

May Lead Belly makes his first recordings for Moses Asch's small Asch label; these are reissued on Folkways in the 1950s and available for decades to come.

1942

February 14 The Almanac Singers are featured singing "Round and Round Hitler's Grave" on the CBS radio program *This Is War;* three days later a major newspaper chain denounced the group for their previous recordings of union songs.

1943

April Woody Guthrie's semiautobiographical novel, *Bound for Glory,* is published to good reviews, establishing the myth of his life as a ramblin' songster.

1946

January 1 People's Songs formed in New York by Pete Seeger and other area folk musicians to promote folk music, to serve as a booking agency (People's Artists), clearinghouse for performers, and to support left-wing causes. The organization also publishes a newsletter and establishes branch offices in cities such as Chicago and Los Angeles.

1949

March 11 People's Songs closes its national office due to lack of funds.

May 1 Folkways Records and Service Corporation is established. Marian Distler is named as "owner," but in fact she serves as a front for her employer, Moses Asch, who had gone bankrupt operating his DISC label in 1948 and was prohibited from reentering the record business.

September 4 People's Artists sponsors a concert in Peekskill, New York, to benefit the Harlem Civil Rights Congress. Paul Robeson and Pete Seeger are to be among the performers. Originally scheduled for August 27, the first concert is cancelled when a large mob shows up, angered by the group's left-wing politics. The next performance goes off as planned, but after the concert the audience and performers are pelted with rocks by the waiting mob.

December 6   Lead Belly dies in Bellevue Hospital in New York City.

1950

January 28   Alan Lomax organizes a memorial concert for Lead Belly, which features the Weavers, Woody Guthrie, Rev. Gary Davis, Frank Warner, and Sonny Terry and Brownie McGhee, among others.

May   First issue of *Sing Out!* magazine is published. It will become the voice of the folk revival movement for decades to come.

August 7   Lead Belly's song "Good Night, Irene" reaches the top five on the pop charts in a version recorded by The Weavers.

1951

Jac Holzman establishes Elektra Records, a key player in the folk revival in the 1950s–mid-1960s.

1952

Harry Smith's *Anthology of American Folk Music* is issued by Folkways Records on six records in three 2-LP sets along with Smith's eccentric documentation. These records become a major resource for folk revivalists, both for songs and for rediscovering key artists of the 1920s and 1930s, including Clarence "Tom" Ashley, the Carter Family, Mississippi John Hurt, Eck Robertson, and many more.

February 6   Harry Matusow, who had worked for People's Songs, testifies that the Weavers had "communist ties"; Decca Records dropped the group from its label soon after, and the group folded due to the blacklist.

May 7   Burl Ives appears voluntarily to "name names" before the Senate Internal Security Subcommittee, saving his career but angering his friends in the folk community.

September 1   Josh White appears before the House Un-American Activities Committee (HUAC), although he does not indict others and claims no allegiance to communism.

1953

Lead Belly's Last Sessions issued on two 2-LP sets by Folkways Records. Recorded by Frederic Ramsey Jr. a year before Lead Belly's death, these important performances include lengthy spoken commentary and help present Lead Belly to a new generation of listeners.

1954

September 16   Woody Guthrie is admitted into Brooklyn State Hospital for treatment of Huntington's chorea; he is never able to perform again.

1955

August   Pete Seeger and Lee Hays, both members of the Weavers, appear before HUAC. Their refusal to "name names" leads to them being blacklisted. In March 1961, based on his refusal to testify before this committee, Seeger is convicted of contempt of Congress.

December 25   The Weavers reunite for an appearance at Carnegie Hall. The hall is sold out, and the unexpected enthusiasm and love for the group leads them to reunite for concerts and recordings.

1956

January 12   Harry Belafonte's "Day-O" (aka "The Banana Boat Song") reaches the top five on the pop charts, remaining in the top 100 for the next 20 weeks, establishing the calypso craze and Belafonte's pop music career.

February   Izzy Young opens his Folklore Center on Greenwich Village's Macdougal Street, which becomes a central hangout for folk performers through the mid-1960s.

March 17 Harold Leventhal organizes a benefit concert at New York's Pythian Hall for Woody Guthrie to help support him and his family during his hospitalization.

1957

Mike Seeger produces the album *American Banjo Scruggs Style* for Folkways, which introduces contemporary bluegrass picking styles to the urban folk revival.

July Albert Grossman and Les Brown open the Gate of Horn folk music club in Chicago.

December 1 Chicago's Old Town School of Folk Music is opened by Frank Hamilton; it is among the first schools devoted to teaching traditional guitar and banjo styles.

1958

January Art D'Lugoff opens New York's Village Gate, to feature folk, jazz, and comedy.

October 6 The Kingston Trio's version of "Tom Dooley" hits number one, launching the folk revival.

1959

April Alan Lomax returns to the United States and presents "Folksong 1959" at New York's Carnegie Hall. Among the performers are Pete and Mike Seeger, Lomax himself, country singer Jimmy Driftwood, and doo-wop group the Cadillacs. The audience is less than impressed by the eclectic program, and some boo the vocal group.

July 11–12 First Newport Folk Festival is held, featuring Odetta, Jean Ritchie, Pete Seeger, Frank Warner, Brownie McGhee and Sonny Terry, the New Lost City Ramblers, and many more. Joan Baez makes a "guest appearance" at the invitation

of performer Bob Gibson, introducing her to the folk revival audience.

1960

Moses Asch and Irwin Silber launch Oak Publications to print songbooks and instructional material.

Chris Strachwitz launches Arhoolie Records, which becomes a leader in blues, Tex-Mex, and Cajun recordings.

March Jon Pankake and Paul Nelson launch *The Little Sandy Review* in Minneapolis, Minnesota, while attending the University of Minnesota, to promote "pure" folk music against the growing commercialization of the music.

July 11 *Time* magazine notes that the "U.S. is smack in the middle of a folk music boom . . ." reporting on the great success of folk pop groups like the Kingston Trio.

1961

Sandy and Caroline Paton and friend Lee Hagerty launch Folk Legacy Records, which would become one of the leaders in the folk revival over the next decades.

February The first University of Chicago Folk Festival is held, featuring primarily traditional performers such as Elizabeth "Libba" Cotton, Roscoe Holcomb, and Frank Proffitt, and revivalists Frank Warner, the New Lost City Ramblers, and Sandy Paton.

February A benefit concert for the Highlander Folk School is held at Carnegie Hall, featuring two civil rights choruses. While in New York, they record an album released as *We Shall Overcome: Songs of the "Freedom Riders" and "Sit Ins,"* linking the folk music revival with the fight for civil rights.

March 25 First concert presented by the Friends of Old Time Music in New York City, a group dedicated to promoting traditional music and its performers founded by Ralph Rinzler, John Cohen, and Izzy Young.

September 29 Robert Shelton of the *New York Times* hails Bob Dylan as a major new talent following Dylan's first performances as a solo artist at Gerde's Folk City in New York City's Greenwich Village.

November 4 Izzy Young produces Bob Dylan's first major concert at New York's Carnegie Hall.

1962

January 29 Peter, Paul, and Mary are signed to Warner Bros. Records.

February The first issue of the topical folk song magazine *Broadside* is published.

May 18 Pete Seeger's conviction for refusing to "name names" before the House Un-American Activities Committee in August 1961 is overturned by the U.S. Court of Appeals. Earlier in the year, he signed with major label Columbia Records, despite still being under the cloud of this charge.

November 23 Joan Baez is pictured on the cover of *Time* magazine; inside this issue is a feature article on the folk music revival.

1963

January 12 The Rooftop Singers' version of "Walk Right In" tops the pop charts.

April 6 ABC-TV launches *Hootenanny,* the first regularly scheduled program devoted to folk music. The network refuses to employ Pete Seeger because of the blacklist, arousing the anger of many in the folk community. Joan Baez refuses to appear, as do other performers, unless this policy is changed. The show is a popular hit nonetheless.

May 20–22 First Monterey Folk Festival held in California, with headliners Bob Dylan, the Weavers,

Bill Monroe, Doc Watson, and Mance Lipscomb (making his first appearance outside of Texas).

August Bob Dylan's "Blowin' in the Wind" as recorded by Peter, Paul, and Mary reaches number two on the pop charts.

August 28 Martin Luther King Jr. leads the March on Washington for Jobs and Freedom, a key moment in the Civil Rights movement. He delivers his famous "I Have A Dream" speech. Folksingers Peter, Paul, and Mary perform at the march.

1964

July–August Mississippi Freedom Summer project attracts pro–civil rights workers from around the country, including many folk performers under the general name of the Summer Caravan of Music. Phil Ochs, Judy Collins, Barbara Dane, and Pete Seeger (appearing separately in August) all participate.

October 1 The Berkeley "Free Speech" movement is born when University of California officials ban protesters from assembling at the main entry to the campus. Protests continue for months and are supported by performers such as Joan Baez, who sings for the protesters and joins them in sit-ins.

1965

April 17 The Students for a Democratic Society (SDS) organize a march on Washington in support of peace. Twenty thousand people gather; Phl Ochs and Joan Baez perform for the crowds.

July 25 Bob Dylan performs with the Paul Butterfield Blues Band as his accompanists at the Newport Folk Festival, enraging his hardcore fans by adopting electric instruments.

September 24 Two "Sing-in for Peace" concerts are presented at Carnegie Hall, with Joan Baez, Pete Seeger, Mimi and Richard Fariña, Bernice Reagon, and others.

1966

April 30   Singer/songwriter Richard Fariña dies in a motorcycle accident on his way home from a book signing for his novel, *Been Down So Long It Looks Like up to Me.*

1967

September 10   Pete Seeger appears on the nationally broadcast *Smothers Brothers Comedy Hour,* his first network appearance since being blacklisted. However, CBS will not allow him to perform his antiwar song "Waist Deep in the Big Muddy" (although, due to the uproar, Seeger is invited back to sing the song in February 1968).

October 3   Woody Guthrie dies after suffering for more than a decade from the effects of the inherited disease Huntington's chorea.

1968

January 20   Memorial concert is held at New York's Carnegie Hall for Woody Guthrie. Bob Dylan makes his first public appearance since his motorcycle accident in summer 1966, accompanied by The Band. Pete Seeger, Judy Collins, Richie Havens, Tom Paxton, and others perform.

Late Spring   Club 47, Boston's center for folk performers, closes.

July   The first Smithsonian Folklife Festival is held in Washington, D.C., programmed by Ralph Rinzler and featuring Skip James, Ralph Stanley, the Georgia Sea Island Singers, Doc Watson, and others.

1969

Autumn   Fairport Convention releases its album *Liege and Lief,* a collection of traditional British ballads and songs written in a traditional style, accompanied by electric-rock instrumentation; the Album goes on to inspire a generation of British folk-rock performers.

1970

October   Last Berkeley Folk Festival is held, featuring Pete Seeger, Peggy Seeger and Ewan MacColl, Ramblin' Jack Elliott, and rock acts Janis Joplin and Big Brother and the Holding Company and Joy of Cooking, among others.

The Rounder Co-Operative of Cambridge, Massachusetts, issues its first album, recordings by banjo player George Pegram. Rounder Records would become one of the most important labels devoted to traditional music over the coming decades.

Peter, Paul, and Mary decide to go their separate ways, not reuniting for eight years.

1971

John Prine records his first album for Atlantic Records.

1972

The original version of Planxty—one of the first new Irish revival bands—is formed around singer Christy Moore, and they record their first album.

1974

Patrick Sky and Wendy Newton launch Innisfree Records to present traditional Irish artists and, soon after, Green Linnet for contemporary performers of Irish material.

1975

Diamonds and Rust, Joan Baez's album of confessional, singer-songwriter songs, is released, her last major hit to date.

1976

April 6 After suffering from depression, singer/songwriter Phil Ochs commits suicide by hanging himself while visiting his sister.

1977

David Grisman releases his first album with his acoustic-jazz group, introducing "Dawg Music," which would be highly influential on new acoustic and bluegrass styles.

1978

March 17 Malvina Reynolds, singer/songwriter best remembered for the song "Little Boxes," dies.

1979

February 6 Rodney and Will Balfa are killed in an automobile accident while touring, ending the classic Balfa Brothers Cajun band.

1981

Sing Out! closes its New York City offices and briefly suspends publication; it is revived by the mid-1980s under new editor Mark Moss.

May 13 Zydeco accordion player Nathan Abshire dies.

July 16 Harry Chapin is killed when his car is rear-ended by a truck.

1984

September Singer/songwriter Steve Goodman dies from leukemia.

1986

June The Smithsonian Institution purchases Folkways Records to establish the Moses and Frances Asch (Folkways) Collection.

July The Newport Folk Festival is revived by promoter George Wein after 15 years of inactivity.

1987

First issue of *The Old Time Herald,* edited by Alice Gerrard, appears, which becomes the voice of the old-time string band revival movement.

1997

Smithsonian/Folkways reissues Harry Smith's *Anthology of American Folk Music* on CD, with an accompanying booklet giving the history of Smith and the project.

December 7 Bob Dylan is named a Kennedy Center honoree for his contributions to American arts.

1998

The Smithsonian Institution establishes the Ralph Rinzler Folklife Archives and Collections at the Center for Folklife and Cultural Heritage in honor of the folklorist/collector, who died four years earlier.

2000

The film *O Brother, Where Art Thou?* uses folk, country, and bluegrass music on its soundtrack, bringing renewed interest in what becomes known as "American roots music."

Martin Carthy awarded an O.B.E. for his service to British folk music.

2001

February 22 Influential acoustic guitarist John Fahey dies.

2002

July 19 Folklorist Alan Lomax dies.

Appendix II

Selected Discography

Abshire, Nathan. Legendary Jay Miller Sessions *(Flyright).* Recordings made in the 1950s and 1960s, many featuring Dewey Balfa on fiddle.

Albion Band. Rise up Like the Sun *(EMI Harvest 4092; various reissues).* Released in 1978, this album represents the Albions with an expanded cast of supporting musicians playing in a pop-rock style.

Albion Band. Shuffle Off *(Spindrift 103).* Early 1980s version of the band featuring a nice selection of dance music.

Alger, Pat. True Love and Other Short Stories *(Sugar Hill 1029, 1991).* His comeback album.

Alger, Pat. Seeds *(Sugar Hill 1041, 1993).* Features Alger performing some of his hits for other performers, notably "The Thunder Rolls," which was a smash for Garth Brooks.

Allen Brothers. Complete Recordings in Chronological Order *(Document 1033–35).* Three CDs collecting all of their 78s.

Allen, Red. And the Kentuckians *(County 710, 1990).* CD reissue of 1966 Melodeon LP (7325).

Allen, Red. 1964–83. Smithsonian/Folkways 40127. Reissue of out-of-print early 1960s album that was quite influential on the second generation bluegrass revivalists, which was produced by David Grisman, plus additional tracks from the late 1970s and early 1980s.

Allen, Terry. Lubbock (on Everything) *(Sugar Hill 1047).* Reissue of what many feel is Allen's best album, originally issued on the Fate label.

Altan. Altan *(Green Linnet 1078).* Debut album for the group.

Altan. The Red Crow *(Green Linnet 1109).* Considered the best album of the original line-up, released in 1990.

Anderson, Eric. 'Bout Changes and Things *(Vanguard 79206).* 1966 album that features many of Anderson's best-loved original songs.

Ardoin Family. First Black Cajun Recording Artists *(Arhoolie 9056).* 78 era recordings by Amédée Ardoin.

Ardoin Family. Musique Creole *(Arhoolie 445).* 1966–early 1970s recordings by Bois Sec Ardoin and Conray Fontenot.

Armstrong, Frankie. Lovely on the Water *(Topic 216).* Her debut album released in 1972.

Armstrong Twins. Just Country Boys *(Arhoolie 5022).* 1981 new recordings by the Twins, now out of print. Some tracks have been reissued on various Arhoolie CD compilations.

Armstrong Twins. Old Timey Mandolin *(Old Timey 118).* 1979 LP reissue of 78 recordings, now out of print.

Ashley, Clarence "Tom." Greenback Dollar, 1929–33 *(County 3620).* Reissue of Ashley's early solo recordings, along with band recordings by the Carolina Tar Heels and the Blue Ridge Entertainers.

Ashley, Clarence "Tom." Old Time Music at Clarence Ashley's *(Smithsonian/Folkways 40029/30).* Wonderful early 1960s recordings by Ralph Rinzler, featuring Doc Watson, Clint Howard, and Fred Price.

Axton, Hoyt. Gotta Keep Rollin': The Jeremiah Years *(Raven 91).* CD reissue of 1979–81 fine recordings that Axton did for his own Jeremiah label.

Baez, Joan. Joan Baez's recorded catalog is very large; here is a selection of albums from varied parts of her career: Joan Baez *(Vanguard 2077).* 1960 debut album for Baez on Vanguard, which introduced her to the folk audience. Farewell Angelina *(Vanguard 79200).* 1965 album focusing on contemporary singer-songwriter material, including the Bob Dylan title cut. Diamonds and Rust *(A&M 65427).* 1975 album of originals in a singer-songwriter style.

Bailes Brothers. Early Radio, Vols. 13 *(Old Homestead 103, 104, 109).* 1930s and 1940s-era radio broadcasts reissued on this series of out-of-print LPs.

Baker, Etta. Instrumental Music of the Southern Appalachians *(Tradition 1061).* Anthology of various artists issued in 1957; Baker's first (and only) appearance on record until her first solo album was released, 34 years later!

Baker, Etta. One Dime Blues *(Rounder 2112).* Her first solo album, released in 1991.

Baker, Kenny. Puritan Sessions *(Rebel 1108).* With Josh Graves.

Baker, Kenny. Master Fiddler. *(County 2705).* Reissue of 1968–83 tracks from various County albums; a good introduction to Baker's music.

Baker, Kenny. Plays Bill Monroe. *(County 2708).* Featuring the big man himself, this is Baker's homage to Monroe, featuring many standards by the father of bluegrass music.

Balfa Brothers. J'ai Vu le Loup, Le Renard et la Belette *(Rounder 6007).* Excellent 1975 recordings.

Balfa Brothers. Plays Traditional Cajun Music *(Swallow 6011).* CD reissue of two Swallow albums, one recorded in 1965 and one in 1974.

E. C. and Orna Ball. E. C. and Orna Ball *(Rounder 11577).* CD reissue of Rounder recordings first made in the early 1970s; includes additional material drawn from their local radio work.

Battlefield Band. Home Is Where the Van Is *(Flying Fish 250; reissued Temple 2006).* This 1980 album was the band's first U.S. release, and established their reputation; many still feel it represents their best work.

Beausoleil. Bayou Cadillac *(Rounder 6025).* 1989 album with a typical mix of traditional and more contemporary sounds, along with several originals by bandleader Michael Doucet.

Belafonte, Harry. Calypso *(RCA 1248).* 1956 album that launched Belafonte's career, with the immortal "Banana Boat Song" as its lead song.

Berline, Byron. Berline-Crary-Hickman *(Sugar Hill 3720).* 1981 album, the first for the superpicker trio. They would record three more albums for Sugar Hill through the mid-1980s.

Berline, Byron. Dad's Favorites *(Rounder 0100).* 1979 album featuring tunes Berline learned from his father; includes a slew of young bluegrass stars, including Vince Gill before he became a country superstar.

Blake, Norman. Back Home in Sulphur Springs *(Rounder 0012).* Cassette-only reissue of early 1970s debut solo album.

Blake, Norman. Blake & Rice *(Rounder 0233/0266).* Two albums cut with hot picker Tony Rice, from 1988 and 1990, respectively, both available on CD.

Blake, Norman. Flower from the Field of Alabama *(Shanachie 6053).* 2001 album that draws on country traditional numbers.

Blake, Norman. Natasha's Waltz *(Rounder 11530).* CD compilation taken from various albums cut with wife, Nancy, and fiddler James Bryant.

Blake, Norman. Slow Train through Georgia *(Rounder 11526).* CD compilation drawn from various Rounder releases.

Boggs, Dock. Country Blues: Complete Early Recordings 1927–29 *(Revenant 205).* Beautifully packaged CD reissue of his classic recordings, including extensive booklet.

Boggs, Dock. Folkways Years 1963–68 *(Smithsonian/ Folkways 40108).* Recordings made by Mike Seeger originally issued on three separate Folkways albums, with complete annotation.

Bok, Gordon. Gordon Bok *(Verve/Folkways 3016).* Hard-to-find but excellent debut album, released in 1965, and produced by Noel Paul Stookey.

Bok, Gordon. A Tune for November *(Folk Legacy 40).* 1970 album, the first in a long series for the Folk Legacy label.

Bothy Band. Old Hag You Have Killed Me *(Polydor 1383417/Green Linnet 3005)* 1976 album that launched the most long-lived lineup of the band.

Bowers, Bryan. The View from Home *(Flying Fish 037).* 1977 debut mostly instrumental album with an excellent supporting cast of bluegrass musicians.

Boys of the Lough. Boys of the Lough *(Trailer).* Debut album featuring Dick Gaughan on guitar and vocals.

Boys of the Lough. Lochaber No More *(Philo 1031).* The group's fourth album; an excellent collection of songs and tunes giving a good feeling for the various traditions that they represent.

Brady, Paul. Welcome Here Kind Stranger *(Green Linnet 3015).* Late 1970s collection that features mostly traditional songs and ballads.

Burke, Joe. A Tribute to Michael Coleman *(Green Linnet 3097).* With Andy McGann on fiddle and Felix Dolan on piano, this album was originally issued in the mid-1960s on a small New York label, and was highly influential on the Irish music revival.

Burke, Kevin. If the Cap Fits *(Green Linnet 3009).* 1978 album recorded while a member of the Bothy Band.

Burke, Kevin. Sweeney's Dream *(Smithsonian/ Folkways 40485).* Recorded in 1973 but unissued (on LP) until 1977, this album was recorded during Burke's first visit to America.

Burnett & Rutherford. Complete Record Works, 1926–30 *(Document 8025).* CD reissue of all of their 78 recordings, including some Burnett made on his own or with other partners.

The Byrds. The Byrds *(Columbia 46773).* Four-CD retrospective set.

The Byrds. Sweetheart of the Rodeo *(Columbia/ Legacy 65610).* Hear the record that started it all! CD reissue of the 1968 album (Columbia 9670) with additional tracks.

The Byrds. Twenty Essential Tracks *(Columbia 47884).* If you can't afford the boxed set, how about buying this single CD and sampling the best of the best.

Carawan, Guy. Sings *(Folkways 3548).* His 1959 debut album.

Carlin, Bob. Bangin' and Sawin' *(Rounder 197).* Banjo and fiddle duets; CD reissue includes bonus tracks not on original LP.

Carlin, Bob. The Fun of Open Discussion *(Rounder 320).* Banjo-fiddle duets with John Hartford.

Carolina Tar Heels. Carolina Tar Heels *(Folk Legacy 24).* "Reunion" album of the original group, 30 years after their heyday.

Carroll, Liz. Liz Carroll *(Green Linnet 1092).* Second solo album for the fiddler, but the first made after her teen years.

Carthy, Martin. Like Joan Baez, Martin Carthy has a large discography stretching over four decades. This is a highly selective list: Both Ears and the Tail *(Gadfly 510).* Live concert recording of Swarbrick and Carthy from 1966.

Martin Carthy *(Fontana 5269/reissued Topic 340).* 1965 debut album featuring fiddler Dave Swarbrick.

Crown of Horn *(Pegasus 12/reissued Mooncrest 8).* One of his strongest solo albums, issued just after he left Steeleye Span.

Crown of Horn *(Topic 300).* 1976 album, produced by Ashley Hutchings, with an excellent selection of songs.

Cephas and Wiggins. Dog Days of August *(Flying Fish 394).* 1986 recordings.

Chad Mitchell Trio. Best of the Mercury Years *(Mercury 534400).* 1963–66 recordings originally issued on Mercury.

Chad Mitchell Trio. Collection *(Varese 5749).* Selections from their first three albums originally released by Kapp.

Chapin, Harry. Anthology *(Elektra 60413).* A good introduction to Chapin's songs, one of many compilations available.

Chapman, Tracy. Tracy Chapman *(Elektra 60774).* 1988 debut album, and still her best.

Chenier, Clifton. Zydeco Dynamite *(Rhino 71194).* Two CD, 40-track compilation of his best recordings.

The Chieftains. The Very Best of Claddagh Years *(Atlantic 83224)*. Compilation of their first recordings from the 1960s and early 1970s.

The Chieftains. The Wide World Over: A 40 Year Celebration *(RCA 63917)*. Gives an overview of their entire recording career.

The Clancy Brothers. Come Fill Your Glass with Us *(Tradition 1032)*. Their second album, from the mid-1950s, which takes as its theme Irish drinking songs.

The Clancy Brothers. In Person at Carnegie Hall *(Columbia 8750)*. 1963 live album representing the group at the height of their success.

Clancy, Willie. The Minstrel from Clare *(Topic 175)*. 1967 recordings.

Clancy, Willie. The Pipering of Willie Clancy *(Claddagh 34/39)*. Two CDs compiling recordings made over several decades.

Clannad. Magical Gathering *(Rhino 78255)*. A good overview of the band's entire recording career, from their traditional folk roots into more pop-rock material.

Clark, Gene. Echoes *(Columbia/Legacy 48253)*. 1970s-era recordings, many unissued at the time.

Clark, Gene. The Fantastic Expedition of Dillard and Clark Plus *(Edsel 708)*. CD reissuing the first LP made by Dillard and Clark in the late 1960s, plus other tracks.

Clark, Gene. So Rebellious a Lover *(Razor and Tie 1992)*. Clark's last recordings made in duet with Carla Olson.

Clark, Gene. With the Gosdin Brothers *(Edsel 529)*. Resissue of wonderful 1967 LP (Columbia 2618) featuring bluegrass backup by the Gosdins, Clarence White, session picker Glen Campbell, and even pianist Leon Russell. This was the first album Clark recorded after leaving the Byrds.

Clark, Guy. Boats to Build *(Asylum 61442)*. 1992 major label recording, with lots of new Nashville folks helping out.

Clark, Guy. Keepers *(Sugar Hill 1055)*. 1996 live recordings, including many favorites as well as a few new songs.

Clark, Guy. Old Friends *(Sugar Hill 1025)*. 1989 comeback album features a star-studded cast, including Rosanne Cash, Steve Wariner, Vince Gill, and many of the folks who appeared on Texas Cooking.

Clark, Guy. Old No. 1/Texas Cooking *(BMG 58813)*. Reissues Clark's first two albums from 1975–76, originally issued by RCA. It features most of his famous songs, including "L.A. Freeway," "Rita Ballou," and "Desperados Waitin' for a Train."

Clayton, Paul. Whaling and Sailing Songs from the Days of Moby Dick *(Tradition 1005)*. 1956 recordings of traditional sea chanteys.

Clements, Vassar. Back Porch Swing *(Cedar Glen 4203)*. 1999 bluegrass-swing session, reprising many tunes from his earlier recordings, including "Hillbilly Jazz."

Clements, Vassar. Full Circle *(OMS 25090)*. 2001 outing that pairs Clements with various folks he has worked with before, including Jim and Jesse, Ricky Skaggs, and other new Nashville luminaries.

Clifton, Bill. Around the World to Poor Valley *(Bear Family 16425)*. A big eight CD, boxed set from the German reissue label, featuring 225 selections made between 1954 and 1991.

Clifton, Bill. Early Years (1957–58) *(Rounder 1021)*. Compilation of 1950s recordings, with sidemen including banjoist Ralph Stanley, mandolin picker Curly Lambert, and ace fiddler Gordon Terry.

Cockerham, Fred. Tommy and Fred *(County 2702)*. Anthology of recordings made from the mid-1970s through the 1980s, compiled by folklorist Ray Alden.

Cohen, John. High Atmosphere *(Rounder 1028)*. Fine 1960-sera field recordings made by Cohen with wonderful photographs and notes.

Cohen, John. Stories the Crow Told Me *(Acoustic Music 34)*. Cohen's first solo album, released in 1998, with Jody Stecher and David Grisman, among others, in the supporting cast.

Coleman, Michael. Coleman's original recordings were issued by various labels on 78 discs. They have been reissued countless times; the best currently available is a two-CD set from Viva Voce that features his complete recordings. It also has extensive biographical notes.

Collins, Judy. Live at Newport (Vanguard 77013). Culled from performances at the famous folk festival from 1959–64, giving an overview of her early career.

Collins, Judy. Maid of Constant Sorrow (Elektra 209). 1961 debut album; a document of the singer at the beginning of her career.

Collins, Judy. Wildflowers (Elektra 4012). 1967 album, arranged by Josh Rifkin, featuring Collins's vocals set against warm string accompaniments. Includes her first recording of "Both Sides Now."

Collins, Shirley. Classic Collection (Highpoint 6008). Career overview with 20 tracks issued in 2004.

Collins, Shirley. No Roses (Pegasus 7/reissued Mooncrest 11). Strong folk-rock album, produced by Ashley Hutchings, with Collins at the height of her vocal powers.

Cooney, Michael. Still Cooney after All These Years (Front Hall 304). Late 1970s-era recordings.

Cooper, Stoney and Wilma Lee. Classic Early Recordings (County 103). Out-of-print LP reissuing late 1940s recordings originally cut for Columbia.

Cooper, Stoney and Wilma Lee. Wilma Lee and Stoney Cooper (Rounder 0066). Bluegrass sessions cut just before Stoney's death. Available now only on cassette.

Copper Family. Come Write Me Down (Topic 534). Two-CD set compiling recordings from the 1950s through the 1990s.

Cotton, Elizabeth. Freight Train and Other North Carolina Folk Songs and Tunes (Smithsonian Folkways 40009). Reissues her first album, first released in 1958. Her playing and singing is a little rough at this point, because she had just been "discovered."

Cotton, Elizabeth. Shake Sugaree (Folkways 30003). 1967 album representing the guitarist/singer at her performing best.

Country Cooking. Bluegrass Instrumentals (Rounder 006) and Barrel of Fun (Rounder 0033). Their two fine albums, now both out of print.

Country Cooking. 26 Bluegrass Instrumentals (Rounder 11551). Compilation from their two albums on CD.

Country Gazette. Hello Operator . . . This Is Country Gazette (Flying Fish 70112). Compilation of "the best" of the band recorded between 1976 and 1987.

Country Gazette. Strictly Instrumental (Flying Fish 446). Later incarnation of the band with Munde and White joined by talented dobroist Gene Wooten along with fiddler Billy Joe Foster.

Country Gentlemen. Country Songs, Old and New (Smithsonian Folkways 40004).

Country Gentlemen. Featuring Ricky Skaggs (Vanguard 73123). Reissue of an album originally recorded about 1976. At the time, Skaggs was just a young bluegrass fiddler on the rise.

Country Gentlemen. Folk Songs and Bluegrass (Smithsonian Folkways 40022). These two CDs reissue the Gentlemen's first two Folkways albums from 1960 and 1961, respectively. This is the so-called classic group, and these albums were highly influential on the urban folk/bluegrass revival.

Country Gentlemen. Twenty Five Years (Rebel 1102). Mid-1990s version of the band celebrating a key anniversary.

Cousin Emmy. With the New Lost City Ramblers (Folkways 31021). Available now on special order CD/cassette.

Crary, Dan. Guitar (Sugar Hill 3730). 1990 album featuring many of the bluegrass/newgrass greats.

Crowe, J. D. And the New South (Rounder 0044). This album, featuring Ricky Skaggs and Tony Rice, was an important and influential 1970s release for the progressive bluegrass movement.

Crowe, J. D. Come on Down to My World (Rounder 610422). 1998 recording with the core band augmented with bluegrass power pickers.

Crowe, J. D. Flashback (Rounder 610322). Compilation of various Crowe albums for Rounder made during the 1970s and 1980s.

Dane, Barbara. And the Chambers Brothers (Folkways 2468). Interesting document from the mid-1960s, when Dane was still primarily performing blues material, although it also includes some folk revival and social-protest songs.

Dane, Barbara. I Hate the Capitalist System *(Paredon 1014).* 1973 album featuring Dane's own compositions and traditional songs of social protest.

Davis, Rev. Gary. Harlem Street Singer *(Prestige Bluesville 547).* 1960 album featuring such strong performances of classics as "Samson and Delilah," "Death Don't Have No Mercy," and "Twelve Gates to the City."

Davis, Rev. Gary. 1935–1949 *(Document 1569).* All of Davis's early recordings; his 1935 recordings (the bulk of the material here) are all gospel material and are marred somewhat by poor microphone placement.

Darby and Tarleton. Complete Recordings *(Bear Family 15764).* All 70 of the surviving recordings of Darby and Tarlton, in a lovingly assembled box set.

De Dannan. Best Of *(Shanachie 79047).* Good compilation of their more traditional-oriented recordings.

Delmore Brothers. Country Music Hall of Fame *(King 3831).* Late 1940s–early 1950s recordings issued in 2001, when the brothers were inducted into the Hall of Fame.

DeMent, Iris. Infamous Angel *(Philo 1138).* This album was originally released in 1992 and then reissued by Warners a year later.

DeMent, Iris. My Life *(Warners 45493).*

DeMent, Iris. The Way I Should *(Warners 46188).*

Denny, Sandy. No More Sad Refrains *(A&M 542747).* Two-CD compilation covering her entire career.

Denver, John. Rocky Mountain Collection *(RRAC 66837).* Two-CD set offering all the hits and a good career retrospective for Denver.

Dickens, Hazel. By the Sweat of My Brow *(Rounder 0200).* 1990 album of primarily original songs by Dickens.

The Dillards. Best of the Darling Boys *(Vanguard 506).* Early recordings when the Dillards were portraying this backwoods group on the *Andy Griffith Show.*

The Dillards. There Is a Time *(Vanguard 131/32).* Classic band recordings originally issued by Elektra between 1963 and 1970.

Dixon Brothers. Volumes 14 *(Document 8046–49).* Chronological reissue of their recordings made between 1936 and 1939.

Donegan, Lonnie. Singles Collection *(Castle 72011).* Eighty six songs on three CDs gives you all of Donegan's hits and much more from his heyday.

Douglas, Jerry. Everything's Gonna Work Out Fine *(Rounder 11535).* Compilation of his Rounder solo albums from early 1980s.

Douglas, Jerry. Restless of the Farm *(Sugar Hill 3875).* 1998 solo outing featuring many of Douglas's regular cohorts.

Dyer-Bennett, Richard. Volume 1 *(Dyer-Bennett Records 1; reissued Smithsonian Folkways 40078).* His first album and his most successful.

Dylan, Bob. Bob Dylan has had a long recording career, and it cannot be summarized here. Here are a few select albums reflecting his folk/social-protest style: Basement Tapes *(Columbia 33682).* Working with the Band, in Woodstock c. 1968, Dylan created roots-rock without really trying. Bob Dylan *(Columbia 8579).* 1961 debut album, featuring mostly traditional folk material. Freewheelin' *(Columbia 8786).* 1963 follow-up, all originals, including the first recordings of many early Dylan classics. Time Out of Mind *(Columbia 68556).* Dylan returns as a rockabilly rebel, singing songs of love gone wrong. Times They Are A-Changin' *(Columbia 8905).* His third album, and his last purely social-protest one.

Eanes, Jim. Classic Bluegrass *(Rebel 1116).* 1970s-era recordings.

Eanes, Jim. Complete Decca Recordings *(Bear Family 15934).* Everything Eanes recorded for Decca between 1952 and 1955.

Eanes, Jim. Your Old Standby *(Starday 3507).* Complete Starday recordings, featuring Allen Shelton on banjo.

East Texas Serenaders. Complete Recorded Works in Chronological Order 1927–37 *(Document 8031)*

Elliott, Ramblin' Jack. Sings the Songs of Woody Guthrie *(Prestige 13016).* 1960 album that features the songs of Elliott's hero—one of the first albums to be devoted to Guthrie's songs.

Elliott, Ramblin' Jack. The Essential *(Vanguard 89/90).* Mostly taken from a 1965 concert, this presents Elliott at the height of his folk career.

Emerson, Bill. Reunion *(Webco 140).* 1991 recordings made with various accompanists who played with Emerson over the years.

Ennis, Seamus. Bonny Bunch of Roses *(Tradition 1023).* Late 1950s recordings of songs and pipe instrumentals.

Ennis, Seamus. Forty Years of Irish Piping *(Green Linnet 1000).* Nice collection of recordings from various sources compiled by Pat Sky in 1970.

Fahey, John. Blind Joe Death *(Takoma 72702).* Fahey issued his first album on his own Takoma label in 1959, pressing only 100 copies. In 1964 he re-recorded the entire album, and it is this version that survives as his first release.

Fahey, John. Essential *(Vanguard 55/56).* Reissues Fahey's two mid-1960s albums for Vanguard.

Fairport Convention. History of *(Island 4/reissued Polygram 846083).* Compilation of their recordings from 1966–72.

Fairport Convention. Liege & Lief *(A&M 4257).* This 1969 album virtually defined British folk rock, taking traditional ballads and songs and performing them with electric guitar, amplified fiddle, bass, and drums. Great vocals by Sandy Denny.

Farina, Mimi and Richard. Complete Vanguard Recordings *(200/02).* Reissues all three albums that they made during their short career.

Fink, Cathy. The Leading Role *(Rounder 0223).* 1990 album highlighting the important contribution of women to country music.

Fisher, Archie. Man with A Rhyme *(Folk Legacy 61).* Mixes traditional with his own compositions.

Fleck, Béla. Crossing the Tracks *(Rounder 0121).* Nice 1979 collection combining bluegrass with original jazz-flavored compositions.

Fleck, Béla. Tales from the Acoustic Planet *(Warner Bros. 45854).* 1995 collection, primarily of Fleck originals, with bluegrass and jazz musicians.

Flores, Rosalie. Honky Tonk Reprise *(Rounder 3136).* Best of her early through mid-1990s recordings.

Flores, Rosalie. Speed of Sound *(Eminent 25090).* Flores returns to a harder-rocking style on this 2001 release, with rockabilly, Western Swing, and Tex-Mex sounds all thrown into the mix.

Fraley, J. P. Wild Rose of the Mountain *(Rounder 0037).* Mid-1970s recordings.

Gaughan, Dick. Handful of Earth *(Green Linnet 3062).* Early 1980s solo album featuring a nice performance of "Song for Ireland." Considered among his best recordings.

Gaughan, Dick. No More Forever *(Trailer 2072).* Gaughan's first solo album from 1972 is still one of the best of the folk-revival; features fiddler Aly Bain.

Gerrard, Alice. Calling Me Home *(Copper Creek 225).* Traditional and original songs.

Gerrard, Alice. Pioneering Women of Bluegrass *(Smithsonian Folkways 40065).* Compiles 26 tracks from two mid-1960s albums made by Gerrard with Hazel Dickens.

Gibson, Bob. Where I'm Bound *(Elektra 239/reissued Collectors Choice 228).* 1964 album recorded as the folk revival was running out of steam; nonetheless, one of his better recordings and representative of his style.

Gimble, John. Texas Fiddle Collection *(CMH 9027).* Mid-1970s recordings with many of the old Texas Playboys on hand.

Goodman, Steve. Essential *(Buddah 55652).* Gathers his best early 1970s recordings.

Goodman, Steve. No Big Surprise *(Red Pajamas 8).* Two-CD compilation of his studio work and a nice live set.

Graham, Davey. Fire in the Soul *(Topic 818).* Compilation of 1960s-era recordings, including his best-known instrumentals.

Graves, Josh. Sultan of Slide *(OMS 2504).* 2000 CD with all-star cast.

Greenbriar Boys, The. Best of the Vanguard Years *(Vanguard 206/07).*

Greene, Richard. Sales Tax Toddle *(Rebel 1737).* 1997 CD featuring primarily bluegrass tunes played by an all-star supporting cast.

Griffith, Nanci. Lone Star State of Mind *(MCA 31300).* Her 1987 big-label debut.

Griffith, Nanci. Once in a Very Blue Moon *(Philo 1096).* Her 1984 breakthrough Nashville album produced by country folkie Jim Rooney.

Griffith, Nanci. Other Voices, Other Rooms *(Elektra 61464).* 1993 album of folkie standards, her most commercially successful to date.

Griffith, Nanci. There's a Light Beyond These Woods *(Philo 1097).* Reissue of her first album, recorded live in 1977–78.

Grisman, David. DGQ 20 *(Acoustic Disc 20).* Three-CD retrospective of the Grisman quintet, with live recordings drawn from its entire career.

Grisman, David. Early Dawg *(Sugar Hill 3713).* Compilation of previously unissued 1960s and early 1970s-era recordings.

Grisman, David. Quintet *(Kaleidoscope 5).* This is the album that started it all, defining "Dawg" music and launching one strand of "new acoustic" music.

Grisman, David. Rounder Compact Disc *(Rounder 610069).* A return to his bluegrass roots; reissues the LP of similar name (Rounder 069).

Grossman, Stefan. Best of the Transatlantic Years *(Castle 72072).* Compiles recordings from the mid-1970s through the 1980s.

Guthrie, Arlo. Alice's Restaurant *(Reprise 6267).* His debut album featuring the first recording of the title story-song that inspired the 1969 film.

Guthrie, Arlo. Best Of *(Reprise 3117).* Overview of his recording career through 1977.

Guthrie, Woody. Asch Recordings, 1–4 *(Smithsonian/ Folkways 40112).* Four-CD set collecting 105 recordings made by Moses Asch of Guthrie in the mid-to-late 1940s. Also available as individual CDs.

Guthrie, Woody. Columbia River Collection *(Rounder 1036).* Recordings made in the late 1930s for the WPA that were never previously available.

Guthrie, Woody. Dust Bowl Ballads *(BMG 57839).* Reissue of Guthrie's RCA recordings.

Guthrie, Woody. Library of Congress Recordings *(Rounder 1041/42/43).* Three-CD collection of recordings made by Alan Lomax for the Archive of Folksong in 1940.

Guthrie, Woody. Struggle *(Smithsonian/Folkways 40025).* Late 1940s recordings commissioned by Moses Asch on political themes.

Hackberry Ramblers. Jolie Blonde *(Arhoolie 399).* 1960s-era recordings.

Hamilton, Frank. Sings Folk Songs *(Folkways 2437).*

Hardin, Tim. Hang on to a Dream *(Polydor 521583).* Anthology of his 1964–66 recordings originally made for Verve/Folkways.

Harrell, Kelly. Complete Record Works, 1 & 2: 1925–29. *Document 8026/27.*

Hartford, John. Aereo-Plain *(Rounder 366).* Reissue of classic 1971 Warner Bros. album (WB1916) that was highly influential on 1970s newgrass bands.

Hartford, John. Good Ol' Boys *(Rounder 462).* Hartford's last studio vocal album, a collection of new songs including a wonderful story-song about the life of Bill Monroe, "Cross-Eyed Child."

Hartford, John. Me Oh My, How Time Flies *(Flying Fish 70440).* Compilation of his mid 1970s through early 1980s recordings.

Havens, Richie. Resume *(Rhino 71187).* A 17-track "best of" collection that serves as a good introduction to his recording career.

Haywire, Mac. Hallelujah, I'm a Bum *(Rounder 1009).* Late 1920s-era recordings, including many of his best-loved songs.

Hester, Carolyn. Carolyn Hester *(Columbia 8596/reissued Columbia Legacy 57310).* 1962 album featuring a young Bob Dylan on harmonica. Hester's recordings have not aged well, but this is representative of her style and repertoire.

Hiatt, John. Bring the Family *(A&M 5158).* 1987 comeback album with great backup by Ry Cooder and company.

Hiatt, John. Crossing Muddy Water. *(Vanguard 79576).* 2000 album of acoustic country and blues numbers; a standout in Hiatt's discography.

Hiatt, John. Greatest Hits. *Capitol 7 2438 59179 2 9.* 1998 compilation mostly drawn from Hiatt's 1987 to current recordings, with some remakes of earlier songs.

Hiatt, John. Y'All Caught *(Geffen 24247).* Anthology of his 1979–85 Geffen recordings, many poorly produced but featuring some good songs nonetheless.

Hickerson, Joe. With a Gathering of Friends *(Folk Legacy 39).*

Highwoods Stringband. Feed Your Baby Onions: Fat City Favorites *(Rounder 11569).* CD compilation of their three LPs from the 1970s.

Hinojosa, Tish. Culture Swing *(Rounder 3122).* Her best recording.

Hinojosa, Tish. Sign of Truth *(Rounder 613172).* 2000 album of new songs returns Hinojosa to solid ground.

Holcomb, Roscoe. Mountain Music of Kentucky *(Smithsonian Folkways 40077).* Anthology featuring Holcomb and other musicians from the area.

Holcomb, Roscoe. The High Lonesome Sound *(Smithsonian Folkways 40079).* Drawing from all of Holcomb's Folkways recordings, a beautifully produced reissue with great notes and photographs by John Cohen.

Holt, David. Grandfather's Greatest Hits *(High Windy 1251).* 1991 album; one of his best.

Holy Modal Rounders. Holy Modal Rounders *(Fantasy 24711).* Reissues their first two (and best) LPs.

Holy Modal Rounders. I Make a Wish for a Potato *(Rounder 611598).* Compilation of several Rounder albums by the Rounders and their disciples and spinoff bands.

Holy Modal Rounders. Too Much Fun *(Rounder 3163).* 1999 reunion of Stampfel and Weber produced this recording, which features remakes of some of their 1960s recordings, along with new "old" (traditional) material.

Hopkins, Al and His Hill Billies. Complete Recordings, Vols. 1–3, 1925–28 *(Document 8039–41).* All of the recordings issued by Hopkins.

Hot Mud Family. Meat & Potatoes (& Stuff Like That) *(Flying Fish 251).*

Hot Rize. Red Knuckles/Hot Rize Live *(Flying Fish 70107).* CD reissue of two 1980s LPs featuring both Hot Rize and their alter ego band, the Trailblazers.

Hot Rize. Take It Home *(Sugar Hill 3784).* 1990 release, the last from the band.

Houston, Cisco. Folkways Years *(Smithsonian Folkways 40059).* Collects his recordings made between 1944 and 1961.

Hurt, Mississippi John. Avalon Blues: The Complete 1928 Okeh Recordings *(Columbia/Legacy 64986).* Although these have been reissued on Yazoo and other labels, this "official" reissue has the best sound.

Hurt, Mississippi John. Best Of *(Vanguard 19/20).* Actually this consists of a live concert from 1965, but it captures Hurt at the height of his powers after his "rediscovery" and does feature most of his best-known songs.

Hutchings, Ashley/Albion Band. Morris On *(Island HELP 5).* 1972 release that helped launch the Morris dance music revival; with John Kirkpatrick on concertina and accordion and Barry Dransfeld on fiddle.

Hutchison, Frank. Complete Recorded Works, 1926–29 *(Document 8003).* Just about everything Hutchison recorded, a treasure trove of white country blues.

Ian and Sylvia. Best of the Vanguard Years *(Vanguard 79516).* Remastered recordings drawn from their classic albums, including live tracks from Newport that were previously unavailable.

Ian, Janis. Janis Ian *(Verve Forecast 3017).* Her 1967 debut album, featuring the hit "Society's Child."

Incredible String Band. Hangman's Beautiful Daughter *(Hanibal 4421).* 1968 album that is considered to be the group's best work.

Irish Rovers. The Unicorn *(Decca 74951).* 1971 album that was their most popular; featuring the Shel Silverstein–penned title track.

Irvine, Andy. And Paul Brady *(Green Linnet 3006).* Mid-1970s album featuring all traditional songs.

Ives, Burl. Greatest Hits *(MCA 114).* Reissues his most popular late 1940s/early 1950s recordings for Decca.

Ives, Burl. Wayfaring Stranger *(Columbia 6474; reissued Collectables 6474). Mid-1950s recordings that introduced many standards to the folk repertoire.*

Jackson, Aunt Molly. Library of Congress Recordings *(Rounder 1002).* Wonderful collection of recordings made by Alan Lomax of the singer in her prime.

Jansch, Burt. Burt and John *(Transatlantic 144).* 1966 duo LP with John Renbourn; still one of the most admired acoustic guitar instrumental albums of the folk revival.

Jansch, Burt. Jack Orion *(Vanguard 6544).* 1969 album featuring all traditional material, with the exception of one song by Ewan MacColl.

Jarrell, Tommy. Legacy of, Vols. 1–3 *(County 2724–26).* Reissues of Jarrell's classic County recordings, beginning with his great solo fiddle album (vol. 1), through his duets with Fred Cockerham (vol. 2), and his solo banjo album (vol. 3).

Jenkins and Sherrill. Snuffy Jenkins: Pioneer of the Bluegrass Banjo with Homer Sherrill *(Arhoolie 9027).* 1962 sessions.

Jenkins and Sherrill. Jim and Jesse 1952–1955 *(Bear Family 15635).* Fine Capitol recordings, their first for a major label.

Jenkins and Sherrill. Y'all Come *(Epic/Legacy 65076).* 1960s-era hits for Epic, in bluegrass and honky-tonk country style.

Johnson Mountain Boys. Favorites *(Rounder 11509).* Selections from their Rounder recordings of the 1980s.

The Johnstons. The Transatlantic Years *(Transatlantic 13).*

Jones, Bessie. So Glad I'm Here *(Rounder 2015).* 1975 album finds Jones in fine voice singing a nice selection of hymns, traditional songs, and children's material.

Kahn, Si. Home *(Flying Fish 207).* A more varied program than many of his other albums makes this a good starting place.

Kazee, Buell. Buell Kazee Sings and Plays *(Folkways 3810).* Early 1960s recordings, now avaiilable on special order CD/cassette.

Keen, Robert Earl. A Bigger Piece of the Sky *(Sugar Hill).* 1993 debut album on the small folk label.

Keen, Robert Earl. Walking Distance *(Arista Texas).* 1998 song cycle.

Keith, Bill. Banjoistics *(Rounder 0148).*

Keith, Bill. Beating around the Bush *(Green Linnett 2107).* 1992 recordings.

Keith, Bill. Fiddle Tunes for Banjo *(Rounder 0124).* Also includes Tony Trischka and Béla Fleck.

Kentucky Colonels. Appalachian Swing! *(Rounder 31).* Reissue of their classic all-instrumental World Pacific album from 1964, with fiddler Bobby Sloan and dobro picker Leroy Mack.

Kentucky Colonels. Long Journey Home *(Vanguard 77004).* 1964 live recordings from the Newport Folk Festival.

Kessinger, Clark. Legend Of *(County 2713).* CD reissue drawn from various 1960s-era recordings.

The Kingston Trio. Capitol Collectors Series *(Capitol 92710).* One of the better compilations of the many that are available of their hits.

The Kingston Trio. The Kingston Trio *(Capitol 996).* Their debut album featuring the big hit, "Tom Dooley."

Kirkpatrick, John. Force of Habit *(Omnium 2015).* 1996 live recording featuring accompaniment from ex-Albion band guitarist Graeme Taylor.

Kirkpatrick, John. Plain Capers *(Free Reed 010; reissued Topic 458).* Nice collection of morris dance tunes, featuring the guitar work of Martin Carthy.

Koerner, Spider John. Blues, Rags and Hollers *(Red House 76).* Reissues Koerner, Dave Ray, and Tony Glover's first album from the mid-1960s. Includes traditional blues and originals by Koerner.

Koerner, Spider John. Nobody Knows the Trouble I've Been *(Red House 12).* 1986 album of traditional blues and songs.

Kottke, Leo. Anthology *(Rhino 72585).* Two-CD set gives an overview of his recordings from 1969–83.

Kottke, Leo. 6 and 12 String Guitar *(Takoma 1024).* This 1972 album introduced Kottke as a great acoustic guitarist in the John Fahey mold; it remains one of his best recordings.

La Farge, Peter. As Long as the Grass Shall Grow *(Folkways 2532).* Original songs focusing on the plight of Native Americans.

Lawson, Doyle. Gospel Collection, Vol. 1 *(Sugar Hill 9104).* Thirteen tracks recorded through 1993.

Lawson, Doyle. Just Over in Heaven *(Sugar Hill 3911).* A cappella and accompanied gospel material, released in 2000 with the latest version of Lawson's band.

Lead Belly. Lead Belly's recordings have been reissued by many different labels. The German Document label has issued all of his commercial recordings on a series of individual CDs. Lead Belly's recordings for Moses Asch have been issued on the Folkways label (later Smithsonian/Folkways) in many forms; his Last Sessions *(Smithsonian/Folkways 40068) presents recordings made by Frederic Ramsey Jr. a year before Lead Belly died and features his discussion of the songs as well as performances. The Library of Congress recordings made by Alan Lomax have been reissued on a LP-boxed set by Elektra and more recently on CD by Rounder. ARC (later acquired by Columbia), Capitol, and RCA material has been reissued in various forms by these labels over the years as well.*

Ledford, Lily Mae. Banjo Pickin' Girl *(Greenhays 712).* Late 1970s recordings.

Lewis Family, The. 16 Greatest Hits *(Hollywood 217).* Compilation of recordings originally made for Starday.

Lewis, Laurie. And Her Bluegrass Pals *(Rounder 610461).* All-star bluegrass album.

Lewis, Laurie. Earth and Sky: Songs of *(Rounder 610400).* Gathers material from her 1980s Flying Fish albums in a country-folk-pop vein.

Lightfoot, Gordon. Gordon Lightfoot's back catalog of recordings is extensive. He first recorded for United Artists records, and these albums, among his best, are collected on The United Artists Collection *(1995; EMI 27015). Rhino Records's* Songbook *(1998; 75802) offers a four-CD overview of his entire recording career to that time. There are many other compilations available, and many of his original albums have also been reissued in various form on CD.*

Lily Brothers, The. Have a Feast Here Tonight *(Prestige 9919).* Reissues two early 1960s albums by the brothers and Don Stover on banjo.

Lloyd, A. L. During his lifetime Lloyd recorded dozens of albums that were issued on various labels, including Topic, Prestige, Folkways, Tradition, Riverside, and many others. Not much of this material has been reissued on CD. A CD of sea chanteys released in the mid-1950s (also featuring Ewan MacColl) is available (Blow Boys Blow; Tradition 1024). Leviathan, first issued in the mid-1960s, is a collection of whaling songs (Topic 497). English Drinking Songs is an earlier collection, also reissued by Topic (496). Most of Lloyd's recordings feature excellent English concertina accompaniment by Alf Edwards.

Lomax, John and Alan. Sings American Folksongs *(Folkways 3508).* John Lomax recorded these songs in the late 1940s; although not a great performer, they are of some historical interest.

Lulu Belle and Scotty. Sweethearts of Country Music *(Hollywood/IMG 289).* Cassette-only issue of recordings of unknown vintage.

Lunsford, Bascomb Lamar. Ballads, Banjo Tunes and Sacred Songs of Western North Carolina *(Smithsonian/Folkways 40082).* Collection of 1950s and 1960s-era recordings.

MacArthur, Margaret. The Old Songs *(Philo 1001).*

MacColl, Ewan. Like A. L. Lloyd, MacColl recorded extensively from the 1950s until his death in the later 1980s. Many of these albums are no longer available. The Real MacColl (Topic 463) collects various recordings made for that label during his prime singing years. Like Lloyd, also, MacColl was often accompanied by ace concertina player Alf Edwards, and often recorded in duet with his wife, Peggy Seeger.

Macon, Uncle Dave. *Uncle Dave's complete recordings have been reissued on a large boxed set, with nine CDs, a DVD, and a beautiful illustrated book, by the German Bear Family label (15978). A smaller, four-CD compilation has been issued by JSP, which is much more moderately priced, but lacks much documentation.*

Mainer, J. E. J. E. *Mainer's Crazy Mountaineers (Old Timey 106/107). Two out-of-print LPs reissuing early recordings by Mainer's band.*

Mainer, J. E. *Run Mountain (Arhoolie 456). 1963 recordings by a later-day Mountaineers.*

Martin, Benny. *Big Tiger Roars Again (OMS 25010). 1999 release, with Earl Scruggs, John Hartford, Jesse McReynolds, Bobby Osborne, and many other legendary players.*

Martin, Benny. *Tennessee Jubilee (Flying Fish 70012). 1970s-era recordings with John Hartford and Lester Flatt.*

Martin, Benny. *Twenty Greatest Hits (Deluxe 7863). 1970s-era recordings from the Gusto label.*

Martin, Benny. *You Don't Know My Mind (Rounder 21). Great 1950s-era recordings in a bluegrass style.*

McCoury, Del. *Classic Bluegrass (Rebel 1111). 1970s-era recordings. Del, Doc, and Mac, Sugar Hill 3888. With Doc Watson and Mac Wiseman; released in 1998.*

McCoury, Del. *Del and the Boys (Hollywood 902006). 2000 album brings Del and his band to a major label; a typical mix of contemporary songs and some older traditional numbers performed in straight-ahead bluegrass style.*

McCurdy, Ed. *When Dalliance Was in Flower (Elektra 170). His most famous album, very influential in its day. Not currently available on CD.*

McDonald, Country Joe. *Thinking of Woody Guthrie (Vanguard 6546). 1969 album that returned McDonald to his folk roots.*

McEuen, John. *String Wizards (Vanguard 79462). His first 1991 solo album, with contributions by*

Vassar Clements, Byron Berline, Jerry Douglas, and Earl Scruggs. Stories and Songs, Planetary 9023. Duet album with Jim Ibbotson features a group of contemporary country-rock songs, along with the "stories" behind them.

McGarrigle, Kate & Anna. *The McGarrigle Hour (Hannibal 1417). Relaxed sessions featuring the McGarrigles and their extended families.*

McGee, Sam. *Grand Dad of the Country Guitar (Arhoolie 9009). Reissue of 1969–70 recordings produced by Mike Seeger (Arhoolie 5012).*

McGee, Sam. *1926–34 (Document 8036). Complete recordings from this period, some featuring brother Kirk.*

McLean, Don. *Legendary Songs of (Capitol 81654). One of many compilations of McLean's hits along with selections from his other recordings.*

Miller, Buddy and Julie. *Buddy and Julie Miller (High Tone 8035). 2001 duet album.*

Miller, Emmet. *Minstrel Man from Georgia (Columbia Legacy 66999).*

Mitchell, Joni. *Mitchell has been recording since 1968 and has an extensive discography. Her early albums are the most "folk" flavored, notably* Song to A Seagull *(aka Joni Mitchell; Reprise 6293) and* Clouds *(Reprise 6341), released in 1968 and 1969, respectively. 1971's* Blue *(Reprise 2038) is recognized as a classic in the self-confessional, singer-songwriter style that became popular in the early 1970s.*

Moloney, Mick. *Far from the Shamrock Shore (Shanachie 78050). Songs that reflect the Irish-American immigrant experience.*

Moloney, Mick. *Strings Attached (Green Linnet 1027). 1980 all-instrumental album.*

Moore, Christy. *Prosperous (Tara 2008). The album that launched the revival group Planxty.*

Moore, Tiny. *Back to Back (Kaleidoscope F-9). With Jethro Burns; recorded in 1979.*

Moore, Tiny. *Tiny Moore Music (Kaleidoscope F-12). Solo album from 1982.*

Morris Brothers. *Wiley, Zeke and Homer (Rounder 0022). 1973 recordings.*

Muldaur, Geoff. *Beautiful Isle of Somewhere (Tradition & Moderne, 25). Live recordings from*

2003 of Geoff Muldaur made in Germany, including blues and pop material.

Muldaur, Geoff and Maria. Sweet Potatoes *(Reprise 2073)*. 1972 duet album, recorded right after the demise of the Jim Kweskin Jug Band.

Muldaur, Maria. Maria Muldaur *(Reprise 148)* Her 1974 debut solo album, which produced the major hit "Midnight at the Oasis."

Muleskinner. Muleskinner *(Warner Bros. 2787).* The 1973 album. Live: Original Television Soundtrack, Sierra 6001. Not the album that made them famous, but the actual soundtrack off the local public television program that was the impetus for forming the band.

Murphy, Jimmy. Electricity *(Sugar Hill 3702).* Out-of-print, fine album; reissued briefly on CD.

Nashville Bluegrass Band. Waiting for the Hard Times to Go *(Sugar Hill 3809). 1993 album that combines contemporary and traditional bluegrass songs and stylings.*

Nesmith, Michael. The Newer Stuff *(Rhino 70168).* Nesmith ventures out into territories only he would explore.

Nesmith, Michael. The Older Stuff *(Rhino 70763).* His great country-rock sessions from 1970–73.

New Grass Revival. Best of *(Liberty 28090).* The later-day band, with Béla Fleck, taken from their Capitol/Liberty albums.

New Grass Revival. Fly Through the Country/When The Storm is Over *(Flying Fish 70032).* Reissues two classic 1970s albums by this influential group.

New Lost City Ramblers. The Early Years *(Smithsonian/Folkways 40036).* Selections from their albums cut between 1958 and 1962 with Tom Paley.

New Lost City Ramblers. The Later Years *(Smithsonian/Folkways 40040).* The band's best recordings from 1963 to 1973.

Newman, Jimmy C. Alligator Man *(Rounder 6039).* 1991 recording in a more traditional Cajun style.

Newman, Jimmy C. Bop A Hula-Diggy Liggy Lo *(Bear Family 15469).* Two-CD compilation of his Dot recordings made between 1953–58, featuring Cajun-flavored country and rockabilly.

Nickel Creek. Nickel Creek *(Sugar Hill 3909).* 2000 debut album, heavily promoted on country music TV.

Niles, John Jacob. Collection *(Gifthorse 100008).*

O'Brien, Tim. Red on Blonde *(Sugar Hill 3853).* 1996 album of Bob Dylan material, which garnered O'Brien a well-deserved Grammy nomination.

Ochs, Phil. Chords of Fame *(A&M 6511).* Career overview including Elektra and A&M recordings compiled by Ochs's brother, Michael.

O'Connor, Mark. The Championship Years *(Country Music Foundation 015).* Mark as a young fiddle-burner performing in various contests.

O'Connor, Mark. National Junior Fiddle Champ *(Rounder 0046).* Cassette-only reissue of his first album cut when he was 12.

O'Connor, Mark. New Nashville Cats *(Warner Bros. 26509).* Fine bluegrass/honky-tonk country outing with Skaggs and Gill.

O'Connor, Mark. Retrospective *(Rounder 11507).* Best of his many Rounder albums.

O'Day, Molly. Molly O'Day and the Cumberland Mountain Folks *(Bear Family 15565).* Two CDs of O'Day's Columbia recordings made between 1946 and 1951. Includes duets with husband, Lynn Davis.

Odetta. The Tradition Masters *(Tradition 1085).* Mid-1950s recordings by the artist at her prime.

Old and in the Way. High Lonesome Sound *(Acoustic Disc 19).* A second album of live recordings, not issued until 1996, although recorded in 1973.

Old and in the Way. Old and in the Way *(Sugar Hill 3746/Grateful Dead 4104).* Reissue of their first album, recorded live.

Osbourne Brothers, The. Bluegrass, 1956–68 *(Bear Family 15598).* All their MGM and Decca recordings from this period, totaling 114 tracks.

Osbourne Brothers, The. 1968–74 *(Bear Family 15748).* Four-CD set covering their later Decca recordings.

Osbourne Brothers, The. Once More, Vols. 1 & 2 *(Sugar Hill 2203).* CD reissue of remakes of their favorite bluegrass numbers originally issued on two LPs in 1985–86.

Paton, Sandy and Caroline. Sandy and Caroline Paton *(Folk Legacy EGO 30).* Their first duet album issued on their own label in the late 1960s.

Paxton, Tom. I Can't Help But Wonder Where I'm Bound *(Rhino 73515).* 26-track survey of 1960s and early 1970s recordings, his best work.

Pentangle. Pentangling *(Sanctuary 86371).* Overview of their late 1960s-early 1970s recordings.

Peter, Paul and Mary. The Collection *(Reader's Digest/Warner Special Products 8505)* Four-CD set selected by Peter Yarrow of the hits and favorites.

Phillips, Bruce "U. Utah." Good Though *(Philo 1004).* 1973 album featuring many of his favorite songs and the notorious recitation "Moose Turd Pie."

Planxty. Planxty *(Shanachie 79009).* 1973 debut album, considered by many to be their best.

Poole, Charlie. Vols. 1–3 *(County 3501/3508/3516).* All of Poole's classic recordings, in pristine sound; County originally issued this material on three albums during the 1970s.

Prine, John. Great Days *(Rhino 71400).* Collection of his best 1971–91 recordings.

Proffitt, Frank. High Atmosphere *(Rounder 0028).* Anthology of 1960s recordings by John Cohen, featuring several fine performances by Proffitt. Proffitt's two albums—on Folkways and Folk Legacy—are currently available only on special order.

Puckett, Riley. Red Sails in the Sunset *(Bear Family 15280).* Bluebird recordings from 1939–41, featuring mostly pop numbers remade in Puckett's unique style.

Red Clay Ramblers. Twisted Laurel/Merchant's Lunch *(Flying Fish 77055).* CD reissue of two fine albums from the mid-1980s.

Redpath, Jean. Frae My Ain Countrie *(Folk-Legacy 49).* 1973 recordings.

Redpath, Jean. Songs of Robert Burns, Vols. 1–6 *(Philo)* Sensitive performances of the Scottish poet's popular works.

Reed, Blind Alfred. Complete Record Works *(Document 8022).* Twenty tracks, all of his Victor recordings cut between 1927 and 1929, with notes by Tony Russell. Supersedes an earlier LP reissue on Rounder (1002), which is worth seeking for its extensive liner notes.

Reed, Ola Belle. My Epitaph *(Folkways 2493).* 1978 recordings.

Renbourn, John. Lady and the Unicorn *(Reprise 6407).* 1970 collection of medieval and early music instrumentals, and music inspired by them.

Renbourn, John. Transatlantic Anthology *(Castle 72140).* Two-CD set of his best mid-1960s–early 1970s recordings.

Reno, Don. Collector's Box Set *(Starday 7001).* Four CDs, 115 classic Reno & Smiley tracks cut between 1951 and 1959.

Reno, Don. A Variety of Country Songs *(King 646).* More 1950s-era recordings.

Reynolds, Malvina. Ear to the Ground *(Smithsonian Folkways 40124).* Recordings from 1970–80 originally issued on Reynold's own Cassandra record label.

Rice, Tony. Devlin *(Rounder 11531).* Compilation of his various new acoustic/instrumental albums for Rounder.

Rice, Tony. Sings Gordon Lightfoot *(Rounder 370).* Compilation of various tracks featuring Rice's interpretations of the Lightfoot catalog.

Riddle, Almeda. Ballads and Hymns from the Ozarks/More Ballads and Hymns *(Rounder 0017/0083).* Two great albums from the 1970s, now out of print.

Riders in the Sky. The Best of the West, Vols. 1 and 2 *(Rounder 11517/11524).* Compilation CDs of their first albums cut for Rounder.

Riders in the Sky. Riders Radio Theater *(MCA 42180).* 1988 album recreating the classic cowboy radio shows of the 1930s and 1940s.

Ritchie, Jean. Live at Folk City *(Smithsonian/ Folkways 40005).* Reissue of early 1960s concert with Doc Watson.

Ritchie, Jean. The Most Dulcimer *(Greenhays 70714).* 1985 recording emphasizing her skills on this instrument.

Roberts, Fiddlin' Doc. Complete Recordings *(Document 8042, 8043, 8044). Everything he recorded between 1925 and 1934.*

Robertson, Eck. Old Time Texas Fiddler, 1922–29 *(County 3515).* All of his classic era recordings; sound quality is variable, but still a must have for fans of Texas fiddling.

Robeson, Paul. Ballad for Americans *(Vanguard 117/18).* Two-CD compilation of recordings made for the Vanguard label in the mid-1950s.

Robison, Carson J. Home, Sweet Home on the Prairie *(ASV 5187).* 1996 compilation of 1928–36 recordings, a mixture of cowboy, novelty, pop, and other styles.

Rogers, Sally. What Can One Little Person Do? *(Thrushwood 5715).* Social action songs for children.

Rogers, Stan. Fogarty's Cove *(Fogarty's Cove 1001).* Rogers's first solo album, a collection of his songs about life in the Canadian Maritimes.

Rooftop Singers. Best of the Vanguard Years *(Vanguard 79749).* Two-CD compilation of their best recordings.

Rooney, Jim. Brand New Tennessee Waltz *(Appaloosa 67).* 1996 collection of country and bluegrass standards.

Rosenbaum, Art. Art of the Old Time Banjo *(Kicking Mule 519).* Cassette-only reissue of mid-1970s album.

Rosenbaum, Art. Georgia Banjo Blues *(Global Village 313).* 2003 recordings featuring Rosenbaum with traditional musicians from Georgia.

Rowan, Peter. Peter Rowan *(Flying Fish 70071).* Reissue of late 1970s solo album.

Rowan, Peter. The Walls of Time *(Sugar Hill 3722).* 1991 bluegrass album with Ricky Skaggs, Eddie Adcock, and Sam Bush.

Rush, Tom. Classic Rush *(Elektra 74062).* 1965–69 recordings made at the height of his career.

Rush, Tom. No Regrets *(Columbia/Legacy 65860).* Mostly taken from his folk-rock albums of the early 1970s.

Sainte-Marie, Buffy. Best of the Vanguard Years *(Vanguard 79750).* Two-CD compilation of her classic 1960s-era recordings.

Savoy, Marc. Oh What A Night *(Arhoolie 5023).* 1981 album of traditional Cajun music on accordion.

Scott, Tom. Now and Then *(Folkways 31078).* 1980 recordings by Scott with Curley Seckler and Marty Stuart.

Seeger, Mike. Southern Banjo Styles *(Smithsonian/Folkways 40107).* 1998 demonstration record illustrating various styles of playing old-time banjo.

Seeger, Mike. Third Annual Farewell Reunion *(Rounder 313).* Seeger performs with a slew of other folk revivalists.

Seeger, Pete. Birds, Beasts, Bugs and Fishes, Little and Big *(Smithsonian/Folkways 45039).* Reissues two 10-inch LPs from 1955, including his famous children's version of "The Cumberland Mountain Bear Chase."

Seeger, Pete. Darling Corey/Goofin' Off Suite *(Smithsonian/Folkways 40018).* Two of Seeger's more innovative 1950s recordings, the first dedicated to traditional banjo songs, the second to instrumental versions of everything from fiddle tunes to classical music and pop songs.

Seeger, Pete. Essential *(Vanguard 97).* Compilation of his Folkways recordings of the 1950s and 1960s.

Seeger, Pete. Folkways Years, 1955–1992 *(Smithsonian/Folkways 40048).* Career retrospective includes recordings made for Folkways and other labels.

Seeger, Pete. We Shall Overcome *(Columbia 45312).* Two-CD set drawn from a Carnegie Hall concert in 1963, during the height of Seeger's involvement in civil rights and other contemporary issues.

Seldom Scene. The Best Of *(Rebel 1101).* Drawn from their first three Rebel albums.

Seldom Scene. 15th Anniversary Celebration *(Sugar Hill 2202).* All-star tribute recorded at the Kennedy Center in 1986.

Shocked, Michelle. Arkansas Traveler *(Mercury 512101).* Shocked takes traditional fiddle tunes and uses them to create new songs on this interesting collection.

Silly Wizard. Best Of *(Shanachie 79048).* The best of their mid-1980s recordings.

Skillet Lickers. Complete Recordings in Chronological Order, Vols. 1–6 *(Document 8056–61).* Everything the band recorded between 1926 and 1934. Includes fiddle tunes, songs, and their famous extended group skits. The earlier material is the strongest, but there's much to enjoy throughout on each disc.

Skyline. Ticket Back: Retrospective 1981–89 *(Flying Fish 664).* Compilation of tracks from their original albums.

Sky, Pat. A Harvest of Gentle Clang *(Vanguard 19054).* 1966 release featuring half originals and half traditional songs, with friends including Mississippi John Hurt on a few tracks.

Sky, Pat. Songs that Made America Famous *(Adelphi 4101).* Famously tasteless collection of satirical songs that scandalized the folk scene on its release in 1973.

Smeck, Roy. Plays Hawaiian Guitar, Banjo, Ukulele and Guitar, 1926–1949 *(Yazoo 1052).* CD reissue of great early sides emphasizing his string wizardry.

Smith, Fiddlin' Arthur. McGee Brothers and Arthur Smith: Old Timers of the Grand Old Opry *(Folkways 2379) and* Milk 'em in the Evening Blues *(Folkways 31007).* 1964 and 1967 recordings of Smith with his cohorts the McGee Brothers made by Mike Seeger.

Smith, Hobart. Blue Ridge Legacy *(Rounder 611799).* Alan Lomax recordings made in 1959 of the great banjo player.

Sorrels, Rosalie. Always a Lady *(Green Linnet 2110).* 1976 recording, mostly of original songs.

Sorrels, Rosalie. My Last Go Round *(Red House 167).* 2004 album marking her retirement from active performing and touring; includes many "favorites" by Sorrels and her close friend, Bruce "U. Utah" Phillips.

Speers Family. Gospel Music Hall of Fame *(Riversong 82708).* Two CDs put together in 1999 to celebrate the family's induction into the Hall of Fame, including recordings from various sources.

Spence, Bill. The Hammered Dulcimer *(Front Hall 302).* Reissues the complete first album by Spence and his band, Fennig's Allstars, which helped launch the hammer dulcimer revival, plus tracks from their other albums.

Spoelstra, Mark. At Club 47 *(Folkways 3572).* Early 1960s live recordings.

Steeleye Span. Please to See the King *(Shanachie 79075).* 1970 album featuring the band's second (and most folk-oriented) lineup, including master singer/guitarist Martin Carthy.

Steeleye Span. Spanning the Years *(Chrysalis 32236).* Two-CD career retrospective takes the band from 1970 to 1995.

Stoneman, Ernest. Edison Recordings *(County 35102).* All of Stoneman's 1928 recordings for Edison, featuring full string band accompaniment with Stoneman's guitar and vocals.

Story, Carl. 16 Greatest Hits *(Starday 3004).* Bluegrass and country material with various accompanists, from the late 1950s and early 1960s.

Story, Carl. Somebody Touched Me *(King 5111).* Ten-song compilation of gospel numbers.

Sullivan Family. A Joyful Noise *(Country Music Foundation 16).* 1991 album by Tammy and Jerry Sullivan, produced by Marty Stuart.

Sullivan Family. Tomorrow *(Ceili 2005).* 2000 release produced by Marty Stuart featuring father-daughter team Jerry and Tammy Sullivan; Stuart also cowrote many of the inspirational songs with Jerry.

Sullivan Family. The family sells a number of tapes and videos of their performances, available through their Web site at http://thesullivanfly.com.

Sweet Honey in the Rock. Selections, 1976–1988 *(Flying Fish 667).* Two-CD compilation of their first eight albums.

Taj Mahal. In Progress, in Motion, 1965–1998 *(Columbia/Legacy 64919).* Three-CD career retrospective giving a good overview of his work in blues and world music styles.

Tashians. Harmony *(Rounder 412).* Their third Rounder album, from 1997, produced by Jim Rooney.

Taylor, James. Sweet Baby James *(Warner Brothers 1843).* His 1970 breakthrough album with much of his best singer-songwriter work.

Taylor, Tut. Friar Tut *(Rounder 11).* Album originally recorded and released in 1972, with Sam Bush and Norman Blake.

Terry, Sonny. Harmonica and Vocal Solos *(Smithsonian/Folkways 32035).* 1940s–1950s recordings.

Thompson, Joe. Family Tradition *(Rounder Select 2161).* Recordings of Joe, Odell, and Nate Thompson from the 1970s through the 1990s, produced and annotated by Bob Carlin.

Thompson, Joe and Family. Old Time Music from the North Carolina Piedmont *(Global Village 217).* Cassette-only issue of Joe and Odell.

Trischka, Tony. Dust on the Needle *(Rounder 11508).* Compilation of his many Rounder albums.

Trischka, Tony. Early Years *(Rounder 11578).* A second compilation, focusing more on his first few albums.

Trischka, Tony. Solo Banjo Works *(Rounder 0247).* Solos by Trischka and Béla Fleck.

Traum, Happy and Artie. Happy and Artie Traum *(Capitol 586).* Their first album as a duo.

Van Ronk, Dave. Folksinger *(Prestige 7527).* Early 1960s recordings when Van Ronk was at his peak both as a musician and personality on the Greenwich Village folk scene.

Van Ronk, Dave. Folkways Years, 1959–61 *(Smithsonian/Folkways 40041).* His first recordings.

Van Zandt, Townes. Anthology, 1968–79 *(Varese 061128).* Two-CD compilation of his best early recordings, originally issued by the British Charly label.

Van Zandt, Townes. Highway Kind *(Sugar Hill 1070).* Posthumous album of 1990s recordings.

Walker, Jerry Jeff. Best of the Vanguard Years *(Vanguard 79532).* Twenty tracks from his Circus Maximus and his first solo albums.

Walker, Jerry Jeff. Great Gonzos *(MCA 10381).* Selected cuts from MCA albums from the mid-1970s.

Walker, Jerry Jeff. Live at Gruene Hall *(Rykodisc 10123).* 1989 live recording.

Ward, Wade. Uncle Wade *(Folkways 2380).* Tribute album featuring fine playing from the 1960s.

Watson, Doc. Doc Watson Family *(Smithsonian/Folkways 40012).* Originally issued in 1962, this collection documents Watson and his family before he became a professional musician; excellent notes by Eugene Earle and Ralph Rinzler.

Watson, Doc. The Essential *(Vanguard 45).* Twenty-six tracks recorded for Vanguard between 1964 and 1967. A four-CD set gives a more thorough overview of his recordings for this label [Vanguard 15558]).

Watson, Doc. Gerdes Folk City, *Sugar Hill 3934.* Doc's first New York appearance recorded live in 1963. He's joined on some songs by the Greenbriar Boys.

Watson, Doc. Memories *(Sugar Hill 2204).* Originally issued in 1975 by United Artists (423), this set saw Doc playing many of the traditional songs and tunes that he grew up with.

Watson, Doc. My Dear Old Southern Home *(Sugar Hill 3795).* 1992 album, recorded with the Nashville Bluegrass Band, comprising country standards.

Watson, Doc. Pickin' the Blues *(Flying Fish 352).* 1983 album inspired by Merle's love of the blues.

Watson, Doc. Third Generation Blues *(Sugar Hill 3893).* 1999 recording with his grandson, Richard Watson.

Watson, Gene. Back in the Fire *(Warner Bros. 23832).* 1989 comeback album.

Watson, Gene. Greatest Hits *(Curb 77393).* His first hits drawn from Capitol recordings made in the mid-1970s.

Watson, Gene. Greatest Hits *(MCA 31128).* Hits from the late 1970s and early 1980s.

The Weavers. Best of the Decca Years *(MCA 11465).* Compilation of their early hits, including full orchestral and choral accompaniments made by

Gordon Jenkins. The Weavers at their most commercial.

The Weavers. Best of the Weavers *(Vanguard 500).* Later 1950s–early 1960s recordings by the reunited group.

Welch, Gillian. Revival *(Acony 201).* Her 1996 debut album, originally released as Almo Sounds 80006.

Welch, Gillian. Time *(*The Revelator*) (Acony 203).* 2001 release, covering more personal subject matter.

White, Josh. Complete Recorded Works, 1929–1933 *(Document 5194).* White's earlier blues recordings, before he became immersed in the folk revival. Document has issued a series of CDs that takes White through the 1940s in this series.

White, Josh. Free and Equal Blues *(Smithsonian/ Folkways 40081).* Compilation of recordings made in the mid- to late 1940s for Moses Asch in the folk revival style.

The Whites. Greatest Hits *(Curb 77498).* Their pop-country hits of the early to mid-1980s.

The Whites. A Lifetime in the Making *(Ceili 2004).* 2000 gospel album, featuring Jerry Douglas.

Whitter, Henry. Grayson and Whitter *(County 3517).* Selection of 1928–30 recordings by the famed duo. Document Records has released their complete recorded output (8054/55).

Williams, Lucinda. Car Wheels on a Gravel Road *(Mercury 558338).* Her best-received album, its roots-rock sound appealing strongly to listeners of the late 1990s.

Williams, Lucinda. Ramblin'/Happy Woman Blues *(Smithsonian Folkways 40042/40003).* Reissues of her two Folkways albums.

Wise, Chubby. An American Original *(Pinecastle 1041).* 1994 recordings with Bobby and Sonny Osborne.

Wiseman, Mac. Early Dot Recordings, Vol. 3 *(Rebel 113).* Bluegrass-flavored sessions from the 1950s; the first two volumes appeared on LP and are now out of print.

Wiseman, Mac. Grassroots to Bluegrass *(CMH 9041).* 1990 recordings.

Wiseman, Mac. Mac, Doc, and Del. *(Sugar Hill 3888).* Nice 1998 recordings with Watson and McCoury, also featuring McCoury's sons and Alison Krauss.

Further Reading and Resources

Books

Abrahams, Roger, and George Foss. *Anglo-American Folksong Style.* Englewood Cliffs, N.J.: Prentice Hall, 1968.

Artis, Bob. *Bluegrass.* New York: Hawthorn Books, 1975.

Atkinson, David. *The English Traditional Ballad: Theory, Method, and Practice.* Aldershot, U.K.: Ashgate, 2002.

Bufwack, Mary A., and Robert K. Oermann. *Finding Her Voice: Women in Country Music, 1800–2000,* 2nd ed. Nashville, Tenn.: Vanderbilt University Press, 2003.

Burton, Thomas, ed. *Tennessee Traditional Singers.* Knoxville: University of Tennessee Press, 1981.

Cantwell, Robert. *Bluegrass Breakdown: The Making of the Old Southern Sound.* Urbana: University of Illinois Press, 1984.

———. *When We Were Good: The Folk Revival.* Cambridge, Mass.: Harvard University Press, 1996.

Carawan, Guy, and Candie Carawan. *Voices from the Mountains.* New York: Alfred A. Knopf, 1975.

Carlin, Richard. *Country Music: A Biographical Dictionary.* New York: Routledge, 2002.

Carlin, Richard, and Bob Carlin. *Southern Exposure: The Story of Southern Music in Pictures and Words.* New York: Billboard, 2000.

Clarke, Donald. *The Penguin Encyclopedia of Popular Music.* New York: Penguin Books, 1990.

Cohen, John, Mike Seeger, and Hally Wood. *Old-time String Band Songbook.* New York: Oak Publications, 1976.

Cohen, Norman. *Long Steel Rail: The Railroad in American Folksong.* Urbana: University of Illinois Press, 1981.

Cohen, Ronald. *Alan Lomax: Selected Writings 1934–1997.* New York: Routledge, 2003.

———. *Rainbow Quest: The Folk Music Revival and American Society, 1940–70.* Amherst: University of Massachusetts Press, 2002.

Conway, Cecelia. *African Banjo Echoes in Appalachia: A Study of Folk Traditions.* Knoxville: University of Tennessee Press, 1995.

Cray, Ed. *Ramblin' Man: The Life and Times of Woody Guthrie.* New York: Norton, 2004.

Daniel, Wayne. *Pickin' on Peachtree: A History of Country Music in Atlanta, Georgia.* Urbana: University of Illinois Press, 2000.

Filene, Benjamin. *Romancing the Folk: Public Memory and American Roots Music.* Chapel Hill: University of North Carolina Press, 2000.

Fowler, Gene, and Bill Crawford. *Border Radio.* New York: Limelight Editions, 1990.

Greene, Archie. *Only a Miner.* Urbana: University of Illinois Press, 1972.

Gruhn, George, and Walter Carter. *Acoustic Guitars and Other Fretted Instruments: A Photographic History.* San Francisco: GPI Books/Miller Freeman, 1993.

Hardy, Phil, and Dave Laing. *The Faber Companion to 20th-Century Popular Music.* London: Faber & Faber, 1990.

Hood, Phil, ed. *Artists of American Folk Music.* New York: Morrow, 1986.

Jackson, George Pullen. *White Spirituals in the Southern Uplands.* New York: Dover Publications, 1965 [reprint].

Jones, Loyal. *Minstrel of the Appalachians: The Story of Bascom Lamar Lunsford.* Boone, North Carolina: Appalachian Consortium Press, 1982.

———. *Radio's Kentucky Mountain Boy: Bradley Kincaid.* Berea, Ky.: Appalachian Center, Berea College, 1988.

Kingsbury, Paul, ed. *The Country Reader.* Nashville, Tenn.: CMF/Vanderbilt University Press, 1996.

———. *Encyclopedia of Country Music.* New York: Oxford, 1998.

Klein, Joe. *Woody Guthrie: A Life.* New York: Alfred A. Knopf, 1980.

Kochman, Marilyn, ed. *The Big Book of Bluegrass.* New York: Quill, 1985.

Lloyd, A. L. *Come All Ye Bold Miners: Ballads and Songs of the Coalfields.* London: Lawrence & Wishart, 1952.

———. *Folk Song in England.* New York: International Publishers, 1967.

Lomax, John. *Adventures of a Ballad Hunter.* New York: Macmillan, 1947.

Lomax, John, and Alan Lomax. *American Ballads and Folksongs.* 1934. Reprint, New York: Dover, 1994.

———. *Negro Folk Songs as Sung by Lead Belly.* New York: Macmillan, 1936.

———. *Our Singing Country.* 1941. Reprint, New York: Dover, 2000.

Lornell, Kip. *Introducing American Folk Music: Ethnic and Grassroot Traditions in the United States,* 2nd ed. Boston: McGraw-Hill, 2002.

——— and Anne Rasmussen, eds. *Musics of Multi-Cultural America.* New York: Schirmer, 1997.

———. *Virginia's Blues, Gospel and Country Records, 1902–1943.* Lexington: University Press of Kentucky, 1989.

Malone, Bill C. *Country Music USA.* Rev. ed. Austin: University of Texas Press, 1985.

Malone, Bill C., and Judith McCulloh, eds. *Stars of Country Music: Uncle Dave Macon to Johnny Rodriguez.* Urbana: University of Illinois Press, 1975.

McCloud, Barry. *Definitive Country: The Ultimate Encyclopedia of Country Music and Its Performers.* New York: Perigree, 1995.

Morton, David C., and Charles K. Wolfe. *Deford Bailey: A Black Star in Early Country Music.* Knoxville: University of Tennessee Press, 1990.

Oermann, Robert, and Chet Flippo. *A Century of Country.* New York: TV Books, 1999.

Paris, Mike, and Chris Comber. *Jimmie the Kid: The Life of Jimmie Rodgers.* New York: Da Capo, 1977.

Piazza, Tom. *True Adventures with the King of Bluegrass.* Nashville, Tenn.: CMF/Vanderbilt University Press, 2000.

Porterfield, Nolan. *John Lomax: The Last Cavalier.* Champaign-Urbana: University of Illinois Press, 1996.

Riddle, Almeda, and Roger Abrahams, ed. *A Singer and Her Songs.* Baton Rouge: Louisiana State University Press, 1970.

Rinzler, Ralph, and Norman Cohen. *Uncle Dave Macon: A Bio-Discography.* Los Angeles: John Edwards Memorial Foundation, 1970.

Rooney, Jim. *Bossmen: Bill Monroe and Muddy Waters.* New York: Da Capo, 1989.

Rorer, Clifford. *Charlie Poole and the North Carolina Ramblers.* 2nd ed. N.C.: Self-published, 1992.

Rosenbaum, Art. *Folk Visions and Voices: Traditional Music and Song in North Georgia.* Athens: University of Georgia Press, 1983.

———. *Shout Because You're Free: The African American Ring Shout Tradition in Coastal Georgia.* Athens: University of Georgia Press, 1998.

Rosenberg, Neil V. *Bluegrass: A History.* Urbana: University of Illinois Press, 1985.

Russell, Tony. *The Carter Family.* London: Old Time Music, 1973.

Sandberg, Larry, and Dick Weissman. *The Folk Music Sourcebook.* Rev. ed. New York: Da Capo, 1989.

Santelli, Robert, and Emily Davidson, eds. *Hard Travelin': The Life and Legacy of Woody Guthrie.* Hanover, N.H.: Wesleyan University Press, 1999.

Seeger, Mike, with Ruth Pershing. *Talking Feet.* Berkeley, Calif.: North Atlantic Books, 1992.

Seeger, Pete and David K. Dunaway. *How Can I Keep from Singing?* New York: McGraw-Hill, 1981.

———, with assistance by Peter Blood. *Where Have All the Flowers Gone: A Musical Autobiography.* Bethlehem, Pa.: Sing Out, 1997.

Shelton, Robert. *No Direction Home: The Life and Music of Bob Dylan.* New York: Morrow, 1986.

Smith, Richard D. *Bluegrass: An Informal Guide.* Chicago: A Cappella Books, 1996.

Stambler, Irwin, and Grellun Landon. *The Encyclopedia of Folk, Country, and Western Music.* 2nd ed. New York: St. Martin's Press, 1984.

Tichi, Cecelia. *High Lonesome: The American Culture of Country Music.* Chapel Hill: University of North Carolina Press, 1994.

Tribe, Ivan M. *Mountaineer Jamboree: Country Music in West Virginia.* Lexington: University of Kentucky Press, 1984.

Webb, Robert Lloyd. *Ring the Banjer! The Banjo in America; From Folklore to Factory.* Boston: MIT Museum, 1981.

Wiggins, Gene. *Fiddlin' Georgia Crazy: Fiddlin' John Carson, His Real World, and the World of His Songs.* Urbana: University of Illinois Press, 1987.

Wolfe, Charles K. *Tennessee Strings: The Story of Country Music in Tennessee.* Knoxville: University of Tennessee Press, 1977.

Wright, John. *Travellin' That Highway Home.* Urbana: University of Illinois Press, 1993.

Web Sites

Individual artists have "official" Web sites, and there are also many semiofficial and fan sites on line. These can be found using standard search engines (Google, Yahoo, etc.). Following are some useful sites of general interest.

All Music
http://www.allmusic.com
Massive database of artists in all musical styles searchable by artist, album name, or song; a wonderful resource.

Folk Alliance
http://www.folkalliance.net
Web site for the Folk Alliance, a service organization for performers of folk music.

Smithsonian Folkways Recordings
http://www.folkways.si.edu
Web site for the Smithsonian/Folkways collection, including more than 2000 recordings.

Southern Folklife Collection
http://www.lib.unc.edu/mss/sfc1
Web site for the Southern Folklife Collection at the University of North Carolina; indexes the collection that includes photographs and other materials related to traditional country music.

The American Folklife Center
http://www.loc.gov/folklife/archive.html
Archive of American Folklife, Library of Congress. Portal to collections of music, photos, and other materials; the premier national collection.

Sing Out!
http://www.singout.org
Main page for the long-running folk music journal, including its archives.

Glossary of Music Terms

a cappella   Literally "in the chapel." Used generally to describe unaccompanied vocal music.

accent   Extra emphasis given to a note in a musical composition.

alto   (1) The lowest female voice, below mezzo-soprano and SOPRANO. (2) In musical instruments, an instrument with a range of either a fourth or fifth below the standard range; the viola is tuned a fifth below the violin, for example. (3) The alto CLEF (also known as the C clef) used for notating music for alto instruments and voices.

arpeggio   A broken CHORD; the notes of the chord played in succession, rather than simultaneously.

ballad   (1) In folk traditions, a multiversed song that tells a narrative story, often based on historic or mythological figures. (2) In popular music, a slow lament, usually on the subject of lost love.

bar   See MEASURE.

baritone   (1) The male voice situated between the BASS (lowest) and TENOR (highest). (2) Baritone is sometimes used to describe musical instruments that play an octave below the ordinary range.

barrelhouse   An aggressive two-handed piano style suitable for a piano player working in a noisy room, a bar, or a brothel. The same word is used to describe such a venue.

bass   (1) The lowest male vocal range. (2) The deepest-sounding musical instrument within a family of instruments, such as the bass violin. (3) The lowest instrumental part.

beat   The basic rhythmic unit of a musical composition. In common time (most frequently used in popular music), there are two basic beats to the measure; the first is given more emphasis, and therefore is called the *strong* beat, the second is less emphasized and thus is called the *weak* beat.

bebop   A form of jazz that developed in the late 1940s and 1950s played by small ensembles or combos, which emphasized rapid playing and unusual rhythmic accents. Many bebop musicians took common CHORD PROGRESSIONS of popular songs and composed new melodies for them, allowing the accompanying instruments (piano-bass-drums) a form that could be easily followed while the melody parts (trumpet, saxophone) improvised.

bending notes   Technique used on stringed instruments where the musician pushes against a string with the left hand, causing the note to rise in pitch. On an electric guitar, which has light gauge strings, the pitch may rise as much as a whole tone (two frets).

big band jazz   A popular jazz style of the 1930s and 1940s featuring larger ensembles divided into parts (brass, reeds, rhythm). Riffs, or short melodic phrases, were traded back and forth between the melody instruments.

"Blue Moon" progression   A sequence of four chords associated with the song "Blue Moon," popularized in 1935 by Benny Goodman and others. The chords are I, VI minor, IV (or II minor), and V. In the key of C, they would be: C, A minor, F (or D minor), and G. Each chord might be held for two, four, or eight beats, but they appear in sequence. The progression is very common in doo-wop music.

blues   An African-American vocal and instrumental style that developed in the late 19th to early 20th centuries. The "blues scale" usually features a flattened third and seventh, giving the music a recognizable sound. The classic 12-bar blues features three repeated lines of four bars each, with the first two lines of lyrics repeated, followed by a contrasting line. The chord progression is also fairly standardized, although many blues musicians have found ways to extend and improvise around these rules.

boogie-woogie   Boogie-woogie is a way of playing BLUES on the piano that was first recorded in the 1920s. Its chief characteristic is the left-hand pattern, known as eight-to-the-bar (a note is played on every one of the eight possible eighth notes in a measure of four beats), which provides a propulsive rhythm that seems to have been influenced by the sound of trains. Boogie-woogie became a fad after the 1938 and 1939 From Spirituals to Swing concerts, and was adapted into big band swing, pop, and country music. From there it became part of ROCK 'N' ROLL. To boogie in general slang (as in "I've got to boogie now") means to leave somewhere in a hurry. In musical slang, to boogie means to maintain a repetitive blues-based rhythmic foundation, particularly one associated with the style of John Lee Hooker, similar to the figure in his song, "Boogie Chillen."

brass   Traditionally, musical instruments whose bodies are made out of brass (although sometimes today they are made out of other metals). Usually used to refer to members of the horn family, including trumpets and trombones.

British invasion   Popular groups of the 1960s that dominated the American pop charts. The Beatles led the charge in 1964, but were quickly followed by many soundalike bands, as well as more distinctive groups like the Rolling Stones, The Who, the Kinks, and many others.

cadence   A melodic or harmonic phrase usually used to indicate the ending of a PHRASE or a complete musical composition.

capo   A metal or elastic clamp placed across all of the strings of a guitar that enables players to change key, while still using the same chord fingerings as they would use without the capo.

CD (compact disc)   A recording medium developed in the mid-1980s that enables music to be encoded as digital information on a small disc, and that is "read" by a laser. Various forms of CDs have been developed since to contain higher sound quality and/or other materials (photographs, moving images, etc.)

chord   The basic building block of HARMONY, chords usually feature three or more notes played simultaneously.

chord progression   A sequence of chords, for example in the key of C: C, F, and G7.

chorus   Most commonly used in popular songs to indicate a repeated STANZA that features the same melody and lyrics that falls between each verse. Perhaps because members of the audience might "sing-along" with this part of the song, it came to be known as the chorus (a chorus literally being more than one voice singing at the same time). See VERSE.

clef   The symbol at the beginning of a notated piece of music indicating the note values assigned to each line of the STAFF. The three most common clefs used in popular music are the G clef (or treble clef), usually used to notate the melody; the F clef (or bass clef), usually used for harmony parts; and the less-frequently seen C clef (or tenor clef), used for notating instruments with special ranges, most usually the viola.

country and western (C&W)   A category developed by the music industry in the late 1940s to distinguish folk, cowboy, and other musical styles aimed at the white, rural, working-class listener (as opposed to R&B, aimed at black audiences, and pop, aimed at urban whites). Later, the *western* was dropped.

cover versions   The music business has always been competitive, and even before recordings were possible, many artists would do the same song, as can be seen by the multiple editions of the sheet music for certain hits, each with a different artists' photo on the front. In the 1950s the practice of copying records was rampant, particularly by bigger companies, which had more resources (publicity, distribution, influence) and which used their artists to cover songs from independent labels that had started to show promise in the marketplace. A true cover version is one that attempts to stay close to the song on which it is based. Interpretations of existing songs are often called covers, but when artistry is involved in giving an individual treatment to an existing song, that effort is worthy of being considered more than a cover version.

crescendo   A gradual increase in volume indicated in music notation by a triangle placed on its side below the STAFF, like this <.

crossover record   A record that starts in one musical category, but has a broader appeal and becomes popular in another category. For example B. B. King's "The Thrill Is Gone" started out as an R&B record, but crossed over to the pop category.

cut a record   Recording a record.

decrescendo   A gradual decrease in volume indicated in music notation by a triangle placed on its side below the STAFF, as in >.

Delta blues   Blues music originating in the Mississippi Delta and typically featuring the use of a slide, intense vocal performances, an aggressive, sometimes strummed guitar style with bass notes "popped" by the thumb for a snapping sound.

diatonic harmony   The CHORDS implicit in the major scale. The sequence of triads is I major, II minor, III minor, IV major, V major, VI minor, and VII diminished. Because the diminished chord is unstable, it is virtually never used in this context. Because major chords are more common, many songs use only them: I, IV, and V.

disco   A dance form of the 1970s developed in urban dance clubs, consisting of a heavily accented, repeated rhythmic part.

Dixieland jazz   Jazz style popularized in New Orleans at the beginning of the 20th century by small combos, usually including three horns: a clarinet, a trumpet, and a trombone. The rhythm section includes a banjo, a tuba, a simple drum set, and a piano, and occasionally a saxophone, string bass, or guitar is added.

DIY (Do-It-Yourself)   An emphasis on homemade music and recordings, which began with the PUNK movement but outlived it. The message was that everyone could make their own music, and record and market it on their own, using simple, inexpensive instruments and technology.

DJ (deejay)   The person who plays records at a dance club or on a radio station. DJs began to create musical compositions by stringing together long sequences of records, and then further manipulated them using techniques such as backspinning (rapidly spinning a turntable backward while a record is being played) and scratching (moving the turntable back and forth rapidly to emphasize a single note or word).

DVD (digital video disc)   A form of optical disc designed to hold video or film, but also sometimes used for higher-quality music reproduction. See CD (COMPACT DISC).

easy listening   See MOR (MIDDLE-OF-THE-ROAD).

eighth note   See NOTE VALUES.

electronic music   Music created using electronic means, including SYNTHESIZERS, SEQUENCERS, tape recorders, and other nontraditional instruments.

falsetto   A high register vocal sound producing a light texture. Often used in soul music.

finger-picking   A style of guitar playing that keeps a steady bass with the thumb while playing melody on the treble strings.

flat   A symbol in music NOTATION indicating that the note should be dropped one-half step in PITCH. Compare SHARP.

flat pick   A pick held between the thumb and first finger of the right hand that is very effective for playing rapid single note passages or heavy rhythm guitar.

flip side   The other side of a 45 rpm record, typically the nonhit song.

folk music   Traditional music that is passed down from one person to another within a family or a community. Often the original composer or songwriter is unknown.

45   A record that plays at 45 revolutions per minute (rpm). Developed in the 1950s by RCA, the 45 or "single" was the main way of promoting individual songs on the pop and R&B charts through the CD era.

gospel music   Composed black religious music.

half note   See NOTE VALUES.

harmony   Any musical composition with more than one part played simultaneously. In popular music the harmony is usually the accompanying part, made up of CHORDs, that complement the MELODY.

heavy metal   Rock style of the mid-1970s and later that emphasized a thunderous sound, simplified chord progressions, subject matter aimed to appeal to teenage boys (primarily), and flamboyant stage routines. Other variants (death metal, speed metal) developed over the coming decades.

hip-hop   The music (rap), dance (breakdancing), and visual expression (graffiti art) originating in urban areas in the mid-1970s.

holy blues   Songs that combine religious words with blues melodies and accompaniments.

hook   A recurrent musical or lyric phrase that is designed to "hook" the listener into a particular song or record. It is often also the title of a song.

interval   The space between two PITCHES. The first note of a SCALE is considered the first interval; the next note, the second; and so on. Thus, in a C major scale, an "E" is considered a third, and a G a "fifth." The I-III-V combination makes up a major CHORD.

jukebox   A machine designed to play records. Commonly found in bars (known as "juke joints" in the South), these replaced live music by

the mid-1950s, and were a major means of promoting hit records. Customers dropped a "nickel in the jukebox" to hear their favorite song.

key   Indicates the range of notes (or SCALE) on which a composition is based.

key signature   The symbol at the beginning of a piece of notation that indicates the basic KEY of the work.

looping   Repeating a short musical PHRASE or RHYTHM. SEQUENCERS can be programmed to "loop" or repeat these parts indefinitely.

LP   A "long-playing" record, playing at 33 revolutions per minute (rpm). Developed in the late 1940s, the LP enabled record companies to present more or longer compositions on a single disc (the previous time limit of 78s was 3 to 5 minutes, while an LP could hold 20 to 25 minutes per side).

major   One of the two primary SCALEs used in popular music. The relation between the seven notes in the major scale is whole step (WS)-WS-half step (HS)-WS-WS-WS-HS. Each scale step has a related CHORD defining major harmony. Compare MINOR.

measure   A unit of musical time in a composition defined by the time signature. In 4/4 time, for example, each measure consists of four beats (and a quarter note is equal to one beat). The bar line (a vertical line across all five lines of the STAFF) indicates the beginning and end of a measure.

melody   Two or more musical tones played in succession, called the "horizontal" part of a musical composition because the notes move horizontally across the staff (as opposed to the HARMONY which is called the "vertical" part because the harmony notes are stacked vertically on the staff). In popular music the melody of a song is the most memorable part of the composition.

meter   The repeated pattern of strong and weak rhythmic pulses in a piece of music. For example, in a waltz, the oom-pah-pah meter is the defining part of the music's style.

MIDI (Musical Instrument Digital Interface) A common programming language that enables SYNTHESIZERS, computers, and SEQUENCERS to communicate with one another.

minor One of the two primary SCALES used in popular music. The relation between the seven notes in the major scale is whole step (WS)-half step (HS)-WS-HS-WS-WS. (There are two variations of this basic pattern found in scales known as the "harmonic" and "melodic" minor.) Each scale step has a related CHORD defining major harmony. Compare MAJOR.

minstrel Performance of African-American songs and dances by white performers in black-face, burnt cork rubbed on their faces beginning in the mid-19th century. Later, black minstrels appeared. Minstrel shows included songs, dances, and humorous skits. Many of these skits and songs made fun of African Americans.

modes A type of SCALE. The two common scales used today (the MAJOR and MINOR) are two types of mode. In the Middle Ages, a system of eight different modes was developed, each with the same intervals but beginning on a different note. The modes are sometimes still heard in folk music, some forms of jazz, and some forms of contemporary classical music.

MOR (middle-of-the-road) Pop music aimed at a wide audience, designed to be as inoffensive and nondisturbing as possible. This term is often used pejoratively by critics. Also sometimes called "easy listening."

movement A section of a longer musical composition.

notation A system developed over many centuries to write down musical compositions using specific symbols to represent PITCH and RHYTHM.

note values The time values of the notes in a musical composition are relational, usually based on the idea of a quarter note equaling one beat (as in 4/4 time). In this time signature, a quarter note fills a quarter of the time in the measure; a half-note equals two beats (is twice as long) and a whole note equals four beats (a full measure). Conversely, shorter time values include an eighth-note (half a single beat), a sixteenth (¼ of a single beat), a thirty-second (⅛ of a single beat), etc.

octave An INTERVAL of eight notes, considered the "perfect" consonance. If a string is divided perfectly in half, each half will sound an octave above the full string, so that the ratio between the two notes is expressed as 1:2.

opus A numbering system used in classical composition to indicate the order in which pieces were composed. Some composers only give opus numbers to works they feel are strong enough to be part of their "official" canon.

percussion Instruments used to play the rhythmic part of a composition, which may be "unpitched" (such as drums or cymbals) or "pitched" (such as bells, chimes, and marimbas).

phonograph A mechanical instrument used to reproduce sound recordings. A phonograph consists of some form of turntable, needle, tone arm, amplifier, and speaker. A record is placed on a turntable, a disc that is set to revolve at specific speeds. The needle "reads" the grooves cut into the record itself. The vibrations then are communicated through the tone arm (in which the needle is mounted) into an amplifier (which increases the volume of the sound). A speaker projects the sound out so that it can be heard.

phrase A subsection of the MELODY that expresses a complete musical thought.

Piedmont blues A form of blues from the Carolinas, Georgia, Florida, and Alabama that uses a restrained style of fingerpicking and soft vocal performances. It also often uses ragtime CHORD PROGRESSIONS.

pitch The note defined by its sound; literally, the number of vibrations per second (of a string, air column, bar, or some other vibrating object) that results in a given tone. Pitch is relative; in most tuning systems, a specific note is chosen as the pitch against which others are tuned. In modern music, this is usually A above middle C, defined as vibrating at 440 vps.

pop music   Any music that appeals to a large audience. Originally, the pop charts featured records aimed at white, urban listeners (as opposed to R&B, aimed at blacks, and C&W or country, aimed at rural, lower-class whites). Today, "pop" is applied to any recording that appeals across a wide range of listeners, so that Michael Jackson or Shania Twain could equally be defined as "pop" stars.

power chords   Played on the low strings of an electric guitar, power chords use only the root and the fifth (and often a repeat of the root an octave higher) of a triad, leaving out the third of the CHORD. With no third, the chord is neither MAJOR or MINOR. With only two notes, it is technically not even a chord, but an interval. The use of power chords was pioneered by Link Wray ("Rumble") and the Kinks ("You Really Got Me"), and used extensively in hard rock (Deep Purple's "Smoke on the Water"), heavy metal (Metallica), and grunge (Nirvana's "Smells Like Teen Spirit").

power trio   Three instruments—guitar, bass, and drums—played at loud volumes.

psychedelic   Popular ROCK style of the late 1960s-early 1970s that featured extended musical forms, "spacey" lyrics, and unusual musical timbres often produced by synthesizers. Psychedelic music was supposed to be the "aural equivalent" of the drug experience. See also SYNTHESIZER; TIMBRE.

punk   A movement that began in England and travelled to the United States in the mid-1970s emphasizing a return to simpler musical forms, in response to the growing commercialization of ROCK. Punk also encompassed fashion (including spiked hair, safety pins used as body ornaments, etc.) and sometimes a violent, antiestablishment message.

quarter note   See NOTE VALUES.

race records   Music industry name for African-American popular music recorded in the 1920s until around 1945.

ragtime   Music dating from around the 1890s and usually composed in three or four different sections. The most famous ragtime pieces were for piano, but the style was also adapted in a simplified form for the banjo and the guitar.

record producer   The person in charge of a recording session.

register   The range in notes of a specific part of a musical composition. Also used to define the range of an individual musical instrument or vocal part.

resonator guitar   Guitars with a metal front and back, often used in playing slide guitar, and prized during the 1930s for their volume.

rhythm   The basic pulse of a musical composition. In 4/4 time, the 4 beats per measure provide the pulse that propels the piece. Compare METER.

rhythm and blues (R&B)   Black popular music that emerged around 1945 and peaked in popularity in the 1960s. It usually included gospel-influenced vocal performances, and a rhythm section of piano, bass, and drums. The lead instruments were often guitar and saxophone.

riff   A short, recognizable melodic phrase used repeatedly in a piece of music. Commonly heard in big band jazz or in electric guitar solos.

rock   An outgrowth of ROCK 'N' ROLL in the 1960s that featured more sophisticated arrangements, lyrics, and subject matter. The BRITISH INVASION groups—notably the Beatles and the Rolling Stones—are sometimes credited with extending the style and subjects treated by rock 'n' roll. Rock itself has developed into many different substyles.

rockabilly   Mid-1950s popular music that combined BLUES and COUNTRY music.

rock 'n' roll   The popular music of the mid-1950s aimed at teenage listeners. Popular rock 'n' roll artists included Elvis Presley, Chuck Berry, Little Richard, and Carl Perkins. Compare ROCK.

royalties   Payments to recording artists based on the sales of their records.

salsa   Literally "spice." A form of Latin dance music popularized in the 1970s and 1980s.

scale   A succession of seven notes. The most common scales are the MAJOR and MINOR.

score   The complete notation of a musical composition.

sequencer   An electronic instrument that can record a series of pitches or rhythms and play them back on command.

78   The first form of recorded disc, that revolved on a turntable at 78 revolutions per minute (rpm). The first 78s were 10 inches in diameter and could play for approximately three minutes per side; later, 12-inch 78s were introduced with slightly longer playing times.

sharp   A symbol in a piece of music indicating that a pitch should be raised one half-step in PITCH. Compare FLAT.

side   One side of a recording disc.

slide guitar   Style of guitar in which the player wears a metal or glass tube on one finger or uses a bottle neck to play notes. It creates a distinctive crying sound. Also called bottleneck guitar.

songster   A turn-of-the-20th-century musician with a varied repertoire that included different styles of music.

soprano   The highest female voice, or the highest pitched instrument in a family of instruments.

soul   A black musical style developed in the 1960s that combined elements of GOSPEL MUSIC with RHYTHM AND BLUES.

spirituals   Traditional religious music found in both white and African-American traditions.

staff   The five parallel lines on which the symbols for notes are placed in a notated piece of music. The CLEF at the beginning of the staff indicates the pitch of each note on the staff.

stanza   In poetry, the basic lyrical unit, often consisting of four or six lines. The lyrics to both the VERSE and CHORUS of a popular song follow the stanza form.

strings   Instruments that produce musical sound through the vibration of strings, made out of animal gut or metal. Violins and guitars are stringed instruments.

suite   In classical music, a group of dances played in succession to form a larger musical composition.

symphony   In classical music, a defined form usually consisting of three parts, played Fast-Slow-Fast.

syncopation   Accenting the unexpected or weaker BEAT. Often used in RAGTIME, jazz, and related styles.

synthesizer   An electronic instrument that is capable of creating different musical pitches and timbres.

tempo   The speed at which a piece of music is performed.

tenor   The highest male voice.

theme   A recognizable MELODY that is often repeated within a musical composition.

thumb picks and finger picks   Guitar picks made of metal or plastic worn on the player's right hand fingers and thumb in order to play louder.

timbre   The quality of a PITCH produced by a musical instrument or voice that makes it distinctive. The timbre of a guitar is quite different from that of a flute, for example.

time signature   In notation, the symbol at the beginning of each STAFF that indicates the basic metric pulse and how many beats are contained in a measure. For example, in 4/4 time, a quarter-note is given one beat, and there are four beats per measure; in 6/8 time, an eighth-note is given one beat, and there are six beats in a measure.

Tin Pan Alley   The center of music publishing on West 28th Street in New York City from the late 19th century through the 1930s (so-called because the clatter from competing pianists working in different buildings sounded to passersby like rattling tin pans). Used generally to describe the popular songs of this period.

tone   See PITCH.

tremolo   The rapid repetition of a single note to give a "quivering" or "shaking" sound. Compare VIBRATO.

turnaround A musical phrase at the end of a verse that briefly outlines the CHORDs of the song before the start of the next verse.

12-bar blues A 12-bar BLUES has 12 measures of music, or bars, and is the most common blues format, though eight bars and 16 bars are also used.

vamp A short segment of music that repeats, usually two or four CHORDs. Two chord vamps are common in GOSPEL and ROCK, especially the I and IV chords (C and F in the key of C).

vanity records Recordings that are conceived and financed by the artists involved. They are called "vanity records" because the motivation comes from the person or group themselves, not from a record company. The reason is to realize a creative project, to promote a career, or just to boost the ego. Previously, singers and musicians would pay to go into a studio and to cover the costs of backup musicians, mixing, mastering, and manufacturing. This continues, but with the rise of home studios, these steps can be done at home, with computerized recording and CD burning. Vanity records now represent perhaps the majority of recordings being made and are more likely to be called independent productions.

verse The part of a song that features a changing lyric set to a fixed MELODY. The verse is usually performed in alternation with the CHORUS.

vibrato A rapid moving up and down slightly in PITCH while performing a single note as an ornament. Compare TREMOLO.

walking bass A style of bass playing that originated in jazz on the upright bass. The bassist plays a new note on every beat, outlining the CHORDs as they pass by in a CHORD PROGRESSION. Chord notes are primary, but passing notes and other decorations enliven the bass line, as well as brief rhythmic variations enliven the bass line. A rock example is Paul McCartney's bass part in the Beatles' "All My Loving" (1964).

whole note See NOTE VALUES.

woodwinds A class of instruments traditionally made of wood, although the term is now used for instruments made of brass or metal as well. Clarinets, flutes, and saxophones are usually classified as woodwinds.

Editorial Board of Advisers

Richard Carlin, general editor, is the author of several books of music, including *Southern Exposure, The Big Book of Country Music, Classical Music: An Informal Guide,* and the five-volume *Worlds of Music.* He has also written and compiled several books of music instruction and songbooks and served as advisory editor on country music for the American National Biography. Carlin has contributed articles on traditional music to various journals, including the *Journal of Ethnomusicology, Sing Out!, Pickin', Frets,* and *Mugwumps.* He has also produced 10 albums of traditional music for Folkways Records. A longtime editor of books on music, dance, and the arts, Carlin is currently executive editor of music and dance at Routledge Publishers. He previously spent six years as executive editor at Schirmer Books and was the founding editor at A Cappella Books, an imprint of the Chicago Review Press.

Barbara Ching, Ph.D., is an associate professor of English at the University of Memphis. She obtained a graduate certificate in women's studies and her doctorate in literature from Duke University. Dr. Ching has written extensively on country music and rural identity, and she is the author of *Wrong's What I Do Best: Hard Country Music and Contemporary Culture* (Oxford University Press) and *Knowing Your Place: Rural Identity and Cultural Hierarchy* (Routledge). She has also contributed articles and chapters to numerous other works on the subject and has presented papers at meetings of the International Association for the Study of Popular Music.

Ronald D. Cohen, Ph.D., is professor emeritus of history at Indiana University–Northwest (Gary). He obtained a doctorate in history from the University of Minnesota–Minneapolis. Dr. Cohen has written extensively on the folk music revival and is the coproducer, with Jeff Place, of *The Best of Broadside: 1962–1988: Anthems of the American Underground from the Pages of Broadside Magazine* (five-CD boxed set with illustrated book, Smithsonian Folkways Recordings, 2000), which was nominated for a Grammy Award in 2001. He is also the author of *Rainbow Quest: The Folk Music Revival and American Society, 1940–1970* (University of Massachusetts Press) and the editor of *Alan Lomax: Selected Writings, 1934–1997* (Routledge). He is also the editor of the Scarecrow Press book series American Folk Music and Musicians.

William Duckworth is the composer of more than 100 pieces of music and the author of six books and numerous articles, the most recent of which is "Making Music on the Web" (*Leonardo Music Journal,* vol. 9, December 1999). In the mid-1990s he and codirector Nora Farrell began *Cathedral,* a multiyear work of music and art for the Web that went online June 10, 1997. Incorporating acoustic and computer music, live Web casts by its own band, and newly created virtual instruments, *Cathedral* is one of the first interactive works of music and art on the Web. Recently, Duckworth and Farrell created Cathedral 2001, a 48-hour World Wide Web event, with 34 events streamed live from five continents.

Index